Case Studies & Cocktails

THE "NOW WHAT?" GUIDE TO SURVIVING BUSINESS SCHOOL

By Carrie Shuchart and Chris Ryan

ISBN-10: 1-935-707-21-3

ISBN-13/EAN-13: 978-1-935707-21-9

eISBN: 978-1-935707-75-2

To order additional copies of this book, please visit:
www.casestudiesandcocktails.com

Published by MG Prep, Inc.

Interior design by Cathy Huang and Dan McNaney

Cover design by Evyn Williams

*This book is dedicated
to our students, without whom
it'd be tough to be teachers.*

Table of Contents

Introduction

Part I – Making the Most of Your Time Before B-School

Part II – Taking Care of Business at Business School

Part III – Grasping First-Year Academics

Part IV – Landing the Perfect Job

Appendix

INTRODUCTION

Welcome!

If you're like the majority of folks reading this book, you've already been through the tough process of applying to business school: the GMAT, the essays, the interviews, and so on.

Hopefully, you've been accepted to at least one program by now, and you're only months or even weeks away from the remarkable adventure of business school.

That's a fantastic—if unsettling—place to be. And we welcome you to it.

Why We Wrote This Book

As instructors for Manhattan GMAT, we have both come to know and love many of our students. These are the ones we hear from right after the test: "You were my first call. I have to call my mom now or she'll kill me."

Later, we hear from the same students again, when they've been accepted to school. Even more joy ensues. After all, the GMAT was always just a means to this end.

Finally, after the excitement wears off a little, our students come back again, this time to ask us, "***Now what am I supposed to do?***"

It's a good question. Back before we each started our respective MBA programs, neither of us spent enough time pondering this issue. We both came from somewhat non-traditional backgrounds, and for us, business school was meant to be a golden ticket to a new career path. But school wound up being much more complicated than we predicted, and in various ways, we each struggled to make sense of it.

Years later, as we heard the *"Now what?"* question from our GMAT students, we began thinking about what would be helpful for them to know. As a start, we looked back on our own experiences. We also talked to fellow graduates of various MBA programs, current students, and some folks just months away from the first day of classes. We began compiling a list of topics that were concerning, frustrating, or downright confusing. It was a long list.

Thus, *Case Studies & Cocktails* was born.

Well, not quite "thus"; it took a bit more work than that. We ran around to 14 of the top US business schools and picked the brains of nearly 200 current students and administrators, gathering wisdom, perspectives, and frequent flyer miles.

Along the way, a self-evident truth was confirmed: if you offer free food, people will talk. More importantly, we gained fabulous insights into how to approach everything from academics to roommate issues, from self-discovery to case prep. Little tips and big ideas came from a variety of sources and made us wish we could re-matriculate.

We hope that *Case Studies & Cocktails* will be a useful reference for you, both before and during your program. Think of this book as a travel guide to a distant country where you're going to spend the next two or more years.

We're excited for you, and even a little jealous.

If you're committed to giving business school your all, the next few years of your life will be some of the most energizing, exhausting, challenging, surprising, and amazing of your life. You will meet people who will inspire and engage you. You will have once-in-a-lifetime experiences, whether around a dinner table or on a trip around the world.

At the end of it all, you will graduate with a master's degree in business administration, the fabled MBA. What you choose to do with that degree is entirely up to you.

And that's pretty cool.

How To Use This Book

This book is organized in four big parts.

- Part I: Making the Most of Your Time Before B-School
- Part II: Taking Care of Business at Business School
- Part III: Grasping First-Year Academics
- Part IV: Landing the Perfect Job

Before school, read Part I closely. Dip in and out of the other parts. Return to them as needed during your first year.

Along the way, you'll find a number of helpful worksheets and exercises. Feel free to copy the blank pages or visit our website, www.casestudiesandcocktails.com, for downloadable versions. We like this web-thing; check it often, as we will post content updates and other nifty extras there.

Filling In The Blank

When talking to students and administrators for this book, we generally opted for unstructured, casual conversations, rather than more formal interviews. However, there was one specific question we tried to end every conversation with.

"Finish this sentence," we'd say. "Business school is…"

The first answer out of people's mouths was nearly always a flippant comment—or a curse word we can't print.

Inevitably, they'd ask for a minute to think. Brows would furrow as people tried to answer an immense question with a sentence fragment.

After a little while, they'd say something. The responses ranged from heartfelt expressions to other words we can't print. But one answer came up time and time again, practically word for word:

"Business school is….a transformative experience."

And half of the respondents added "…if you let it be."

Speaking from personal experience, we have to agree.

It's not so much that business school shaped each of us into something specific and fixed. Rather, the experience left us forever changed—in some ways, *less* fixed than before.

To hear that others shared our sentiment left us both reassured and nostalgic. There may be better laptops and smartphones around campus now, but school hasn't really changed since we left.

The Hardest Thing About B-School

...is getting in. Let's be honest: classes are usually graded on a curve, socializing is expected, and being caught on campus with a beer in your hand doesn't result in a trip to the principal's office.

That's not to say that business school is easy. But the admissions process is rigorous, and if you made it past the gatekeepers, you're clearly doing something right. Admissions committees are pretty good at choosing people. They picked you and your classmates because, among other reasons, you're smart and you work hard. And you'll need both of these attributes to persevere when the seas get stormy. Which they will. Despite rumors to the contrary, people don't sail through MBA programs.

So what *is* the hardest thing about b-school—at least, once you've been admitted?

Some folks say it's *managing your time*. Others say it's *finding a job*.

Yes, both of those things are legitimately difficult to do. They require your full effort. But they're both symptoms of a deeper tension for you to resolve.

While you're in business school, you have to strike a balance between **changing** and **staying the same**. In fact, paradoxically, you must do both at the same time.

This is actually the hardest thing about b-school.

Is that too touchy-feely for you? Then think about it another way—by taking a look at where you're *not* going: dental school.

D-School vs. B-School

Welcome to dental school! What are you going to do when you graduate?

Umm…be a dentist?

Exactly.

No one goes to dental school for any other reason. The sole purpose of dental school is to produce dentists. In fact, there's no other way to become a dentist: students must pass national board exams to graduate, and you can't take those exams by signing up off the street. Dental school is really what licenses you to be a dentist.

Of course, these observations are not to denigrate dental education in any way. We are grateful that smart, talented people have gone through extensive training to keep our teeth from falling out of our gums. In fact, none of us is grateful enough, so take a break to floss right now. You know your dentist would want you to.

Most graduate professional schools function this way: they produce licensed professionals who join a profession. Law schools produce lawyers. Medical schools produce doctors. Even PhD programs produce professors, who in essence are licensed to teach at the university level and to conduct research within a particular field.

Since there's no way to become a dentist without going to dental school, everyone starts out in a similar state: that of not being a dentist. Your classmate might have spent a summer in high school making brittle plaster casts of teeth for his orthodontist (as one of us did), but any differences in background pale once you get on board the dental curriculum train. And every dental student has to ride that train to the end of the line.

Visually, this is what d-school does:

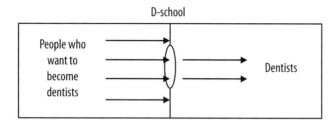

D-school is a ***focusing lens*** with a single purpose. Every year, dental schools generate a tight beam of trained professionals. Kind of like a Waterpik of dentists.

Now consider what business schools do—or don't do.

The biggest thing they *don't* do is license you in any way. Your MBA is not a license to practice business. There is no certification, no board exam.

What, or whom, do b-schools produce? The best you can say is "leaders" or "general managers," but those aren't professions with strict member-ship criteria. You can certainly be a leader or a manager without an MBA. Plenty of folks start or run businesses without one.

So what b-schools produce is really just people with the MBA degree, a degree that doesn't license you to do anything. The world does not demand a yearly supply of MBA graduates in the same way that it demands a yearly supply of freshly minted dentists.

We're not trying to get you to freak out, now that you're about to spend a bunch of money and time getting this no-license degree. The lack of licensing is both the weakness and the glory of business school. No one's going to hire you just because you have an MBA. There's no MBA equivalent of a crappy school that needs licensed teachers or a crappy hospital that needs a staff of MDs. As a result, you are forced to create the meaning and value of your MBA—and that's ultimately a good thing.

Visually, this is what b-school does:

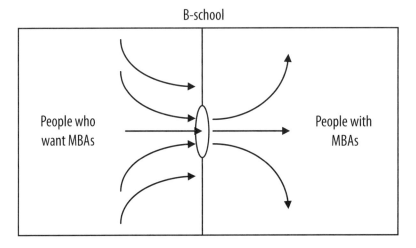

B-school is a ***mixing lens.*** Every year, business schools mash together folks with all sorts of different backgrounds and goals. Clashes are inevitable as students struggle to work together. In the end, folks come out and head in a variety of directions, again without a license of any kind, but empowered by their experiences to take on unspecified challenges. Insofar as one can train leaders and general managers, business schools do just that.

Again, The Hardest Thing About B-School

You are free to treat b-school like d-school. You can arrive with absolutely fixed notions of what you want to learn and what you want to become, and you can leave with those notions intact.

But if you ask us, that's taking an impoverished view of what business school is for. It's *meant* to shake you up some. It's *meant* to create clashes between folks with different backgrounds and goals, and it's *meant* to change you as a result of those clashes.

At the opposite extreme, you can be *too* open to change. Every week, you'll be presented with numerous opportunities. Your classmates, with their various backgrounds and goals, will influence your thinking about your own life and career, but if you try to do everything, you'll be overwhelmed. In the end, you must make choices; you must say no to many appealing paths.

Again, the hardest thing about business school is striking a balance between changing and staying the same. Somehow you need to do both.

PART I:
MAKING THE MOST OF YOUR TIME BEFORE B-SCHOOL

Congratulations! You've just gotten into business school!

What are you going to do now?

If you're a marketer, you know the answer: *I'm going to Disney World!*

Well, probably not. Instead, you'll celebrate with friends and family. You'll put on the Kellogg t-shirt or the Sloan baseball cap that you've been hiding in your closet. You'll build a bonfire with your GMAT books. And, if you haven't already, you'll start fantasizing about your last, glorious day at the office.

That's all well-deserved. But before you get too far on that victory lap, you have some work to do.

This section is designed to help you get through all of the stuff that you need to do *now*, or at least *soon*—like making the final decision on schools, establishing a budget for the next couple of years, and more. You will be amazed at how fast the time goes. Whether you have nine months, nine weeks, or nine days, you need to use your time wisely. Once orientation begins, you'll be off to the races. Classes, clubs, recruiting, socializing…it all starts at breakneck speed.[1]

---

1   In researching this book, we reached out to a number of friends who were just beginning their MBA programs—and got almost no responses at first. These folks weren't avoiding us; they were just so inundated that they couldn't catch up on personal email until the weekend (and that's if we got lucky).

What follows will be most relevant to those beginning full-time pro-grams, but part-timers should look over this material anyway. Taking on an MBA is a big life change, no matter how you do it.

Here's your to-do list from now until you show up for orientation. Each numbered bullet below corresponds to a chapter in this section. So grab your favorite beverage and get comfortable as you scan the list and the associated chapters.

Pre-MBA To-Do List

❏ 1. **Choose your school & accept the offer.**
- ❏ Go to Admit Weekend(s).
- ❏ Compare schools if you have multiple offers.
- ❏ Make up your mind and send in your deposit to your future alma mater.
- ❏ Make a calendar of key dates (e.g., FAFSA submission, class bidding deadlines).

❏ 2. **Say your farewells—and celebrate.**
- ❏ Decline offers from other schools.
- ❏ Tell your boss you're leaving and lay the groundwork for a possible return.
- ❏ Let your network know where and when you're going.
- ❏ Send thank-you notes to everyone who helped you along the way.

❏ 3. **Rest, relax, & search your soul.**
- ❏ Spend real time with family and friends.
- ❏ Take a trip somewhere you've always wanted to go.
- ❏ Reflect on the big picture: why you're going back to school.
- ❏ Sleep, exercise, and get healthy.

❑ **4. Get to know your future classmates.**

    ❑ Go to Admit Weekend if you haven't already done so.

    ❑ Join email lists and online groups.

    ❑ Attend or host social events.

❑ **5. Firm up your career knowledge.**

    ❑ Read *The Wall Street Journal* and other publications regularly.

    ❑ Learn about typical and atypical post-MBA career paths.

    ❑ Conduct informational interviews.

    ❑ Attend pre-MBA career conferences.

    ❑ Reevaluate your own interests using formal assessment tools.

    ❑ Do additional summer reading on topics that are of interest to you.

❑ **6. Prepare for class.**

    ❑ Plot out your first-year course schedule.

    ❑ Find out how to place out of core classes.

    ❑ Skim Part III of this book.

    ❑ Consider taking courses to fill in your knowledge gaps.

❑ **7. Find housing & move.**

    ❑ Assess your housing preferences and investigate options.

    ❑ Interview potential roommates.

    ❑ Make your housing selection and sign a lease.

    ❑ If you have a roommate, agree on key issues and ground rules.

    ❑ Move in and stock the refrigerator.

    ❑ Get your school-related paperwork ready (health insurance, vaccinations, etc.).

❑ **8. Figure out your finances.**

    ❑ Determine your spending style.

    ❑ Make an honest budget.

    ❑ Figure out how you are going to pay for school and file the necessary forms.

    ❑ Submit the FAFSA and apply for private loans as well.

    ❑ Get other funding sources lined up.

CHAPTER 1:
CHOOSE YOUR SCHOOL & ACCEPT THE OFFER

First things first. If you're sitting on multiple offers, you need to decide where you're going to go. That's a great problem to have. There is no one "right" school, but you should consider a few issues as you make up your mind.

Even if you've decided on which school to attend, don't skip this chapter entirely. Read the next section on events for admits, then turn to page 30 and read from "Say Yes" onward.

Admit Activities (a.k.a. MBA Rush)

Admit weekends are largely sales events. The school pulls out all the stops to convince you to spend your tuition dollars *there*. After all, you're already in. Your "yes" increases the school's yield numbers and thus improves its position in all those nifty business school rankings.

Despite the sales pitch element, admit weekend should be at the top of your to-do list, even if you are already committed to attending the school. Admit days give you a real taste of campus life, even if artificially sweetened, and provide an opportunity to meet many potential classmates. Visits made while applying don't count. You need to be on campus when you know you're already in; you'll be much more objective in your assessments when you're a buyer, not a seller.

Admit weekend gives you a good feel for how well you fit into the school and the caliber of the kids you'll be in class with. I had a lot of question marks about this place before the weekend but left totally solid in my decision to attend.

-- John, Kellogg '12 (Northwestern)

Typical activities include mock classes, financial aid presentations, happy hours, lunches, and parties. Be prepared to be whisked from spot to spot by current students wearing matching shirts, happy to regale you with highlights of their MBA experience.

Even if you don't need the sell job—you already own the t-shirt, sweatshirt, and coffee mug—admit events are a terrific way to network with your future classmates. Some tips:

1) **Don't be shy** about joining in for happy hour or an after-party; admits tend to go en masse. Most everyone is a bit unsure in this bizarre new social situation. Go ahead and join (or lead) the herd.

2) People will repeatedly ask you your name, where you're from, where you went to college, and what you do. **Deal with it nicely.** Rob from Minnesota doesn't know you've already introduced yourself fourteen times. Don't take it out on him.

3) **Be interested** in your prospective classmates. For every person you meet, there's a subject, somewhere between boring small talk and weird personal stuff, that intrigues or amuses you both. Your job is to find that subject in five minutes.

4) **Spend time both with people who are like you and with people who aren't.** It's easy to gravitate to other XYZs, whatever "XYZ" means to you. Sure, do that. But also have a drink with some ABCs. And if you can throw in some other letters, too, go for it.

5) If you aren't sure that this is the school for you, you can **be honest.** But don't lament the school's failings. Be open to the positive aspects of the program. If you want to compare schools in discussions with other admits or current students, do so sensitively.

6) If you think you might want roommates, **talk to people about living arrangements.** If you've already decided on a school, it might even be possible for you to go apartment hunting while you are in town.

7) Enjoy the party—but **don't party TOO much.** Remain above reproach. There will be plenty of opportunities to, um, enjoy your classmates' company in the future. This is not the time to make *that* sort of name for yourself. Let someone else become the focus of the *TMZ* recap.

8) **Ask questions.** Why do the current students at Admit Weekend all wear the same shirt? So you can spot them in the crowd. Current students are your best resource for nearly everything related to preparing for your MBA. Moreover, these student hosts have volunteered for the job—they really want to help you out. Ask them:

    - the hidden upsides and downsides of the program
    - which clubs attract the best guest speakers
    - what surprised them when they arrived on campus
    - what they didn't budget for
    - where to live
    - how to game the class bidding system
    - who that hottie in the corner is
    - …and anything else on your mind.

Remember, you're already in the club. Don't hang back because you're afraid that your question might be "stupid." Just ask it nicely.

This is What You'll Be Remembered For
(at least, for the next few months)

Networking truly begins at admit events. Many lasting friendships are formed early on—as are reputations. Be yourself, knowing that others are watching. If you want everyone to know that you're going to be "that guy," be obnoxious to the professor teaching your mock class. Want to be the class social chair? Collect email addresses and bring as many people as you can to the party. Your entire b-school career will not be determined within a few hours. But do be aware that if you wind up coming to this school, you will see many of these people again…and again…and again over the next two years. And while only some will be lifelong friends, it's helpful to have friendly faces to recognize right at the start of your first semester.

You Like Me! You Really, Really Like Me!

When Sally Field won the Best Actress Oscar for her performance in *Norma Rae*, she bounded up to the podium and proclaimed to the Academy, "You like me! You really, really like me!" For Sally, that little gold statue wasn't just about this particular film; it validated her entire body of work.

Getting acceptance letters (or emails) can feel like the same thing, only without the ball gown and after-parties. The "Welcome to the Class of 20XX" email doesn't just invite you to a school; it tells you that what you did during college and what you've done since then have been worthwhile. On the basis of your essays, test scores, and all the rest, a bunch of people somewhere think that you'll be an asset to their community.[1]

Seriously, that's pretty great.

---

1   We know someone who lists on his resumé a couple of stellar graduate schools he has been *admitted* to. He has never attended any of these schools, not even for a single day. We love this guy, and we admire the brilliance and chutzpah of this move, but we do not recommend it for most mortals.

But what happens when too many people want you? How do you decide where to go?

You may have gone into the application process already knowing which school is your first choice. However, the prospect of being disappointed may have been so daunting—after all, many programs have low acceptance rates—that you applied without a true "favorite" in mind. Or your criteria may have shifted, inspiring you to reconsider your list with an open mind.

You might like all the schools for a variety of different reasons. But pick one program you must.[2]

You might have a very strong gut instinct that one particular program is for you. If so, it is still worthwhile to take a bit of time to think through the attributes that tend to distinguish schools, just to make sure that you've covered all the important areas.

All of this means just one thing: it's time to do more research. And if you haven't been to a particular school yet, you really should go. Then compare the schools across the areas described on the next two pages.

---

2   By the way, don't expect to be able to transfer. One of us was in the class below a guy who, after his first year, managed through devilish arts to transfer to another school. However, he had to repeat his entire first year; meanwhile, his effigy was burned at the stake at his old school. It is probably easier to levitate yourself by the power of your mind than to transfer to a top program, so don't think of transferring as "Plan B," should you not get into your first choice.

Eeny, Meeny, Miny, Moe…

At some point in your MBA studies, you will encounter *decision analysis.* Companies use this sort of process when making big decisions (e.g., which target company to acquire, where to build the next billion-dollar plant, etc.). We explain how to use decision analysis in Chapter 26 to help you choose between multiple job offers. If you're debating between several schools, consider flipping ahead to page 612 and adapting the process presented there to this decision. After all, the ramifications are colossal: two years, $200,000, and the permanent branding of your resumé.[3]

Formal analysis may seem mechanical, but the driving force is your own judgment; no one is telling you what to think or feel. The whole point is to help you understand what you are *truly* thinking and feeling, outside of the influence of friends, family, and bloggers. A structured process can clarify your own goals, desires, and values, which need to be paramount.

Issues To Consider As You Gather More Intelligence

Timing of School Visits—Be aware what is going on during your visit. Stress levels on campus change like the weather. Is this a relatively easy time academically, or is everyone in the midst of midterms? Are recruiting deadlines fast approaching, or have offer letters begun to arrive? As you compare schools later, remember any differing conditions and put your impressions in context.

Location and Social Life—Consider the size of the school's city or town. What fraction of the student body lived in that city before school? What social outlets exist outside of school? Schools in large cities may have more fragmented social environments than schools in smaller locales, where almost everyone is an outsider and folks band together.

---

3   No matter how much you love your school, keep the actual branding on paper. We know an Ivy Leaguer so in love with his alma mater that he tattooed a school logo on his inner thigh. Decision analysis says: *really bad idea.*

Comfort vs. Challenge—Too much comfort (collegiality among your classmates, ease in the classroom, home-cooked meals) and you won't learn or grow much, except around your midsection. But too much challenge (competitiveness, academic difficulty, overall workload) can also be detrimental. We all need some of both, but you should contemplate the right balance for you.

Size—Bigger may or may not be better for you. Either way, size definitely influences several factors such as social life, alumni network, and on-campus recruiting. Ask yourself what about a school's size matters to you, and consider how the school divides itself into smaller units. Are there assigned sections or groups? How important are they to classroom work and social interactions?

Rankings—Every ranking system has flaws. The numbers vary from year to year and among the different raters much more than they should. Furthermore, rankings are based on past performance and statistics, not on how things will be while you are enrolled. Large differences in rankings may be meaningful, but small differences are essentially noise. If you care about rankings, use more than one year's worth of numbers and more than one source.

Cost—Most business schools cost about the same—a lot—so there may not be a large difference between programs. However, public schools generally cost less than private schools, and you may have been offered scholarships at one program or another. Also, take into account the cost of living in a particular location; it's a lot cheaper to live in Hanover, New Hampshire for two years than in New York City.

And last but not least…

Name—School names loom large over the decision process. Names are important, no doubt, because they embody brand and reputation. But try not to let the name *itself* be the final deciding factor. You don't go to a "name"; you go to a school. The name should be just one part of the equation.

We promise—you can get any university's name embroidered on a very comfortable sweatshirt. Or underwear, if you'd rather keep your alma mater on the down low. Regardless, the clothes feel the same.

Even if you have already mailed your deposit and locked in football or basketball tickets for next season, reassess your decision. Consider it due diligence. In the end, it will let you rest assured that you made the right choice.

Counteroffers

Some folks hang on to offers of admission, particularly if fellowships or scholarships are attached, and even try to play these offers against each other. However, few schools are able or willing to adjust aid in response. It is not particularly useful, or couth, to dangle one school's aid offer in front of another. Loan amounts are set by federal guidelines (see the section on Financial Aid in Chapter 8 for more info). This is why different schools have slightly different budgets and why aid officers can't do much to match packages.

Scholarships, which are scarce to begin with, tend to have particular criteria attached and are rarely comparable across schools. If you have been offered a fellowship or scholarship, be grateful, but recognize that schools do not have equal resources or equal ability to share those resources with you.

What If You're Still Waiting To Hear?

While multiple offers are nice, the timing of these offers often isn't. Schools usually require you to submit a deposit within a short window of time, which may be before you have heard final decisions from other programs. Sadly, there is little you can do about this squeeze play.

You may be able to convince one school to give you a bit of leeway if you know for a fact that you will hear from another program soon. More than likely, you will have to decide whether to plunk down a deposit at School B (and lose that deposit if School A takes you later) or give up your space at B (and cross your fingers tightly for A, which may never take you). If you do submit a deposit, in many cases you are not bound to attend.[4] But it does mean that someone has your money, whether you show up for class or not.

---

4   Schools have different deposit and commitment requirements, some of which may be associated with an "early decision" process. With early decision, you have to pony up more money and agree to withdraw all other applications; your acceptance is considered binding. Check with the schools for the particulars, and be 100% aware of what you are committing to.

In the grand scheme of this expensive degree, it often makes sense to submit a deposit at a school that you will be happy to attend, while you wait to hear back from another school you prefer. A thousand bucks or two—or even six, in some cases—is (unfortunately) a small drop in the ~~bucket~~ mammoth lagoon of MBA expenses.

If you are on the waitlist at your dream school, realize that there is no rhyme or reason to whether or when you might be accepted. Schools differ as to what, if anything, you are allowed to do to influence the process. Follow the explicit guidelines and do your best to contain your anxiety.

Meanwhile, make your plans on the basis of the offers you have in hand. It's up to you whether to keep the waitlist option open, but proceed as if you are going to a school that has already accepted you and that you are happy to graduate from. Do everything else on your pre-MBA to-do list.

You may decide to take yourself off the waitlist at some point so that you can fully commit to another school and mentally prepare yourself for the next two years. Embrace that school you're going to wholeheartedly and without regrets. *If you cannot do so, then you should not attend this school.* The next two years will be tough enough without self-doubt and bitterness undermining your every effort. Find something else to do and reapply next year.

If you decide to stay on the waitlist at your dream school, be as Zen as possible while your fate lies in the hands of others. Realize that if you are admitted at the last minute, you'll be behind in some ways (e.g., housing), but you'll catch up just fine. And there will be others in the same boat.[5]

---

5   One of us did get in off the waitlist two weeks before orientation. The logistics were a little hairy at first, but everything worked out. And we now hold a special place in our hearts for waitlist folks. It's like another club, only without t-shirts.

> ## Why Am I Here?
>
> If we heard it once, we heard it a thousand times talking to students and administrators: know why you're going to business school well before you show up on any campus. This is not to say that you have to have a full plan for the future, but you do want to know what your personal goals and aspirations are. Without this, it is otherwise impossible to evaluate which school will best meet your needs.
>
> In a nod to the professional therapists out there, you never can know yourself too well. And given the number of times we've heard this refrain, maybe they're on to something…

Say Yes

At the end of the day, commit to a school. Not just on paper, but in your head and heart. It feels good, doesn't it?

Take a moment to let it sink in. In a couple of years, you'll be a graduate of… [fill in your future alma mater here]. Go Fighting Artichokes![6]

Okay, now on to the next thing.

Say No … Nicely

Declining an offer of admission isn't like breaking up with a significant other. There's no deep emotional bond, and you don't have to worry that you'll never see your favorite sweater again. All you need to do is let the school down politely: "Thank you very much, but I have decided to pursue my studies elsewhere/continue along my professional track."

---

6   The mascot of Scottsdale Community College is Artie the Fighting Artichoke. The Sixties and Seventies produced some really weird names of college sports teams.

However, since you and the school have been casually dating, use the following etiquette when you figure out that the relationship is going nowhere.

First, **inform the school as soon as you know** that you will not attend. People on the waitlist covet your spot.

As a courtesy, **write a short email to thank the admissions committee** for the offer. Avoid comparing the program you are declining to the program you will be attending. You would, one hopes, never tell a soon-to-be-ex that you're ending the relationship because she is less attractive than the model you just met; you'd say it's not her, it's you…

In short, treat the school the way that you would want to be treated. Be prompt, be honest, and be polite. You may never apply to business school again, but admissions karma has a way of paying off. Respecting all admissions committees may allow you to reach out when your best friend applies in the future.

Make a Calendar

Print a copy of the acceptance email and stick it in a folder along with copies of any paperwork the school has sent you physically or electronically. Read through everything, make a list of what you have, and input key dates into a calendar. Note any firm deadlines, such as when you have to submit financial aid forms, housing and parking requests, and petitions to waive out of classes.

Of course, send back anything needed right now (including the deposit) to hold your place in the class. It should actually feel nice to complete this sort of paperwork—think back to when you were first applying, and now you're signing a piece of paper saying "I accept my place in the class of 20XX…"

In addition, you may come across forms that you can't or won't fill out right away. For instance, the school will almost certainly require you to go on its student health insurance plan or show proof of alternate coverage. Likewise, you'll need to prove that your vaccinations are up-to-date. Can't remember your pediatrician's name? Moved a few times over the years? Generally, your undergraduate institution required that you file the same sort of documentation, so call up the registrar's office and see whether they can help you track it down.

These issues may seem minor and annoying, but they'll be way more annoying if they cause you to miss an orientation session and have a student nurse stick needles in your arm. Remove the stress by putting these items on your master to-do list.

Also, your school may conduct a background check on you. Yes, private eyes are watching; they're watching you. No, you don't have any choice in the matter. These checks are generally routine and simply ensure that you didn't fabricate your previous degrees or work experience. Assuming you were on the up and up when you went through the application process, you should have nothing to worry about here. And if you weren't…well, good luck.

And while it might not be the most modern way of doing things, do make a physical calendar. Use paper or one of those awesome dry-erase wall calendars that plagued your working days. This way, you can see at a single glance everything you need to get done, and you can strategize effectively about what to do with this unique time that you have before school starts.

As you read through the other chapters in this section, add items to your calendar. Block out sufficient time for it all; that first day will be here before you know it.

Silence Shouldn't Be Scary

Depending upon when in the admissions process you receive your decision, you may hear a lot from your school, or you may not hear much at all. If the latter is the case, don't panic! Your school will let you know about every administrative requirement well in advance, although you have to pay attention. Some students report being very anxious when the whole admissions frenzy dies down and, suddenly, no one's telling you to check your updated status.

Relax. You're still in. It's fine.

However, if you're going to be out of email or phone contact for an extended period of time, let the school know. Also assume that if you have been told something once, you might not be told it again. For better or worse, your graduate program has no desire to be your parent; you won't necessarily get multiple reminders for everything you have to do. It's not the school's fault if you miss a deadline.

Chapter 2:
Say Your Farewells— and Celebrate

The philosophy behind this chapter is simple: **get the uncomfortable tasks out of the way.** Then crack open the champagne. Trust us; it's much easier to do things in this order. Much, much easier.

Breaking the Bad (or Good) News to the Boss

Remember those "Choose Your Own Adventure" novels that were popular in the 1980s and 90s? In the spirit of those novels, we offer the following vignette, especially for those who've had to keep their application process hidden from their coworkers.

As you read, remember: *have a little boilerplate language ready for when you make your announcement.* Go in with a few semi-rehearsed lines so that you don't stumble over yourself. The more awkward the situation is, the more you should stay on message. Be a gracious broken record about how much you appreciate what your boss has done for you, without going overboard.

****

It's 5pm on a Friday. After a long week and an even longer day, you wander over to your boss's office.

"Bob?" you say hesitantly from the threshold. "Got a minute?"

"For you, I've got five!" he booms back.

You exhale and slowly find your way to the armchair on the near side of the desk, where you've sat countless times over the past few years.

Bob smiles at you expectantly. His eyes dart to his computer screen.

"Um," you say, clearing your throat. "You know how we talked a while back about potential next steps in my career?"

"You mean, playing outside linebacker for the Patriots?" he says with a chuckle, his eyes still on his monitor.

"Right," you say, a little flustered. "Maybe in my next life! Anyway, I wanted to tell you I've learned a great deal over the past three years here. I'm very grateful for all you've done for me. You gave me responsibilities I wasn't sure I could handle, but you always had faith in me. And now, I wanted to let you know—"

Bob's full attention is now on you. You can see the wheels turning—are you leaving for a competitor? About to demand a raise? Asking to marry his daughter?

"—I've been accepted to the Haas MBA program," you say, confidence returning to your voice.

If you decide to continue this friendly conversation and tell Bob that you are leaving for a full-time MBA, turn to the next page.

If you decide to continue this friendly conversation and ask Bob to accommodate you as you complete a part-time or executive MBA, turn to page 39.

Telling Bob You're Leaving for a Full-Time Program

You watch Bob take in the news. "The program will be full-time for two years, and it'll be a ton of work, but it's an investment in my future."

Bob's face is blank, so you plow ahead.

"Over the past year or so, I've realized how much I have to learn in order to progress in my career, and business school is the natural next step. I'm excited to be building off of what you and others here have taught me, and I believe I'll represent Corporation, Inc. well among my classmates. I hope you'll—"

"That's great news!" Bob interjects. "Congratulations!"

"Thank you."

"Of course, now I have to replace you. With the hiring freezes and all, who knows what corporate will let me do. But that's not your problem, now is it?"

You smile, relieved. "Well, whatever I can do to help with the transition, you know I'll do it."

Bob's face hardens. "What I don't understand is why this is the first I'm hearing about all this. Who wrote your recommendations?"

You gulp and answer him as honestly as you can.

"I never told you that I was applying to business school because I didn't want you to think that my focus was ever on anything other than this company. I believe that my work product has remained excellent over the past several months. Now that I am sure of my future plans, I wanted to give you plenty of notice, since this place and the people here matter to me, and I'd like to make the transition as smooth as possible for everyone's sake."

You do not tell him that you believe that if you'd asked him for a recommendation last fall, he would have moved you off the fast track—or even let you go. Instead, you stay on point and take the high road.

You avoid apologizing for not asking him for a recommendation. If you need to take the lumps, though, you can say something like, "Maybe I made the wrong call in not asking you at the time I was applying and, for that, I apologize. Again, I have always wanted to do right by you and this place and I believe that I have."

Bob glances back at his computer. "How much longer are you planning on sticking around?"

"I'd like to stay for another two months. That should give me plenty of time to wrap up the projects I am currently working on and help train my replacement. How does that work for you?"

Bob nods, frowning. "I think that can work." Then he stands, indicating that the meeting is winding down. "So tell me, what will you be doing with this MBA? Any chance we'll see you back around these parts in the future? Are you going to grace us with your presence again?"

Whatever your true feelings, you just smile and nod.

"Maybe," you say. "If I'm lucky."

Congratulations! Now turn to page 40.

Telling Bob You're About to Start a Part-Time Program

You watch Bob take in the news. "The program will be part-time for about three years, and it'll be a ton of work, but it's an investment in my career here at Corporation, Inc. and in my future more generally."

Bob's face is blank, so you plow ahead.

"Over the past year or so, I've realized how much I have to learn in order to progress in my career, and the part-time program at Haas is the natural next step. I'm excited to be building off of what you and others here have taught me, and I believe I'll represent Corporation, Inc. well among my classmates. I hope you'll—"

"Why, that's wonderful news!" Bob interjects. "But what does 'part-time' mean exactly? Leaving at noon every other day?"

"No, no," you assure Bob. "Nothing like that. Most of my classes will be in the evenings and on weekends. I will have to leave on time a few nights a week but, other than that, I don't foresee needing all that much in the way of special accommodations. I imagine that an occasional conflict or time crunch might arise, and I'll do my best to predict those and develop workarounds. I'd really like to have your support to make this work."

"Well…you've been here long enough to know what we expect of our employees."

"And I fully intend to keep up the quality of my work. I was able to maintain our standards while completing a time-consuming application process, and I see no reason why being in school should prevent me from doing the same. In fact, I see my MBA studies as a great complement to my work here."

"Oh?"

"Sure! I'll learn new insights and approaches I can take to our clients. I'll also be honing my leadership and management skills. What I'm learning in the classroom one week, I'll be able to put into practice here the following week, at least some of the time."

"So, basically you're after my job?" Bob asks.

Whatever your true feelings, you just shake your head, smiling.

"No, of course not! I could never replace you."

Well done! Now keep reading.

****

However this conversation pans out, it will probably go more smoothly than you imagine right now. Even mean people like to think of themselves as nice. If you are polite and appreciative, you take the wind out of their sails. Don't rise to their bait and don't let yourself be bullied; you know that this is the right decision for you, so feel good about it. This goes for co-workers too. Most will be sincerely happy for you, but a few might feel "left behind" and even a little rejected.

If pushed, take a lesson from *Bull Durham*. As Crash tells Nuke when he gets that first call up to the major leagues, you simply repeat the lines: "I'm just happy to be here. I just hope I can help the ball club."

Above all else, maintain a professional attitude. Do not tell Bob off or post a YouTube video in which you reveal his nasty eating habits. Keep the *Fight Club* and *Office Space* fantasies as just that—fantasies. And no, don't try to take the Swingline stapler with you.

I'll Be Back

If you haven't dropped the MBA bomb on your employer before now, you may think it is too late to discuss issues such as getting a sponsorship or returning to the company after you complete your degree. However, if you are interested in pursuing these goals, don't shy away from bringing them up. It may in fact be too late, but why not ask? A "yes" could be game-changing for you.

With sponsorship, your employer agrees to pay some or all of your tuition.[1] In return, you agree to work for the company for a set amount of time after finishing your program. It's not unlike indentured servitude, but the pay is better. Some employers allow you to work for another company during your MBA summer; others will firmly request your presence back in their offices. Clarify this matter and any other expectations before you leave for school.

> *I knew I wanted to leave early and travel, so I asked my boss if I could accelerate my options and leave when I wanted to [as opposed to sticking around just to let them vest].*
>
> *-- Ed, HBS '12 (Harvard)*

Even if your company is not willing to foot your MBA bill, it may be open to keeping a seat warm for you or giving you preference in future hiring. The conversation might end in a handshake, but try to get something in writing, if at all possible. Two years is a long time. You never know who will still be hovering around the water cooler when you want to cash in on your agreement.

---

1   One thing to take note of: sponsorship is like winning the lottery—in that you have to pay taxes on the money. Before you jump into any agreement, you need to carefully weigh the costs and benefits. Also, be aware that whatever aid an employer gives you will most likely change what you are eligible to get from the school and/or federal government. And if you decide not to go back to your employer after you're done, you will have to come up with a large chunk of cash very quickly to reimburse the tuition. You'll need to dig deep into your own pockets or find a private loan, which might carry a hefty interest rate.

Before you leave your job, make sure to get final results from every one of your projects. You'll want this information for your resumé and interviews down the line.

-- Jen, Ross '12 (Michigan)

Thanks For All The Fish

This last task isn't uncomfortable; it just takes discipline. Well, your hand might cramp a bit, but you can get through that.

You need to show your gratitude to each person who helped you—the people who wrote your recommendations, the roommate who read your crazy essays, the alum who interviewed you, that beloved GMAT instructor, and the co-worker who covered for you when you wigged out the week before applications were due.

Honestly, an email is not enough. It's not *quite* the least you could do (which would be nothing at all), but it's barely a notch above. A batch of electrons never comes across as heartfelt. A call is nicer, but take at least one more step:

1) **Buy a pack of thank-you notes.** A handwritten thank-you note is magic. It doesn't have to take any more time to write than an email—you can knock out at least one during a commercial break while you're watching television. (You remember what a commercial break is, right?) A physical note has much, much more impact than an email.

2) **Send a gift.** A bottle of wine or a box of chocolates is always appropriate and is always appreciated.

3) **Take the person out for a meal.** This works best for a roommate or friend to whom you might feel weird sending a handwritten note or a tub of bonbons. Don't just buy him or her a drink, though. Make it an occasion, and go somewhere nice.

Now that you've finished your task list, you can break open the Dom Perignon and really celebrate your admission to business school.

CHAPTER 3:
REST, RELAX,
& SEARCH YOUR SOUL

This chapter has a simple philosophy: get some rest. You can do that, right?

The Virtues of Downtime

If you are entering a full-time program, you have a financial incentive to keep working right up until the first bell chimes. After all, you are leaving the workforce for close to two years, while incurring a very large expense. Whether you are supporting a family or just yourself, you may be tempted to work a little longer for one last paycheck. The benefits are tangible, while the costs are hard to measure.

> *Four weeks of pay is nothing in the grand scheme of things, and you need to do some soul searching outside of your comfort zone before school.*
>
> *-- Emily, Fuqua '12 (Duke)*

We understand the financial pressure of business school; we've lived under that pressure ourselves. Just remember that business school is an investment. Yes, that is a truism, but that's because it's true. Over the next two years, *you* are the asset you're investing in. And it's tough to hit the ground running if you are burnt out before the race begins. To make the most of school, you need some time to:

- Physically recover from a job that has been running you ragged.
- Put some juice back in your psychic and emotional batteries.
- Wrap up your life in one place and (maybe) move to a new one.

So schedule yourself a break. You've earned it.

What you do with that time is, of course, up to you—visit a Buddhist monastery, engage in a charitable project, repaint your home, take trapeze lessons, or just vegetate. Regardless, spend at least a little time doing whatever you like to do. The challenges that lie ahead of you are numerous and daunting. You will benefit from being rested and ready when you start.

Homeward Bound

One way to relax may be to go home. See Mom, visit with Dad, sleep in your sister's guest bedroom, entertain your toddler nephew. For some folks, time with family is the opposite of relaxing. So define "family" broadly to include old friends. If a bunch of college buddies live in another city, go crash on some couches. The important thing is to spend some time with folks who know all your foibles and don't care, folks you can completely let your hair down around, folks you aren't worried about impressing.

I took a road trip to visit my family and friends and, in essence, to say goodbye because I knew I wouldn't be seeing them for the next two years. Not like, never seeing them, but I knew I'd be moving to school and then... who knows.

-- Craig, Stern '11 (NYU)

When you get to school, you may feel as if you always need to be "on" in all kinds of ways, including socially. Over the course of two years, you will make lots of new friends. That takes work, so reconnect with some old friends first; it's good for your soul.

It's also good for your mind, and even for your career. As you catch up over a bottle of wine with your friend from ninth grade, you will get past all that application-essay malarkey. You'll lay it all out there—your real concerns, your fears, your dreams. Don't expect that he or she will have all of the answers for you. Rather, through the conversation, you'll get back in touch with the bedrock principles by which you've always lived your life. The better you reconnect with those principles, the better able you'll be to navigate business school, which demands that you arrive with both clear career direction and openness to personal development and growth. That's quite a tension.

Later on, once you're in the thick of school, you'll draw on those tried-and-true friendships. Even from afar, your buds will help keep you grounded over the next two years. It's worth reinvesting in those friend-ships when you've got more time in your schedule.

> *The other day, I called my best friend from home and told her that I was feeling overwhelmed. She asked me when was the last time I was on a horse, and I was like, oh, right, I miss that. Who here would know to ask me about stuff like that?*
>
> *-- Sara, Fuqua '12 (Duke)*

Fly Like an Eagle

Feeling the urge to cash in some of your frequent flyer miles? Want to take advantage of your airline status while you still have it? The summer before business school is an optimal time for many to travel somewhere cool. Be prepared to take your own adventure or be left to hear about those of your classmates.

Some quick words about pre-MBA travel:

1) This is hardly your last opportunity to travel. If resources are tight, you might want to postpone major trips so that you can take advantage of treks offered during school.

2) Consider meeting up with future classmates, whether as travel companions or as hosts. (If you are staying home, consider inviting others to check out your neck of the woods.) While it may seem odd to backpack around Europe with total strangers, you will only be total strangers for a few more weeks, even if you wait until school starts. Why not begin building friendships now?

3) Travel doesn't have to mean "keep moving." It can mean "go somewhere different and stay put for a while." The summer before b-school, one of us took a conflict resolution course in Switzerland and spent three weeks in a gorgeous mountain village above Lake Geneva. Hands down, a great decision. (And the other one of us wishes she'd done something half as cool.)

4) Whether your plans involve summiting Mt. Kilimanjaro, swimming across the English Channel, visiting all of the churches in Italy, or enjoying Grandma's cooking in south Florida, get back home with time to spare. The last thing you want to do is show up for your first day of orientation exhausted. Your program could be down the road, across the country, or on another continent; regardless, allow plenty

of time to arrive and get settled. Give yourself more than a weekend to make the transition. You will thank yourself for this, we promise.

Also on this note, a number of schools offer pre-term trips, usually run by second years. While participation varies from school to school, these trips are generally highly enjoyable, both for the travel itself and for the bonding that ensues.

> *The first month of business school is mayhem. You meet 300 people and have two minutes to converse with each of them. On a trip, you get to know a small group of people really well. It gives you a sort of "safe zone" once you start school.*
>
> *-- Mike, Booth '12 (Chicago)*

Sleep, Work Out, Eat Healthy, Sleep

If you've been working madcap hours, burning both ends of the candle and the midnight oil, then you're probably physically, as well as mentally, worn down.

Your body is the foundation on which everything else rests. Think of how you feel when you're sick. You don't want to start business school that way. Rather, you want to be in as good physical shape as possible.

Schedule yourself real sleep. Get eight hours in a row for once. And then do it again. Take some afternoon naps on the weekends (if you're still working) or during the week (if you're not…or if you have a very generous boss). There is no substitute. Yes, quite often you'll be sleep-deprived in school. Unfortunately, you can't "stock up" on sleep like it's canned soup or toilet paper, but at least you can go into school without a (sleep) deficit.

As for exercise, you *can* get yourself in better shape. Coffee may have propelled you through some long workdays, but it's best if the energy comes from the core. You don't have to become a poster child for the local gym, but spend some time on the bike or the yoga mat.

Finally, take the time to eat better. Choose a salad (without the creamy dressing) instead of pizza. You'll get enough pizza on campus. Figure out healthy options and change your habits now, so that you'll stick to them once school starts. And speaking of good alternatives…

Learn how to cook. It'll save you money.

-- Aderly, Booth '12 (Chicago)

Get to Know Yourself (Again)

Hi! Hello? Over here! Yup, I'm the one in the mirror. And yes, I'm talking to you. And no, this isn't a scene from Taxi Driver. *Things have been pretty nutty over the past couple of years, and I thought maybe we could take some time to get to know each other again before you run off on your next great adventure. Maybe we could also set some goals and priorities for the next couple of years. I'm not asking for a formal contract; I just want us to know what it is we're doing and why we're doing it. Sound good? Great! Think maybe you could grab some Windex next time you come by? Thanks. I'm a little smudgy.*

Even if you've already set your sights on a particular career, pinpointed which activities you want to take part in, and decided how valuable grades will be to you, there is still merit in taking time to refocus on yourself and who you are. Chances are good that you've changed quite a bit since you left college, which was probably the last time you did any real introspection. (And if you missed it…then whoops!) So schedule a little self-reflection; you'll be glad that you did.

CHAPTER 4:
GET TO KNOW YOUR FUTURE CLASSMATES

To begin with, go to Admit Weekend. See page 21 for details. But if you missed it, fear not; there are plenty of other ways to meet the kids in your new sandbox.

So-and-So Wants to Be Your Friend

Regardless of your feelings about Facebook, LinkedIn, or even email, you should plan to join and contribute to whatever email lists or networking groups your fellow admits drum up. Or take up the mantle of leadership and start one yourself. Consider a name that will work for the long-term (e.g., Stanford GSB Class of 2013 rather than Stanford GSB 2013 Admits) and publicize it.

Despite some annoying banter, these lists and groups can be wonderful ways to connect with future roommates, travel partners, and movers.[1]

This may also be a good time to do some much-needed culling of your

> *Don't send emails out to the whole school and don't Facebook the whole school before you get to campus.*
>
> *-- Tripp, Ross '11 (Michigan)*

---

1   One of us happened to arrive at her new home a day after all her belongings, which had been left under a tarp in her building's courtyard. Truly unable to move an entire apartment's worth of stuff by herself, she posted a class-wide offer of pizza and beer for anyone willing to schlep boxes on a lovely 102° day. Four hours and a couple of six-packs later, the courtyard was empty (in a good way) and new friends filled the living room.

social networking pages. Make sure you want all of your future classmates to see the pictures that are posted before you give them access…and maybe adjust your relationship status (depending on your expectations).

Finally, recall what we said about "what you may be remembered for" at admit events, back in Chapter 1. This goes triple for online, where people are nastier to each other and nothing is ever, ever forgotten (or truly deleted). As the ex-girlfriend says in *The Social Network*, "The Internet isn't written in pencil … It's written in ink." Stay above the online fray. As much as possible, keep your praise public and your complaints private. Do the same once you arrive on campus.[2]

Shake Hands

Attend any events for admitted students that you possibly can. Happy hours and mixers with current students and/or alums in your city are invaluable. Not everyone you meet will be your best friend, but it bears repeating: look for that topic that you're both genuinely interested in. And give people the benefit of the doubt. They are not defined by their previous or current occupation any more than you are yours.

> *If alumni contact you after you get in, meet them and use them as a resource.*
>
> *--Kevin, Ross '12 (Michigan)*

If no one is throwing a social event in your city, volunteer to do it yourself. It can be as simple as emailing the list or posting to a Facebook group that every-one should come by the Parrot Bar at 7 pm next Thursday night. You might try to get sponsored by the local alumni club or the admissions office—see whether they will buy the first round or get you a

---

2   When one of us was a second year, a first year found himself stranded without a ride home from a distant Halloween event organized by the student government. After trudging for hours along dark streets and highways in his floppy costume, he posted a furious rant attacking the organizers. This rant gave rise to an all-too-memorable brouhaha. The costumed trudger would have been much better off approaching the organizers personally and privately to vent his frustrations.

private room. Either way, ask people to RSVP. (According to the "commitment and consistency" principle that you'll learn about in school, folks are more likely to come if they've made public their plans to attend.) Wear a school t-shirt, tie a school sweatshirt around a pillar, or just describe yourself in the post so attendees know where to congregate.

Once you arrive at the location, stay in communication. Use Foursquare to announce that you are there. Tweet it and change your Facebook status.

Admittedly, taking charge of this sort of event is a brave thing to do. But a party is nothing more than one person publicly committing to being somewhere and having fun. This is a great way to kick off friendships (as well as your campaign for class social chair). Others will be grateful to you for taking the initiative. If you build it, they will come.

CHAPTER 5:
FIRM UP YOUR CAREER KNOWLEDGE

Your first day of business school is the first day of your post-business school job search.

If you are using school to switch fields, or if you are considering more than one possible career route, you have to start your research long before you get to campus.

Just as colleges looking for top athletes send scouts to middle school games, a few companies sponsor events *before* classes even begin. And once you're on campus, the bell dings and the gloves come off.

"C'mon," you may be saying right about now (if you are one of those people who speaks out loud while reading). "The whole point of business school is that I'm going to be able to experiment and test out a number of different careers."

Nope. Sorry. That's all a myth.

While business school will offer you sneak peeks at a variety of career paths, you won't have the time to explore many of them before you have to begin winnowing down the list of summer internship possibilities. It will be physically impossible for you even to attend all of the recruiting presentations, even for just one sector, whether it's consulting, brand management, investment banking, sales and trading, general management, venture capital, or whatever else you're considering.

> *Students think that they have two years to decide what they want to do,*
> *but you can't just come in, go to class, and then figure it out. Day 1 is*
> *when you start your career search; the whole thing just takes two years.*
>
> *-- Jennifer Brooks, Senior Associate Director, MBA Career*
> *Management Center, Kenan-Flagler (UNC)*

So, before you arrive at school, you need to know as much as possible about which path you want to take with your MBA, while giving yourself room to learn and even change your mind later on. The more you can clarify in advance what you really want, deep down, the better off you'll be.

Even if you're already sure about your goals, you should take this opportunity to question them. Right now, you have a momentary hiatus between sprints. Why not make sure that you are running in the right direction?

Part IV of this book is all about recruiting. In the meantime, here are a few avenues for early career exploration.

Learn the Buckets—and Think About What's Not in Them

As a simplification, "MBA jobs" tend to fall into a few buckets in terms of industry and function. Three popular tubs are finance, marketing, and consulting. But there are other buckets as well, such as general management, operations, and entrepreneurship. Each of these buckets is split into subdivisions—e.g., sales and trading, equity research, mergers and acquisitions—that make for a variety of career tracks. Chapter 23 goes into much more detail.

It is worth knowing what these buckets (and specific jobs) entail, if for no other reason than you'll know what to avoid come recruiting season, when your classmates are scurrying from corporate presentation to corporate presentation.

> *On-campus recruiting defines the student's world—and it's only "this" [holds thumb and index finger very close together] big.*
>
> *--Sheryle Dirks, Associate Dean for Career Management, Fuqua (Duke)*

All that said, there really is no such thing as an "MBA job." MBAs can fill many different roles in traditional and non-traditional industries. Spend some of your time looking into positions that may fall outside of the typical buckets. Not only do you want to arrive on campus with a knowledge of what's possible, but you need to know what truly interests you and whether you will be focusing your recruiting efforts on or off-campus (or potentially both).

Read Everything

If you don't already read *The Wall Street Journal*, start now. Skim the whole thing rapidly, then actually read 5–7 articles that interest you. That's the first point of the exercise—to figure out what in the wide world of business you find compelling. Is it Russian mining or Brazilian media? Sales or supply chain? Know before you go. Keep the exercise to 15-20 minutes daily, and you'll actually make it a habit. That's far more useful than trying to read the whole thing cover to cover every day, a target you're more likely to shirk.

Through your daily reading, as you focus on industries and arenas that intrigue you, you will naturally pick up bits of the language. You'll gradually learn who the players are and how they compete. This kind of historical awareness can't be crammed in just before a second round of interviews—you need to build it over time.

By the way, buy physical copies of publications. Online is great for search, but *search* is not the same as *browse*. And true browsing is not what you do with a browser. Following links won't expose you to as much breadth of content as flipping through a paper newspaper. (Yes, we know we're old school.)

If you get really into the "Reading Is Fundamental" vibe, then add any of the following:

- *The Financial Times*, the international business daily
- *The Economist*, the international business weekly
- *Harvard Business Review* or *McKinsey Quarterly*, for more theoretical articles

Apply the same "skim, then dive" approach. Do not feel guilty about reading only a few articles closely. If you already know what industry you're most interested in, supplement with industry-specific publications and blogs.

> *In school, you'll want to treat* The Wall Street Journal *like a 5th class. When it comes to interviewing, you will want to be able to tell an entire business story to a recruiter.*
>
> *-- James, Fuqua '12 (Duke)*

Start a list of areas and functions that seem most interesting or that you keep reading about. Who are the players? Highlight the names of key companies and individuals. Of course, this beginning research begets much more. After you have your lists, hit the web, the library, and your local career service office in search of more materials. Career guides provide great overviews and background information, but often aren't updated with the most recent information. Use the Internet (and not just Wikipedia) to ascertain the latest on who's who and what's what.

When you have found a few people that interest you, delve into how those people got to where they are. What was the career path? Are there common threads or a particular experience that seems to be required to get to whatever your coveted spot is? As much as you will learn in school, no one gets hired to be the CEO of a *Fortune* 100 company days before graduation. You'll have to spend some time climbing the corporate ladder first.

Examine what each rung looks like and decide for yourself whether you really want to climb this specific ladder. Maybe the end is appealing, but you are just not willing to stomach the particular work that you have to do to get there. Say you want to be a managing director at an investment bank. You will go through a semi-formal process or timeline before you are even considered for MD.[1] And yes, that is "considered." Nothing is guaranteed and, as you move up in the organization, the competition will grow fiercer. With that in mind, would you be happy not making it to MD? Is there an off-ramp you can see yourself taking at some point along the way, and where would that off-ramp lead you?

Call it your personal Yellow Brick Road. Make a map of what your future career might look like, given a variety of scenarios.

---

1   If you hear "MD" and think about skin rashes and blood tests, rather than "Managing Director," now's the time to get your b-school vocabulary straightened out.

Get the Inside Scoop

If you're at all interested in marketing as a career, you will have to know what a brand manager does.

Uh, manage a brand?

Sorry, that's not good enough. And recruiting will likely start well before you've finished your first marketing course. You need to understand the role of brand management within consumer packaged goods companies such as Procter & Gamble and Coke. You also want to have a good idea of how brand managers spend their time and how the career track works (which is not usually covered in class).

First, do some more reading. Chapter 23 in Part IV describes brand management briefly. If this piques your interest, go through a book-length guide to this career path, such as those published by *Vault* or *WetFeet*. You might also pick up a guide to specific companies that recruit MBAs for brand management positions.

Once you know the book definitions of the typical career paths, you're ready for the next step: talking to people who've actually walked the walk and lived the life.

Talk to Everyone

When was the last time you were trapped in the middle seat on an airplane? What did you do? Listen to your iPod? Read the Sky Mall catalogue? Watch *The Notebook*? Or did you have a conversation with the person sitting next to you?

One of the best ways to explore professions and career paths is to talk to those who have walked them already. Casual conversations and more formal informational interviews can help you explore different segments of a particular industry or get an overview of a larger field, such as operations management or consulting (which always sounds nebulous).

It doesn't matter exactly where you get your information; just get lots of it from a variety of sources. Call up your second cousin who's a brand manager or your neighbor who has spent years trading natural gas. And that guy in a "Deloitte" embroidered polo shirt sitting next to you on the airplane? Strike up a conversation about where he's been, what he's doing, and what he likes (and dislikes) about his job. You want an "in the trenches" account, so find out if this trip was a rarity or if he's on a first-name basis with the flight attendants. (If he is, see whether he can score free drinks for the both of you.)

Casual conversations can be incredibly useful, since they tend to be fairly unfiltered. That being said, know that you will be getting this one person's particular truth, which won't be all wine and roses. Take everything you hear with a grain of salt; every individual's experience will be different. Also remember that no job is perfect; to paraphrase e.e. cummings, there's some s**t to eat in every job. So don't rule things out too quickly.

> *Being a student is a license to ask anyone anything.*
>
> *-- Nate, NYU Stern '12 (NYU)*

Ask for Informational Interviews

In an informational interview, you're the one leading the discussion. The stated purpose of this kind of interview is for you to get information about the career, the industry, the company, and the position of the person across from you. This is probably the most formal research you'll be doing at this point.

For you, the potential benefits are enormous. As Suzanne describes for you her particular responsibilities, the skills she uses daily, her lifestyle, her growth trajectory, the challenges she faces, and so on, you can evaluate whether Suzanne's path is one you'd like to follow. Indeed, this is the prime time to search for the answer to one of business school's $1,000,000 questions: *What does a consultant actually do???*

In an informational interview, you're talking to someone in a position of power who is further along in a field or role that attracts you. That's potentially game-changing for your career. But you should *not* ask for a job at this juncture; rather, think of this meeting as the beginning of what could be a beautiful relationship. The need for professionalism here should be obvious—even though you're not looking to start work right away, you always want to create a positive impression. Get your dumbest questions out of the way with safe channels, such as your college roommate who works at a hedge fund (in our cases, Josh and Adam). Ask the bigwigs smart questions, and the sky's the limit.

> *You say the word "networking" and people cringe because they think it's just about the schmooze and the schmaltz, that you're not being genuine. But you can be; you're building your professional and personal network. The reality is that it's not so transactional—just don't expect that someone will have a job for you.*
>
> *-- Sheryle Dirks, Associate Dean for Career Management, Fuqua (Duke)*

While the benefits of informational interviews are legion, people often balk at one necessary component: networking.

Yup. We said it. It's the four-letter-word of business school, despite having ten letters.

Believe it or not, "networking" is not inherently disingenuous or burdensome. And yet, most of us have a fear, small or large, of contacting someone we may not know well and asking for a favor. We do not want to impose, particularly when we feel that we have nothing to offer in return for the favor we are requesting.

But think about it this way: we all love to talk about ourselves. Moreover, most of us like to help others, especially someone in an earlier stage of our own career path. An informational interview is the perfect way for someone to do both at the same time, while letting you buy her a nice meal or a round of drinks. Additionally, the person you're talking to probably has some role to play in recruiting. From his or her point of view, it's always good to have a sense of the young talent out there.

You will be amazed at how well-received your request will be. It's also a great way to find mentors for the future, because the people who are willing to help you remember what it was like to be in your shoes.[2]

Opening Doors Early, Very Early

In recent years, there has been a rise in pre-MBA conferences or "industry camps" aimed at attracting minorities and women. Companies want to be the first to get their paws on those who have yet to matriculate but who will potentially be populating the next year's intern class. Admissions organizations focused on women and/or minorities, such as The Forte Foundation and MBA JumpStart, sponsor or hold these events for their members. Even if you did not use these organizations during the admissions process, it may still be possible for you to get in on these and other future events.

Less well-known to future MBAs are pre-MBA internships. Some traditional MBA employers are starting to take on interns who have left their jobs but have yet to start their MBA studies. These internships can sometimes result in offers for the following summer. Don't feel, however, that you must get such an internship to have a shot at a summer gig next year.

You can also explore other career paths and companies by offering to intern for little or no money. Clearly, if you've been accepted to an MBA program, you have an interest in business and a skill set to offer, so companies may be willing to take you on—particularly if it won't cost them anything. If you want to make a dramatic career switch, any relevant experience will greatly enhance your odds of being successful.

---

2   Chapter 24 covers informational interviews in great detail.

Reassess Your Own Interests Using Formal Tools

More than likely, you will have to complete some sort of personality or leadership assessment early in your business school career. However, if you're really interested in this sort of thing, you might begin your own formal assessment of the sorts of environments and tasks that work best for you.

The Myers-Briggs Type Indicator (MBTI) is probably the most well-known of the different personality tests—and one that kicks off the alphabet soup of business school. ENFJ? ISTP? The letters correspond to psychological types originally described by Carl Jung. Knowing your Myers-Briggs type can help you understand yourself better.

The test classifies your personality along four dimensions. Each dimension is a spectrum: few people fall hard to one side or the other. The first dimension, extraversion vs. introversion (E/I), indicates whether you're more outwardly or inwardly focused. Sensing vs. intuition (S/N) addresses preferred ways of processing information—do you build up from concrete details or work down from the big picture? Decision-making is based either on feelings (F) or on thinking (T). The last dimension, judging or perceiving (J/P), describes whether you tend to think convergently (focusing on a specific goal) or divergently (exploring a variety of possibilities).

Don't think of your MBTI type as a straitjacket. It simply describes your comfort zone; it doesn't restrict your movements. For instance, if you're an I (introverted), you're not by definition antisocial. All it means is that you tend to draw energy from solo or small-group activities. You probably enjoy large groups too, but they can exhaust you over time.

You can find the MBTI and other tests online, as well as a number of tools for interpreting the results, if that's your sort of thing. Another way to get more feedback is to simply ask for it. As you leave your job, ask people who worked with you what they see as your strengths and weaknesses. Do this in the classic "360" manner; that is, ask people who work all around you, not just those above you. Sure, get feedback from your boss, but also ask colleagues and direct reports for their opinions. You can even ask support staff or clients with whom you have a close relationship. Just be sure that you are open and accepting of their comments, both good and bad. You asked for it, so be prepared to take it.

Do Summer Reading

We are often asked what books are worth reading before business school. Simply put, read the stuff that interests you. If you like management, read in that area. If you like finance, hit those shelves. This is a way both to learn more about the career paths that attract you and to confirm (or challenge) that attraction. Check out books on different industries or biographies of those who have worked in them.

Over the years, we have developed a list of some personal favorites that we suggest you check out (but only after you've finished this book).

- *Good to Great* by Jim Collins - For those interested in management, leadership, and innovation, as exemplified by companies that transformed themselves from good to great.

- *The 7 Habits of Highly Effective People* by Stephen R. Covey - One of the classics.

- *The Innovator's Dilemma* by Clayton Christensen - This book sheds light on how new technologies can disrupt industries.

- *Crossing the Chasm* by Geoffrey Moore - Learn how to get new products to "cross the chasm" from bleeding-edge adopters to mainstream users.

- *Financial Statement Analysis* by Martin Fridson - You'll know if this is something you're interested in or not; it's great for those going into related fields.

- *Securities Analysis* by Benjamin Graham and David Dodd - Probably the best known book out there on investing, but does require you to understand a fair bit about analyzing financial statements.

- *Hedgehogging* by Barton Biggs - This isn't so much a text as a good book on finance and investing.

- *Valuation* by McKinsey & Co. - Again, if it's up your alley, it's a fantastic guide to techniques for valuing companies.

- *Only the Paranoid Survive* by Andy Grove - The former CEO of Intel discusses the "strategic inflection points" that businesses face.

- *The Big Short* by Michael Lewis - For those interested in understanding the recent financial crisis.

- *Too Big to Fail* by Aaron Ross Sorkin - And another one on the recent financial crisis.

- *Freakonomics* by Steven D. Levitt and Stephen J. Dubner - For those interested in consumer behavior and wacky stories.

- *The Art of Strategy* by Avinash K. Dixit and Barry J. Nalebuff - Practical game theory in well-written layman's terms.

- *Getting Things Done: The Art of Stress-Free Productivity* by David Allen - One can always dream.

CHAPTER 6:
PREPARE FOR CLASS

For all of the talk of socializing, networking, and recruiting, business school is, in fact, *school*. While the effort expended in class will vary from individual to individual (and from course to course), you aren't going to avoid the academics. So think about what you really want to get out of the classroom experience. What fields do you want to learn about? What skills do you want to develop? What professors do you want to study under? What sort of class schedule do you want, assuming you get control over your calendar? And how much do you want to challenge yourself?

When That First Bell Rings

The amount of flexibility you will have will be particular to your program. Regardless, there are a few general areas to consider as you think about the upcoming term:

1) **Are you trying to switch fields?** If you don't have the requisite knowledge for an internship in your desired area, then you need to get it—and fast. Not a lot of finance in your background and you're gunning for a banking job? See if you can't swap a marketing class for one on capital markets in your first term. Moreover, you'll need to prove your chops in that class. Career switchers should obviously try to ace courses related to their goals.

2) **Does your school have a grade disclosure/non-disclosure policy?** Some MBA programs have a policy that students may not reveal their grades during the job search. If this is the case, the pressure to get all A's (or whatever the top grade is) diminishes substantially.[1]

3) **Is there a forced curve?** If your school allows you to talk about your GPA, a forced curve means that the vast majority of the class does well. Some curves are middle-biased; for instance, there might be 10% A's, 80% B's, and 10% C's or lower. These curves give you a reason to challenge yourself with a class, knowing that the risk/ reward proposition is slanted in your favor. It's hard to fail a class.

4) **Are you allowed to test out of classes?** Schools with set core curricula sometimes allow students to waive out of certain courses. If you've been a CPA for the past five years, you should investigate what's involved in getting out of Managerial Accounting. You might get to *credit* your core and *debit* your electives.[2]

Testing out of a class not only frees you up, but also helps others who might not know the subject. Professors tend to play to the level at the top, which makes it hard for people who are new to the material and really need to learn it.

-- A.J., Kenan-Flagler '11 (UNC)

---

1   Truth be told, there are a limited number of employers who really care about fine grade-point distinctions: namely, the top-tier banks and consulting firms. Random other companies, such as Google, also like to play the GPA numbers game, but most won't focus on your transcript. At the same time, the companies that do care, *really* care. Talk with second years to find out how students deal with the pressure to reveal grades, if your school has a non-disclosure policy. Remember that companies that don't recruit on campus can ignore any such policy.

2   Painful. Sorry.

If You Don't Know Where You're Going, Any Road Will Take You There

…but if you do know where you're going academically, it helps to have a plan (or be willing to stop and ask for directions a lot). Set aside some time before you even get to campus to think about what courses you want to take during your b-school tenure. Do certain classes have pre-requisites that you need to pass? Are there classes that are only taught every other year or term? Is a top professor on sabbatical or about to be?

The last thing you want to do is get to your final term and realize that the one class you were dying to take isn't being taught or that you're ineligible because you never got around to taking some intro course. That just sucks.

$2 + 2 = 5?$

The months before matriculation are also good for getting rid of some of the rust that may have accumulated on your study and academic skills. Last time you took a math class was in high school? Haven't written a paper in many a year? Is the GMAT already just a distant, bad memory?

Spend some time with Part III of this guide. Maybe even think about enrolling in a class at your local college, not necessarily for credit, but to get back into "school" mode. You remember how hard it was to go back to school after summer vacation, right? It's probably been a bit longer than three months since you last set foot in a classroom, so it's worth knocking the dust off of your Trapper Keeper.

Even if you are not looking to exempt out of classes, you may be lacking a presumed background in a few key areas. Business school classes are masters-level courses, so if you only think of statistics in terms of batting averages, you have some work to do.

> *Business school assumes that you have some basic familiarity with business concepts. There are no "101" classes and you're not going to get the "college" version. Familiarize yourself with terms and concepts so that class isn't the first time that you are exposed to them.*
>
> *-- Christine Gramhofer, Director of Academic Services,*
> *Booth (Chicago)*

Part III of this book is designed to give you an entry-level conceptual foundation for a number of required topics. Part V contains a glossary of some b-school specific jargon and basic business language. Use these sections to prep. Additionally, check with your school about any pre-term programs. These "MBA camps" vary from school to school: some are required, some are optional, and some are by invitation only. Many of them focus on basic quantitative skills that you may be missing.

Pre-term programs actually serve two purposes —introducing academic material and also providing a way to meet some of your classmates early. Most students who attend camp report that it was a benefit to their social life, if not their academic life. Even if you don't qualify for camp, you may want to inquire about attending. Besides, what else are you going to do with those last couple of weeks? Blow through your Netflix queue?

> *Talk to current students and try to gauge, depending upon your background, what training you need before you get to campus.*
>
> *-- Ed, HBS '12*
> *(Harvard)*

Alternatively, if you want to keep hanging around home, look into classes at your local community college or university. This is one way to get back in the academic swing, brush up on your algebra, and establish a bit of a foothold on those topics you've never studied before. By the end, you might be in a position to test out of the intro accounting course—or you just might be a bit better prepared to discuss debits and credits on a higher level. Either way, taking a non-credit course before the real school work begins can be a great way to ease the transition.

CHAPTER 7 :
FIND HOUSING & MOVE

The transition to business school may be major (e.g., moving across the globe/country/state/city) or minor (e.g., changing your commuting route). In either situation, it's most likely time to address some of the fundamentals of your life, such as how you live and spend your money. If you are like most MBAs, the next couple of years will require a rather dramatic change in your cash flow, so you may not be able to continue that swashbuckling lifestyle to which you have become accustomed. Or maybe you can ... It all depends on the sacrifices you are willing to make.

Living Arrangements

Returning to school often means reexamining your living arrangements. Is it time to strike out on your own or to go back to having roommates? Is on-campus housing available, or will you be hunting for an apartment? Every community presents a variety of different options, but choosing can be quite difficult—particularly if you are moving from another locale.

When thinking about housing preferences, consider your current and presumed lifestyle:

> *I was already living in Boston, so I stayed in the same apartment I was in. My environment didn't change—but I did.*
>
> *-- Juliet, HBS '12 (Harvard)*

- How social do you want to be, and in what way?

- How much distance will you want from campus, physically and psychically?

Some folks need to keep home a separate sphere from school. Others are happy to have case discussions and keg parties pour into their living rooms. Just be sure that, given the very few hours you'll spend in your bed, you'll be happy there.

To Dorm or Not to Dorm

For many future MBAs, the first housing question is whether to apply for on-campus housing. Housing styles, availability, and policies vary widely from school to school, further complicating the matter. For example, Harvard Business School offers a variety of on-campus living options that more than 80 percent of the student body takes advantage of. Columbia's business school, in contrast, has extremely limited on-campus housing, with priority going to students coming from abroad or extreme distances (think Alaska). Meanwhile, Fuqua students tend to live in off-campus apartment complexes, which become their own centers of social activity.[1]

Even programs that offer housing may provide an array of choices, such as dorms, apartments, or university-owned houses. Some dorm-like arrangements may come with access to dining halls or even meal plans. (Remember those days of the all-you-can-eat cereal bar in college?) Other arrangements resemble subsidized or standard apartments, often with lease terms that bar you from subletting to anyone other than university affiliates (a key thing to think about if you are planning on a summer internship in another city).

---

1   One thing to keep in mind if you do live in one of these more contained communities—people will see you. They will see you at the drug store, they will see you stumbling home at night, they will see you on your walks of shame. If you're fine with that, great. If you're not, think about ordering your more personal supplies online so your next trip to the CVS doesn't end in a checkout line discussion of Church & Dwight's latest marketing strategy.

On-campus housing options may feature buildings reserved for business school students or those open to a wider array of graduate students. Being married or having a significant other may also limit your options; kids definitely put you in a special pool. Check with your program and evaluate your options. But you should also think about whether you are looking to take on roommates or if you need to be king/queen of your own castle.

Thinking Outside the Typical Four Walls

Non-traditional housing options may also exist; it is up to you to check them out. Many universities use grad students as resident advisors, offering up a room to those willing to tell the underage to stop drinking and turn down that stuff they call music. If you think you are up to the challenge, dorm life can save you money on housing and even food, if you can score a meal plan. If you don't want to live with the little ones, you can still look into other advisor roles that come with perks such as office space or free meals. Remember, though, that nothing's truly free. The accompanying commitments may turn out to be more costly than what you're saving on room and board.

Me, Myself, and I vs. Larry and Balki[2]

Having your own place can be quite nice. You decide the cleanliness standards, you own all of the groceries, and you can never get sexiled.[3] At the same time, you probably pay more for rent, have to cover utilities on your own, and have no one to blame but yourself for the dirty dishes in the sink.

For many MBAs, post-college life consisted of solo living or a lot of time spent on the road. The idea of having roommates again can feel akin to

---

2   Larry and Balki, respectively portrayed by Mark Linn-Baker and Bronson Pinchot, were the lead characters in the classic 1980s sitcom *Perfect Strangers*. Add it to your Netflix queue.

3   MBA roommates almost never share bedrooms, so the physical situation would rarely be as appalling as when you were a freshman in college. That said, your sensitivity to these matters has probably heightened over the intervening years.

> *Business school is ideal for having a roommate because you're never home; you don't have to see each other. It's very different from an undergraduate roommate situation.*
>
> *-- Cassandra, HBS '12 (Harvard)*

returning to college—which may be the best idea you have ever heard or your worst nightmare. Living on your own during grad school does allow you to separate your work from your home in much the same way that you did when you were a professional. Many find it to be more conducive to establishing boundaries and maintaining a good school/life balance.

At the same time, living alone may make it more difficult to share books, course notes, and hangover remedies. You may be more inclined to stay in on nights when others go out, and you will have to remember what you did with your keys when you come back after a long night at the bar. But no one will interrupt your study time, steal your lucky tie, or accidentally erase that episode of "Jersey Shore" or the finals of the U.S. Open from your DVR.

Life with roommates who are classmates has its ups and downs as well. It is easier to get help late at night with that corporate restructuring

> *It's nice to be a little removed from the whole scene by living in a non-business school dorm.*
>
> *-- Fareeda, GSB '12 (Stanford)*

project if a friendly tutor is sitting on the couch next to you, and impromptu case prep can pay dividends the following day. If your roommate runs in a different social circle, you can double your party invites. You can also help each other navigate recruiting, tag-teaming events and picking up extra swag.[4]

---

4   Swag = free stuff branded with company names. Years from now, you'll own at least one t-shirt from a company gone kablooey.

Roommate living often means more space and lower costs. The cable bill gets split multiple ways, and the individual burden of kitchen supplies and general furnishings is lighter (although you have to figure out which one of you actually gets to contribute the television, couch, and olive oil).

On the downside, it becomes harder to get away from b-school if it follows you home. You have to contend with a roommate (or mates) on a similar pressure-cooker schedule as you, with mid-terms, recruiting, finals, etc. And then there's the really annoying part of trying to keep your social life private; what happens in the apartment may not stay in the apartment.

That being said, sometimes it pays to have an open-door policy on your home. It's all too easy just to meet up with your classmates on campus or at the pub, but you really get to know someone in his or her living room—or in yours. If you have a pad close to campus, invite friends who live far away to take a shower before an interview, nap on your couch during a free period, or just relax and recharge their cell phone. Geographical cliques can form unintentionally; singles congregate in dense apartment complexes, while married students with kids tend to gravitate to more open spaces. Make an effort to cross the train tracks, figuratively and literally.

Yes, It's Animal House

At some schools, certain houses are social institutions. These renowned party locales are stewarded by second-year students, who turn over the keys and keg-erators to the next generation in an annual rite of passage. The occupants change, but the "Love Shack" and the "Moon Tower" live on.

Living in one of these houses may be tradition, but it is not for everyone. Think long, hard, and sober about jumping into one of these arrangements. It can be a lot of fun and make for an easy move, but you should take the social responsibility seriously. And you'll want to get a hotel room for your mother when she comes to visit.

Bunkmates and Bathrooms

It is rare that you would meet someone, go out on a single date, and declare that you are moving in together.[5] Yet, when it comes to finding a roommate, you are often left with little choice. Many MBAs meet at admit events and decide, there and then, to live together the following school year. Others find each other through online bulletin boards, meeting for the first time over the threshold of their new abode.

While fun and exciting, this rush to find housing buddies has a few potential issues: (1) ensuring roommate compatibility and (2) finding a living space.

While the first issue may seem obvious, the second one comes into play if neither or none of you live near campus. In some housing markets (particularly those that are university-friendly), you may be able to sign an August lease in March or April, but don't count on it. Will you all return for a house-hunting trip in the summer? Will one person be designated to find the space and, if so, what parameters must he/she follow?

> *I was surprised at how many people wanted roommates at this age, but there are a lot more advantages to having them in school than when you're working. For one, it helps to give you a better sense of what's going on. For another, you'll be less likely to be lazy if you see people up and moving around.*
>
> *-- Mike, Kellogg '12 (Northwestern)*

To help guide you through the very difficult roommate evaluation process, we offer the following questionnaire. Think of it as Speed Dating— you have 10 minutes to figure out if you really are compatible. This may not be the time to discuss religion or

---

5   One friend did, in fact, do this. A week later, we were boxing up her things and moving them into her beau's place. A month after that, we were again boxing up her things…and moving them out of her now-ex's place.

politics, but you definitely need to air your thoughts on soap scum, keg parties, and houseguests.

This kind of discussion can help the both of you to commit to good behavior ahead of time. No one is going to tell you, "I handle conflict terribly." Why ask about conflict management, then? So that the other person verbalizes his or her ideal—which makes him or her more likely to live up to that ideal, whether or not you actively enforce it. Long story short, it's worth getting this stuff out in the open now.

Everything You've Always Wanted to Know About a Potential Roommate*

Previous Relationships
- Have you ever had a roommate or roommates? What were they like?
- How and why did your last roommate experience end?
- What makes for a successful roommate experience?
- How would your previous roommates describe you?
- What are your pet peeves with regard to roommates? How have roommates ever gotten on your nerves?
- How have *you* ever gotten on a roommate's nerves?

Logistics
- What's your price range? Does that include utilities and other expenses?
- What luxury items or amenities are you willing to pay for? (e.g., premium cable channels, doorman, on-site gym)
- How do you like to split the cost of kitchen supplies and other miscellaneous expenses? How do you like to keep track of joint expenses, and how closely? How often do you want to settle up?
- How many people are you willing to live with?

---

*   And Should Not Be Afraid to Ask

- Are you looking for a fully-furnished place? If not, what furnishinga do you wish to contribute/anticipate contributing?
- What do you value in housing—size, location, amenities, etc.?
- Are you more into cooking, ordering in, or eating out? What's your typical eating pattern? [This can help you assess kitchen usage.]

Socializing and Other Standards

- How do you like to relax? What do you do for fun?
- What sort of socializing do you plan to do at home? What sort of socializing will you tolerate?
- How do you feel about houseguests? How many is too many and how long is too long?
- How often are significant others allowed to stay over? What about insignificant others?
- What are your standards for cleanliness? Does this just apply to your space or to common spaces, too? Are you willing to pay for cleaning help? How much? How often?

Personality Issues

- How do you handle conflict? If I have an issue, how would you want me to raise it? If you have an issue, how would you typically raise it?
- What are you type A (more anal) about, and what are you type B (more relaxed) about?
- What is your general schedule like? That is, are you a morning person or an evening person?
- Are you a homebody or someone who goes out a lot?
- Are you more likely to study at home or elsewhere? Do you care where others are when you are studying?
- What is your noise tolerance like?
- Do you generally involve others in your disagreements or do you prefer to handle things yourself?

MBA Profile
- What are you looking to do with your MBA?
- Which classes do you suspect will be easier for you? Which ones will be harder?
- How focused on grades do you think you'll be?
- Which school clubs or associations do you see yourself involved with?

There's No Place Like Home

Now that you have found the perfect living companion(s) or decided to go it solo, you have to find the perfect place. Having already laid out your priorities, you may be set to hit the real estate listings … or you may have to deal with a few more issues first.

If you do have roommates, who is going to take the lead in finding the apartment? For many, starting a full-time MBA program means moving to a new city. Will you have to arrange a special trip to look at places? When will this need to happen? Timing the housing market varies from city to city; look to your program for guidance on this issue. If not, bug some current students—they are often your best resource when it comes to housing (and may have a great place they need to unload).

Landlord negotiations tend to be pretty simple and largely focused around price. However, you should also consider the length of the lease and whether you are allowed to sublet. Pets, co-signers, and credit history are often part of the dance, so know where you stand on these issues before you get too attached to that place you found on Craigslist.

What Lease Terms Work for You?

It's hard to imagine ahead to your MBA summer or your second year right after you are admitted, but you should take different possibilities into consideration when you think about lease terms.

Are you likely to stay the summer, or do you need a lease that will allow you to sublet? Even if your landlord signs off on a sublet, will your roommates?

Are you considering going abroad for a semester? If so, will you want to sublet or simply move out?

Can you negotiate a lease for a non-traditional length of time? Twenty-two-month leases are often optimal for students starting pre-term in August and wanting a place through the end of May nearly two years later, but not a lot of landlords like that arrangement.

Be willing to offer different concessions to get what you want. You may not have taken Negotiations yet, but it's never a bad idea to start working on those skills. And given that your BATNA[1] is living in a van down by the river[2], you should be able to find some common ground.

---

1   Best Alternative to a Negotiated Agreement.

2   Best Chris Farley line from *Saturday Night Live.*

Splitting the Rent Without Splitting Skulls

It's possible to pick places from afar or trust one roomie to do the digging. However, few bedrooms are created equal. So you have to figure out how to divide up the rent—and the rooms—in an equitable way.

Given that this is real life and not just some academic exercise, we realize that there are a number of different approaches. You can use the shotgun method, draw straws, or simply fight it out old-school style.[6] You can

---

6   Three words of advice, courtesy of the Cobra Kai dojo: "sweep the leg."

also divide up the rent in a roughly proportional way, using factors such as square footage.

While all of these methods will result in an outcome you can probably live with, we happen to be big fans of something called the **Indifference Point Model**, which draws from economics and game theory. This method generates an outcome that you and your roommate(s) will recognize as fair. It works like this:

Say there are two roommates, Joey and Chandler, looking to live in an apartment that rents for $2,000. There are two bedrooms: a small one and a large one.

Without discussion, Joey and Chandler each secretly write down their respective indifference points. What is an indifference point? It's the split where the person would be happy getting either side of the deal.

Chandler decides he's indifferent between getting the larger room for $1,200 and the smaller room for $800. How does he figure this out practically? He considers different splits at opposite ends of the spectrum. For instance, he knows that at $1,000/$1,000, he'd take the larger room but at $1,500/$500, he'd take the smaller room. He tests different splits until he finds one where he'd be happy with either arrangement.

 Meanwhile, Joey figures he's indifferent between getting the larger room for $1,100 and the smaller room for $900. Notice that both numbers must sum to the rent total. Chandler and Joey put their indifference points on paper, then reveal their sealed bids.

Now both people get a "deal."

As Chandler is willing to pay more for the big room ($1,200), he gets that one. Joey gets the small room, because he was willing to pay more for it ($900). However, if they each pay those amounts, there would be an extra $100 (= $2,100 − $2,000) collected each month. Given that they're not going to just turn that extra money over to their landlord, each guy gets a discount of $50 off of what he was willing to pay.

In the end, Chandler gets the big room for $1,150 and Joey gets the small room for $850. Both are happy because they each ended up with cheaper rent than what they were willing to pay for the rooms they got. How Monica and Rachel divide their rent is entirely up to them.

The model works for larger groups, too. Jack, Janet, and Chrissy[7] have found a great place with three different rooms and a total rent of $3,500. They all secretly write down indifference points for the three rooms, making sure each set of numbers sums to $3,500:

	Large	Medium	Small
Jack	$2,000	$1,000	$500
Janet	$1,500	$1,100	$900
Chrissy	$1,700	$1,200	$600

Since Jack is willing to spend the most for the large room ($2,000), he gets it. Chrissy offers the highest for the medium room ($1,200), so that's hers. Janet put the highest price tag on the small room ($900), so that's hers.

Their winning bids total to $4,100, which is $600 more than is needed to cover the monthly rent. Divide this overage by 3 to calculate the discount for each roommate: $200.

So, when the dust settles, Jack is in the large room, paying $1,800. Janet is in the small room, paying $700. And Chrissy is in the medium room at $1,000. Everyone's whistling a happy tune.

---

7   *Three's Company.* Another Netflix addition, if necessary.

Game Theory Rent Splitter

The following worksheet is filled out with Chandler and Joey's preferences, so you can see how the process works.

Game Theory Rent Splitter Example

	Room A - **LARGE**	Room B - **SMALL**	Total Rent = **$ 2,000**

(1) Chandler finds his Indifference Point.

(a) Make Room A a bargain $ 1,000   + $ 1,000   =   Total Rent
definitely pick A

(b) Make Room B a bargain $ 1,500   + $ 500   =   Total Rent
                                              definitely pick B

(c) Adjust toward the middle in steps of $200, $100, or $50. Keep the total rent correct.

	Room A	Room B
Your Bargain A scenario *from above*	$ 1,000	$ 1,100
You would probably pick A	$ 1,100	$ 900
You would flip a coin	$ 1,200	$ 800 ← **Chandler's** Indifference Point!
You would probably pick B	$ 1,300	$ 700
Your Bargain B scenario *from above*	$ 1,500	$ 500

(2) **Joey** also finds his Indifference Point, using the same process. **$ 1,100 for large, $ 900 for small.**

(3) They both submit their bids.

(4) They open the bids, determine the winners, and split the savings.

	Room A	Room B
Chandler's bids	$ 1,200	$ 800
Joey's bids	$ 1,100	$ 900
	circle the winning bid for A	*circle the winning bid for B*

Add up the winning bids:		$ 2,100
Subtract the total rent:	−	$ 2,000
Total savings:	=	$ 100

Chandler bid $ **1,200** for room **A** and won. He actually pays $ **1,200** minus $ **50**   = $ **1,150**.
                                                                    his bid   *½ the savings*   *his rent*

Joey bid $ **900** for room **B** and won. He actually pays $ **900** minus $ **50**   = $ **850**.
                                                             his bid   *½ the savings*   *his rent*

Use the following worksheet to go through the same exercise with your future roommate.

Game Theory Rent Splitter Worksheet

	Room A	Room B	Total Rent = $

(1) Find your Indifference Point.

(a) Make Room A a bargain $ _____   + $ _____   =   Total Rent
definitely pick A

(b) Make Room B a bargain $ _____   + $ _____   =   Total Rent
definitely pick B

(c) Adjust toward the middle in steps of $200, $100, or $50. Keep the total rent correct.

Your Bargain A scenario *from above* $ _____ $ _____

You would probably pick A $ _____ $ _____

You would flip a coin $ _____ $ _____   ← Your Indifference Point!

You would probably pick B $ _____ $ _____

Your Bargain B scenario *from above* $ _____ $ _____

(2) Your roommate also finds his or her Indifference Point, using the same process.

(3) You both submit your Indifference Points as sealed bids.

(4) Open the bids, determine the winners, and split the savings.

	Room A	Room B
Your bids	$ _____	$ _____
Your roommate's bids	$ _____	$ _____
	circle the winning bid for A	*circle the winning bid for B*

Add up the winning bids:		$
Subtract the total rent:	−	$
Total savings:	=	$

You bid $_____ for room ___ and won. You actually pay $_____ minus $ _____ =$ _____ .
your bid   *½ the savings*   *your rent*

Your roommate....

bid $_____ for room ___ and won. He/she actually pays $_____ minus $ _____ =$ _____ .
roommate's bid   *½ the savings*   *his/her rent*

If the two sets of bids are identical, flip a coin to determine who wins which room. There are no savings in this case: you each pay what you bid.

Moving in and Getting Settled

Regardless of your final decisions, you'll eventually have to start packing boxes (or hire someone to do it for you, if you happen to be in that post-MBA, big money mindset already). When should you actually move? Pre-term courses and trips often necessitate earlier-than-anticipated move-in dates. Work backwards from when you are required to be on campus—and then give yourself at least an extra week.

You want to be as moved in as possible before school activities start. (Pre-term is, by all accounts, akin to military boot camp...only with more vodka, fewer pushups, and more members of the opposite sex to mingle with.) Those who arrive the day before orientation will be scrambling to screw together their IKEA bookshelves while others are profitably exploring the local dives.

If you are set up with some time to spare, offer to help your fellow classmates. You are probably a pro at unwrapping dishes by this point, and you know where the hardware store is. Share this tidbit of information now, and someone might be willing to show you how to use the F4 key in Excel a couple of weeks from now.

Most utilities can be turned on from afar with phone calls, except...the cable. Someone has to wait around during a four-hour window for the cable guy to show up. Since that also affects high-speed Internet access, take care of this fun task as early as possible.

> *You don't want to say that you can't go to dinner with your friends because you have to wait for the cable guy to show up.*
>
> *-- Jessie, Wharton '11 (Penn)*

Find all the stores you typically need. Figure out the best grocery store, deli, pharmacy, and dry cleaners. Set up a local bank account and get checks with your new address on them. If you have a car, find a mechanic and gather any local parking permits you need. Find a few go-to restaurants as well. Between Google Maps and Yelp, you have more information than ever before at your fingertips, so you can always figure it out on the fly. But you'll look so much cooler if you just know these things.

CHAPTER 8:
FIGURE OUT YOUR FINANCES

~~~~~~~~~~~~~~~~~~~~

Budgeting

There's no doubt about it: business school is an expensive proposition. Full-time tuition at private universities can cost more than $50,000 a year. And that's just what you pay for the privilege of showing up to class. Your school will provide you with an estimated budget for the year, breaking down additional costs for books, housing, food, travel, and assorted other items. This budget will be too low by 20–30 percent.[1]

Even if you live with roommates, subsist only on the food provided at recruiting events, and go home after every happy hour, you will, in all likelihood, still be spending over the official estimates. And let's face it: you are almost certainly not going to live a completely Spartan lifestyle. You may have roommates, you may watch your food budget, but you are also going to go out every so often, buy a new suit for recruiting, and take a spring break trip. You hardly need Excel's sum function to know that the costs will add up.

As a point of comparison, take a look at Wharton's 2010-2011 budget for first years on the next page.

---

1   In fairness to your school, the budget presented is largely limited by federally-mandated guide-lines. Financial aid offices are required to use modest figures and can only include the items you see.

Wharton MBA First Year Student Budget
2010-2011 Academic Year (10 Months)

Expenses	Fall Semester Aug 10 - Dec 10	Spring Semester Jan 11 - May 11	Total Budget
Tuition/Fees			
Tuition	$ 24,275	$ 24,275	$ 48,550
General Fee	$ 1,076	$ 1,076	$ 2,152
MBA Program Fee	$ 772	$ 772	$ 1,544
Pre-Term Fee	$ 1,715	-	$ 1,715
Total Tuition & Fee Expenses:	$ 27,838	$ 26,123	$ 53,961
Books & Supplies			
Books, Bulk Packs & Supplies	$ 1,000	1,000	$ 2,000
Total Books & Supplies Expenses:	$ 1,000	1,000	$ 2,000
Room & Board			
Rent	$ 6,525	$ 6,525	$ 13,050
Rental Insurance	$ 150	$ 150	$ 300
Utilities	$ 750	$ 750	$ 1,500
Board	$ 3,333	$ 3,333	$ 6,666
Total Living Expenses:	$ 10,758	$ 10,758	$ 21,516
Miscellaneous			
Health Insurance	$ 1,340	$ 1,340	$ 2,680
Transportation	$ 390	$ 390	$ 780
Clothing/Laundry	$ 500	$ 500	$ 1,000
Phone/Internet	$ 500	$ 500	$ 1,000
Personal	$ 531	$ 532	$ 1,063
Total Miscellaneous Expenses:	$ 3,261	$ 3,262	$ 6,523
Total MBA Expenses	$ 42,857	$ 41,143	$ 84,000

When it comes to attitudes towards expenses, MBA students can be anywhere between carefree and terrified:

A. "I'll be making major bank when I get out, so why not just rack up the debt now and worry about it later?"

B. "What do you mean, I'm not earning anything for the next two years? Does anyone want to split a membership to Costco?"

C. "My employer/school/government/grandparents are paying for this. The least I can do is buy a round every time we go out."

D. "Sallie Mae set a budget for me, and I'm going to do my best to stay within that. If I go a little over, I guess that's why I've been saving the past couple of years."

E. "Maybe I'll play it safe my first year, but if I get a job offer after the summer, all bets are off."

F. "I'm going to eat PB&J sandwiches every day for lunch…and dinner while we're at it. These loans give me bloody ulcers."

G. "I only withdraw $40 at a time from the ATM, and I try never to touch a credit card. I can't stand watching my bank balance drain away."

At one time or another during your program, you may adopt every one of these attitudes. A signing bonus can make you feel as if you won Powerball. On the other hand, a protracted job search can leave you eating ramen three times a day.

As with so much in life, the key is moderation. Aim to average somewhere in the middle. Neither carefree nor terrified is a healthy long-term stance.

Before you sit down to budget for yourself, take some time to consider what sort of lifestyle you envision over the next two years, and which end of the spectrum you tend toward by nature. Are you someone who will be going out a lot and, if so, will you be following the crowd to the nearest hotspot or chilling at the local coffee joint? Spring break in Rio or visiting the folks? Will your job search be largely on campus, or will you have to travel around the globe for informational interviews? You live in a warm-weather climate now, but do you have a down parka to get you through the next two years in the frozen tundra?

> *Money is constantly on your mind, but if you're going to make business school a transformational experience, you have to expect it.*
>
> *-- Pete, HBS '12 (Harvard)*
>
> *You have to watch what you spend, but it's more about the tens of thousands than the small stuff. Do you want to save a few bucks or really enjoy the experience?*
>
> *-- Ed, HBS '12 (Harvard)*

The "moderate lifestyle" that US schools are required to use to estimate costs is significantly more restrained than is realistic. Take the first-year number that the school provides and break it down into the areas listed below.

Use the worksheet following this list to tally up. It can be helpful to consider certain expenses on several time scales: a $3 daily coffee is $20 per week, $90 per month, $800 per 9-month academic year, and $1,100 per calendar year. We're not trying to scare you into living in a miserly way; just budget realistically, allowing for some discretionary spending. The natural basis for irregular expenses may not be monthly, but convert them to a monthly spend for an apples-to-apples comparison.

Also notice that the school number often accounts only for nine or ten months of living. For an extra dose of depression, run the numbers including an extra two or three months of expenses, assuming that your summer internship won't pay you a dime.

- **Housing** – Are you on campus? Off? Living on your own or with roommates? If you don't have firm housing costs at this point, try to approximate. Find out typical rents from second years. Include utilities, phone, and Internet, as necessary.

- **Food** – What is your current food budget? Now think about where you spend money on food. Are most of your dinners currently covered by your employer because you work late? Do you bring lunch every day? Think you will keep that practice up when you are in school, or are you likely just to buy something at the cafeteria? Will you bake a big lasagna and eat it for a week or pop a frozen pizza in the oven every night? If you are used to getting coffee for free at the office, will you now buy it (setting aside a $1,000 annual Starbucks budget) or brew it at home?

- **Clothing** – What's your current wardrobe like, and will it last you for the next two years? You will need casual clothes for class, business casual for daytime activities, and business formal for interviews.

- **Books and Supplies** – This figure rarely includes newfangled technology like an e-reader or iPad. Is that Blackberry yours, or do you have to return it to your employer when you leave? You may need a new laptop, too.

- **Transportation** – Do you need a car? Mass-transit? The costs here can vary widely, so think about all the different components and act wisely. If you have a car, will you need an expensive on-campus parking permit? How often will you park in the $2/hour visitors lot because you're running late for class?

- **Travel** – What are your travel plans? Many schools offer treks for groups of students to go abroad, visiting companies in São Paulo and Buenos Aires for ten days, for instance. These school-sponsored trips tend to be

> *Looking in the parking lot, you see 15-year-old Civics and $100K cars. There's a definite range in terms of the resources people have.*
>
> *-- Maya, GSB '12 (Stanford)*

both popular and expensive. The good news is that you can usually get a bump in loans for this purpose; the bad news is that you just increased your loan burden. Additionally, completely non-school-sponsored trips are, of course, not reflected in the school's suggested budget. But as extravagant as they may sound, such trips may be a part of your overall school experience that you don't want to sacrifice.[2] Finally, if you plan to conduct an off-campus job search, you will likely incur significant airfare and car rental expenses. Estimate these costs as best you can—and then add 20 percent.

- **Lifestyle expenses** – Entertainment, no matter your chosen variety, is never included adequately in the estimated budget.

- **Major milestones** – Many people in business school are of an age when major life events take place. Allow yourself a budget for non-missable commitments (e.g., weddings, baby showers, family needs), considering both travel and fancy schmancy clothes.

Try estimating your expenses on the next page. Use any numbers your school has given you, then think about your own spending needs, as well as costs you might encounter early on, such as those involved in actually finding a place to live (e.g., a trip to hunt for a place, money to cover a broker's fee, security deposits, move-in fees, etc.).

Check with your school before you buy things. I would have saved 120 bucks on a backpack and 100 dollars on Office 7 if I had known that they'd be giving me those things.

-- Mike, CBS '12 (Columbia)

---

2   Beach Week at the end of the year is a big deal at Fuqua. If that's where you are, consider it a class. If you're not at Fuqua, organize your own Beach Week and tell people it's a class.

	School Projections	Self-Projections	Percent +/-
Upfront Expenses for the Year			
Tuition			
General fee			
MBA program fee			
Pre-term fee			
Health insurance fee			
Other university fees			
Computer/technology purchases			
Books/supplies			
Moving			
Misc. big purchases (car, etc.)			
Upfront Total:			
Monthly Expenses			
Rent/rental insurance			
Utilities (electric, gas, water, etc.)			
Phone/Internet/cable			
Groceries			
Restaurants/on-campus meals			
Transportation			
Clothing/laundry/personal care			
Entertainment/recreation/gym			
Travel (personal/international)			
Misc. expenses (gifts, etc.)			
Monthly Total:			
10 Months:			
Upfront + 10 Months Total:			
Dollar Difference:			

Have you done the math? Did that sum function help? How does the result compare to what your school said?

Yeah, we thought so. Your overall number is almost certainly higher by some percentage—probably around 20-30%. You won't be able to get federal school loans for this overage; you'll have to cover it some other way (more on that to come).

As a point of comparison, here is the same worksheet filled in for Wharton 2010 first years, with several key assumptions:

- You buy a new laptop and smartphone.

- You need to move from one city to another. You don't need a new car, but you do need new furniture. Miscellaneous upfront expenses also include various on-campus club memberships.

- You live with a roommate and get a cable/Internet combo package. Your smartphone plan is not so cheap.

- Restaurants and on-campus meals work out to less than $150 a week, or about $20 a day. Two cafeteria meals can easily run that amount.

- You have to buy some new professional clothes and a winter coat. Dry-cleaning is a non-negligible expense, since you're attending regular business events.

- Entertainment includes drinks out with classmates and friends, movies, gym membership, tickets to school-sponsored charity events, and anything else you do for fun on less than $100 a week, total.

- Travel includes one international school-sponsored trip, one domestic school trip, and two wedding weekends.

- Miscellaneous includes gifts for those weddings, etc.

	School Projections	Self-Projections	Percent +/-
Upfront Expenses for the Year			
Tuition	48,550	48,550	0%
General fee	2,152	2,152	0%
MBA program fee	1,544	1,544	0%
Pre-term fee	1,715	1,715	0%
Health insurance fee	2,680	2,680	0%
Other university fees	0	0	
Computer/technology purchases	0	1,400	
Books/supplies	2,000	2,000	0%
Moving	0	1,500	
Misc. big purchases (car, etc.)	0	2,000	
Upfront Total:	58,641	63,541	8%
Monthly Expenses			
Rent/rental insurance	1,335	1,400	5%
Utilities (electric, gas, water, etc.)	150	75	-50%
Phone/Internet/cable	100	225	125%
Groceries	333	400	20%
Restaurants/on-campus meals	333	600	80%
Transportation	78	100	28%
Clothing/laundry/personal care	100	300	200%
Entertainment/recreation/gym	106	350	229%
Travel (personal/international)	0	500	
Misc. expenses (gifts, etc.)	0	100	
Monthly Total:	2,536	4,050	60%
10 Months:	25,359	40,500	60%
Upfront + 10 Months Total:	84,000	104,041	24%
Dollar Difference:	20,041		

As you can see, these reasonable projections wound up 24 percent over the official Wharton budget.

If you have a significant other and/or offspring, you have even bigger budgeting fish to fry. Most schools will help you take on additional loans to cover your dependents; adjust the numbers appropriately. Find out if your family can be covered under the university's health plan and if there is reduced-fee childcare available through the school. Clubs for significant others can help you calculate these sorts of numbers. Reach out to current members for advice.

Words From the Wise

According to Marilena Botoulas, Director of Financial Aid at Columbia Business School, the key to budgeting successfully is to make sure you have enough money to start and end each semester.

Key things to remember:

- Aid checks often arrive late and take time to process. That is, they may not be available exactly when you need the dough. If you are planning to quit your job in May, make sure that you have enough cash at the ready to survive the summer and at least the first month of school.

- Renting a place often requires you to pony up a lot of money in the beginning. First and last month's rents, plus a security deposit, can mean a large chunk of change flowing out early on. Also, if you're going to have to rent a second place for the summer, you may again be required to hand over a very large check before you have begun earning any income.

- Your balance is declining. Financial aid typically arrives in two chunks—at the beginning of each semester. It is great to see your checking account balance suddenly have multiple zeros, but remember, you are going to be whittling that number down over the next few months. Plan ahead and don't let the balance convince you that you're richer than you are. It is unlikely that you've had to live this way recently, so know your monthly spend, and make sure that this simple-looking but scary equation holds:

Big lump sum ÷ Months to spend it = Monthly spend

If your spend goes up, then the months go down. The math is unforgiving. Don't zero out with five weeks to go. Cup-a-Noodles three times a day is not a nutritious foundation for finals.

- Use your credit card judiciously, and pay your balance in full each month. Avoid using your credit card as an "emergency student loan," except in an absolutely *true* emergency. Once the storm has passed, immediately find cheaper financing and pay off your balance.

I have always worked hard to have a large nest egg and now I'm living off of Campbell's soup. I just upgraded to Campbell's Select because of the sodium content, but still…

-- Lisa, Anderson '12 (UCLA)

Some guys go to Costa Rica because it's Friday.

-- Seth, Stern '11 (NYU)

Tips for Saving $$$ Here and There

- **Brown-bag it**. Those PB&J sandwiches of your youth? A couple of those a week can save you thousands over two years. If nothing else, buy boxes of energy bars at the grocery store and keep them in your locker at school. Carry an aluminum water bottle and refill it at a fountain (drinking, not splashing). Avoid unnecessary expenses, such as bottled water and those chichi energy drinks.

- **Share a book or two**. Often the same class is taught on different days. Find someone in another section and split the cost of the book, alternating who gets it on different days. Before you do this, make sure you don't need the book every day because the class is killing you. But professors sometimes over-assign. One of us had a finance class with a mandatory coursepack and *two* separate textbooks. Years later, the second textbook still has the uncracked spine of a pointless $100 investment.

- **Hoof it. Or pedal it. Or pool it.** Living right next to campus can be lovely—and also expensive. Check out slightly more distant "grad ghettos" and assess the cost of housing, taking into account any extra transportation cost. A longer walk to public transportation or to school itself may be worth it. Likewise, biking occasionally to and fro can save gas and car repair costs, while trimming your waistline and sparing the planet. If you must drive to and from school, consider buying a permit for a cheaper, more distant lot, and get your exercise sprinting to your 8 am class. Finally, if you have friends who live near you and are on similar class schedules, consider carpooling once a week or more. You can discuss the Marketing case on the way in.

- **Purchase in bulk**. Learning about economies of scale? Put that lesson into action by buying as a large group. This works for computers, printers, airplane tickets, toothpaste, etc. You've got a whole group of potential customers at the ready; just get them to work together, exercising your leadership skills and gaining a resumé bullet. Or join Costco.

- **Use your student status**. Remember those neat student discounts you used to get back in high school and college? Guess what? You are now eligible for a lot of them once again! Flash that student ID round town and see what it will get you (like 15 percent off at J. Crew). And don't be shy about taking advantage of the student subscription rate for *The Wall Street Journal*.

- **Check with your alumni club**. A lot of alumni clubs have discounts at local or national merchants. See if you are eligible for membership while you are a student (many will let you join at a reduced rate).

- **Make the most of your summer internship**. This is a *big* fish if you land it. Your summer employer may be willing to pay your second year tuition if you sign up then and there (and promise to stay for a certain length of time post-graduation). Work to negotiate such perks into your contract.

- **Take advantage of tax breaks**. While it is debatable whether your MBA is tax-deductible, many education-related expenses are. Be sure to speak with your school's financial aid office or your favorite CPA to see what benefits you can reap when you file next April.

- **Drink when it's free (or nearly so)**. Pre-game at cheaper spots. Happy Hour on campus or at a local dive is always a great jumping off point. Just don't put those pictures on the Internet, no matter what your study buddy tells you.

Following the Money Trail

Just thinking about the cost of an MBA is enough to give you a case of angina. But before you start searching for your insurance card and calling 911, remember that this is an investment in your future, an investment that should teach you the practical application of calculating an ROI.[3]

Funding for an MBA can come from a variety of sources:

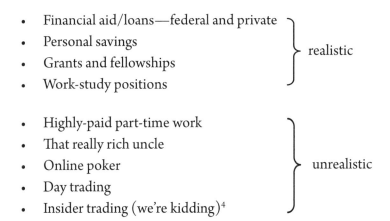

- Financial aid/loans—federal and private
- Personal savings
- Grants and fellowships
- Work-study positions

realistic

- Highly-paid part-time work
- That really rich uncle
- Online poker
- Day trading
- Insider trading (we're kidding)[4]

unrealistic

And while everyone has to figure out how to pay, there is no universal approach. This part of MBA planning is unique to you. Your resources, school, citizenship, and credit history will all play major roles in defining your payment approach.

Don't be afraid to ask for help. Check with your school for the latest in advice and resources; opportunities (particularly for international

---

3   Return on Investment. If you need to convince a significant other of the value of your MBA, say that the ROI, while hard to estimate, is almost certainly positive. By the way, spell this acronym out as R-O-I; don't pronounce it like Roy (as in Rogers or G BIV) or like *roi* (as in the king of France). And while we're on the subject, always find out whether a jargony acronym is spelled out or pronounced as a word. For instance, EBIT, Earnings Before Interest and Taxes, is pronounced "EE-bit," not E-B-I-T. The Acronym List in Part V provides pronunciations so that you can avoid unnecessary embarrassment.

4   In all seriousness, stay away from this. One particular classmate lost his summer job after he was accused of this. He also nearly got kicked out of his MBA program. And it's not like insider trading did wonders for Martha Stewart either, so it's best to keep your trading all on the up-and-up.

students) will differ from place to place.[5] This is a massive undertaking, it's complicated, and there are people throughout your school who have much more experience with this stuff. Just because it has to do with money and you're in an MBA program doesn't mean that you're expected to know all of the answers.

Financial aid officers, as well as other students, are great resources. Ultimately, though, finding the right mix of loans will take time and effort on your part. At least there are a lot of free pizza lunches in your future.

Financial Aid from Uncle Sam

The majority of funding for loans comes from the federal government. However, times (and terms) have most likely changed since you last applied for federal student loans. As of the 2010-2011 school year, many loan products will be appearing under new names:

- The Stafford Loan is now called the **Direct Loan**

- The Grad PLUS Loan is now called the **Direct Grad PLUS Loan**

These name changes are a result of changes in the law: all future Stafford and PLUS loans will come *directly* from the US government.

Federal Perkins Loans, which are common for many undergraduate students, are much less useful for business school students since these loans require demonstrated financial need, are limited to $8,000 a year, and are capped by a $60,000 lifetime limit. If you have Perkins loans at this amount from your college days and/or are unable to show need, you need to look at the other loan products. However, one of us had a little Perkins loan for business school; he always felt good paying it since it was administered directly by the university and came with an

---

5 The federal financial aid information is geared for those enrolled in US-based programs. MBA programs operating overseas and across borders have their own menagerie of different payment options, so please follow the relevant guidelines closely.

old-school booklet with tear-out coupons for payments. With a fixed 5-percent interest rate, Perkins loans are as safe as houses and cheaper than the Direct loans, so if you qualify and you want Uncle Sam's money, take this type of greenback first.

Many students rely on a compilation of the two Direct loans for the bulk of their financing, since these loans, in theory, can get you all the way to the school's estimated budget. How much you can borrow is limited by the government and varies from school to school.[6] The chart below lays out a few of the characteristics of the key federal loans:

	Direct Loan (Stafford)	**Direct Grad PLUS Loan**
Max amount (per year)	$20,500 ($8,500 may be subsidized)[7]	The school's student budget minus any other financial aid received (including a Direct Loan)
Interest rate	6.8% (1.0% origination fee), fixed	7.9% (4.0% origination fee), fixed
Interest accrual (how your overall bill grows while you're in school)	Subsidized portions accrue no interest during enrollment, grace, and deferment periods Unsubsidized portions accrue interest over the loan's lifetime	Interest accrues over the entire lifetime of the loan, regardless of your student status

---

6   Remember that the "student budget" your school provides is computed in accordance with federal requirements that assume a "modest" lifestyle. Your school is not trying to be disingenuous when its room and board figures seem to imply that you will live with an actual roommate. That is, a person sharing your bedroom.

7   Subsidized loans are great if you can get them, but it's all about your Adjusted Gross Income. According to www.finaid.org, more than ⅔ of subsidized loans are given to those with family AGIs under $50K, ¼ go to those who have an AGI between $50–$100K, and the rest (less than 1/12) go to those with higher AGIs. Obviously, it is worth asking about, but don't hold your breath.

	Direct Loan (Stafford)	**Direct Grad PLUS Loan**
Eligibility	Subsidization is based on demonstrated financial need Available to US citizens and eligible non-citizens enrolled with half-time or greater course load	School must partici-pate in the program Available to US citizens and eligible non-citizens enrolled with half-time or greater course load Must not have adverse credit history
Repayment Terms	Standard repayment is 10 or 25 years Repayment begins 6 months after graduation or when enrollment drops below half-time	Standard repayment is 10 or 25 years Repayment begins 6 months after gradua-tion or when enroll-ment drops below half-time

In an era of exceptionally low interest rates,[8] it's annoying that the rates are so high on these federal loans. After all, you're getting a very marketable degree, and the government is at low risk because it has greater power to collect on these loans than lenders have on most other kinds of loans.

But the gubment does what the gubment wants, and we all gotta deal. Many other MBAs will use these borrowing options, so don't feel as though you are alone in feeling the burn. None of these federal loans penalizes you for prepayment, so if you make big bank on your summer internship or first job, you can take swipes at the federal debt load with-

---

8   As of winter 2011, the Federal Reserve has been taking aggressive steps to keep interest rates low, in an effort to spark the economy and head off deflation, which doesn't sound all that bad (after all, isn't inflation bad?) except that a deflationary spiral can cause a Great Depression. You'll learn more in macroeconomics, or earlier if the crap really hits the economic fan—then we'll all know a lot about deflation and its ills.

out penalty. If you can't get cheaper private loans, the federal loans are a sturdy backup.

To start figuring out your options, you first need to fill out the FAFSA, the Free Application for Federal Student Aid. (Unlike business school, you don't have to pay to apply—the title guarantees it!) The FAFSA becomes available on January 1st for the school year that begins the following fall. You must have completed your tax return for the year before you can submit the FAFSA, so you might have to wait until after April 15th. Check the due date; you will probably have to submit the FAFSA no later than July 15th prior to enrollment.

Your FAFSA should be processed in 3–5 business days, at which point you will receive an email Student Aid Report, detailing how much aid you are eligible and in what forms. The same form should show up in about 7–10 days via snail mail.

That July 15th date also applies to a number of different things, including the date by which you must file a Master Promissory Note if you are taking out any federal loans. These loans, if approved, also require that you undergo counseling. Not on-the-couch, talk-about-your-mother kind of counseling. But you do have to do an online workshop before they will cut you a check for tens of thousands of dollars.

Key in all of this process is to follow the suggestions and recommendations of your school. And definitely remember to pay attention to deadlines, since that's what they are. Just like with that whole April 15th deal we American citizens have come know (and not love), when the federal government wants something on a particular date, it means it.

If you are approved for loans, they will come in two chunks, one for each semester. As we've mentioned, this means that you will be starting the semester very, very flush and finishing it substantially less so. Be sure that you always have enough cash on hand if your loan checks are late or you incur unexpected expenses at the end of the semester.

Your loan amounts may also be adjusted if you decide to take on additional education-related expenses. Most schools are able to increase your federal loan amount to cover school-sponsored, educational trips, such as those to visit businesses in other countries. Trips to Rio for Carnival, though perhaps highly educational in a variety of ways, are not considered legitimate reasons to increase loans. Sorry.

Paying the Piper

While having money to pay your tuition is lovely, some day you will have to think about repaying those loans. As described before, most federal loans have a six-month grace period from the time that you complete your degree or drop below a half-time enrollment. After that, payments must be made. So, what does that look like?

Funny you should ask. The chart on the following page is a simple model based on Wharton's 2010–2011 budget of $84,000 a year. To compute two years, we simply doubled all of the numbers, even though we know that the likelihood is that the second year will be more expensive than the first, given both increases in tuition and cost of living.[9]

---

9   This doubling also assumes that your summer internship exactly covers your living expenses for those two or three months, and that you start working right after graduation and paying your loans three months later. Finally, we're assuming that loan fees are capitalized and that interest accrues for a year and a half, the average while you're still in school, on the each Direct PLUS loan and on all but $8,500 of each Direct Loan. Ah, technical caveats.

Here is a 10-year repayment estimate:

	$20,500 Direct Loan	$63,500 Direct PLUS	Sum of two loans	Doubled to cover 2 years
Loan Balance	$20,500.00	$63,500.00	$84,000.00	$168,000.00
Loan Fee	1%	4%		
Adjusted Loan Balance	$21,970.84	$74,018.32	$95,989.16	$191,978.32
Loan Interest Rate	6.8%	7.9%	*Effective* 7.65%	
Loan Term	10 years	10 years	10 years	10 years
Monthly Payment	**$252.84**	**$894.14**	**$1,146.98**	**$2,293.96**
Cumulative Payments	$30,340.94	107,294.82	$137,637.75	$275,275.51
Total Interest Paid	$9,840.94	$43,796.82	$53,637.75	$107.275.51

At a 25-year repayment estimate:

	$20,500 Direct Loan	$63,500 Direct PLUS	Sum of two loans	Doubled to cover 2 years
Loan Balance	$20,500.00	$63,500.00	$84,000.00	$168,000.00
Loan Fee	1%	4%		
Adjusted Loan Balance	$21,970.84	$74,018.32	$95,989.16	$191,978.32
Loan Interest Rate	6.8%	7.9%	*Effective* 7.65%	
Loan Term	25 years	25 years	25 years	25 years
Monthly Payment	**$152.49**	**$566.39**	**$718.88**	**$1,437.77**
Cumulative Payments	$45,748.04	$169,917.23	$215,665.27	$431,330.54
Total Interest Paid	$25,248.04	$106,417.23	$131,665.27	$263,330.54

Those are mortgage-sized numbers. And you can't live in your diploma. But rest assured, there are ways around expensive government debt. Legal ways, too.

I see it as borrowing against future vacations I won't be taking.

-- Tony, Kellogg '11 (Northwestern)

Private Loans

You know how every corner in America seems to have a branch of some national bank on it? You know how the banks fund those branches? By taking in deposits and lending the money back out to people like you.

As interest rates and origination fees have risen on federal loan products relative to commercial interest rates, private banks have come back as a popular source for student loans. Unlike most federal products, these will have different qualifications and depend substantially more on your personal credit history and that of any guarantor. This is why it is key to get your financial house in order as quickly as possible.

Spend the $15 to get a copy of your credit score and credit report. Double check to make sure that there aren't any errors and approach your local banks to see what sort of products are available. Don't be shy about shopping around and ask your classmates about how they're structuring their own loans. Ask current students if they know of a friendly banker you should approach.

> *No financial aid office is allowed to publish information about private lenders on its website. You need to explore all of the different loan vehicles that are out there. Go on to the blogs with other students and ask what is out there in the private market. Schools can't tell you what's out there but your peers can. There are different cultural norms when it comes to talking about money, but be aggressive and ask where someone got their loan and what the terms are.*
>
> *-- Debbie Berechman, Executive Director, MBA Program, Sloan (MIT)*

The nice news about private loans is that if you have good credit, you may be eligible for lower rates at banks than you are through the government.

You can't do much to change your credit score now; it is what it is for the near term. If your credit is weak, you might even swallow your pride and ask a family member with better credit to co-sign. For example, if

> *Pay off as much debt as you can before you go to school.*
>
> *-- Susan Brooks, Financial Aid Assistant Director, Kenan-Flagler (UNC)*

the interest rates you can obtain are half of the federal rates, then all else being equal in the Wharton model (and if those rates never changed at all), you'd pay almost $500 less a month over 25 years, saving nearly $150,000 in total interest paid. The difference between a set of loans at 7.65% and another at 3.82% is enormous. You may not have taken finance yet; you need this finance lesson now.

Additionally, private loans can be used to close the gap between federal loans (capped by that horribly inadequate "moderate lifestyle" budget) and the real budget you've determined, since there is no predetermined cap to the amount that can be borrowed.

Still, think through the ramifications of over-borrowing. In this case, the piper always gets his money, no matter what it costs you. Even in catastrophic circumstances, student loan debt is as hard as child support or alimony to get rid of—normal bankruptcy doesn't shake it. So don't bite off more than you can chew.

> *I reduced my stress level by having already saved a bit and using less in loans. I figure that if I need supplemental loans, I can always get them.*
>
> *-- Michael, HBS '12 (Harvard)*

Another key difference between federal and private loans is that private loans are usually variable-rate loans—they pass interest-rate risk on to you. So, although rates are beautifully low right now, understand how the rates could go up in the future. You think the numbers for 7.9% fixed are bad? Wait till you have a private loan at a 10% variable rate.

This is why it's good to think of building a portfolio of debt. Have some fixed government loans (which you can only obtain while you're in school) and some private loans, lower interest but variable. If interest rates stay low, you pay off the fixed federal loans faster. If interest rates shoot up, you pay off the private debt faster. Over the period of time you're going to be repaying these loans, interest rates will do a lot of things. They're not going to stay low forever, so reduce your risk by taking your loans in a few different flavors.

We have to note that private loans for international applicants may be much harder to come by now than they were in the past. In the fall of 2008, Citibank canceled the CitiAssist Student Loan Program for several top business schools. Before then, this program was funding over 60 percent of the private student loans at many schools. Hopefully, banks will step up to fill this need in the future. Until then, international students would be wise to speak with financial aid officers early and often to learn what aid, if any, will be available.

Grants and Fellowships

Grants and fellowships are the holy grail of grad school. What's better than free money? Unlike loans, grants do not have to be repaid and often go directly to offset tuition and/or living expenses.

If you are a current or former member of the United States Armed Forces, you should definitely check out the latest GI Bill, which covers some or all of your MBA tuition. You must serve beyond your 4-year military commitment, and funding is capped by state school tuition figures, but you could save boatloads. In even better news, many programs may waive any tuition not covered under the GI Bill as part of the Yellow Ribbon Program, so ask your financial aid office. Now is the perfect time to reap some of the rewards of your service.

Groups traditionally underrepresented in business school have a number of fellowships geared towards them. For instance, women can look to the Forté Foundation and the American Association of University Women. The Consortium, which has historically supported underrepresented minorities in management, is technically open to all U.S. citizens and permanent residents who can show that they are committed to the organization's mission and offers a variety of resources.

At the end of the day, though, MBA candidates will likely discover that they have a harder time finding outside sources of free money than other graduate students. Sadly, there isn't the same support for an MBA as for a PhD student studying ethnomusicology or trying to save the spotted lemur. Let's face it—most of you are getting your MBAs with the intention of going on to higher-paying corporate jobs. Yes, if you are currently in a socially-conscious field and/or intend to go into one, you may come across organizations willing to provide a little assistance. Even in this case, though, it may be best to focus on longer-term loan forgiveness, since that's the practical way many schools and even the government have tried to address the gap in earning potential for social entrepreneurs (more on this to come).

Most first-year fellowships at particular schools are handed to you with your acceptance letter or shortly thereafter. Such fellowships range from the $1,000 So-and-so Family Scholarship to straight-up full rides wherein the limo whisks you from matriculation to graduation: your feet never touch the earth.[10]

---

10   Must be nice, playa!

Unfortunately, odds are that if you haven't heard by now that your school wants to give you free money, you probably aren't getting any. Fellowships vary dramatically from program to program, both in terms of availability and the various criteria/strings attached. In most cases, some alum or his/her family established a grant requiring you to meet various demographic or interest criteria.[11]

Later, if you did well in your first year, you might receive a small second-year fellowship.[12] Again, this is the kind of bonbon that just shows up on your plate courtesy of the chef; rarely is there an application process. If you are interested in such bonbons, speak with your financial aid office, cozy up to your administrators, and be sure that you are someone whose name rings positively across campus. Just realize that second-year fellowships rarely cover a huge portion of your tuition costs. But money is still money and if your school offers it to you, be happy. And gracious.

Loan Forgiveness and Other Acceptable Schemes for Not Repaying

The Health Care and Student Affordability Reconciliation Act of 2010 (yes, you can laugh) created several provisions by which federal loans could be forgiven in whole or in part. Depending upon what you do after business school, you may be eligible for public service forgiveness or income-based repayment programs. These can make all the difference as to whether you can enter certain fields after your expensive MBA.

Be forewarned. As socially important as well-functioning capital markets are, investment banking is not regarded as a public service profession.

---

11   This is why schools can hardly ever match grants as a way of enticing you to choose their program. Just because you were offered $20,000 by one program because you are an Asian woman from the southwestern United States who is interested in real estate development in Eastern Europe, you cannot assume that another school will be able to offer you similar funds, regardless of how much the admissions committee may like you.

12   One of us would like to thank the Class of 1987 again, as he was living near poverty level as a high school teacher before school. The Class of 1987 gift was one of the four basic food groups for him.

For practical details on loan forgiveness, check with your financial aid office. More and more schools have developed loan assistance programs for graduates who pursue less lucrative, more socially-conscious careers. Usually, you have to stick it out for some time, so the relief is not immediate, but it'll trickle in.

Is Your MBA Tax-Deductible?

In 2009, the U.S. Tax Court ruled that a Maryland nurse could deduct the cost of her MBA tuition from her taxes. Of course, this got us thinking—if a nurse can do it, can the rest of us?

Before you take our word on anything, consult your accountant or other trusted tax professional. But, in brief, the ruling seems to indicate that, if an MBA is an "ordinary and necessary" expense in your profession, you might get away with it. In other words, if you are using your MBA in the way that others would use continuing education classes, there is reason to think that you may qualify.

That being said, career switchers need not apply for this exemption. There is no continuity of career when you move, say, from consulting to marketing or from banking to operations management. Moreover, if you are not making much money while you are in school, it hardly seems worth the audit trouble to try to fight The Man on this one. But that's just our two percent of a dollar.

Other MBA Money Trees to Consider

If you have exhausted the grant and loan pipelines, do not despair. There are a number of other ways to think about funding your graduate studies.

Before school:

- **529 plans.** Originally designed to help folks save for college, you can also apply the funds to grad school. Have a relative who's done with schooling but still has money in his/her account? See about having the balance transferred over to you.

- **Formal loans from family members.** This is a great way to get some help from family—but you want to make sure it's not just a gift, or the IRS is going to crack the whip. You need to have real contracts and real promissory notes, along with a legitimate interest rate if the loan is over $10,000. Set it up as a "demand loan," and keep the overall amount small. Virgin Money US will set up the loan and act as the intermediary, if the amount is non-trivial. Or just draw up a contract by finding a form from Nolo Press or another vendor.

During school:

- **Assistantships**. Talk to your professors if you're interested in teaching or research assistantships. Someone's always looking for another person to help crunch the data for an upcoming paper or hold Friday review sessions. Realize that the per hour rate is usually crappy.

- **Tutoring**. Schools will often pay second years or those who have waived out of classes to tutor other classmates. You need to be a good teacher for this one, but it's usually a very convenient gig. Also consider tutoring undergrads—or working in the test-prep industry (it can be much more lucrative than you think).

- **Publications and other activities**. Some schools pay the publisher of the school newspaper or other publications. Also see if there are paid roles within the admissions or other campus offices.

- **Part-time outside work**. No, you don't have a lot of time, but you can think about getting a small job to pick up a few extra bucks. And if you can finagle a paid internship, you're clearly doing something right.

After school:

- **Tuition reimbursement**. Some employers will reimburse tuition or pay hefty signing bonuses. If you are so lucky, immediately send a check to the student loan. Knock some right off the top. Otherwise, it'll go into the second-year money pit.

A Final $0.02

Money is a huge issue, both in b-school and in life. But the fact is, he who dies with the most toys still dies. So don't let the numbers run (or ruin) your life. As with everything else during this period, you need to stick to your own values, your own priorities, and your own metrics for gauging what is important to you.

Living richly doesn't depend upon the number of digits in your bank account balance, now or in the future.

PART II:
TAKING CARE OF BUSINESS AT BUSINESS SCHOOL

It's hard to believe, but you've finally made it to business school. No more baffling tests, no more jump-through-the-hoop applications to fill out, no more frustrating colleagues…oh wait. Well, still you made it!

This section will help you prepare for life in business school. You'll need to know how to manage your time, interact in class, work with your learning teams, and balance your social life. We also threw in a hangover remedy for good measure.

Time management is truly the key. It can determine your success in your classes, clubs, and career search, not to mention the non-school portions of your life. Figure out your priorities early and stick to them. Remember you're the same person that you were when you got your offer of admittance. Just a lot busier.

Unlike Part I, this part doesn't lead with a checklist, because there's no finite set of tasks to accomplish. What we offer instead is a simple diagram. Once you're in the thick of school, you're often going to feel like you're trying to put out a five-alarm fire with a cup of tea. It can be easy to stay down in the weeds, but every so often, pop up like a prairie dog for ten minutes and look around (to change metaphors again).

You know how the classic game *Trivial Pursuit* forces you to go around and around a circular board, gathering wedges to signify mastery of certain topics? Geography, Entertainment, History, Arts & Literature,

Science & Nature, and Sports & Leisure cover pretty much everything there is in life. In that spirit, we offer our own six wedges in a game we like to call *Trivial Purse/Suit*:

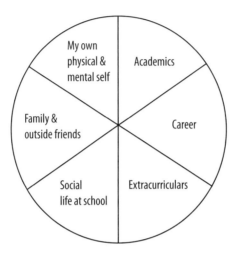

Once a week, go around the wheel and ask yourself, for each area:

- How did last week go?

- What do I need to do next week?

- What would I like to do next week?

- How can I make all of those things happen?

You might resist confronting the reality of everything you have to juggle. After all, if you feel that you're constantly in fire-fighting mode, how can you possibly take a break to glance at the big picture? It's easy to let the enormity of your task list scare or depress you.

Fear not. You can afford to take a deep breath; air's free. Planning ahead is a great way to lower stress and, if you're honest with and forgiving of yourself, you'll recognize that you're doing better than you think. And if you're really having that bad of a day, gather some friends, a few bottles of Jack, and enjoy a game of drunken *Trivial Pursuit.* You can check off two wedges with this one—*My own physical & mental self* and *Social life at school.*

> *The most surprising thing about business school is how empowering it's been. I suddenly have all of these tools at my fingertips. Just being exposed to all of these people who have done all of these amazing things creates this mental shift that I can do things that I never thought I could.*
>
> -- Jen, Fuqua '12 (Duke)

Chapter 9:
Time Management 101

It's the first day of 17th (or thereabouts) grade. Surely you have your new notebooks ready, your pencils sharpened, and your first-day outfit picked out. Take a picture and send it to your mother; she'll be overjoyed.

This is a very exciting and slightly nerve-wracking time. Whether you are kicking off your b-school with pre-term classes, orientation, or a school-sponsored trip, it all starts now. You have opportunities galore at your fingertips, so go take advantage.

The most successful b-school students, the ones who report having the most fulfilling experiences, are those who truly commit to being a part of the school. They are active in clubs and social events, participate in class and in competitions, and work to foster a supportive, collaborative environment. They recognize that the best way to get ahead is to help others (and the only way to ensure you get a beer is to take a turn running the tap).

The old adage rings true—you get out of business school what you put into it. Think about what your goals are as you read further. And as long as you have all of those new pens sitting about, feel free to take notes.

Off to the Races

There are a few incontrovertible truths both in life and in business: gravity pulls things downward, taxes can't be avoided forever, and the third part of a trilogy is never the best part. The incontrovertible truth about business school is that it is overwhelming, particularly in the beginning. Academic, social, and recruiting commitments ramp up immediately. Even orientation is full-time (including for part-timers). And, for many, your liver is put to the test.

First-year MBAs across the US report near-universal shock and awe at how much of one's life a full-time program encompasses. *Everyone* ends up gobsmacked by the experience. Simply accepting this fact is the first coping mechanism.[1]

> *The first thing you lose is sleep, then exercise, then weight, then sex. Hopefully, that turns around at some point.*
>
> -- *Dean, Fuqua '12 (Duke)*
>
> *You're constantly in a state of running out of battery on something.*
>
> -- *Patty, Wharton '12 (U Penn)*
>
> *You think you have a 3-day weekend and that's going to be awesome but, in reality, it's a no-day weekend.*
>
> -- *Matt, Ross '11 (Michigan)*
>
> *I see people posting on Facebook that they're going to some event or another and I wonder, "How do they do it?" I can't even make it to the grocery store.*
>
> -- *Geoff, Anderson '12 (UCLA)*

---

1   Try to communicate this forthcoming avalanche to your non-MBA friends and loved ones. No one will understand when you go completely AWOL, but some forewarning decreases the odds that they'll send out a search party to track you down.

Although it is extremely useful to think of school as a job—and to be every bit the "professional" student—it is very different from an office job. When you work for someone else, you are told, implicitly and explicitly, what to do and how to prioritize the different demands on your time. In other words, you have a boss. The good news about business school? No one's going to tell you what to do. The bad news? No one's going to tell you what to do.

You must decide what your priorities are; you are now the boss.[2] Define those priorities and stick with them. Check your status regularly on the *Trivial Purse/Suit* wheel. If you are too easily swayed from your goals, you will find yourself running around like a headless chicken—and that's never pretty.

> *First quarter sucks because everyone's trying to figure out what they're doing. Are we really working hard or not? And it turns out, everyone's working—but they're like ducks. They try to keep a calm appearance above the water, but they're working like hell under the surface to stay afloat.*
>
> *-- Alexander, GSB '11 (Stanford)*

---

2   However, you are not Bruce Springsteen, Tony Danza, or Judith Light.

When There are Only 24 Hours in a Day

At first thought, b-schoolers have it made. You've got about 15 hours' worth of class each week, a few club meetings, some reading and homework, and a slew of social events. How bad can your schedule really be?

Bad. Really bad.

> *The intensity of business school was surprising. My calendar is more full now than when I was working more than 80 hours a week.*
>
> *-- Alexander, GSB '11 (Stanford)*

While you may have few standing obligations, you will be amazed at how quickly your schedule gets booked up. Group work always takes longer than you think it will. Club meetings run over. Recruiting activities mean that you're always revising your resumé or sending follow-up emails. Those kinds of tasks are never finished; you can always be doing more (but that doesn't mean that you should). Even coffee chats may not seem like a huge stress, but they eat up an hour of scheduled time. And, as one student put it, "It's always someone's f$#ing birthday."

> *There are a million different things that sound awesome and interesting. You just need to stay focused.*
>
> *-- Mike, Booth '12 (Chicago)*

And we haven't even discussed reading tomorrow's cases yet.

The fact is that there are more things to do than there are hours in the day. You have to balance class work with club obligations, recruiting events with social events, friends with study groups, and alcohol with water.[3]

---

3   This last one is key. Try to do the 1:1 ratio and you'll be a much happier camper the next day. Also, before you fall asleep, take some B-12 with as much water as your stomach can handle.

No matter how good you are at multi-tasking, you've got a lot of balls to juggle. You have no choice but to manage your time well.

Check out the sample first year schedule on the following page. Take notice of what's there—and what's not there. Large chunks of time are blocked off for events, but note how many times there are multiple events scheduled at the same time that you might want or need to go to. How do you decide between going to a speaker or a corporate presentation? A club meeting or a study group meeting? Your new best friend's birthday drinks or a review session?

These conflicts can make you even more stressed than simply being over-scheduled will, so it is imperative that you know what your priorities are and balance accordingly.

> *There are 36 hours of things to do but only 8 hours in which to do them. People are afraid of missing out on something, so they try to do it all and you just can't.*
>
> *-- Anna, HBS '12 (Harvard)*

	Monday	Tuesday	Wednesday
8		- Drop off dry cleaning	
9	Strategy	Learning team mtg. - Strategy case - Corp. Fin. problems	Strategy
10			
11	Informational w/ Tom @ Citi--phone call		Learning team mtg. - Finish problem set
12	Statistics	J & J mkt. campus pres. India trip mtg.	Statistics
1			
2	Corporate Finance	Macro Economics	Corporate Finance
3			
4	coffee w/Cathy re: summer internships	Managerial Accounting	
5			
6	Stein Club Booz & Co. campus pres. Deloitte @ Pub Bar	Pepsi Co. rotational program BCG meet & greet	Speaker Series: Jeff Daniels McKinsey small group dinner Kraft campus pres.
7			
8	Marketing conference phone call	- Laundry - Call home	
9			
10			
11			

	Thursday		Friday	Saturday	Sunday
8					
9	- Resumé Review w/2nd year		Coffee chats w/Amex	Learning team	
10	- Prep Micro case				Brunch w/ Scott, Carol & Steve
11	- Send thank-you notes - Call speakers for conf.		- Flu shots @ clinic		
12					
1	Statistics		Marketing club conference committee		Learning team
2					
3	Macro Economics		Corporate Finance review session		
4	Managerial Accounting				Rugby Club Practice
5			- Get wedding gift for Chris & Becky - Book ski trip		
6					
7	Pub night	Bain pres.			
8			Birthday dinner for Sarah @ Dali		Las Vegas trek reunion drinks
9				Rohit's Birthday Party	
10	Salsa Party				
11					

A Positive Outlook (or Google Calendar or Whatever Else You Choose)

It's ridiculous to think that you can keep all of your appointments, obligations, and assignments straight in your head. Plus, you have to remember those pesky little things like your sister's birthday, your parents' anniversary, and the date your credit card bill is due. Having a system— a formal calendar—is key.

> *I've been surprised by how busy business school is. You don't really get it until you're in it. It's like invest- ment banking; people tell you it's crazy and you think you know what that means, but you can't until you get there.*
>
> *-- Rob, CBS '12 (Columbia)*

But what system or calendar to choose? First, talk to second years and ask what's popular around the school. If everyone is linked up on Outlook, take the path of least resistance and join in. If yours is a Google world, go that route. At many programs, students opt to share their calendars to make it easier to set meeting times.

If you're an old fashioned, pen-and-paper lad or lass, that's great—but it may behoove you to print out regular copies of an electronic calendar and keep things updated both on screen and in your notes.

As soon as you have your calendar in front of you, start filling it up with as much information as possible. Don't just block off class times; use your syllabus to add in assignment due dates.[4] Make sure to mark off major recruiting activities, and don't forget about school events, financial aid deadlines, and other key dates for course bidding and trip registrations.

---

4   Some schools have taken to doing this for their students, or a random first year might create a calendar and then share it with her classmates. This student clearly rocks and deserves free drinks for the rest of the semester.

Calendars can also help you reclaim some time for yourself. If you want to go to the gym, you have to write it in. Time with your significant other? Block it off on the calendar. Calling home on Sunday nights? That should read as "busy" to anyone who might see your schedule—including you.

But having a well-kept calendar isn't the only thing: you have to manage your time well, too. With so many things on your task list, it's often tough to know which ones to do when and it's easy to let things slide. Check out the following rules for time management and start incorporating them as appropriate into your regular activities.

> *The stress of business school is self-inflicted. Sometimes, I've never been so stressed and then, six hours later, I'm having the best time of my life.*
>
> *-- Pat, Ross '12 (Michigan)*

Rule #1: If it's only going to take you two minutes to do it, do it now. Whether it's paying your phone bill or answering a quick email, if it's the sort of thing you can get off your plate quickly, just do it. You don't want to overload your "To Do" list with things that take just as long to write down as to get accomplished. Working this way will save you time and stress.

> *Decide when you're actually working, not "working/playing." If you really need to get stuff done, sit where people can't bother you and check your email every six hours, not every six minutes.*
>
> *-- Seth, Stern '11 (NYU)*

Rule #2: Use a daily system to check the status of your calendar and tasks. Set aside ten minutes, either every morning or every night, to look at what's coming up in the days and weeks ahead. This is not the same as checking your inbox, by the way. Not every commitment or opportunity sends you an email reminder. Are you on track for all of your projects? Any big deadlines around the corner? Midterms loom-ing? Cover letters due?

Your task-tracking system needs to be failsafe. If you remember that you need to pick up your dry cleaning while you're in Financial Accounting or if you come up with a splendid insight for your paper while picking up your dry cleaning, you need a method for logging it and finding it later. Sticking it in the recesses of your brain isn't enough. You'll remem-ber that you had a brilliant idea; you just won't remember what it was. Dang nab it.

If you have a smartphone (and you should), keep memos such as shop-ping lists, paper ideas, career-related tasks, and personal stuff at your finger tips. You can also carry one of those sporty pocket-sized spiral notebooks (but that involves using an actual pen to write stuff down).

In addition to keeping up with your school and career search calendars, periodically look at the other wedges on the wheel and see how well you're keeping up. Have you talked to your family this month? When was the last time you hit the gym (honestly)? And shouldn't you really get a doctor to take a look at that thing on your back? If you're falling behind on the rest of life, schedule time on your calendar to take care of the things you need to take care of. Life doesn't stop because you're in business school.

I set a bare minimum for certain categories and consider anything above that to be icing on the cake. I need six hours of sleep, I need to read my cases, I need to have one meeting a week with a second year, etc. At least I know that I'm covering my bases.

-- Alison, HBS '12 (Harvard)

Rule #3: Break big tasks into smaller chunks with defined goals.
Work backwards from the open space in your schedule: what do you
want to accomplish between 2 and 3pm? Rather than "Work on cover
letters," try "Incorporate Career Service's suggestions into my Goldman
cover letter." Give yourself a clear goal (e.g., the letter will be ready for
proof-reading at the end of the hour). Turn activities into accomplishments. Once you're done, look at your "To Do" list and check the task off.
If it wasn't on the list already, write it down now and cross it off. Ahh...

Rule #4: Get creative about multitasking. Are there activities that
you can combine, knocking off multiple birds with one stone? If you're
recruiting for CPG marketing jobs and equities research, think about
focusing your stock research on CPG companies. Have to create a presentation for a communications class and you have the option to do it
on any subject? Why not make it about the material that will be covered
on your upcoming Statistics midterm?

*You have to figure out how to do three things at once. For example,
I'll try to get a group together to discuss a case on a bike ride.*

-- Sarah, GBS '12 (Stanford)

If you walk to class, use that time to get caught up on phone calls. Have
folks over to practice interview questions while you cook dinner. Watch
Glee and answer emails at the same time. You get the idea.

Rule #5: Maintain balance. B-school can be all-consuming. You
begin to speak a crazy language based on acronyms, you think that a
dinner of wine and gherkins is acceptable, and the word "widget" will
mean something other than an application for your smart phone. But
a key to staying grounded is to keep in contact with your non-business
school friends. Your hours are likely to be both long and erratic, but it
is extremely important to stay connected. Make a point of checking in

with a handful of friends at least once a month. There is a real world out there, even if you are taking a temporary vacation from it.

It's easy for me to get caught up, thinking my classes suck. But then I'll talk to a friend of mine who's a doctor and he'll tell me, "Six of my patients died today." It helps to have a new perspective.

-- Monica, Booth '11 (Chicago)

Rule #6: Take a break here and there. As overwhelmed and overscheduled as you may feel, it is important that you take time out to focus on non-school-related activities. Whether you play basketball for an hour, go to a museum for an afternoon, or just zone out in front of *The Daily Show*, a little downtime is essential. So, too, is sleeping and eating well. And by "well," we don't mean those 36-ounce porterhouse steak dinners recruiters will treat you to.

At the end of each day, give yourself permission to "be done" once you've met reasonable goals for the evening. As much of a time-suck as sleep is, failing to get it isn't an option. You need to be able to function well, think coherently, and not fall face-first into your soup when you're trying to impress your future boss.

Technology 101

It's hard to believe there's anyone out there who was born after 1970 and doesn't have a smartphone, but every year a few souls try to brave business school without one. Don't be one of them.

Your peers assume that you are always on email and will use this as a primary form of communication. (Your professors, advisors, and future employers will, in all likelihood, do this too.) Someone's going to be late to a meeting? Expect an email five minutes beforehand. Last-minute invite to hear an awesome speaker? No one's going to ring you; better check your email. And with most schools either not allowing computers in class or blocking Internet access, a smartphone might be the only way you can check your inbox for hours at a time.

One caveat to the smartphone culture: don't be rude. The person right in front of you is more important than the email or text that just buzzed in. And don't assume that it's just the older generation that gets royally pissed off by the "duck and type" maneuver; even your most tech-savvy peers get irked when you're making more eye contact with the table than with them.

If you are expecting an urgent email/text/call, warn the people you're with ahead of time and put the damn thing on vibrate.

To Thine Own Self Be True

We know that you've already pondered what you want to get out of your business school experience. Why are you here (forgetting about what you wrote in your application essays)?

Revisit the *Trivial Purse/Suit* diagram and name your objectives for each wedge. How do you want to prioritize the wedges themselves? Just like in the real game, you can attack them in any order.

> *Know yourself. You're going to get the directive from on high and the directive from your peers. Everyone says "don't follow the herd" but then everyone is applying to the same three companies. Life is about tradeoffs; so is business school.*
>
> *-- Juliet, HBS '12 (Harvard)*

In the abstract, you'd do it all, but in the real world, you need to make compromises. Just make them explicitly, rather than by chance.

Pinpoint where you are willing to make sacrifices and where you aren't. If academics are important to you, be prepared to forgo some social and recruiting events to spend time reading in the library. If you go out every night, accept that showing up hung over to class may negatively impact your participation grade. And if you're locked into recruiting events, you might have to miss a few classes and Happy Hours. This is the price you pay for going after what you want. You must be firm in your desires and consistent in your priorities.

> *We're all here because we want to over-achieve. No one doesn't want to learn —but I don't want to sacrifice time towards finding a job or knowing people just to get an A. Because I go out and have made friends, I'll have connections at other companies for the rest of my life.*
>
> *-- Jennifer, Ross '12 (Michigan)*

Now, if you're like some b-schoolers, you initially think that you're the exception to this rule, that you can score every wedge. If that's what you want to believe, go right ahead… but don't say we didn't warn you. It's too late to learn to swim when you're already drowning.

> *Sometimes you have to lower your standards. Sometimes a B is fine. That's not to say that grades and classes aren't important, but those that are successful prioritize and don't expect perfection. Know what you're willing to give up. You will have to give something up.*
>
> *-- Jennifer Brooks, Senior Associate Director,*
> *MBA Career Management Center, Kenan-Flagler (UNC)*

The Truth About Academics

It's a little secret that business school administrations don't really want to admit: grades aren't the most important part of business school.

We know you're shocked. Take a minute to catch your breath.

Of course, it's called business *school* for a reason. Academics are a critical part of the equation and, for many MBAs, a primary reason they've taken a hiatus from the workforce. Classes are important; you are paying an awful lot to learn a particular skill set. But the operative word in that sentence is *learn*. Given the different grading schemas and policies of the various programs, grades themselves will have more or less importance at particular institutions and to folks targeting particular career paths or employers.

You are in business school because you want to expand your knowledge, whether the academics are your number one priority or not. Focus on learning from all sources: your professors, guest speakers, your classmates, your travel experiences. This means that you may often sacrifice one type of learning for another, and that's okay.

> *Don't let a good grade get in the way of your education.*
>
> *-- Chris, GSB '11 (Stanford)*

It's a University, Not Just a Business School

Once you've decided to relax a bit about grades, think about the classes you want to take. First, sign up for those you are most interested in, not necessarily those you will skate through.[5] You may not have much choice about core classes (depending upon your school), but as your schedule opens up, consider a stretch elective in Derivatives or Decision Models.

If you really want to expand your horizons, take advantage of the fact that you're at a major university with gamut-running courses and other resources. Take Introductory Mandarin or Photography 101.

Don't feel bad if you can't take immediate advantage of these opportunities; you can always hit them second year. You can, however, sign up for additional email lists to keep track of events and speakers appearing across the university's campus. When you can, venture out of the business school bubble and see what else you can learn.

Aiming for the Middle

No matter where you go to school, you can bank on someone telling you during orientation how fabulous you and the rest of your classmates are. Indeed, you will be surrounded by some remarkably accomplished people; that's part of the reason you're in school in the first place.

Think about what that means: *You are in the midst of greatness.*

In other words, your competition is pretty stiff.

Most people who go to business school, particularly highly selective programs, did really well in high school and went on to prestigious universities. Those folks did better than the average bird at their respective universities and went on to land impressive jobs. They excelled in those

---

5   And speaking of skating, we know one MBA who was able to join the undergraduate synchronized ice skating team at her school. We never knew that there was such a thing as competitive Ice Capades, but it was a fantastic opportunity for her.

jobs and in other aspects of their lives, and now they have landed in the seat next to you. Say hello. Be impressed. (Don't worry—we're telling them the same thing about you.)

This is often the first time that these people have ever been "average." But "average" is okay when you're with the best and the brightest.

-- Kembrel Jones, Deputy Vice-Dean of Student Life,
Wharton (U Penn)

Everyone in your class will have varying levels of experience with the material that you're about to encounter. Supply chain guys have an advantage when it comes to operations; former investment bankers have a leg up in corporate finance courses. The playing field isn't level—but that's part of the design of b-school. Just cut yourself some slack and respect the experience and knowledge of those around you.

In most grad schools—law school, medical school, etc.—everyone's a novice. But at business school, you're sitting in Accounting next to this guy who's a CPA.

-- Chike, Wharton '12 (U Penn)

You need to know what your strengths are. When you start feeling average, it's good to know why you're in school and what you're good at.

-- Bridge, Booth '12 (Chicago)

Relax. Your admission wasn't a mistake. You make your class great, too.

Chapter 10:
Social Graces

Humans are social creatures. Business school students tend to take social creature-hood to the next level. Your goal? Do it the right way.

Welcome to Middle School

Some people who have never attended business school tell you that the experience will allow you to relive college or even high school. That's not exactly true. In reality, business school allows you to relive your *middle school* years—although doused in more alcohol. (You can pass your own judgment on whether this is a good thing.)

You may not have braces on your teeth, but you will have lockers to store your things.[1] You and your classmates will tend to move in herds between classes. And just like in middle school, the gossip chain

> *There's this funny thing that happens when you take a group of people who were gainfully employed and successful and then make them unemployed and tell them how hard it is to find jobs. And then you pour alcohol over the whole thing...*
>
> *-- Julie, Wharton '12 (U Penn)*

---

1   Like an extra set of nice clothes. No lie. You never know when you're going to need at least an extra pair of slacks and a shirt to attend a corporate presentation. And those little stain wipes are handy for when your shirt is introduced to a sticky glob of burrito.

will be fierce. There will be cliques and cool kids and nerds with all of those lovely tween traits. You can expect to know far more about your classmates than you want to; likewise, they will know far more about you and your personal business than you ever dreamt they could (or should). Remember that low-level social uncertainty that nipped at your sneakers in 7th grade? It comes back to nip at your loafers (or pumps).

On top of that, you're all out of work.

It is the rare MBA student who survives the first semester without some sort of minor breakdown. When it happens, know that you're not alone, you're not a freak, and you're not the first person to cry over a broken Excel cell.

> *Bring as many costumes as you can.*
>
>   *-- Chris, Haas '11*
>   *(Berkeley)*
>
> *I cleaned out my closet before I came to business school—big mistake.*
>
>   *-- Della, Haas '11*
>   *(Berkeley)*

On the bright side, just like when you were younger, you've got oodles of time to goof off. At least, little oodles. It's like recess, only without the four-square games. Instead, various theme parties, choreographed dances, comedic videos, and section cheers keep you entertained. And when you're at b-school, Halloween comes more than once a year.

Making a Name for Yourself… or Not

Reputations are built in days (often during orientation) but stick around for years. Everyone will remember the guy who couldn't hold his liquor and the girl who slept with him before the first day of class. They will also remember who led the charge to the next bar. They will know who made sure everyone got home safe and who they had to call a cab for.

Have fun during those early days, but know that you will be known and judged by your behaviors.

> *Be a professional student. Part of your goal is to enhance your network and launch your career forward. One bad move can ruin your reputation. 24 hours a day, seven days a week, you're in this program.*
>
> *-- Debbie Berechman, Executive Director,*
> *MBA Program, Sloan (MIT)*

The long and short of it is this: don't do *anything*, both inside and outside of the school, that you wouldn't want your classmates to know about. It is amazing the way someone always finds out about that undergrad at the bar or that late night trip to a professor's office, no matter how stealthy you thought you were.

Soul Searching

As you start anything new, you get a fresh chance to take stock of who you are and what you want. You also get to make some decisions about who you want to be in this new setting. Even if you have always been the life of the party, do you want to fill that role now? If you have generally been more introverted, is now a time to test out some extroverted behaviors?

We are not trying to suggest that you "reinvent" yourself exactly as you enter school, but that you see it as an opportunity to push yourself in different ways. You only get so many chances to start over, so take advantage of this one.

Also think about expanding your circle. We all tend to gravitate towards people who are most like us, in terms of personality, background, or shoe size. Your new environment will offer you a chance to get to know people who are vastly different from you. Be willing to stray from your social comfort zone.

Okay, off the soapbox now.

Hello! My Name is…

Andy Warhol envisioned a future in which everyone would be famous for fifteen minutes. In our version, everyone will have a small-talk bio-chip. When Alice meets Bob, their bio-chips will instantly exchange introductory info: name, age, hometown, degrees, and romantic status. However, until this technology becomes universal, we will all have to put up with introducing ourselves over and over and over and over and over again.

The best intros are like miniskirts: long enough to cover the subject and short enough to still be interesting. With that in mind, consider the following points:

1) **Don't introduce yourself with your fraternity nickname.** No doubt, others will learn about your antics and develop their own name for you in short order. But don't be the guy who introduces himself as "The Cowboy," "The Dilemma," or, god forbid, "Ox" unless you honestly want us to call you that.

2) **Neither brag nor beat around the bush.** If you went to Yale, it shouldn't be the first fact anyone learns about you. But don't tell us you went to school in "New Haven" either. If your last name is carved into stone anywhere on campus, own up to it if someone asks. It will come out eventually.

3) **Don't give your whole life story.** Sure, your memoirs are being published next month, but no one has asked for an advanced copy. Or even a copy of your resumé, for that matter. Offer a couple of headlines and then cede the floor to someone else.

4) **Actually listen to what the other guy is saying.** So, you've given your spiel and now the other guy is rambling on about his past. Blah, blah, blah. Your eyes start to wander around the crowd, looking for someone more interesting or attractive to talk to, like that redhead in the corner… Stop that! Focus on the conversation going on in

front of you. If necessary, excuse yourself only at an appropriate pause in the conversation.

5) **Be nice about repeating your name to folks you've already met.** Some people are great at remembering names and faces; others still ask their mothers to show IDs. If Lori asks your name for the fourth time, gently refresh her memory without getting agitated. Conversely, go ahead and admit up front when you've forgotten someone's name. The drawn out "Heyyyy!" or "What up, Chief?" fools no one.

Keep in mind that you're all having so much data thrown at you in the beginning. You want to introduce yourself in a way that lets people know you.

-- Julie, Wharton '12 (U Penn)

Find people you can "debrief" with after social events.

-- Jessica, Wharton '12 (U Penn)

The Art of Mingling

You are only in class about 15 hours a week. The rest of your time, you may find yourself milling around in one fashion or another. Yes, there are corporate presentations to attend, guest speakers to hear, projects to complete, and clubs to support. But you will also spend hours in lounges, cafeterias, and libraries, chatting with friends and colleagues about your Econ professor's sartorial habits and the really hot second year in your Entrepreneurial Selling class.

In addition, there is formal mingling to be done at recruiting and alumni events. For every hour of pure presentation, you will spend at least another hour chatting with associates of the visiting firm, wine in one hand and cheese in the other (or both in one, if you're really masterful).[2]

To kibitz successfully, you need just one skill: shut up and let the other person talk.

> *The people I respect the most are the ones who have the right to be arrogant by business school standards and aren't. Humility is everything.*
>
> *-- Will, Wharton '11 (U Penn)*

You might think that your quips are wittier and your stories are more fascinating than the ones you're hearing, but no one enjoys a conversation that feels like a competition. It's called a "dialogue" for a reason—it takes two. If you want to mingle successfully, ask the other person questions, inviting her to speak. If she tells you that she just got summer offers from eleven of the top twelve banks, congratulate her. You don't have to drop the fact that you actually got an offer from the twelfth—unless she specifically asks.

The key here is modesty. You need not be coy, but there is no reason to play all of your cards all of the time (or walk around with them stuck to your forehead, unless you're playing a drinking game).

Cornered

During some Happy Hour, you will be trapped in a corner with the most boring members of your section. They will not stop arguing about that day's accounting case. If you can, chug the rest of your beer and make a move towards the keg for a refill. However, if you really are blocked in, try to make the most of it and steer the conversation towards something

---

2   If you have a stemmed glass, wrap your pinky around the stem and grip the cheese between your thumb and middle finger. Presto—you can now eat and drink one-handed. My, that blue cheese goes well with this Pinot Noir.

that you are interested in. This isn't to say that you need to be the one talking, but change up the topic.

If Joe Longwinded, an ex-Marine, is pontificating about recent changes to financial regulations, see whether you can engage him with another hook.

> "I've been meaning to ask you, Joe, you went through basic training, right? Is it really like what you see in *Full Metal Jacket?*"

Get the guy talking about something you might actually care about. It is a good way to get to know someone better, enjoy the conversation more yourself, and perhaps even learn something. And it gets the speaker off whatever dreadful topic he'd been droning on about.

Remember to cut everyone some slack. Other people talk about themselves about 20% less than you think they do, and *you* talk about yourself about 20% *more* than you think you do. It's not a quant question; it's just a fact.

Mean Girls (and Guys)

In a class of two hundred or nine hundred, you are not going to be friends with everyone, not even on Facebook.[3] Cliques will inevitably develop. However, you reap what you sow in business school and beyond. If you are thought of as exclusive, rather than inclusive, you will be remembered that way years from now, when you are looking for

> *During orientation, the administration told us, "We want you to be competitive, but not competitive with each other."*
>
> *-- Jen, Fuqua '12 (Duke)*

---

3   Don't friend every one of your classmates, particularly not on the first day. It'll make you look like some weird, obsessive stalker.

investors for your start-up or someone to help get you back on your feet after a period of "economic recovery." It pays to play nice in the sandbox.

Best Friends for Now or Best Friends Forever?

The madness of b-school often forces relationships to form very quickly and very intensely. It is easy to find yourself a part of a small clique, often made up of folks who have been drawn together by their shared background or some particular characteristics. We'll say it again: go out and meet other people. You can strike up a conversation with anyone in your program. You've got at least one topic in common: school.

> *What am I going to learn from people who want to be just like me?*
>
> *-- Tushar, Wharton '11 (U Penn)*

The intense (and often alcohol-fueled) socializing can make it difficult to get to know people on a deeper level. Pull people together for small-group dinners apart from the mayhem. Having folks you can truly feel comfortable with is essential for making it through the next two years.

> *After the third day, it's very painful to have the "What city are you from?" conversations. You have to have genuine conversations where you can be vulnerable and know it's okay.*
>
> *-- Valerie, GSB '11 (Stanford)*

Chapter 11:
The Finer Points of Being an MBA

At some time in your life, especially in the wake of the current financial crisis, you may have run across one or more of the following impressions of business school students:

- Entitled
- Elitist
- Self-interested
- Only motivated by cold, hard cash

Now, that hardly seems like a fair assessment of you, does it?

We don't think so, either. After all, you are someone who has worked hard to develop your academic and people skills, you have a passion for whatever it is that interests you, and you want to use your talents to make living conditions better for you, your family, your colleagues, and perhaps even others around the world. You weren't lying about those things you wrote about in your essays. We believe you and, if you're reading this when you are supposed to, some admissions committee did as well.

The ugly truth, however, is that business school is a place that is filled with people who are going to judge you: professors, classmates, recruiters, speakers, potential significant others, career counselors, etc. Don't act so surprised—you are out to judge as well. But if you want others to assess you fairly, you need to make sure that your presentation doesn't get in the way of your true talents.

In short, don't be a jerk.

You need to prove that you are not the stereotype. The key here is to show, *through your actions*, who you really are. If you want to be the guy who gets things done, get things done. If you want to be the girl with the great ideas, don't be shy about sharing your great ideas (but let other people label them as "great"). Don't try to wow your classmates or profs by talking about all of the awesome things that you have done up until now. Wow those folks by doing awesome things in front of them.

> *During the application process, you have to prove you're this great leader. When you're finally at school, there is a tendency to keep [trying to prove this point]. Don't do it. You can learn a lot more by sitting back and listening to your classmates.*
>
> *-- Sinead, Ross '11 (Michigan)*

Take, for example, the great tale of David vs. Goliath; only think of yourself as David and your MBA program as the giant. It doesn't matter if you have a history of slaying lions, tigers, and managing directors. All that matters is that you are here now, just one small person, taking on a massive obstacle with nothing but a slingshot and a little rock (or, in your case, your supafly Excel skillz). If you can use your tools to tame the terror and master Managerial Economics, the masses will respect you.

But if all you do is tell the stories of previous feats, good luck building a following. What matters is not what you've done in the past but what you can do right here, right now.

Particularly in the beginnings of the program, people do a lot of jockeying, trying to secure a position in the social hierarchy. You'll hear name-dropping (e.g., where you did your undergrad, who you worked for, what deals you have been involved in, etc.) and stories that begin, "When I was explaining to Bill Gates…"

If Steve Jobs took you aside at some point and revealed the secrets of the latest iGadget, then by all means tell the story. But tell it in such a way that you are sharing some fun anecdote, relating a foible of your own, or letting your audience know how to get inside Apple's doors. Be magnanimous, not self-promoting.

"That guy."

There's one in every section. Someone who thinks that he knows more than everyone else, more than the professor, more than the guest speaker, more than God. And he needs to make sure that you know it.

"That guy" speaks in every class more than once, as if marking his territory. "That guy" regularly throws around his favorite topics, multisyllabic words, and obscure acronyms. "That guy" likes to refresh your knowledge of his past achievements and current connections. "That guy" happily informs you of all of his job offers; he name-checks all of the employers who are still banging down his door for the opportunity to interview him.

Don't be "that guy."

Your job is to do the work, share your ideas, and challenge some of the positions that are offered. You do not need to teach the teacher. Your experiences do not trump all conventional wisdom.

Everyone is made uncomfortable by the student who directly confronts a professor or guest in a disrespectful manner. Just watch—you will see the entire class exchange glances and a large portion sink lower in their chairs. You surely won't win points from anyone, so why do it? If you want to engage in a debate because of a valid disagreement, by all means do so. Just make sure that you keep your comments topical, not personal, and that you back up your argument with solid facts, not conjecture.

> *Friendly disagreement with a professor is okay but there's a limit you need to grasp. In general, if a point is up for debate, the professor will ask a question. Remember, they're like actors and [the classroom] is their stage. Don't try to dethrone the professor.*
>
> *-- Michael, HBS '12 (Harvard)*

You can also avoid being labeled "that guy" by carefully choosing the times that you speak in class. Sixty of you or more all want to get a word in, whether to pick up participation points or to contribute meaningfully to the discussion. When you speak, be succinct and then yield the floor, if only because you want to be called on when you can make your best contributions.

Don't just wait impatiently with your arm raised for your turn to speak; really listen to what your colleagues have to say. They might actually have good points to make. And even when they don't, class discussions are supposed to be conversations between the lot of you. No one is interested in a give-and-take between just one student and the professor.

If you want to challenge the professor, do so professionally. And briefly. Few questions require a four-minute run-up. A simple "What do you think about…?" will demonstrate respect and give the professor room to answer. Questions should be about the subject at hand, not about you. (Try therapy for that.)

While we are on the subject of speaking in class, here's a fun game: Count how many times you hear someone start a comment with, "When I was at Company X …" If you had a nickel for every time, you'd be able to pay off your student loans.

It all boils down to the "Golden Rule": act the way that you would want others to act. And remember that the professor leading the discussion earned that position. It might be you at the helm one day—but it isn't you right now.

> *A professor may only be there for one semester but your fellow students will be a part of your network for the rest of your life. You need to manage your social capital.*
>
> *-- Mark, HBS '11 (Harvard)*

Mind Your Ps and Qs (as well as Your Four Cs and Five Forces)

When you were in college, probably one of the first things that you figured out was that classroom attendance was largely optional, particularly in large lecture classes. Show up, don't show up, no one notices; it is the beauty of no longer being in high school.

Again, business school is more like middle school: you are expected to show up to class.

You may be back in a large lecture class—but this is one in which you display a name card. You'll be called on. And everyone will know exactly who said what.

Think about it this way: theoretically, you are in graduate school because you have a desire to learn the material being presented. You were also accepted to your program because you possess a particular combination of abilities and experiences that make your opinions relevant to your classmates. If you aren't there to share, you are cheating your classmates out of a huge part of their expensive education. You need to show up and participate.

You may or may not have a choice; some schools (and some classes) make participation a large portion of your grade. In those situations, we recommend that you have a "participation buddy," someone in the class who keeps track of when you speak, what you say, and whether you sounded like a loon. Debrief with your pal after class to see how you might have contributed better. If you simply answer "facts of the case" questions or provide summations of others' points, you want to work on finding more compelling ways to add your voice to the class discussion.

Showing up to class also means that you will be present for the time-honored business school tradition of the cold call. Yes, you have heard about it. Yes, you are dreading it. And yes, you will screw it up at least once.[1]

You need to be present in class, both physically and mentally. Whether or not you have a laptop in front of you (a lot of professors won't allow it), turn off your cell phone or, at the very least, put it on vibrate. Now is not the time to update your Facebook page or read Gawker.com. And only check your stock portfolio if (a) you want everyone sitting around you to know your net worth or (b) you really need to know what the Dow Jones did that day as it relates directly to the case you are discussing.

To that end, there is something to be said for taking notes on actual (gasp!) paper. Sure, it makes it a bit harder to share your notes with classmates, but paper doesn't offer the volume of distractions that a computer does. Also, no matter how much of a PowerPoint wiz you are, it is still easier to outline, draw arrows, or sketch flow charts when you have a pencil in your hand. Furthermore, without a computer screen to hide behind, you will be able to engage more with your professor—and hopefully avoid being cold called. If you really crave a techy solution, you might try a smart pen, such as Livescribe, to record audio to synch with your notes.

---

1   For more discussions of cold calls, please see page 162.

(Being on) Time is of the Essence

Showing up to class doesn't mean that you walk in (or out) at the break. You are expected to be there on time, just as if class were an important board meeting or client appointment.

Coming into class midway through is disruptive and, frankly, egotistical. What do you have going on that makes you incapable of showing up in a way that is respectful of your professor and your peers?

Speaking of the money you are spending, do the math. Figure out what you are paying per class hour and the odds are good that you will never be late again. For example, if tuition is $50K for two 12-week semesters, and each semester has the equivalent of five three-hour classes per week, you are spending a whopping:

$50,000 / (2 \times 12 \times 3 \times 5) = $138.89 *per hour* or $2.31 *per minute* or $0.04 *per second*.

Fine, so the last number isn't that scary—but there are 10,800 seconds in your three-hour class, and that works out to be over $400. Check, please.

Location, Location, Location

Once you have made it to class on time, the question becomes one about seat selection. You won't always have this luxury—you may be assigned seats or told to sit with your group (in which case, you may have already decided if you are a "front" or "back" kind of group). But most of the time, it will be up to you.

Is there really an advantage to being in the front or the back of the class? Is there a place that is key for hiding out and a way to avoid being called on when you just didn't get a chance to prep the case? The sad answer is, usually, no.

Most larger MBA classrooms are structured Roman Coliseum-style, with tiered seats rising in a semi-circle above the speaker's podium and the blackboard. Seats are often fixed and placed at regular intervals, allowing for a fair amount of space to spread out your casebooks and computer or notebook. Usually, there is a notch carved in the desk for you to place your name card, which you will carry with you from class to class and which allows the professor to easily identify you, Mr. John Q. Smith, as the guy who just started snoring in the middle of his lecture. It is extremely hard to hide in the classroom, and absences are very conspicuous.

While we have never done a statistical correlation study, anecdotal experience suggests that there is little relationship between where you sit and grades. The lower you sit, the more people who can see your computer from above, so you might want to guard your surfing. On the plus side, it can be easier to see the board or read a professor's expression from the front. And if you want to be first in line to ask a question after class, proximity to the important folk can definitely work in your favor.[2]

Actually getting into the physical seats can be the most difficult part of the whole classroom experience, as there is limited space between one row and the next. Polite classmates will file in neatly and fill the seats from the middle out to the end, not forcing their colleagues to climb over them. Those inclined to make a beeline for the bathroom at a break or to sneak out of class for an urgent phone call will claim the rare aisle seats, much to the annoyance of all.

Thus, the key to seat selection actually has far less to do with front vs. back than it does with *where in the arc* you sit. If you are in the middle of a row, it is not easy to get out. You're trapped, unless you want to climb out from behind a dozen of your classmates who can't even scoot in their chairs to help you pass. If you're tiny, you might be ok. But you

---

2　　　　　This sort of behavior, running up to the professor or speaker the second class has ended, is often referred to as "pit diving," a nod to the physical set-up of the classroom. Routine pit diving is a no-no, as it makes you seem like an over-eager Labrador who needs immediate, special attention.

will never make this move look graceful, and there is no way to escape without having everyone notice.

Those who have mastered the art of seat selection manage to walk into class with barely 30 seconds to spare, grabbing the last aisle seat and whipping out their pencils moments before the professor utters the word "Acme."

The Salad Girl

There was a girl in one of our sections who almost never spoke in class and rarely showed up at activities, making her one of the more forgettable members of our 65+ person group. No one but her study group members would have known who she was had it not been for one distinguishing fact: her salad.

It could be 10 in the morning, but there she was, perched in the front row with her salad bowl. She often walked in late, presumably because there had been a line at the Eat More Veggies counter. Other times, she left class in the middle to fetch her mixed greens with assorted crunchy toppings.

To begin, she would yank her bowl out of a paper bag, which crinkled like a flag snapping in the wind. Then she would fanatically stir the contents about, even though the salad had clearly been tossed back at the deli. Eventually, she would sit up, fork elevated like a baton, and commence chomping for all to hear.

Everyone has occasions to eat in class—you're starving, there's no break in your day, etc. It happens. But salad symphony happened every day, distracting both professors and students alike, until one prof called her out. She refused to moderate her salad-devouring ways and became branded "The Salad Girl." We were the section with The Salad Girl.

What's the point of this story? Just because you can do something, doesn't mean you should. Also, it is up to you, as part of your school, to define what norms and standards of behaviors are acceptable.

A final warning: don't let legumes be your legacy.

> Students need to hold each other accountable. You're the brand; you're the ambassadors.
>
> *-- Anna Millar, Senior Associate Director,*
> *MBA Program, Kenan-Flagler (UNC)*

It's the Case That...

INDUSTRIAL INDUSTRIES

Abner Wallace sat in his 14th floor corner office, gazing out the window at the rolling hills below him. It had been a long day, preceded by an even longer week, preceded by an even longer month. In fact, things at Industrial Industries had been tough for some time. Costs were rising, revenues were falling, and, to top it all off, Abner's wife had run off with his vice president of finance. With the Board of Directors' meeting only a month away, Abner knew he had to make major changes if he wanted to keep his job and keep the company afloat.

Case studies are, in many ways, the heart of business education. They are true stories in which you see the world through the eyes of the CEO or another key player. You are given information about a particular situation, and asked to come up with how you would have responded in the protagonist's shoes. Cases are role-playing games—Excel-enhanced versions of *Dungeons and Dragons*, if you will.

Some MBA programs use the case method of instruction exclusively; others use it alongside lectures and simulations. Regardless, you can expect to encounter numerous cases over the course of your studies. As you'll see, Harvard Business School has cornered the market on writing these.[3]

Cases typically work in the following way. The syllabus tells you that in Session #6, you'll discuss the Wal-Mart case. You may be asked to prepare some sort of written summary and crunch a few numbers, or you may be left to your own devices. Depending upon your personal diligence, capabilities, and interests, prepping a case can be a five-minute task or five-hour ordeal. (If you happen to care about your grades, you may want to shy away from the shorter end of the spectrum.)

Not to be a broken record, but you're not going to have time to read everything, so you need a system for tackling cases efficiently and effectively. Fortunately for you, we've already figured this one out. The following recipe should take about a half an hour.

Step 1: Read the exhibits in the back first. Determine whether the case has a more quantitative or qualitative focus.

Step 2: Read the intro, the conclusion, and any questions in the back. Try to home in on three or four issues of concern.

Step 3: Read the actual case—quickly. This is not beach reading. You don't want to get bogged down with ancillary information and unnecessary details (which cases deliberately contain in an effort to mimic real life). You are reading to get a lay of the land. If you know where information is housed, you can easily locate it when necessary.

Step 4: Prepare your comments/numbers. Cases aren't meant to be read; they're meant to be discussed. So think about what you have to say—and also how your particular class functions. Most case discussions

---

3   It does make you wonder why HBS tuition is so high, given all of the revenue they generate from selling cases to other schools.

start out with someone giving a brief overview of the situation and the key points. Then it's usually on to numbers or some smaller issue that must be resolved before the larger picture can be looked at. Where does your professor usually focus? Are you expected to be able to answer the questions at the end of the case? When do cold calls usually come? Part of your preparation should be strategic in this sense.

Consider the following generic issues:

Case Mapper

1) The basics

    a. Who are the players?

    b. What are their options?

    c. What's the dilemma?

    d. How would you "bucket" the issues into 3–4 categories?

2) The issues of the case

    a. What's surprising/doesn't quite fit together?

    b. What would you do to resolve the discrepancy?

    c. If it were your money or your business at risk, what would you do? What else would you want to know?

3) The case and your class

    a. Why were you assigned this case/how does it relate to other material you've been reading or discussing?

    b. What frameworks from class can you apply?

    c. Is there a specific analysis you can do? (If so, do it.)

4) Getting ready to participate

    a. What are your three best insights?

    b. What are your two best questions?

The Sims

With everyone clamoring for more "real world" practice, it's no wonder that simulations can make up a sizable chunk of your work in courses such as Negotiations, Marketing, and Game Theory. Some simulations last only part of a class period and are designed to teach a particular point. Other simulations function as the "lab" component of the course; the experiment may take weeks. The key to a successful simulation is to take it seriously enough. Of course, you should have fun, and sometimes you have to laugh at cheesy aspects of the game. Just don't completely pooh-pooh the exercise as silly. Simply determine the strategy you would employ in a real setting and execute based on that strategy.

All the same rules about classroom behavior apply in simulations. Your classmates will be around a lot longer than the game, so avoid getting branded as overly self-interested or as a cheater. Think about how your actions will play out in the short-term (this assignment) and long-term (ten years down the line). Be ethical, be thoughtful, and be willing to compromise.

The Cold Call

It's going to happen. Cold calling is as inevitable as death, taxes, and the sock gap.[4]

You've just sat down in your seat with your caramel macchiato when the professor announces, "Pat, why don't you open the case for us?" Problem is, you're Pat.

You'll encounter a variety of cold calling techniques. Some profs start a class off by singling out a random student to begin the discussion; others wait until the number of volunteers has dwindled. Some instructors even target students who are more reticent to speak or who may have a particularly key insight on the topic.

How and why you have been called doesn't matter at the moment you hear your name slice through the air, Pat. What does matter is whether you can answer the question in some legitimate form and, if not, how you can best deflect attention. Thus, it is imperative that you pay attention at all times. Even if your mind is prone to wander, keep distractions to a minimum and your gaze on whoever is speaking. If it is physically obvious that you are off in Lala Land, daydreaming about your upcoming ski trip to Tahoe, you are a sitting duck for a peevish cold-calling professor. You might even jot down ideas to prepare yourself. If you have two points to make, a few notes can keep you from the embarrassing "I lost my train of thought" cop-out.

When you are cold called, you might be prepared but have a sudden attack of nerves. To buy a moment, ask for clarification of the question. Rephrase what was just said, but only as a means of buying time, not as your sole response. It is also both acceptable and expected that you may not have a clear-cut answer to every question; wrestling with different issues is a good thing. And never underestimate the power of the word "interesting," (e.g., "I find it interesting that Five Crazy is actually a player

---

4   Look it up.

in some cola markets. Personally, the stuff scares me"). However, avoid the response typical of a politician (i.e., trotting out your canned answer to a question that wasn't asked). Professors bare their fangs in response to this tactic and swoop in for the jugular.

If you're stuck, try putting on the "CEO hat."[5] Sometimes the best approach is to take a step back and examine the big picture, not the minutiae that may have been the focus of the previous ten minutes of discussion. Quickly summarize what you as a class have learned up to this point and look for a lasting takeaway. The learning is rarely limited to the specific managerial/marketing/strategy/operations problem at the heart of the case.

All of the above presupposes that you actually did the work and know what the case or problem is about. What if you read the title, and that's it? You won't always be the most diligent student, so check out the following tips for those times when you aren't ready for the spotlight:

1) **Listen extra-carefully to the opening of the case.** You haven't seen this movie, so you need to glean everything you can from the trailer. If you're called on to open the case, though, see #6 below.

2) **Second something someone else just said and add to it.** *"To piggyback on Michelle's point, I think the true problem is with the lack of communication between sales and marketing."*

    Build on some idea that was previously well-received. It might be a bit unoriginal, but at least you're not flat-out admitting that you don't know what's going on.

3) **Ask a question.** *"You know, what really had me concerned was why the company was even thinking of selling space heaters in Dubai. Did I miss something?"*

---

5   We mean this figuratively, not literally. We have seen baseball hats actually embroidered with "CEO." Don't ever wear such a hat. Even ironically.

You may still be forced to answer the original question. Only try this manuever if your professor can be swayed by tangents; if she's a stickler for the topic, this is *not* the best tactic.

4) **Reference an earlier case.** *"This kind of reminds me of the 'Contact Lens for Chickens' case, where the problem was product adoption."*

Did you pay attention two sessions ago? Are there any similarities between the case you talked about successfully and this one? Try to expand on lessons learned.

5) **If you honestly have no idea, say so.** *"To tell you the truth, I'm not sure why the current ratio fell in the fourth quarter."*

You don't score points for bullshit, either with your classmates or with your professor. If you didn't do the homework or you don't understand the material, own up to it. Apologize that you were not prepared—and be ready to be called upon in the next class. Or even better, raise your hand and voluntarily join the discussion in future meetings.

6) **Quick! Switch your name card with your neighbor's.**

Now duck.

In all seriousness, learn early on what sort of caller your professor is, and strive to work the system in your favor. Once you've said something, you may fall off of the cold call list, so leap in early to talk about the one exhibit you did take a look at. Some professors opt to call alphabetically or according to some other pattern that you can figure out. Plan accordingly.

Finally, remember that the more confidently you say something, the more likely people are to believe you. And to make fun of you when you are obviously full of crap.

> *Luck favors the well-prepared.*
>
> *-- Mark, HBS '11 (Harvard)*

When You Know You're Right

It's happened to all of us all: you know, beyond a shadow of a doubt, you are right and that someone else is wrong. Maybe it's a disagreement over a shade of green or maybe you know that someone's math is fuzzy. Debates are par for the course in class, but how you deal with them can have huge implications for the outcome of a particular situation, as well as for your reputation.

Whether it is a classmate, professor, or guest speaker, it is acceptable to disagree and challenge whatever point has been made... *tactfully*. Need some help with that? Try these guidelines:

1) **Show respect for the other position.** Calling someone or his/her opinion stupid is the fastest way to elevate a confrontation. Avoid negative comments or remarks such as "that's ridiculous" or "that makes no sense." Instead, reiterate the other's position so it is clear that you understand that which you are opposing. "If I understand you correctly, you're claiming that the moon is made of green cheese, but I'd have to argue differently..."

2) **Don't be contrary just to be a contrarian.** It's a "that guy" move: someone wants to disagree with the professor just to get noticed. Look, the professor isn't necessarily correct about everything, but she was given license to stand in front of the podium because she generally knows what she's talking about. When you argue, have a factual basis for your position. Otherwise, you are going to look like an idiot—and, more than likely, be proven one as well.

3) **Don't think of someone else's mistake as your victory.** Sun Tzu's *The Art of War* may be a heavily referenced text in business school[6], but the classroom isn't a battlefield. You should not look to exploit or take down your fellow classmates. If someone makes an error in a calculation, be kind about correcting him. "I think you may have misplaced the decimal point on that beta" or "Can we look at that again? I found that revenues increase by a factor of 6" are graceful ways to open discussion.

Who Gave This Guy The Lectern?

Your professors are accomplished academics and/or practitioners. However, their teaching abilities can vary, because academia primarily rewards research. Business schools tend to be more responsive to student concerns than other, less market-driven divisions of universities, but they can still stick you with a newbie who's never led a case discussion in English or an old fart who delivers confusing and inaudible rants.

When you're faced with an unskilled professor of any shape, size, or subject, you have to figure out the best course of action to take. There are a few steps you can take on your own or with your classmates.

1) **Talk directly to the professor in a constructive manner.** If you have specific ideas about how to enhance the classroom experience (e.g., additional explanatory handouts of the slides, more time set aside for questions, etc.) and you believe that the professor will be receptive, approach him or her in a polite, private way. Avoid sweeping criticisms and stay focused on concrete proposals. During the conversation, assume good intentions on the other side; professors do want to teach well. Also, be ready to meet the prof partway and to facilitate any changes. Whatever you do, don't raise the issue in front of the whole class; calling someone out in public won't help your case.

---

6   Has anyone ever actually read this?

2) **Seek out the Teaching Assistant (if there is one).** TAs, often second years or grad students, are your first line of defense in a class. They have the professor's ear and can communicate your complaints (if legitimate). TAs can also be a good resource as *Teaching Assistants*, people who have already mastered the material. If you need extra help, attend office hours or ask for a group review session.

3) **Nominate a classmate as an informal teaching assistant.** By now, you've figured out which of your fellow students are racing ahead and which ones are completely adrift. Approach a classmate who clearly gets it and ask him or her to lead a review session, either for a small group of you or the whole class. A bottle of wine or artisanal six-pack for an hour of statistics refreshment is a pretty fair trade.

4) **Steal from the other guys.** If another professor teaches the same class, get your hands on notes and other materials from that class. Have friends from the other class explain things to you; their professor's explanation of CAPM may actually make sense.

5) **If it's really that bad …** Talk to your class representatives or whoever is appointed to deal with academic issues. That doesn't work? Speak with someone in the academic affairs office. Again, be constructive, not overly critical, and you're likely to garner more support for your cause.

Most professors tend to be very open to making changes if you speak with them. And remember, the problem may not be with the professor but with your level of preparation.

-- Naomi Tschoegl, Senior Associate Director,
MBA Program Office, Wharton (U Penn)

When the Going Gets Rough

If academics have you down, ask for help. It's as simple as that. It can be hard to ask if you're used to succeeding on your own. Remember, though, that business is primarily a team sport. Think of getting academic assistance as equivalent to delegating authority and marshalling resources for a project in the working world. It's a strategic move.

Everyone at the school wants you to succeed. Know what your resources are and seek them. The biggest hang-up that students have is thinking that they have to know the answer—but you just need to know where to go to find it.

-- Jilliann Rodriguez, Director of Student Life, CBS (Columbia)

Most programs have tutors available at little or no cost to students. And while it may be humbling if you've never before found yourself struggling in a class, remember that you're in school to learn. Later in life, your colleagues and managers will expect that you will already have this base knowledge. If you don't understand a key concept now, you may have to learn it on the fly when you're working. Not fun.

Think also about using your professors' and/or teaching assistants' office hours and review sessions. These tend to be woefully under-attended, especially office hours. Why not grab the opportunity to break down material with the experts? They rarely bite.

Don't forget to approach your friends. Chances are, someone in your learning team, section, or club really grooves on this stuff and would be happy to help out.

Don't wait for matters to spiral out of control. You know how a guy deep in debt hates looking at his credit card statements, so he shoves them deep into a drawer? Don't do that with your courses. Suck it up, admit that you need a bailout, and go get one. You can't eliminate a semester's worth of confusion three days before the final exam.[7]

> *You may have only one professor, but you have a lot of teachers at business school.*
>
> *-- Neil, Kellogg '11 (Northwestern)*

---

7   We say this from unhappy experience. Lesson learned. Well, at least this lesson was learned.

CHAPTER 12:
LEARNING WITH & FROM YOUR TEAMS

We Are Fam-i-ly!

For all of the decimal points, graphs, and spreadsheets that you trip over in business school, you'll also have plenty of occasions to hum "Kumbayah." Case in point: The Learning Team.[1]

The business school environment is permeated by a variety of learning teams/study groups. They can be formal or informal, assigned or self-selected; they can last for a project, a quarter, a semester, or even the entire year. Most importantly, some teams function, while others "dysfunction" in epic ways. The difference will affect your life immensely. Get a bunch of first years together and, right out of the gate, Jack will start moaning about his crazy team. Meanwhile, Jill keeps quiet in the corner, counting her lucky stars because her team is fabulous.

> *Don't be judgmental up front. You lose an opportunity to learn if you think you have the best approach. If you're open, someone just might have a better idea that will allow you to accomplish more.*
>
> *-- Chris, GSB '11 (Stanford)*

---

1   "Learning Team" is the new, hip term for what used to commonly be referred to as a "Study Group." Driving the rebranding is the notion that you are there to do more than simply study with this group; you are to *learn* from them as individuals and from your experiences as a *team*. Next, they'll be called "Self-improvement Communities."

Some of the best experiences you have in business school can happen because of your team. Ideally, your study buddies will help get you through that difficult accounting project, spur you to pull an all-nighter on your marketing simulation, and explain, for the 47th time, what a currency swap is. They will clue you in when you failed to read the case, and they will give you notes from the operations class you missed so that you could attend your best friend's wedding. They will also challenge your intellect and your patience. They will demand that you do things differently. They will bluntly correct you when you're wrong and ignore you when you're right.

Learning teams are themselves part of the whole learning experience. They force you to balance your own priorities with those of others. You can resist this—or you can learn to compromise. We recommend the latter.

> *Study groups are more about the implied tasks than actual tasks. We all want to be leaders, but we also need to learn to be followers. Even though that's not expressly given as a task, it's why you're there.*
>
> *-- Jeff, Kellogg '12 (Northwestern)*

So what makes for a successful learning team? Part of it is luck, particularly if you are talking about an assigned study group. You may think that a great team has the smartest kids in the room, the business school equivalent of the Justice League *(Fiona Finance! Edward Excel! Marcos the Marketing Maven! Cathy Strategist!)*. But while striking the right balance of strengths is definitely helpful, that's not what defines a successful group. The most functional teams are the ones in which every member is on board with the operation. Everyone respects everyone else and believes in the collective mission. It is much easier to make up for a group-wide Excel deficit than to rein in a member who has gone off the reservation because he or she hates the manner in which the group operates.[2]

The trick? **Discuss expectations early and revisit them often.**

This will feel hokey and awkward, no doubt. But a study group is like a royal marriage without a pre-nup: you need to work together because breaking up really sucks in and of itself, plus it hits the tabloids.

Just as you should never get married without first discussing fundamental issues surrounding finances, faith, and family, don't consummate your team union without talking about organization, priorities, work habits, and general expectations.

> *It doesn't work if two people understand the project and want to leave early; we all need to understand and we all need to be on the same page.*
>
> *-- Jessica, Marshall '12*
> *(USC)*

To that end, the following team questionnaire can provide a structure. Take ten minutes to have everyone answer these questions on his or her own, *in writing*. Only then open it up for discussion around the campfire. This way, all team members will be heard equally. Often those who speak the loudest drown out everyone else, but this is *the* most important time for hearing everyone's respective voice. Really.

This questionnaire can be downloaded from our website or you can just photocopy the next page (we give you permission). So hand around some pencils and start jotting down answers. We'll reconvene in a few moments to discuss.

---

2   Or because he or she is acting like a self-centered schmuck, dang it.

Team Questionnaire

1) When do you prefer to meet? Day? Evening? Weekend? Do you have any regular obligations that prevent you from meeting at certain times?

2) Do you prefer to work in longer sessions or shorter ones?

3) What are your primary strengths with regard to the subject matter we will be covering? What are your concerns about that material?

4) Would you prefer to work on projects that play to your strengths, your weaknesses, or both?

5) How do you prioritize your goals for the team? For instance, what is your target grade for team projects?

6) How hard do you want to work for this class or classes?

7) How should decisions be made (e.g., lengthy consensus-building vs. quicker majority votes)?

8) How should leadership on a project be decided?

9) How should other roles and responsibilities be divided?

10) Are you willing to split up tasks, or should all members be involved with all projects?

11) If not everyone can attend a meeting, can the people there make decisions for the group?

12) How should the team deal with members who do not fulfill their obligations?

13) If there is tension within the team, how do you prefer to deal with it?

Everything answered? All right, go around now and share your answers, one question at a time, stopping to talk and reach some general agreements. Let someone take notes so that there is a record of what the group has agreed to.

No doubt, certain issues may be easier to come to a consensus on, such as when and where you want to work. But how will you decide an acceptable work level or even a basic decision-making process? Be prepared for some intense discussions—you might even agree to put aside a particular topic until the group has had some experience working together. Success isn't starting with consensus but ending up with it.

At the end of your discussion, read back over your notes and make sure that everyone is comfortable with the expectations as established. Then set a date by which you will reexamine this list and make any necessary adjustments.

Ongoing study groups, like any relationship, require ongoing counseling. Do monthly check-ins to make sure that everyone is still satisfied with how things are going. As you revisit these issues, it is always a good idea for people to lay out their thoughts on paper first—again, it ensures that everyone will be able to articulate his/her position freely. The lone voice of dissent deserves to be heard.

> *Commit to having these conversations and build into the process clear communication channels. [If you do have problems,] assume that nobody is intentionally trying to sabotage you, the team, or themselves; people aren't repeatedly stupid. Revisit your rules and see what's working and what's not…*
>
> *-- Dr. Timothy Flood, Associate Professor of Marketing and Corporate Communication, Kenan-Flagler (UNC)*

A few hours spent creating a well-run study group can save you numerous all-nighters down the road. Think of it as a positive ROI.

It's a Small World After All

Whether or not it's growing flatter, the world is definitely shrinking. MBA programs increasingly emphasize the global aspects of a complete business education, proudly enrolling large numbers of international students. And while this diversity increases the range of perspectives in the classroom, it also means that a lot more languages, customs, and cultures have to be harmonized.

Learning teams are a prime way in which schools try to "manage" the diversity of the student body and mix cultures. As microcosms of the whole class, teams often highlight sharp cultural differences. For example, in some cultures, it is only acceptable to express an opinion after you are asked multiple times; in other cultures, you are expected to interrupt frequently. How you manage these cross-cultural issues will affect how functional your group is.

Language barriers can be serious. A common issue in US business schools is that, in discussions, the native English speakers sometimes leave the non-native speakers in the proverbial dust. Understanding everyone's comfort level with spoken English is critical.

> *We worked out a system in our group where our international student simply raises her hand when she wants to speak. She can then talk without being interrupted, so she can contribute without having to fight so much to get into our discussions.*
>
> *-- Jen, Fuqua '12 (Duke)*

If you're a native English speaker, don't confuse fluency in English with intelligence. Think back to the last time you studied a foreign language. You probably understood more in that language than you could say, but your thinking wasn't hampered by your inability to express yourself clearly. Realize that your teammates may be in a similar position, formulating awesome thoughts in their native language but struggling to translate them into English at your rapid-fire pace. It's not surprising that a number of foreign students prefer to correspond in writing or to know that they have a protected space in which to articulate their ideas aloud.

Look, you're not out to make peace in the Middle East. But if MBAs can figure out how to break the cultural divide, there just might be hope for the rest of us.

While There's No Place Like Home…

The international roadway is a two-way street. While non-native English speakers may lament that fast-talking Americans leave them out of conversations, US students can find themselves wondering the proper way to insert themselves into a lunch table full of Portuguese-speaking Brazilians.

It's understandable that foreign students from one country or region tend to flock together. After all, they share a common language, food, and culture, all of which can be extremely reassuring thousands of miles from home. These students may have met back in their native land before school, or their significant others have become fast friends in their new communities. However, the insularity of such groups can be intimidating to outsiders. Meanwhile, generally speaking, US students can afford to do a better job of rolling out the welcome wagon for their international colleagues.

The point is simple: if you want to grow globally, you have to start locally. So get to know your peers, no matter where you and they hail from. If you're from the US, sit down with the Brazilians at lunch and don't leave until you've learned a few words of Portuguese. If you're from Brazil, share your beautiful language with the rest of us, and be patient as we mangle it.

Are Two Heads Better than One? Or Five?

> *Writing is not a group process. Don't try to write a paper with five people.*
>
> *-- Chitra, Haas '11 (Berkeley)*

Even though much of the learning team experience helps you, well, learn about teams, you still have to get some actual work done. In the name of efficiency, your group will sometimes have to divide and conquer. Not everyone will be able to be involved with every aspect of every project. You should figure out in advance how you will divide up the work when crunch times come a-crunchin'.

For some groups, expedience rules. Give the job to whoever knows how to do it the best. For others, the learning process carries more weight. To strike a balance, you may want to pair folks up, one stronger and one weaker, on particular tasks. This way, there is real knowledge transfer going on while the project gets done.

> *My group agreed that we would each do what was challenging, so I wrote the first draft of a case so I could get feedback. The group's comments helped me improve before I had to go and do it all on my own.*
>
> *-- Miguel, Haas '11 (Berkeley)*

If you do have the luxury of time, think about rotating "teaching" responsibilities through the group. People might even take the lead on subjects they don't really know. That may seem strange, but if you have to explain some completely foreign concept, you'll learn it really well beforehand. One of the best ways to hone your knowledge of a subject is to plan to teach it to someone else.

Time is probably your scarcest resource, but don't lose sight of your obligations to your team members. You won't receive a higher grade for explaining for the tenth time exactly why a yield curve might flip, but it will make you a better person.

> *It is your responsibility to help out the other students; that's part of being an MBA.*
>
> -- Matt, Fuqua '12 (Duke)

Cookies and Cases

While formal teams are a hallmark of many first-year MBA experiences, informal study groups spring up all over the place. These little groups get together on a regular or as-needed basis to prep cases, review home-work, or study for exams. As voluntary assemblies of individuals with different strengths, ad hoc groups can be a godsend. Case outlines and study sheets often pass freely around these groups, with everyone con-tributing to the pool.

However, these groups are "informal," not "freeloading." All members are expected to hold up their respective end of the bargain. It is extremely off-putting when folks don't come through with their share of the work. It can be even more frustrating when a member finds that her outline of chapters 3–10 has been forwarded to the entire class—and that she never got the other outlines she was expecting.

> *The people you go out with are not necessarily the people you want in your study group.*
>
> -- Nadiyah, Booth '11 (Chicago)

Informal study groups are like potluck dinners. Don't show up with a hunk of Velveeta and some saltines. On the other hand, you don't have to bring caviar and blini. A rough parity of contributions is best.

Again, it is important to set expectations even in the most informal of settings. Agree on when work will be turned in and whether it is acceptable to share notes with those not in the group. Be a good team player in one group, and there is a high likelihood you will find yourself inundated with offers to study with other buddies.

Older, Wiser, and (Potentially) a Lot Less Interested

Second-year friends are extremely valuable. They can tell you who the better professor for Capital Markets is, teach you strategies for bidding for interviews and classes, and even provide you with last year's final exams.[3] Second years can be great tutors, as they may be less pressed for time than some of your first-year colleagues and won't see themselves as being in direct competition with you.

Having second years in your study groups, however, can be a bit of a different story. Say your second-year study buddy received an offer from his summer employer. He may be mentally checked-out of school and focused on enjoying a final year out of the daily grind, while the first years, who are often on the hunt for summer internships, are busting butt on every assignment.

If you are assigned to a group that includes second years or if you choose to work with them in elective classes, it will behoove you to lay out your expectations at the beginning. If the grade is important to you, don't be shy about saying so. The more that you can remind your colleagues that they were in your position not all that long ago, the more you will get them to contribute.

Of course, you may need to accept a certain level of unconcern from your second-year teammate. Don't expect someone to come through

---

3   Make sure that this falls within your school's honor code. Didn't know you had one? Better go look it up.

suddenly at the last minute if he hasn't done so already. You can't teach an old dog new tricks, and you can't make a second year share your urgency.

Houston, We Have a Problem

No matter how much advance planning you do, things can still go awry. You may have a particularly rogue study group member or someone who has a personal crisis that drags her away for some time. Dealing with and managing these sorts of problems is, in fact, one of the key learning components of business school.

Study groups are a part of your general management education. You should come out of business school with an ability to work in groups. And most things aren't truly disasters if they're talked about, but it takes courage to do so.

-- Nayla Bahri, Assistant Dean of Student Affairs, CBS (Columbia)

If your teammate Brian is dropping the ball, first address the issue internally. Call a team meeting. Start by stating the facts in a non-accusatory manner (e.g., "The executive summary that you agreed to write, Brian, didn't get done in time, so Jorge had to write it"). Revisit your team rules and create a group-approved strategy to remedy the issue. Give Brian the benefit of the doubt and be ready to offer assistance. Remember that you're still in this together.

Keep criticism concrete and actionable and keep it focused on a particular situation. When you use a specific context, it becomes a lot less threatening.

--Jakub, Booth '11 (Chicago)

If the situation persists or if you are unable to reach any sort of agreement, enlist outside facilitation help. Different schools will have different protocols. Often the first people to approach are second years or peer leaders trained to help you deal with conflict. You can also seek out administration officials who deal with student life or academics.

Try to avoid approaching a professor unless you absolutely have to. If you are confronting a problematic classmate, you do not want that person to fear that his/her grade is at stake. Furthermore, you do not want to look like a tattle-tale. No one, not even a four-year-old, wants that.

CHAPTER 13:
THE SOCIAL LIFE
OF THE MBA

We all know that the real reason you are going to business school is to advance your career. You want to build a certain skill set, you want to have certain leadership experiences, and you want to have opportunities to network with likeminded folks. You want to delve deeply into the world of financial modeling and accounting, to establish a highly nuanced understanding of the global economic environment and the factors that shape it, and to explore the theories that undergird all manner of market forces.

What? Did we lift that directly from your application essay?

Okay. No matter what you wrote, you are also in business school for one other very important reason: the social scene.

As you well know, the social aspects of the MBA experience are very important. It is in the non-class hours that you build those relationships, people skills, and networks that will serve you for the rest of your life. An IPA now may impact an IPO years in the future.[1]

You ought to know a few things about the business school social scene, some good and some bad. And yes, it is a scene—the clubs, the study groups, the recruiting activities, and, occasionally, just a night out. So pop open a bottle of something or other as you read the next section; it is the appropriate thing to do.

---

1   IPA=India Pale Ale. IPO=Initial Public Offering.

The Lush Life

For many people, "business school" is synonymous with "drinking." And yes, a disproportionate amount of the socializing does include, or even revolve around, a beer tap. Does this mean you have to drink? *Absolutely not.*

> *Many events revolve around drinking. If you aren't a big drinker, you just have to work harder. People won't judge you for not drinking but drinking is a part of the social setting.*
>
> *-- Rachel, Haas '11 (Berkeley)*

Non-drinkers in b-school can get tired of being around the drunkards, a completely understandable feeling. So create other events where drinking isn't the primary activity. Dinner parties, bowling, and movie nights are all great ways to bring folks together. This is one group that will clearly be up for marathon games of Jenga or Apples to Apples.

Do what you are comfortable with. And if that means you drink sparkling water rather sparkling wine, that's just fine. You just want to have something in your glass when your classmates start toasting in six different languages. To which we say: Cheers!

Join the Club—We Have T-Shirts

Are there more students or more clubs at your MBA program? It's a legit question. The proliferation of clubs—professional and social—is a universal business school phenomenon. Nearly everyone has membership in multiple clubs, and most students hold more than one office. Think you had a lot of t-shirts from your college days? As your club memberships rise, so will your ownership of silk-screened 100% cotton tees.

With so many clubs to choose from, it is worth taking a strategic approach to your activities. Be methodical and a little picky.

Step 1: Diversify your membership. Divide clubs into four categories: *professional, identity, volunteer,* and *recreational.* Professional clubs tend to sport obvious names such as "Finance Club" and "Marketing Club." Be on the lookout for "cute" acronyms, too—those clubs can still be pretty serious about their career planning services.

> *Try to be an officer for at least one club because it's the quickest way to meet people who are interested in the same things you're interested in and who you won't necessarily meet otherwise.*
>
> -- Brian, Stern '11 (NYU)

Identity clubs are those that try to draw together members who have similar pasts or who check the same boxes on census forms. Examples are "Military in Business," "Black Business Students Association," "Association of Women in Business," and "The Italian Society." These clubs promote networking for both students and alumni. Additionally, these clubs tend to throw the best parties and often host additional study sessions before exams.

Volunteer or community-oriented clubs often focus on the school or the surrounding area. Included in this group is the club for students who want to assist the admissions office or provide tours to prospective students. You'll also come across community outreach clubs that help local small businesses or are chapters of larger organizations such as Junior Achievement. Adding one or two of these to the mix is a way to give back to your community. It also reads nicely on your resumé.

Recreational clubs provide more clothing and fewer serious discussions. "The Rugby Club," "Microbrewers Association," and "Top Chefs of Business School" can provide great outlets for letting off steam and getting to know your peers in more casual settings.

Some activities may fall under a couple of categories, such as Columbia Business School's *Follies* and Duke's *FuquaVision*. While more recreational than professional, these kinds of entertainment organizations do not simply "amuse" students; they improve the way life is lived on the planet we call home.[2]

> *Turn business school into a resumé builder beyond the three lines under your "Education" section.*
>
> *-- Jake, Haas '11 (Berkeley)*

Step 2: Schedule your commitments. Decide which clubs to be active in and which ones to join simply for the mailing lists. You can't be an officer in every club and, frankly, you don't want to be.

Go ahead and sign up for clubs you may only be mildly interested in, but joining every club can get awfully expensive. (Most clubs require dues, which can vary from the price of a beer to the price of a rather nice bottle of vino.) Ask yourself: *Do I want to get emails from The Argentine Tango Society on a regular basis? Will the Association of Snake Performers provide opportunities that I might partake in?* Also, talk to second years about which clubs tend to limit events to members.

Narrow down your list to a handful of clubs that you do want to become active in. Many first years gun for leadership positions in professional clubs. Don't kid yourself, though—being co-chair of the Investment Banking Society's Casino Night does not guarantee you a summer internship at Goldman Sachs, nor does it even necessarily mean that you will get an interview slot. At the same time, demonstrating initiative and responsibility can impress recruiters. Furthermore, professional clubs often host speakers and coordinate informational interviews. Getting involved in these activities and acting as a liaison between various

---

2   Our publisher insists that we disclose a personal bias—Chris co-ran *FuquaVision* and Carrie was the director of *Follies*.

firms is one way to build personal connections and broaden your own network.

Don't discount taking roles in other types of clubs. These can be rewarding on a personal level, and they can facilitate relationships with people across different years and class sections. Look to club activities for leadership positions, and not just for resumé bullet points or interview stories; you want the actual experience. Want to manage a budget or spearhead an outreach effort? Such opportunities exist in all varieties of clubs and organizations; it is up to you to seek them out.

> *You get this completely exaggerated sense of self-importance because you've been running some club.*
>
> *-- Gemma, Wharton '11 (U Penn)*

Before you sign on for a plethora of responsibilities, check your clubs' schedules. For instance, most professional organizations host conferences. What weekend is the Operations Club's symposium? Is that the same weekend as the rugby tournament? If you want to be highly involved with several organizations, you will want to spread out your activities and commit to events in different seasons. Avoid obligations that all hit at the same time. Also, compare dates with both the academic and recruiting calendars. School- and admissions-oriented clubs tend to have a "high season" with lots of activities and commitments. Ask second-year representatives of these clubs for a list of dates or general time periods when you can expect to be booked.

One advantage of becoming active in a club with a front-loaded calendar is that you will have tangible accomplishments to speak about during recruiting season. So, while you will be overwhelmed that first semester, you may want to consider taking on one more project. That's one—not twelve.

Step 3: Choose your roles wisely. If you want to thicken your resumé with club experiences, you need actual accomplishments. There are two key ways to get some on your record. The first is to have an on-going leadership role (i.e., Assistant Secretary) through which you can take credit for long-term planning and steering of the organization. The other is to take on specific tasks and projects, such as initiating a speaker series, organizing an outing to visit the local bourbon brewery, creating an "Intro to Business" seminar for the local high school, or planning the annual BBQ cook-off.

> *If you don't win an officer role, it's a testament to the people you're working with. Just find another way to make an impact.*
>
> *-- Mark, Kenan-Flagler '11 (UNC)*

What offices do you want? Consider both this year and next. Most clubs are structured such that first years come in as "Assistant X" or "Vice-President X," while second years hold the title of "President," "Chair," or "Grand Poobah." The natural feeders to the top roles are the lower-level roles. It's hard (though not impossible) to land a presidency in your second year if you haven't previously been a leader in some capacity.

Before you throw your name into the ring for any position, talk to people who currently hold the role. Clarify what the job entails and when your responsibilities will peak. Find out when can you expect to see the results of your actions (so you can talk about them in interviews). Gauge the

> *Participate as if [the school] was your own organization; you're not just a customer.*
>
> *-- Al Cotrone, Chief Administrative Officer, Ross (Michigan)*

first year vs. second year breakdown of the workload. In a setup quite reminiscent of corporate life, much of the actual work falls to first years, while the high-ranking second years show up primarily to enjoy the party. However, this is not really a bad thing for first years, since you can truly take ownership of a project.

When crafting a bullet for your resumé, choose an activity that shows how you took action in a particular situation and produced a spectacular outcome. Look to quantify the impact of what you have done, emphasizing the size of the undertaking and the success you achieved. To that end, if you are running an existing event, be prepared to discuss why your event was better than the previous year's. For example, if you run a charity auction, know exactly how much money you raised, how many donors you had, and by what sort of margin these numbers exceeded previous high-water marks.

> *Pick your activities based on what you'll get out of them so that you'll be more likely to follow through and do them.*
>
> *-- Gemma, Wharton '11 (U Penn)*

In truth, club leadership is all about finding opportunities to prove that you can have a positive impact. Membership is easy; you just have to write a check or toss your name on a list. But if you want a potential employer to give you real credit, you have to produce results. That will take time and energy. Be passionate about whatever it is that you choose to do club-wise, both so that you will stay committed through thick and thin, and so that you can talk about it with genuine enthusiasm.

Everyone is an Entrepreneur

Business school students tend to think that little counts if you don't start it yourself. As a result, hundreds of new clubs are born every year at business schools across the world.

Does this mean that you *have* to start an organization to get noticed? Nope. From a resumé-padding perspective, starting a club can accomplish the same thing as initiating a project in an existing organization. Do you spot a need? Can you do something about it? Great! It does not matter whether you launch a whole new organization or simply extend the purview of a club to which you have already shown devotion. Honestly. Ask a recruiter.

If something is clearly lacking from your school's extracurricular offerings, then you might gather a group of like-minded people and build something new. But make sure you have support before you light the fuse on the rocket. The last thing you want an interviewer to ask is how many members you have recruited to your new club when the answer is one: you. You'd be admitting that no one showed up to your party (cry if you want to).

If you are dead set on starting something "new," think about bringing back something old, like a club or event that existed in the past but isn't around now. B-school organizations naturally churn because, unlike in college, students turn over very quickly; in one summer, "freshmen" become "seniors." Institutional memory exists with administrators, not the student body. Resurrecting an old club is great for a number of reasons: (1) you don't have to be creative, (2) you have a model to follow, and (3) you can contact a bunch of alumni on a perfectly good pretext. Not to mention the fact that it is incredibly cool to bring something worthwhile back from the dead, like a zombie barbershop quartet.

CEOs and CMOs and COOs... oh my!

Going to hear high-falutin' guest speakers is both a rite of b-school passage and a privilege of your MBA student status. While it may be insane to contemplate squeezing another item onto your already jam-packed calendar, be insane and try to do so as often as you can. A CEO you've always admired from afar shows up and paces around a lectern a few yards away from you. Yes, a fair bit of the talk will be canned, but you might hear a golden insight—maybe even in response to your own question. And there's something, dare we say, inspirational about seeing and meeting these folks in the flesh. If nothing else, there's probably free pizza.

> *One thing I'm really glad I did was go to hear speakers. People often only go to hear those in industries that they're interested in, but you can learn so much regardless of the field.*
>
> *-- Barr, Fuqua '11 (Duke)*

As part of your time management strategy, check your school's calendar of upcoming events and block off time in advance for the bigwigs. If someone who is really up your alley is coming to campus, find out how the invitation came about. Maybe the host club or professor can slip you into the green room for a few minutes. Small groups of students often have lunch with the speaker or act as escorts (in the literal sense of accompaniment, of course) to and from the airport or around campus. Figure out how to be one of the lucky few.

Remember that your school's Board of Directors boasts some pretty impressive folks, too. These people are often around town and may be accessible to you. You might also check out any sort of student liaison roles that you can fill. The food at board meetings is much, much better than what you're used to on campus.

Happy Hour, Pub Night, Etc.

Whatever you call Happy Hour, you should know four things about it:

1) It's rarely just an hour.

2) Despite all evidence to the contrary, it is not actually a frat party.

3) The drinks are usually cheap or free.

4) You should go.

Happy Hour is one of the time-honored, universal traditions of business school. Though practices vary, an evening of beer, wine, music, and general debauchery at the end of a long week looms large at most fulltime programs. Different weeks often sport different themes (e.g., 80s Hair Bands, International Alcohols, Valentine's Day: a.k.a, Mergers and Acquisitions, etc.). Whether you partake in the Bon Jovi sing-a-long or you are just there for the food, showing up to "Drinkety Drinks" is a way to solidify your MBA relationships.

The idea that business school, or for that matter business itself, is all work and no play is silly. Gone may be the days of the three-martini lunch, but the social components of deal-making are as alive as ever. If you need justification, consider that events such as Happy Hour provide opportunities to interact with your colleagues in more relaxed settings and talk about non-business topics. Casual discourse skills will be vital in your career, and it never hurts to have an awesome karaoke rendition of "Sweet Child o' Mine" up your sleeve.

Since many schools only have class four days a week, Happy Hour often falls on the night before the "off" day, so you should have nothing pressing to do that night (and nothing to be hung over for the following morning). Spending the evening in the library, huddled over an Operations case as the smell of cheap beer wafts past, is not a good use of your time. The work can wait. There are second years you can meet and maybe even some alumni floating around. And hey, there's beer. Probably food, too. You've got to eat.

Proms, Parties, and Other Merriment

In addition to regular social events, you can expect a fair number of one-off parties hosted by various clubs and organizations. There will be a formal dance or two, too, with expensive tickets, loud music, and a degree of forced jollity.[3] As such, these dances fall lower on the totem pole of necessary attendance. Don't get us wrong—b-school proms can be great fun—but if you have to choose between attending Happy Hour regularly and just going to the Spring Fling, opt for the former.

Ideally, of course, go to both. You need one last chance to wear that teal tie and cummerbund set you bought for your senior prom, right? Corsages are optional.

I Don't Speak Alphabet Soup

You're what people call a connector. You like to introduce new people and get your friends to be friends with each other. One of the things that you're most excited for is bringing together your non-MBA buddies and your new classmates, so they can join forces and take over the world.

But after an outing or two, your non-school friends don't really want to go to bar night. What gives?

Like an Amazonian tribe, b-school students speak their own tongue, hunt in packs, and sprawl all over each other. Face it: you're a tough crowd. You're insular, and you're crazy energetic. If you were an outsider still working for a living, would you really want to try to break into that sort of incestual beehive?

Don't take your friends' hesitance personally; rather, make time for them away from the b-school buzz. And talk about things of interest to all of you—i.e., not business school.

---

3   Business school is technically more like high school than middle school in this respect. No curfews, though.

> *One day, after 45 minutes of listening to my husband talk about his day, I had to ask if he wanted to hear about mine. He'll have a million things to talk about but they're all related to school.*
>
> *-- Maura, wife of a Sloan '12 student (MIT)*

Cancún, Baby!

Another added perk of business school is that it comes with vacation days built in. Winter Break, Spring Break, assorted other three-day weekends and university holidays make for fantastic getaways. Add in padding between school and your summer internship, and you've got tickets to ride.

> *Take every opportunity to travel. We're all "NPV-minded" so we're all worried about cash flow, but the travel is something you're not going to get to do until you're retired. And even then, it won't be the same. Don't make excuses not to do it; just take out a loan. These are memories you can't replace. A few hundred dollars will be meaningless in the future.*
>
> *-- Della, Haas '11 (Berkeley)*

Travel can be a big part of many MBAs' social experience, with a variety of trips and locations to choose from. Some excursions nobly focus on business and industry; others make you feel like you just turned 21. While budget may constrain you, the trips themselves are invaluable experiences.

Many schools or clubs sponsor treks to different countries or regions so that students can meet with local business leaders and tour the facilities. The thought of traveling with a professor or administrator may make you cringe, but these sponsored trips are often led by students native to the area. Why not visit the Taj Mahal with an Indian classmate or the Kremlin with a Muscovite? Imagine inspecting a Ferrari assembly line in Italy or a cutting-edge Samsung plant in South Korea; these are places that no guidebook will get you in to see.

The academic component of these trips is (1) easy, (2) informative, and (3) money, in that you may be able to increase your student loans to cover the costs. Sure, you will have to pay the bill off eventually, but you can just add it to your tab.

In contrast, the federal government does not subsidize recreational trips, like spring break in Rio or the Sailing Club's adventure in the Keys. Shocking. Don't let this prevent you from going. You have earned (and need) a break. Large-group trips are also common in some schools, with Beach Week or Atlantic City drawing more than half the class. Like a never-ending Happy Hour, these are once-in-a-lifetime vacations with stories that you will tell your grandchildren. Or not tell, as the case may be.

The MBA Meat Market

Question: What happens when you get a bunch of successful, like-minded, slightly tipsy 20- and 30-somethings together in tight quarters for months at a time?

Answer: They do it like they do on the Discovery Channel.[4]

If nothing else, they date around.

Whether you enter business school attached, single, or celibate, the sexual current will be all around you. Those who are single are likely on the prowl, curious as to what (and who) their new social life will

---

4   Name the one-hit wonder. Give up? Answer: The Bloodhound Gang. Now name the song. Answer #2: *The Bad Touch.*

include.[5] For those in relationships, the tension of school and learning teams has led to a phenomenon known as Black Monday.[6]

Now, just because the rabbits are hopping all over each other doesn't mean that every interaction has to be sexual in nature or that platonic relationships are impossible; in fact, those are by far the most common. But, as social norms are often jumbled in school, you may want to clarify if you're going out to drinks with your new friend *because* he or she is "your new friend" or because you're hoping he or she might be *more* than just "your new friend."

> There is a tension between the girls and guys because most everyone wants to get laid, but it's not as casual as college because of the risk to your reputation. There's concern that if I hook up with one person, I'm stuck with them for the rest of the time.
>
> -- Alexander, GSB'11 (Stanford)

We thought of creating a list of Dating Dos and Don'ts, but then we realized you wouldn't follow them. Despite our warnings, you will go after someone in your section or even your learning team. You will try to keep a dalliance a secret and you will fail. If you are a hetero guy, you will try to use your MBA status as a way to pick up a girl at a bar.[7]

---

5   The business school dating environment often seems to have a heterosexual bent to it, but LGBT students should not, in any way, shy away from dating or bringing their partners to school events. While business school is still pervaded by a classic frat/sorority vibe, most members of the LGBT community we spoke with were surprised to find out how much of a non-issue their sexuality was with the vast majority of their classmates.

6   "Black Monday" is the Monday following Thanksgiving, when all of the rest of the America is buying its Christmas gifts online. At business school, this is the day when many of your first year colleagues will announce that they have broken up with their significant others (and thus why at least one school refers to it as "The Turkey Drop"). Long-term relationships, engagements, and marriages are all put through the wringer during those first few months—and sadly, not all survive. But at least you can still find an online deal for that toaster you've always wanted.

7   Good luck with that. Granted, in any college town, a few undergrads may fall for it. If you yourself just graduated from college, knock yourself out. If you've been out in the working world long enough to have a 401K, the undergrads are jailbait.

So go forth and, well, don't multiply, but we know that you'll know each other in the biblical sense. Just realize that your personal life is school property. If things don't work out perfectly, you could have the better part of two years to still see your ex every day, so keep things peaceful for the benefit of all. Death stares across the aisle don't count towards your class participation grade.

Beyond the Ivory Tower

Had enough of resumés and REITs? Sick of discussing queueing theory and corporate structures? Then you may want to try to date off campus—or at least at a different graduate school. It's a running bad joke that's made its way into reality. MBA guys clamor to invite students from the schools of social work, education, and nursing to campus parties. Ladies, if you're in search of a man, it's not easy since women now make up more than 50% of most other graduate programs. Our suggestion? The school of engineering. Or the local fire house.

Making the Most of Your Partnership

Have you already merged your assets with someone? Have you and a partner integrated corporately?[8]

If you are in a committed relationship, you and your significant other need to discuss some issues before you arrive on campus since the nature of your relationship will surely change. As the one going off to school, you need to be cognizant of the sacrifices your partner is making. He or she may have to move, change jobs, support you, pick up the housekeeping slack, or simply be more flexible about spending time with you. At times over the next two years, you will be stressed to the point of myocardial infarction. To avoid death, you will undoubtedly need understanding and chicken soup.

---

8   These are business-dork ways to refer to romantic commitment. As pickup lines in bars, b-school puns fail with p=1. That's 100% probability.

While you have probably already figured out the answers to some of the questions below, you need to have a discussion about them before school actually starts. As with your learning team, set expectations early and revisit them often.

1) How involved do you want your significant other to be in your school life? How involved does he/she want to be?

2) How will you resolve schedule conflicts? What happens when you each need the other one to be somewhere at the same time?

3) What expectations do you have about time spent together, both with regard to quantity and quality?

4) Are there any underlying trust issues to bring up? Now's the time. You will be working closely with a number of attractive people, and additional obligations will pop up at the last minute. If such situations are likely to lead to altercations, better plan for it now.

Travel is often a flashpoint for couples. Be aware that your calendars are going to be different and your partner may not be able to join you. You have to make the big choices together.

-- Ari, HBS '11 (Harvard)

To Move or Not to Move, That is the Question

For many b-school-bound couples, the question arises as to whether both partners should relocate. We can't tell you what to do here. What we can tell you is that a move places a lot of stress on both parties, but it can also result in a much stronger partnership.

If it's not too late, bring your partner into the discussion of which school to attend. You want your partner to be committed to the plan and to understand why you're in school. (Now's a good time to share those essays, if you haven't done so already. You were able to convince a few complete strangers that you know what you're after, so maybe it'll work on the person who knows you best. And, if not, it's a wonderful place to start a discussion.)

> *The difference is so small between two schools that you don't want to sacrifice your life or your marriage just for 2 years. Even if I had preferred somewhere else, half of my decision has to be based on my wife.*
>
> *-- Miguel, Haas '11 (Berkeley)*

If your partner does decide to move with you to school, mull over what he or she will be doing while you're in school. Working? Taking care of the kids? Pursuing other academic goals? Clearly, the student has a purpose and a myriad of time-sucking activities. The partner also needs a purpose and stuff to occupy the day. Find out what outlets will exist for partners, including clubs and classes. A number of on-campus jobs tend to be held by S.O.s; there may also be networks to help them find employment. Check into travel policies—can S.O.s join on trips?—and any other special opportunities for families.

> *A lot of partners are frustrated when they move and don't have a job;*
> *they end up by themselves a lot of the time.*
>
> *-- Carolyn, wife of Kenan-Flagler '11 student (UNC)*

It's Actually All About You

If you have a partner, you're probably pretty familiar with the upsides of your romantic commitment.[9] A downside is that you just can't be as selfish as some of your single classmates. As much as you'd love to close out the bar, fly off to some exotic locale every weekend, and stay out till the wee hours of the night with your learning team, you just can't. There's someone else you need to think about, someone who is making great sacrifices to support you through this time.

So stop and think about what it must be like for your S.O. Now talk to him or her about it.

For many S.O.s, the experience is just as overwhelming as it is for you. New people, new places, new lingo … and on top of it all, partners are largely on the periphery. They don't get the jokes. For some, the constant discussion of careers and of b-school life in general can be hard to handle, particularly if they're currently looking for work or not thrilled with their own careers.

> *The flip side of school being so social is keeping up with it all. For students, its hard but they are all on the same schedule. The students move in packs and its harder to go out and meet up with them when you're working.*
>
> *-- Tim, significant other of Haas '11 student (Berkeley)*

Clear and constant communication is key to any successful relationship, but perhaps never more so than during a stressful situation like

---

9   And if you're not, reassess the relationship.

b-school. Some couples share online calendars to keep track of each other's whereabouts; others check in periodically through the day via text message, particularly as phone calls are often difficult to return and emails pile up. Decide how and for what reasons you can interrupt each other, as well as what activities can more or less easily be interrupted. Set aside a regular date night or time to be together—and refuse to let anything interfere. Convey what's coming down the pipeline—is this a busy week for recruiting? Are midterms around the corner? The more a partner knows the sources of your stress, the better he or she can help you manage them—or simply stay out of the way.

It's a sordid joke that MBA stands for "Married But Available." Even if your relationship is as solid as a Treasury bond, the rate of business school divorces and breakups is high enough to jar even the most committed of partners. Be aware of anything that might cause your S.O. anxiety and work to alleviate it. Your efforts will pay dividends in the long run.

Finally, not that we should have to include this, but make sure your partner feels like you're taking care of his or her needs. We all know you're tired...but you're not *that* tired.

A Letter to All B-School Significant Others

Dear S.O.,

Congratulations! After what has probably been an agonizing period of watching your loved one study for the GMAT or GRE (or maybe even both), scour the Internet for information on schools, write draft after draft after draft of silly essay after silly essay, and then wait for a decision, your loved one has finally been admitted to business school! No doubt, you have played a part in his/her success. You both deserve kudos.

Whether you are married or not, you are involved. It's important that you know what you and your partner are signing up for if you want your relationship to survive business school.

We are here to tell you all the stuff that your beloved b-school admit needs you to know but (a) either doesn't know yet or (b) doesn't know how to tell you. Please recognize that everything here is said with the best of intentions. Relationships do survive b-school, and we want yours to be one of the triumphant ones.

1) The next two years are not about you.

One key lesson that your partner will (hopefully) be learning in business school is that all partnerships are about compromise. Sadly, you will probably have to learn this first.

Your partner's focus is going to be all over the map for the next long while—classes, activities, recruiting, travel, etc. He/she will have a very erratic schedule. Projects will take longer than expected and involve other people whom you will hear about constantly and sometimes see at your home. Abilities will be doubted, career plans will change. In all likelihood, you will have to bear the brunt of the frustration and anxiety that your partner experiences.

> *Honestly, I feel like my relationship is on hold for now—I don't have the time to talk about it and I feel bad about that. I don't expect anything in particular from [my boyfriend] but I also can't give anything right now. The best thing I can do is integrate him with my friends so that he feels better about how I spend my time and knows who the people are whom I am referencing.*
>
> *-- Alison, HBS '12 (Harvard)*

Thanks for having your partner's back through this time. You will be asked to provide any or all of the following: financial support, emotional support, life-management support, and even bodily support (after a night out). It will be an unbalanced relationship during this time, and the best you can do is accept it as such, trusting that in times to come, your partner will be there for you. If it helps, have a discussion with your b-schooler about how you will balance things over the long haul. And, ideally, the haul will be a long one.

> *You should recognize that this schedule isn't really just for the next two years. Regardless of what job [your partner] gets next, he's going to be expected to hustle. It's not like it will suddenly change and he won't be busy anymore.*
>
> *-- Maura, wife of Sloan '12 (MIT)*

2) Your partner is not picking other things over you.

Business school, done right, is all-consuming. You may be thinking back to your own college or graduate school days, when you had a few hours of class, a few hours of work, and plenty of time to participate in whatever activities you wanted.

MBA programs, while seemingly similar, are actually very different. While classroom hours are limited, class projects can extend far beyond normal working hours. Having to work around the schedules of five other people often means that a business school student has to make sacrifices within his/her personal schedule. Moreover, things that feel like recreational activities (e.g., clubs, company presentations, social events) are integral parts of the b-school experience, and attendance should be considered mandatory.

The last thing you want to do is make your partner (already super-worried about debt burdens and job prospects) feel guilty for having to choose between you and school priorities. He/she may not realize all that you are giving up now but you will be thanked aplenty later. (We're insisting on it.)

On a related note, prepare yourself to hear a lot about various classmates and learning team members. Don't assume that any of them are a threat to your relationship.

3) Happy Hour is a class.

It's Thursday night at 10pm. Do you know where your b-schooler is?

Chances are, he/she is at Happy Hour, drinking a couple of cold ones. Meanwhile, you're at home, taking care of the bills/laundry/kids/work/TiVo and holding the short end of the stick. The truly tough pill to swallow is that he/she actually needs to be at Happy Hour. Socializing is a non-negligible part of the MBA curriculum. Your partner can skip events here and there, but he/she needs to be part of the social scene.

> *Please understand that we're going to be busy with things that don't sound stressful or difficult. Part of the reason we're here is to always be saying "yes" to an opportunity.*
>
> *-- Jim, Sloan '12 (MIT)*

Recruiting-related events are mandatory, whether it's a Sunday on the golf course or a six-course meal on a Tuesday night. And if you do get to join, your job is to make your partner look like partner material. Be an asset, not a liability. Get a little dressed up and play by the rules for the night.

4) Feel free to join in.

Most schools have Significant Others' clubs or allow you to join student clubs. Give these a try, particularly if you are accompanying your partner to a new location. You can meet others in your position and become a real part of the business school community.

> *Enjoy the fact that your social life is planned for you for two years. Be open to joining things.*
>
> *-- Julian, husband of Haas '11 student (Berkeley)*

Talk to your partner about what events you should attend. Want to come to Happy Hour? How about organizing a dinner for the study group and their respective S.O.s? Participating in school life is another way to show your support—and for you to sneak in some time with your partner, too.

> *If my wife wasn't willing to be involved, I'd be very unhappy and constantly stressed. She doesn't hold it against me when I stay out late and I try to make it up to her by doing things around the house because so much now rests on her shoulders.*
>
> *-- Luis, Sloan '12 (MIT)*

5) Don't be afraid of being the CEO.

Just because so much of this time is focused on your partner, you still get to call the shots half the time. Don't be afraid of asking for particular time to be set aside or for help in various activities. Make demands, but be reasonable. You and your happiness are every bit as important as your partner and his/her happiness.

We recognize what a huge role you play in the life of your b-schooler and we think that he/she is incredibly lucky to have you. And you're lucky, too…at least, most of the time. Take a deep breath and know that this is a very unique time for both of you. Good or bad, it'll be over before you know it.

Sincerely,

Carrie and Chris

Study Time is Not Quality Time

If you and your partner are both in MBA programs, you have your own challenges to work through. Sure, it's great to come home to someone who's already done the finance homework, but who's cooking dinner? How do you define "time together" when you spend so many hours poring over a problem set? And what happens when your stressors—academic, recruiting, etc.—all hit at the same time?

Most everything from the letter for significant others applies to both of you. Plus, we've got two more unique suggestions for you. (1) Hire a housekeeper, no question. (2) Take a short but nice vacation together during winter break. The two of you should spend at least three days somewhere warm, isolated, and free of emails, cell phones, and in-laws. As for the rest, good luck...

It's wonderful to share the experience with my husband and he gets what I am going through in a way that other partners can't, but it makes it impossible to escape business school.

-- Rachel, Haas '11 (Berkeley)

Some Final Words of Wisdom

Find what makes you happy amid all of the noise and do a little more of that.

Remember to eat when you drink.

Pace yourself, in life and at the party.

Carve out a dollop of time for yourself.

Just make sure you're having fun. If you're not having fun, you're doing something wrong.

-- Jared, CBS '11 (Columbia)

PART III: GRASPING FIRST-YEAR ACADEMICS

During orientation, you might at times forget that business school is actually school. Once classes start, this illusion will evaporate like the dew. Whether you're gunning for the top of your class or just looking to make it through, you've always got to deal with the *school* business of business school.

A Complement, Not a Substitute

These chapters are not meant to replace any course. You don't need an "MBA in a box"; after all, you're getting a real MBA. Rather, these chapters are intended to introduce the **quantitative concepts involved in typical introductory courses**.

Our focus is on "quant" because that's where we can do the most good in the fewest pages. Even if you have a serious math background, we think you'll find this material useful.

Our focus is also on concepts because you'll get plenty of applied practice in your classes. The upcoming chapters attempt to paint the big picture, clarify the lingo, reveal assumptions, and point out traps.

Checklist for Academic Prep

Chapter	Topics
14: Excel & PowerPoint	❏ Excel ❏ PowerPoint
15: Economics & Game Theory	❏ Microeconomics - Supply, Demand, & Elasticity ❏ Micro - Cost Curves ❏ Micro - Profit Maximization ❏ Macroeconomics - Circular Flow & Production Function ❏ Macro - Money Supply & Money Demand ❏ Macro - Investment, Savings, & General Equilibrium ❏ Game Theory
16: Statistics	❏ Descriptive Statistics ❏ Probability ❏ Distributions ❏ Sampling & Hypothesis Testing ❏ Correlation & Regression
17: Accounting	❏ The Big Three Financial Statements ❏ Transactions ❏ Managerial Accounting
18: Finance	❏ Time Value of Money ❏ Net Present Value (NPV) & Discounted Cash Flows (DCF) ❏ Capital Asset Pricing Model
19: Marketing	❏ Big Picture & Quant Tools
20: Operations & Supply Chain	❏ Process Analysis ❏ Queueing ❏ Inventory Management
21: Common Threads	❏ Common Threads & Key Tensions

What's Left Out

Lots of interesting, valuable stuff is minimized or omitted, because you'll learn it just fine in school. For example, here's what you won't see much of in this book:

- Social psychology, organizational behavior, behavioral economics & finance, negotiations
  - E.g., systematic cognitive and emotional biases that affect decision-making
- Strategy & management theory
  - E.g., Porter's Five Forces and generic strategies
- The history of various companies and industries
- Leadership

Many of these subjects require hands-on application (e.g., negotiations and leadership). Moreover, you'll pick up bits and pieces of "business history" with every case that you do.

This isn't at all to say that these topics are less important than those listed on the opposite page. Rather, they don't lend themselves as well to guidebook treatment (and this book is already thick enough).

As you get into recruiting season, depending on your goals and the structure of the first-year curriculum at your school, you may need to accelerate your learning in some of the areas listed above. For instance, general strategy courses are sometimes placed as "capstones" at the end of the first year, but you should know about Porter's Five Forces long before any consulting interview. (By the way, these mysterious Five Forces are very easy to learn.) If necessary, borrow last year's strategy syllabus from a second year and review the highlights. Moreover, the consulting club at your school will almost certainly be aware of any sequence issues such as this one and will be able to help you out.

How To Use This Part

Before school begins: Only glide through these chapters. Do *not* try to master them. Just get the big picture. Skip around as you like.

Once school begins: Reread the material relevant to courses you're currently taking. It's that simple.

The Big Picture of Business

If you're like we were, you might not have much of a business background before school. Or you might have deep expertise in a specific industry or two. Either way, you're smart, but there is at least some knowledge of the business world that you lack. (Otherwise, why go back to school? Go conquer the world, since you already know everything.)

Your strategy and general management courses will seek to give you the "big picture of business." However, we want to get you started with a slightly different take on that picture.

Multiple Lenses

Bear with us, as a brief digression into physics is in order (when is it ever not?). *Wave-particle duality* is the idea that you can regard visible light either as a stream of particles[1] or as a rippling wave of electromagnetic fields.

Particle Model of Light   Wave Model of Light

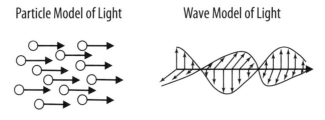

---

1   These particles are called photons. Science!

Which concept of light is right? Both and neither. They're competing metaphors that capture important aspects of the underlying phenomenon, but neither model is complete on its own. In fact, these models are complementary. When one is too limiting, the other works well.

Likewise, when you are a general decision-maker, you need to be able to apply *multiple lenses* to an issue. This "general management perspective" lies at the heart of the MBA degree. For instance, if you are deciding whether to launch a joint venture with another company, you need to consider many aspects of the venture—financial, operational, marketing, and so on—by gathering and synthesizing a variety of specialist opinions and analyses. No single analysis would be enough for this complex and weighty situation.

In the same vein, there are three simple models of that one basic thing you study in business school: a *company*. Frankly, none of these models is that interesting by itself. Each is almost so simple as to be silly. That's why they're worth making explicit as a trio. The whole key is to have all three in your hip pocket and be ready to switch among them, like a particle physicist.[2]

What is a Company?

Just remember **EFG: Entity-Factory-Group**.

A company is...

1) A Legal **Entity** or "person"	2) A **Factory** or machine	3) A **Group** of people
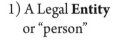	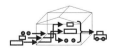	

---

2   Presumably a better-dressed particle physicist.

1) *A Legal **Entity** or "person"*

The law considers a corporation an actual, living person in many respects. The root of the word *corporation* is *corp*, meaning "body." When you in*corp*orate your company, you turn it into a single *body* from the law's point of view.

But this is not the only reason to look at a company this way. When a business does something, you typically use a singular verb: *Coke **is** entering three new markets this year*. Of course, you don't picture some giant Coke can with feet storming into three new markets. But in analyzing the strategic actions of some company from the outside, you often need to simplify matters by thinking of the company as a monolithic actor with a single brain. (Yes, some companies seem to act as if there were only one brain on the premises, but that's a different matter.)

2) *A **Factory** or machine*

Peeling back the layers, you can also picture a company as an operating factory, which is itself really just a big machine with walls and a roof. Processes involving all kinds of stuff happen within the factory, which takes in raw materials and turns them into products for its customers. Money flows around as well: customers pay the company, which turns around and pays its suppliers.

The factory model can represent a literal factory making cars or a conceptual factory making ideas (e.g., a software company). Either way, in this functional view, you examine the way all the parts interlock.

3) *A **Group** of people*

Finally, of course, a company is made up of people. Back on the etymology kick, the word *company* means "a group of folks sharing bread." This is not to be touchy-feely. In a way, there is very little to any firm *but* its people. Every company decision, every company agreement, every company success or failure is ultimately the responsibility of some*one*, not some*thing*. You might even say that a company is a kind of shared idea, a web of expectations and promises among huge numbers of people (both those within the company and those on the outside). At all times, a company carries with it all the possibility and immense complexity of human interaction.

You can answer two other key questions about a company according to which of the three EFG models you're using.

What does a company do?

1) *Entity*: It plays a game in a complex ecosystem.

2) *Factory*: It produces products, selling them to customers.

3) *Group*: Nothing. It's the people, individually and collectively, who do everything.

Why does a company exist?

1) *Entity*: To survive and grow.

2) *Factory*: To produce and sell products at a profit.

3) *Group*: To fulfill various roles in society (a larger group of people) and meet people's needs.

You might naturally gravitate to one of these models more than the other two. That's fine; it tells you something about yourself.

You'll also find that your classmates take different positions. Some very existential arguments you hear in class boil down to clashing perspectives about what a company is, what it does, and what its purpose is.

These arguments get old very fast, as if you heard physicists arguing this way:

> Physicist #1: "Light's really a wave!"
> Physicist #2: "No, dummy! It's a bunch of particles!"
> *Repeat.*

Now replace the players with your classmates.

> Banker: "This company's just a legal entity."
> Engineer: "No, dummy! It's a bunch of interlocking parts!"
> HR Specialist: "Look, morons, it's all about the people."
> *Repeat.*

Ideally, when your classmates lock themselves into just one underlying model, you can recognize the stalemate and sail above the fray.

Common Threads—Later On

Chapter 20, at the end of this section, will draw together themes from across the next several chapters. Some important ideas will rear their beautiful heads more than once, as you'll see.

CHAPTER 14:
EXCEL & POWERPOINT

This chapter provides an introduction to two mission-critical Microsoft applications: Excel and PowerPoint. While you're reading, pop open each application on your laptop, so you can play along.

Excel = Machine Shop

You might think of Excel as a glorified calculator or as a table-maker.[1]

Period	Sales (in millions)
Quarter 1	$270
Quarter 2	$230
Quarter 3	$260
Quarter 4	$240
Full Year	$1,000

Nice ⟶ (table!)

⟵ Nice calculation!

That's all valid, but you should also think of Excel as a ***machine shop***, where you build machines. (Stay with us on this for a few minutes—the analogy will help.) These machines act like little factories, taking in raw materials and spitting out finished products.

---

1   The program has all kinds of uses. Excel might even land you on the reality TV show "America's Next Top Modeler" (thanks, Follies).

The Excel Machine Shop

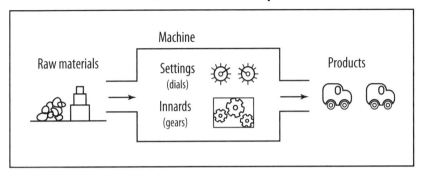

These machines are known as *models*. Models typically have four components:

1) Raw materials for the machine = *inputs* for the model.
   These are the numbers you start with, also known as the data.

2) Settings on the machine = *assumptions* for the model.
   These are *also* numbers you start with, but ones you will change less often. A typical example is a general interest rate. Sometimes, the distinction between inputs and assumptions doesn't matter at all. Other times, it can be conceptually helpful to make this distinction.

3) Innards of the machine = *intermediate calculations* of the model.
   These are formulas that transform your raw numbers according to your settings. By definition, the innards are in the middle of the machine, so if the machine's working, you're just going to *watch* them as they spin around. Wheee!

4) Products of the machine = *outputs* of the model.
   These are the final calculated numbers you care about, the results of your last formulas.

Say you wanted to build a super-simple model that would tell you how much money you'd have in 2 years if you invested it at 5% interest, compounded annually. One version of the model has a single input and a single output.

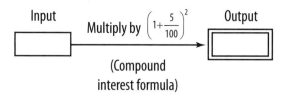

You plug in a dollar amount as the input, and you get the output.

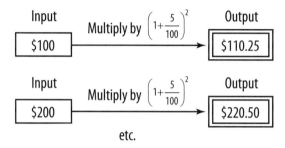

etc.

This model is equivalent to a ***function*** $y = f(x)$, where y is the output and x is the input. Specifically, this function $f(x)$ would be equal to $x \cdot \left(1 + \dfrac{5}{100}\right)^2$; in other words, you multiply the input x by $\left(1 + \dfrac{5}{100}\right)^2$.

This model is fine, but not very flexible. What if you want to change the interest rate or the number of years? You should make them into assumptions that you can adjust:

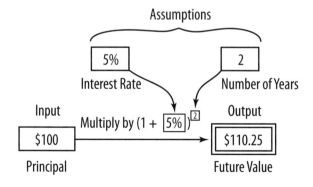

Optionally, you could consider those two assumptions to be inputs instead, so that you have a total of three inputs. The difference is only stylistic, not substantive. You can even introduce "innard" steps in the middle, so you can see intermediate computations. It's up to you.

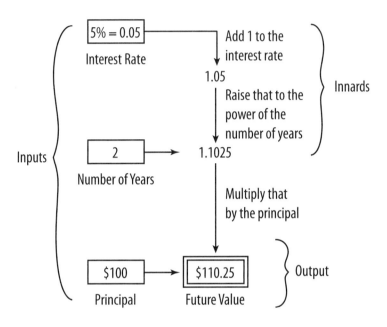

The key to making good models in Excel is ***deciding on the four components*** and then keeping them very straight. For instance, color-coding is amazingly helpful (assuming you're not color-blind).

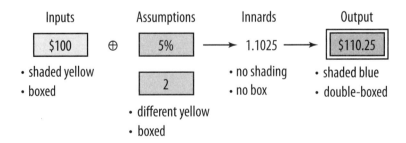

One of us got this specific shading and boxing advice over a decade ago. He can still easily decipher models he built back then, because the path from input to output is completely clear.[2] Models can be built in very different ways to accomplish the same goals, as shown by the simple examples above. Spend time up front to figure out what you want the inputs, assumptions, innards, and outputs to be, and you'll build the model faster and better. Plus, later on you'll be able to make adjustments easily, because you can figure out what you did.

The Structure of Excel

When you open a new Excel file, you'll see a rectangular grid with lots of little boxes.

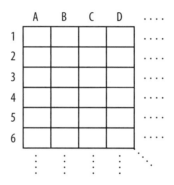

Each little box is called a *cell*.

Cells are arranged in *rows* and in *columns*.

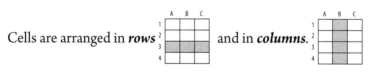

Each cell is named by its column and row.

---

2   His Friday-night examinations of decades-old Excel models for proper shading and boxing reveal a thrilling social life.

Remember Battleship? When you want to hit a target, you announce the coordinates ("B6"). Cells are just like Battleship coordinates.

The whole grid is called a **worksheet** or a **spreadsheet**, and you can have several worksheets in a **workbook**.

A cell can contain one of three things:

1) A cell can contain a **number**, such as an input or an assumption.

	A	B	C
1			
2			
3		14	
4			

Cell B3 contains the number 14.

You can change the **format** or **display** of the number without changing its **value**.

	A	B	C
1			
2			
3		$14.00	
4			

Cell B3 still contains the number 14, but B3 now has the currency format, so you see $14.00 in the cell.

You can always see the actual content of any cell in something called the **formula bar**, which lives between the ribbon at the top and the spreadsheet (on a PC). Click on the cell, and the formula bar will tell you what's "really" in it.

Ribbon							
B3 f_x 14							← Formula bar shows 14.
	A	B	C	D	E	F	
1							
2							
3		$14.00	←				— Cell B3 shows $14.00.
4							

A few formats travel to the formula bar as well, such as percents and dates (which are actually numbers from Excel's point of view).

Percents   Dates

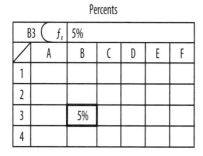

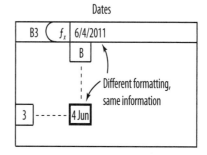

Different formatting, same information

2) A cell can contain **text**, obviously useful for labeling your model.

	A	B	C
1			
2			
3	Rate	5%	
4			

A3 contains the text "Rate."
B3 contains the number 5%.

There's no technical connection between these two cells, but if you know what's good for you, you'll add labels as you build. Spreadsheets that only show numbers become cryptic to you and infuriating to your teammates.

3) A cell can contain a **formula**, which uses information from other cells to do a computation.

This is where it becomes really important to distinguish between what a cell *displays* and what it truly *contains*.

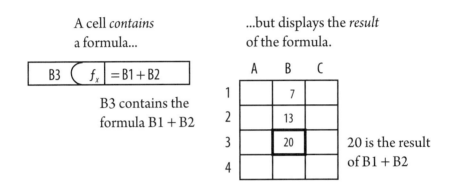

The formula in B3 contains references to other cells (B1 and B2). This is how you take raw material and turn it into finished products.

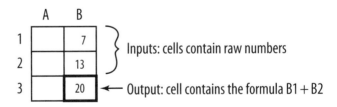

If 20 isn't your final output, then another cell can pick up that value and do something further with it. That cell would contain a formula with B3 in it.

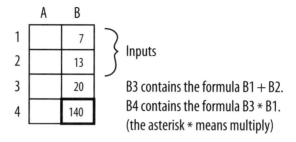

B3 contains the formula B1 + B2.
B4 contains the formula B3 * B1.
(the asterisk * means multiply)

Normally cells do not display the formulas themselves, just the results of those formulas. So at a glance, you can't tell whether a number is **hard-coded** (you literally typed it in as a number) or **computed** by a formula. To reveal the true contents of a cell, you can highlight the cell and look at the formula bar.

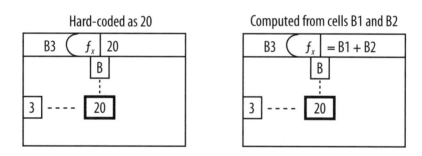

To tell Excel you want to put a formula in a cell, type an equals sign (=). You can also use a plus (+) or a minus (-) sign, but only under limited circumstances, so get used to starting with the equals sign. If you just type "B1 + B2" into a cell, Excel thinks you want that *text* in there.

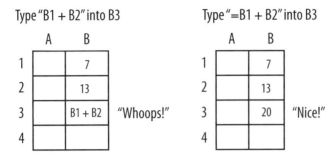

Excel can do all the common math operations:

What you type into B3	What you're telling B3 to do
=B1 + B2	Add B1 and B2
=B1 − B2	Subtract B2 from B1
=B1 * B2	Multiply B1 by B2
=B1 / B2	Divide B1 by B2
=B1 ^ 2	Square B1
=B1 ^ B2	Raise B1 to the B2[th] power

Parentheses work as you'd expect: to control the order of operations.

=B1 * (B2 + B3)	Add B2 and B3 first, then multiply by B1.

What if you want to take a square root? You don't use the radical sign (as in $\sqrt{9} = 3$). Instead, you use a pre-named **function** that Excel has defined for you. The function is SQRT.

What you type into B3	What you're telling B3 to do
=SQRT(B2)	Take the square root of B2

Functions always look like this:

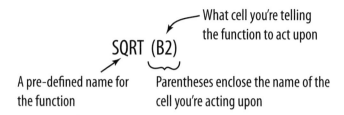

That format is similar to what you've seen in the math world: a function $f(x)$ has the name "f," and it acts on x in some way (maybe it takes the square root). Excel just uses more descriptive names for its functions. You can find lists of all the functions (financial, statistical, etc.) by clicking on the $f(x)$ button on the function bar:

Some functions just take one cell as their **argument** (the input):

What you type into B3	What you're telling B3 to do
=SQRT(B2)	Take the square root of B2
=FACT(B2)	Take the "factorial" of B2

Other functions take more than one cell as arguments. Just separate each argument with a comma.

What you type into B3	What you're telling B3 to do
=AVERAGE(B1, B2)	Take the average of B1 and B2, which is equal to $(B1 + B2)/2$.
=SUM(B1, B2)	Add B1 and B2
=SUM(B1, B2, B3)	Add B1, B2, and B3

Where the functions AVERAGE and SUM really come into their own is with **ranges**—whole rectangular groups of cells.

Name

B2 : B5

"B2 to B5" — the
colon is a "to" in this
context, meaning you want
Excel to be inclusive of these
cells in the operation.

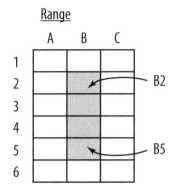

Name

B2 : C4

Notice that B2 is the upper
left corner, while C4 is the
lower right corner.

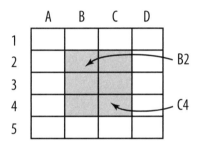

So now you can write powerful formulas like this:

What you type into B3	What you're telling B3 to do
=SUM(B2: B100)	Add up all the cells between B2 and B100, inclusive.
=SUMPRODUCT(B2: B100, C2:C100)	Multiply B2 by C2, then B3 by C3, then B4 by C4, all the way down to B100 and C100, then add up all the results.

The SUMPRODUCT function is extraordinarily useful for computing the weighted-average return (or performance) of a portfolio of stocks, as in the example below.

	A	B	C
1	Stock	Return	Weight
2	IBM	5%	1.2%
3	AT&T	−1%	0.8%
4	Google	+10%	0.5%
5	Microsoft	−3%	1.5%
⋮	⋮	⋮	⋮
99	Exxon Mobil	+3%	0.9%
100	Du Pont	−2%	0.6%

$$\text{SUMPRODUCT(B2 : B100, C2 : C100)}$$
$$= (5\% \times 1.2\%)$$
$$+ (-1\% \times 0.8\%)$$
$$+ (+10\% \times 0.5\%)$$
$$+ ...$$
$$+ (-2\% \times 0.6\%)$$
$$= \text{total return of portfolio}$$

As you work with formulas and functions, you'll notice that the references to input cells and ranges show up outlined in color—and the cells and ranges themselves are temporarily displayed with those colors as well. This helps you make sure you're adding or "sumproduct-ing" the right cells. In fact, to edit the formula, you can grab the colored highlighting on the worksheet itself and move it around.

What if you wanted to add up a range of cells and take the square root? You can do this in two steps.

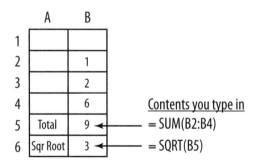

	A	B	
1			
2		1	
3		2	
4		6	Contents you type in
5	Total	9	= SUM(B2:B4)
6	Sqr Root	3	= SQRT(B5)

Or you could do it in one step with a ***nested*** or embedded formula.

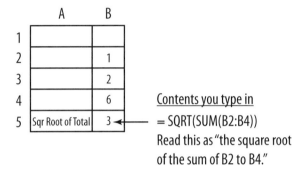

Contents you type in
= SQRT(SUM(B2:B4))
Read this as "the square root
of the sum of B2 to B4."

Which should you prefer? Some Excel jockeys love nested formulas. Our advice? Avoid them (the formulas, not the jockeys) as much as you can. Nesting quickly becomes inscrutable to you and to everyone else who has to follow the logic of your model. Let Excel do what it's great at—showing the innards. You can always hide rows or columns for a presentation.

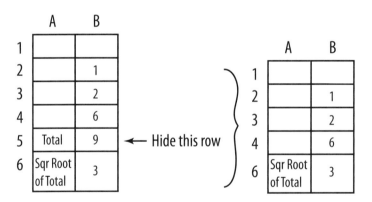

Likewise, avoid hardcoding input numbers *inside* formulas and functions. Keep your work transparent and adjustable by putting inputs in separate, visible cells—shaded in sunburst yellow.

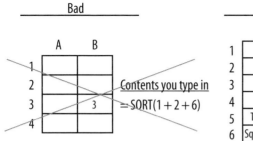

	A	B		
1				
2				
3		3		Contents you type in
4				$=$ SQRT$(1+2+6)$

Bad

Good

	A	B	
1			
2		1	
3		2	
4		6	Contents you type in
5	Total	9	$=$ SUM(B2:B4)
6	Sqr Root	3	$=$ SQRT(B5)

- Completely hidden work
- Inflexible—you have to go inside the function to change anything

- Open layout
- Flexible—you can change the output by editing the contents of B2, B3, or B4

It's Not Always Relative

Say you have a big column of data, and you want the square of every number in that column.

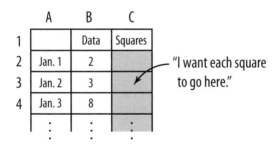

	A	B	C	
1		Data	Squares	
2	Jan. 1	2		"I want each square
3	Jan. 2	3		to go here."
4	Jan. 3	8		
	⋮	⋮	⋮	

All you have to do is write *one* good formula and copy it.

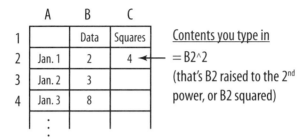

What happens when you copy the content of C2 down the column? Amazingly, the formula adjusts to find the right cell—the cell immediately to the left.

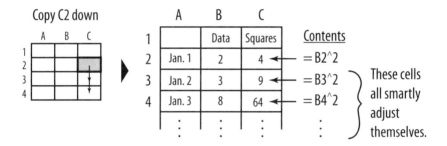

That adjustment happens because of something called **relative addressing** or **relative references**. When you typed "=B2^2" into C2, you *thought* you were telling Excel to square B2. In fact, you were really telling it to square whichever cell is **one space to the left**.

	A	B	C
1		Data	Squares
2	Jan. 1	2	4
3	Jan. 2	3	
4	Jan. 3	8	

In cell C2, the formula "=B2^2" *really* means "square the cell to my left."

Excel assumes you want relative addressing, because it makes big spreadsheets much easier to build. The opposite of relative addressing is **absolute addressing**, which means "refer back to such-and-such a cell, no matter where I copy this formula." Absolute addressing is useful when you're computing percents of a whole. You use dollar signs ($) in front of the column letter and row number to lock the cell reference absolutely.

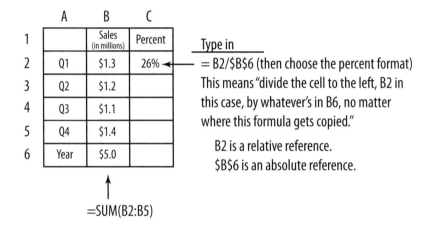

Type in
= B2/$B$6 (then choose the percent format)
This means "divide the cell to the left, B2 in this case, by whatever's in B6, no matter where this formula gets copied."

B2 is a relative reference.
$B$6 is an absolute reference.

=SUM(B2:B5)

Watch how the formula changes as you copy it down. The ugly dollar signs keep the second part locked.

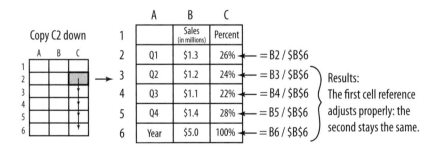

If you have "=B2/B6" in C2 by mistake and then copy down, you get "=B3/B7" and other incorrect formulas, so be careful.

Play with relative and absolute addresses on a scratch worksheet by copying simple formulas around. You'll see how dollar signs keep cell reference locked, while relative addresses (no dollar signs) adjust to each new position. If you're in the formula bar, you can use the F4 function key to toggle between relative and absolute addressing, instead of typing in dollar signs (which also works). By the way, function keys in Excel are pretty useful. The more you can keep your fingers on the keyboard, the faster you'll go.

One other point on absolute references—to avoid ugly dollar signs and make your formulas more readable, **rename** important cells. For instance, you can rename cell B6 as "Total." Just highlight cell B6, then type over the "B6" on the left side of the formula bar:

Now you can refer to B6 in formulas as "Total." That's an absolute reference that will never change, so only rename important cells.

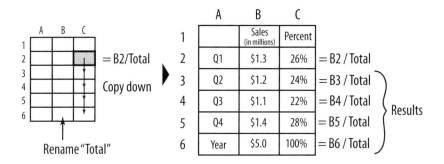

Goal Seek and Solver

Remember the four components of a model?

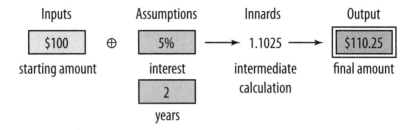

To get $200 in 2 years, how much money do you need right now? You have four ways to figure this out:

1) Build a brand new model. Ugh.

2) Do the math outside of Excel. Double ugh.

3) Plug various inputs in on the left until you get $200 out on the right. Feasible but a pain.

4) Tell Excel to plug different inputs in on the left until you get $200 out on the right. Much better.

This life-saving Excel tool is **Goal Seek**—you tell Excel to seek a goal.

Click on your output cell to highlight it, then choose Data → What-If Analysis → Goal Seek. You'll get a little dialog box:

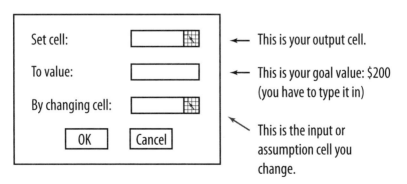

Type in cell references, or click to insert them, then hit OK. Excel plugs a bunch of numbers in, faster than the eye can see, and proposes an answer. In this case, the input that works is $181.41 (rounding). The bigger your model, the more pain the Goal Seek tool can save you.

Solver (an add-in on the Analysis section of the Data ribbon) does the same thing as Goal Seek, but it lets you vary more than one input or assumption at once. With that freedom comes responsibility. Solver is a very powerful tool, but you have to use it wisely. For instance, in the model above, if you try to vary both assumptions at the same time to find a particular goal, Solver goes off the rails because many combinations of years and interest rates give you the result you want, and Solver doesn't know which combination to pick.

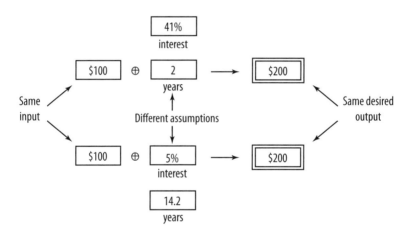

"The Scenario" Is Not On The Jersey Shore

If you want to keep track of different *scenarios* (which are, well, "situations" with whole sets of inputs and assumptions), then you can use the *Scenario Manager* tool or the *Data Tables* tools. In Scenario Manager, you create combinations of inputs labeled "worst case," "best case," etc., while the Data Tables tool lets you vary one or two assumptions through a whole range of values and observe what happens to the output.

Scenario Manager

5% interest
2 years
} Worst case

10% interest
4 years
} Best case

7% interest
3 years
} Likely case

Data Tables

Interest	Output
5%	$110.25
6%	$112.36
7%	$114.49
8%	$116.64
⋮	⋮

Finally, an add-in program called **Crystal Ball** (CB) lets you run *thousands* of scenarios in Excel and aggregate the results. Crystal Ball generates the scenarios at random, but according to guidelines you give it. For instance, you might tell Crystal Ball to pick interest rates between 5% and 10%, with any interest rate equally likely...

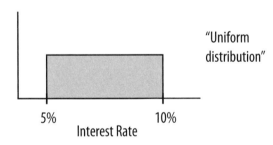

...or with a peak of some kind around 7.5%, so that more scenarios with interest rates close to 7.5% occur.

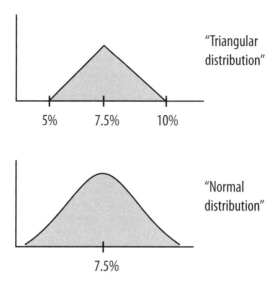

For more on distributions, see Chapter 16: Statistics.

Crystal Ball generates its many thousands of scenarios by rolling the dice, so to speak, over and over again according to your casino rules. For each scenario, an output value comes out, and Crystal Ball collects all those results into a chart.

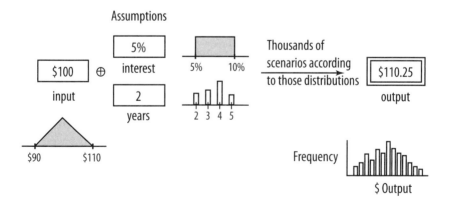

That frequency chart of outputs (or histogram) can tell you a lot—what your average output is, how likely you are to make over $120, etc.

Yet again, Spidey, with great power comes great responsibility. Crystal Ball is only as good as its assumptions. Without any further direction from you, CB assumes that all the random numbers in the scenarios are independent of one another, like coin flips. That may or may not be true. For instance, housing prices throughout the US didn't all move in the same direction very often until, one day, they did. Despite the name, the power of Crystal Ball (and, more broadly, Excel) to predict the future is limited, and it's dangerous to forget those limits. In fact, what Crystal Ball does is called **Monte Carlo analysis**, after the famous European gambling destination. Never forget you're spinning a roulette wheel with CB.

Data Management

You can also keep track of lots of data in Excel. Just be sure to organize the data in a clean table:

	A	B	C	D
1	First Name	Last Name	Date	Purchase
2	Anne	Bancroft	7/10/11	$100
3	Clark	Gable	7/12/11	$150
4	Anne	Bancroft	7/13/11	$70

Each row should represent a separate *record*—a purchase, for instance. Each column should represent a separate *field*—some bit of data you want to track about each purchase (customer first name, customer last name, etc). Make sure that there are no gaps in the table and that it's not touching anything else. Put field names in the first row.

Excel is not truly a "database" program, but if you set up the table this way, you can do a lot:

- *Sort* by any field (say, from earliest to latest)

- *Filter* by field (say, you just want to look at purchases on a particular date)

- Create *subtotals* by field

- Create *pivot tables*

Pivot tables are super-flexible tools for exploratory data analysis. Imagine that you're a store owner, and you have a big list of purchases all scrambled up. You have a lot of repeat customers, even on the same day. You can total up the purchases by customer *and* by day at the same time, using a pivot table. It's a jiffy to set up. Just click the Pivot Table button on the Insert ribbon, hit OK, then drag the field names into position.

Purchases

Full Name	Date	Purchase
Anne Bancroft	7/10/11	$100
Clark Gable	7/12/11	$150
Anne Bancroft	7/13/11	$70
Anne Bancroft	7/11/11	$80
Sam Spade	7/12/11	$100
Clark Gable	7/11/11	$50
Clark Gable	7/12/11	$25
Anne Bancroft	7/12/11	$75
Sam Spade	7/11/11	$100
Sam Spade	7/10/11	$75

Pivot Table of Purchases

Full Name	7/10	7/11	7/12		Subtotal
Anne Bancroft	$100	$150	$75	···	$1,000
Clark Gable	$0	$50	$175	···	$1,250
Sam Spade	$75	$100	$100	···	$750
	⋮	⋮	⋮		⋮
Subtotal	$1,200	$400	$500		$10,000

Total

Last Thought

If Excel starts to beat you down, do one simple thing—remove gridlines from the display. Go to the View ribbon and uncheck gridlines.

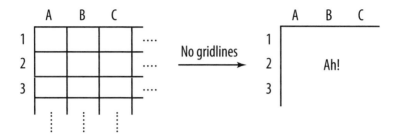

Suddenly Excel looks like a blank sheet of paper. If you're more a Word person than an Excel person, the visual shift will be surprisingly uplifting.[3]

---

[3] One of us sat down with her study group for the first time to tackle a Corporate Finance project. The other three team members (all of whom were guys named Mike) opened up their PCs and launched Excel. The author cheerfully flipped open her MacBook and began typing into a Word table. Finally someone mentioned the F4 key. Needless to say, this author could have used an Excel primer before school.

How To Do PowerPoint

Agenda

1) What is PowerPoint?

2) Principles of Good PowerPoint

3) Principles in Action

What is PowerPoint?

- Most common presentation software
  - Projected on screen
  - Printed for handouts
- Based on slideshow analogy

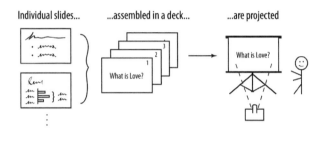

Individual slides...   ...assembled in a deck...   ...are projected

Agenda

1) What is PowerPoint?

2) Principles of Good PowerPoint

3) Principles in Action

Principles of Good PowerPoint

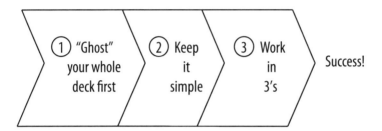

(1) "Ghost" your whole deck first → (2) Keep it simple → (3) Work in 3's → Success!

1) "Ghost" Your Whole Deck First

a)   Draw 9 squares on a blank sheet of paper.

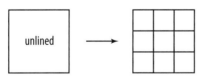

b)   Put 1 big message per slide and "ghosts" (placeholders) for details

Focuses you on the overall storyline—

forest

not trees

2) Keep It Simple

Whole Deck

- Use clear signposts
  - Agenda slides
  - Trackers in corners

Each Slide

- Fewer words = better
- Large enough for the back row
- Modest animations/transitions

3) Work In 3's

Government

- of the people
- by the people
- for the people

- Memorable balance
- 2's and 4's work as well
  - Don't be *too* predictable

Agenda

1) What is PowerPoint?

2) Principles of Good PowerPoint

3) Principles in Action   ← This very presentation!

Principles in Action - Ghosting

Actual Ghost of this Deck

How To Do PowerPoint	Agenda ⌇⌇⌇⌇ ⌇⌇⌇⌇ ⌇⌇⌇⌇	What is PPT? · Presentation · Slideshow ▢ → ▱
Principles 1) Ghost it out 2) KISS 3) Threes?	1) How to Ghost [grid] sample	2) Keep It Simple Deck Slide ▱ ▢ Clear Not every place word
3) Threes · A · B haha · C	In Action this actual ghost deck!	Kiss ⌒⌒⌒

- Done with pencil and paper

- Took only a half-hour subway ride

- Prevented "story creep"

Principles in Action - Simple

- Clear signposts throughout

Slide

Agenda
1) ~~~~
2) ~~~~
3) ~~~~

Slide

Tracker for principles

Slide

- Clear signposts throughout ☐ ☐
- Few words ⊟

- Few words

Principles in Action - 3's

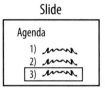

- Three items on agenda

- Three principles of good PowerPoint

- Three bullets, in most places
  - Sometimes two
  - Not averse to four

Can You Ever Deviate From Plan?

- Of course you can

- Try to anticipate objections beforehand
  - Plan your responses and work them into the deck
  - Or have "hip-pocket" extra slides ready

- During the presentation, deal with questions as they arise
  - Audiences hate waiting till the end

Final Thoughts

- Recap the big takeaways—the short "so-what's"
  - Any that you planned to make
  - Any that came out of the discussion

- Lay out next steps

And Don't Do This...

 Swooshing animations!!!

Crazy transitions!!!

Crowded tiny text that no one can read from the back row, so that you have to say, "Sorry, I know you can't read this, but..." That's terrible. This includes graphs with tiny labels.

The entire text word-for-word of what you're going to say, so you stare at the screen and read it aloud to your audience as if they were five years old.

Clip art unless you are a legitimate graphic artist (and you're probably not)

...Do This Instead

Nothing

CHAPTER 15:
ECONOMICS & GAME THEORY

This chapter has three major sections:

1) **Microeconomics** – "small-scale" economics of individual buyers and sellers
2) **Macroeconomics** – "large-scale" economics of nations and governments
3) **Game theory** – the study of certain formalized "games" between players

Depending on your program, these topics may be dealt with in more than one course. They may also use different names, such as "Managerial Economics" or "Global Markets," just to sound cool.

Microeconomics

Microeconomics attempts to describe the *physics of markets*[1], where buyers come to buy what sellers have to sell. Somehow a *price* gets set and a *quantity* of the product gets sold. The buyers and sellers are assumed to be acting *rationally* (i.e., intelligently) and in their own *self-interest*—that is, each one wants to get the best deal for himself or herself. That might not always be 100% true, but the *"neoclassical"* version of microeconomics, which is what you'll be taught, assumes that everyone is smart and selfish in a marketplace. It's often a good assump-

---

1   Yes, one of us used to teach high-school physics. Is that obvious?

tion: just think of the New York Stock Exchange, where many intelligent, self-interested investors bust tail every day to eke out thin advantages. Competitive financial markets such as those for US "large-cap" stocks (those of big companies) are considered relatively **efficient**—most advantages are temporary, as information rockets around the investing community.

Demand Curve

A lot of microeconomics is done by drawing lines and curves on graphs. A single curve (we'll use this term whether the line is actually curved or straight) can represent a variety of real-world situations.

For instance, a **demand curve** captures the following two scenarios:

1. At a high price, only a few people want to buy.

2. At a low price, lots of people want to buy.

This is shown by plotting the price P on a vertical axis and the quantity Q that people demand on a horizontal axis. (Q might be written as Q_D, where the subscript D means "demand.")

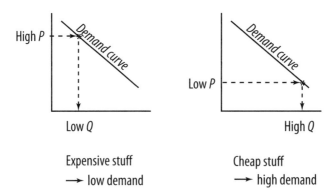

For some historical reason, even though P is the "independent" variable, it goes on the vertical axis. Quantity Q, which depends on P, goes on the horizontal axis. Usually graphs go the other way. When you see a curve plotted on x and y axes, the x variable is what typically determines y. But here, it's P that determines Q, most logically. Not a big deal, but it's worth pointing out.

Imagine that at a price of $10, the buyers demand 200 units of whatever the product is. If those 200 units are sold at that price, then the sellers have collectively made ($10 per unit) × (200 units) = $2,000. That $2,000 is **revenue R = PQ**. On a demand curve, revenue is the area of a rectangle.

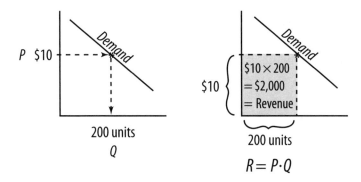

By the way, sometimes prices are written just in dollars ($10), but you should always be ready to think of them as dollars **per unit** ($10/unit). This will help you remember that you multiply per-unit prices by units (quantity) to get a total amount in dollars (revenue in this case).

Supply Curve

A demand curve captures how much buyers demand at various prices. In contrast, a **supply curve** captures the behavior of sellers: how much they're willing to sell at various prices, or how many sellers there even are. Simply put, lots of people want to sell at a high price. On the other hand, if prices are low, only a few people want to sell. (On this graph, Q can be written as Q_s for "quantity supplied.")

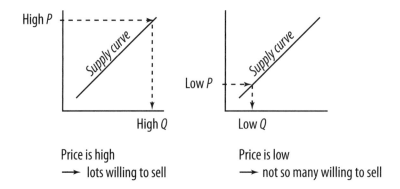

Price is high
→ lots willing to sell

Price is low
→ not so many willing to sell

Supply and Demand

Put supply and demand on the same set o' axes, and presto, they cross.

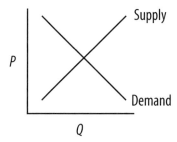

The magical intersection point represents a state of **equilibrium** or balance. At that point, supply equals demand. Every buyer who wants to buy does so; every seller who wants to sell does so. The *market clears*, as they say—there are no unfulfilled desires at the equilibrium price, or **market price**.

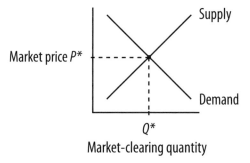

Market-clearing quantity

You always assume that you have **perfect competition,** which means having lots and lots of buyers and sellers, none of whom can corner the market. Under these conditions, supply and demand converge at a specific price and quantity.

If the price is momentarily too high, more quantity is supplied than demanded. Buyers are scarce, so sellers cut their prices to stimulate demand.

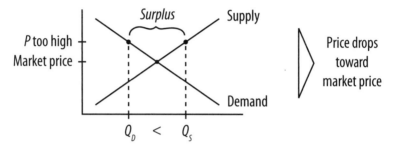

On the other hand, if the price is momentarily too low, more quantity is demanded than can be supplied. Sellers are scarce, so buyers offer higher prices to encourage sales:

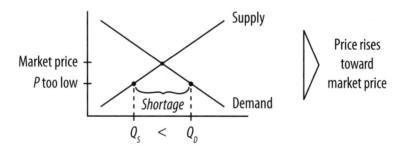

Thus, the **market mechanism** creates a stable equilibrium, in theory.

You can model various "shocks" to the system with these curves. For instance, the entrance of a new supply of product pushes the supply curve to the right, leading to a lower market price at a greater quantity sold. This should make sense. In general, when you move these curves around, the results should not be surprising. Imagine a real-world scenario (or even a fictional one). Anyone who's watched HBO's *The Wire* can picture what happens to the market price and quantity when a new supply of heroin hits the street:

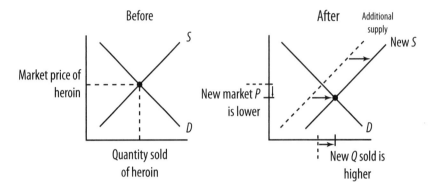

The price drops, and more heroin is sold.

Substitutes and Complements

Substitute products, like butter and margarine, can replace each other. Do you care whether you're using one or the other? Probably not.

So if the price of butter goes up, lowering demand for butter, the demand for margarine goes up:

$$\text{If } Q_D \text{ for butter} \downarrow \text{ then } Q_D \text{for margarine} \uparrow$$

That will push up the price of margarine. It's as if the demands for each of the two products add up to a constant:

$$\begin{matrix} Q_D & + & Q_D & = & \text{some overall demand for} \\ \text{(butter)} & & \text{(margarine)} & & \text{yellow fatty spreads} \end{matrix}$$

On the other hand, products that are **complements** go together and aren't worth as much without the other. Think about butter and toast…

Butter by itself
"What am I going to
put this on?"

Toast by itself
"Yuck, dry toast."

Buttered toast
"Yum!"

With complementary products, the demands move in the same direction. So if the price of butter goes up, lowering demand for butter, the demand for toast also goes down:

$$\text{If } Q_D \text{ for butter } \downarrow \text{ then } Q_D \text{ for toast } \downarrow$$

This will push down the price of toast. The difference between the demands is always the same:

$$Q_D \underset{\text{(butter)}}{} \quad - \quad Q_D \underset{\text{(toast)}}{} \quad = \quad \text{a constant}$$

Elasticity

Elasticity answers the following questions.

- If you change the price a bit, how much does demand change?

- Under the same conditions, how much does supply change?

Elasticity is a measure of how much supply and demand stretch in response to price shifts. Think of a rubber band that you hang a weight from. The more elastic the rubber is, the further the weight hangs down.

When you are trying to determine how elastic supply or demand is, you usually increase the price by 1% and watch what happens to the quantity. This way, you can compare the elasticities of $20 haircuts and $20,000 cars. Likewise, the change in quantity is measured as a percentage.

High elasticity = big response to price shifts = shallow slopes

A 1% increase in price shifts quantity by 5%

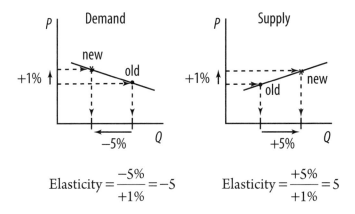

$$\text{Elasticity} = \frac{-5\%}{+1\%} = -5 \qquad\qquad \text{Elasticity} = \frac{+5\%}{+1\%} = 5$$

Low elasticity = small response to price shifts = steep slopes

A 1% increase in price shifts quantity by only 0.2%

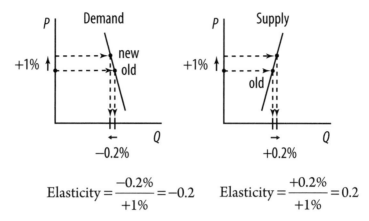

$$\text{Elasticity} = \frac{-0.2\%}{+1\%} = -0.2 \qquad \text{Elasticity} = \frac{+0.2\%}{+1\%} = 0.2$$

The formula for elasticity is this:

$$E = \frac{\%\Delta Q}{\%\Delta P} \qquad \begin{array}{l}(\text{"percent change in } Q \\ \text{over percent change in } P\text{"})\end{array}$$

Percent change in Q is the actual change in Q divided by Q (expressed as a percent). The Δ ("delta") means "change in" something, so $\%\Delta Q = \dfrac{\Delta Q}{Q}$ and $\%\Delta P = \dfrac{\Delta P}{P}$.

If the result is greater than 1 or less than -1, then demand or supply is considered highly elastic. If the result is between -1 and 1, then demand or supply is considered inelastic.

Deviations from Perfect Competition

One way the market mechanism can be distorted is through **cartels** of sellers or of buyers. A cartel of sellers bands together to limit supply and keep the price high. Likewise, a cartel of buyers tries to limit demand to keep the price low.

If supply is truly limited *and* a cartel of sellers can enforce its policy, then the scheme might work. For instance, the oil producers' cartel, OPEC, seems to do just fine. But cartels are **anti-competitive**, so they can run afoot of **antitrust** laws in the United States. Moreover, cartels are unstable, because every member of the cartel has a strong incentive to cheat. For example, if you're an oil-producing country, you can make piles of money if you convince everyone *else* to obey the cartel. Overall supply is limited, prices stay high, and then you secretly sell more oil on the side. Cartels fly in the face of the market mechanism, so they always have to be enforced by fundamentally non-economic means (eg., threats of violence). Again, the show *The Wire* is instructive here.

Taking anti-competitive behavior even further, you can have a **monopoly** (just one seller) or **monopsony** (a much less common word meaning "just one buyer" and not a mutant Milton-Bradley game). If you have a monopoly, you're your own cartel. It's generally going to be in your interest to limit supply and keep prices high, all else being equal. Monopolies are typically illegal as well, unless there's a **natural monopoly**, in which the characteristics of production (such as enormous fixed costs or long-term contracts between any buyer and the seller) push the market toward having just one seller. Think electric utilities—at the end of the day, it only makes sense to run *one* power line to your house, and building a power plant costs loads of dough. When a market has the characteristics of a natural monopoly, government regulators may step in, as they do with utilities, to set prices and quantities.

In contrast, the US government has a natural monopsony for certain kinds of military equipment produced by domestic manufacturers, such as Lockheed Martin. The US is the only (legal) buyer of these products, thereby dictating the overall demand.

Taxes and **quotas** (artificial limits on quantity, either minimums or maximums) also distort markets, meaning that the resulting P and Q are not the theoretical P and Q you'd have without the taxes or quotas. That's not a value judgment; the taxes or quotas may serve a greater good, or they may not. Either way, they impact the market.

Finally, some markets have **network externalities**, meaning that buyers don't act independently. With **positive** network effects, buyers want the product *more* when there are more buyers; the product is worth more to the millionth buyer than to the first. Facebook, the fax machine, and the telephone all work this way, since the more people you can friend, fax, or call, the better for you. In contrast, products with **negative** network externalities are worth *less* when more people use them. Think of anything exclusive, anything with snob appeal—as soon as the masses get the new Louis Vuitton bag, it's no longer cool. Likewise, overcrowding can diminish your enjoyment of an amusement park (or your broadband connection).

Cost Curves

And now for something completely different…cost curves.

Before diving in, you should know that "cost" in microeconomics is not quite the same things as "cost" in accounting, though the concepts overlap. Cost in micro is forward-looking—specifically, you need to remember to consider **opportunity costs** (the benefits of paths you're not choosing) and ignore **sunk costs** (the pain of past choices), when you're making a rational economic decision.

Here's a rogue's gallery of cost variables you might plot on a graph (usually against quantity Q's on the horizontal axis).

Total Cost	**TC**	The total cost of making Q units.
Fixed Cost	**FC**	The fixed constant cost you incur, whether or not you make any units at all—say, the cost of building a plant.
Variable Cost	**VC**	The cost that varies with the number of units you produce—e.g., raw materials costs.

These first three variables are related by a simple sum:

$$TC = FC + VC$$

For instance, a simple formula for TC as a function of quantity Q might be this:

$$TC = 800 + 2Q$$

Plugging in various values for Q, you can see the total cost of making various quantities:

Q	$TC = 800 + 2Q$
0 units	$800 + 2 \cdot 0 = \$800$
100 units	$800 + 2 \cdot 100 = \$1,000$
200 units	$800 + 2 \cdot 200 = \$1,200$

The fixed cost is $800, and the variable cost depends on the quantity made (e.g., at $Q = 200$ units, the variable cost is $400). This particular formula for TC can be decomposed into FC and VC on inspection:

$$TC = \underbrace{800}_{} + \underbrace{2Q}_{}$$

$$TC = FC + VC$$

$$FC = 800 \ (\text{constant})$$

$$VC = 2Q \ (\text{varies with } Q)$$

Here's how these look on graphs versus Q:

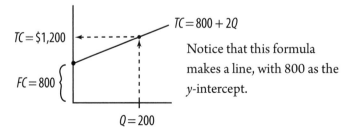

Notice that this formula makes a line, with 800 as the y-intercept.

You might envision *FC* as a horizontal line stretching over from $800 on the vertical axis:

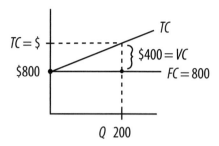

In that view, *VC* sits on top of the horizontal *FC* line. Alternatively, you might plot *VC* against *Q* as well. This way, the constant difference between the *TC* and *VC* curves is *FC*, or $800:

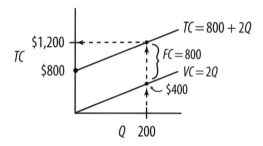

Marginal Cost

This concept is super-important. **Marginal Cost**, MC, is the extra cost of making *one more* unit. For instance, you already know that the cost of making 200 units is $1,200. How much would it cost to make one more unit? Well, first figure out how much it would cost to make 201 units:

$$TC = 800 + 2Q$$
$$TC = 800 + 2(201)$$

to make
201 units

$$= \$1,202$$

Now subtract the cost of 200 units (which we know is $1,200):

TC	$-$	TC	$=$	MC
to make 201 units		to make 200 units		to make 201st unit

$$\$1,202 \quad - \quad \$1,200 \quad = \quad \$2 \text{ (per unit)}$$

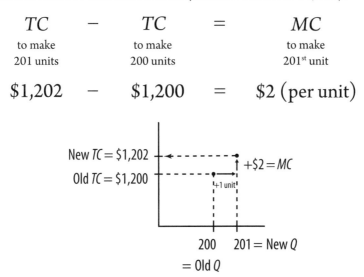

This should not be surprising, if you think about the formula $TC = 800 + 2Q$. If Q goes up by 1 unit, then TC goes up by $2, at any level of production.

Marginal cost is the change in total cost over a small change in quantity, usually taken to be 1 additional unit:

$$MC = \frac{\Delta TC}{\Delta Q} \quad \longleftarrow \quad \text{usually taken to be 1 unit}$$

Visually, MC is the slope of the TC curve when TC is plotted against quantity Q.[2] Since the formula $TC = 800 + 2Q$ represents a line with constant slope, the marginal cost is always the same in this case, meaning that it always costs $2 to make one more unit, no matter how many you've already made:

---

2   If you know a little calculus, you'll recognize that marginal cost is the derivative of TC with respect to Q. That is, $MC = \dfrac{d(TC)}{dQ}$.

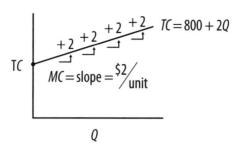

More generally, if the *TC* curve is actually curved, then *MC* will be different depending on where you are:

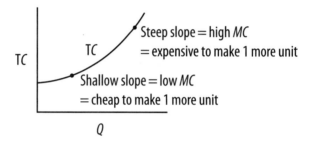

Average Costs

Average cost is calculated just as you'd expect. **Average cost**, *AC*, is the total cost divided by total units produced (Q). For instance, if you make 100 units, then the total cost $TC = 800 + 2 \cdot 100 = \$1,000$, and the average cost is $\$1,000 \div 100 = \$10$ per unit.

$$AC = \frac{TC}{Q}$$

$$\$10\!\!\diagup\!\!_{\text{unit}} = \frac{\$1,000}{100 \text{ units}}$$

If you make 200 units, then $TC = 800 + 2 \cdot 200 = \$1,200$, and the average cost falls to $6 per unit:

$$AC = \frac{TC}{Q}$$

$$\$6\big/\text{unit} = \frac{\$1,200}{200 \text{ units}}$$

Visually, average cost can be seen as the slope of a line *from the origin to the TC curve*, not the slope of the TC curve itself:

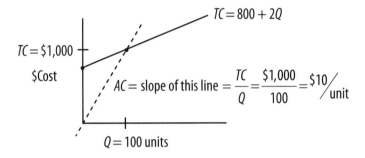

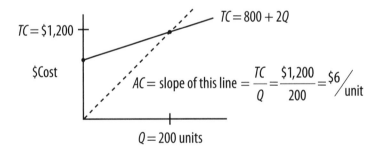

Notice the difference between marginal cost and average cost. Both are "costs per unit," but marginal cost is just the additional cost of producing a single extra unit. In contrast, average cost *includes* both fixed and variable costs, since *AC* is the total cost divided by total quantity.

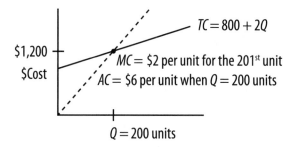

Earlier, we saw that the average cost was $10/unit at 100 units but only $6/unit at 200 units. This drop in average cost per unit can represent *economies of scale*, which occur when you have a high upfront fixed cost (expense of building a pharma plant or writing Windows software) but a low marginal cost (expense of making one pill or Windows CD):

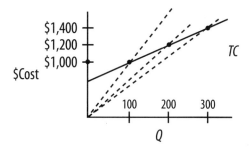

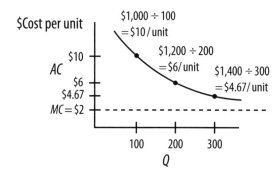

The second graph above plots costs per unit against units. On such a graph, you can think of total cost as the area of a rectangle, since total cost equals average cost (one side of the rectangle) times quantity (the other side of the rectangle):

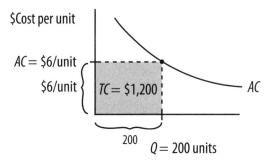

Up to now, only average *total* cost has been mentioned. You can also compute average fixed cost and average variable cost. To keep everything straight, you'll need three letters:

Average total cost	***ATC*** ***(= AC)***	Total cost divided by total units produced (Q)
Average fixed cost	***AFC***	Fixed cost divided by total units produced (Q)
Average variable cost	***AVC***	Variable cost divided by total units produced (Q)

$$ATC = \frac{TC}{Q} \qquad AFC = \frac{FC}{Q} \qquad AVC = \frac{VC}{Q}$$

By the way, when you see these two and three-letter variable names, say them to yourself with their full names: "average total cost," not "Ay-tee-see." Full names make sense. Letters get scrambled up in your brain.

These three averages add up, just like their big brothers:

$$TC = FC + VC$$ ("total cost equals fixed cost plus variable cost")

Divide everything by Q to take the average:

$$\frac{TC}{Q} = \frac{FC}{Q} + \frac{VC}{Q}$$

$$ATC = AFC + AVC$$ ("average total cost equals average fixed cost plus average variable cost")

For large quantities, *ATC* often falls, because you're spreading the fixed cost over more units. Again, this phenomenon is called economies of scale (= "savings as you scale up").

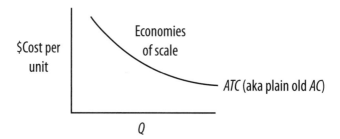

However, *ATC* can curve *back up* if you have ***diseconomies of scale***—at some point, you have to build another plant, you have exhausted cheap supplies of raw materials, etc.

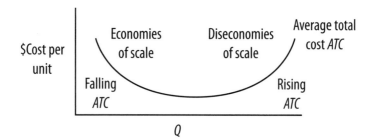

Here's what the corresponding total cost might look like:

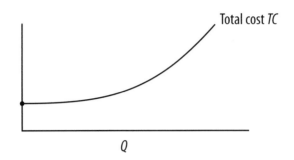

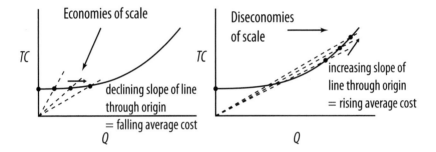

The lowest ATC corresponds to the shallowest slope of the line that goes from the origin to the TC curve:

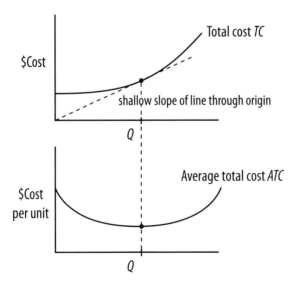

Notice that this point also corresponds to where marginal cost equals the average total cost. Here's why: remember that marginal cost tells you the slope of the *tangent* line to the total cost curve. There are three cases:

1) Economies of scale at low quantities

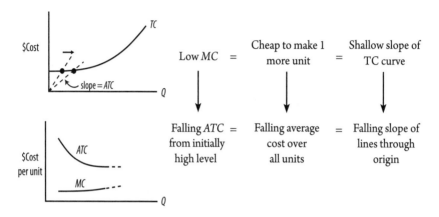

Low MC	=	Cheap to make 1 more unit	=	Shallow slope of TC curve
↓		↓		↓
Falling ATC = from initially high level		Falling average cost over all units	=	Falling slope of lines through origin

2) Diseconomies of scale at high quantities

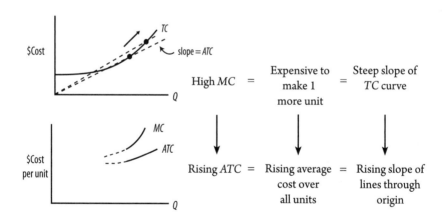

High MC	=	Expensive to make 1 more unit	=	Steep slope of TC curve
↓		↓		↓
Rising ATC =		Rising average cost over all units	=	Rising slope of lines through origin

3) $MC = ATC$ (Economies are about to turn into diseconomies)

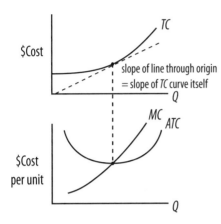

slope of line through origin
= slope of TC curve itself

Cost of making 1 more unit (MC) equals average total cost (ATC) exactly when ATC is at its lowest point

How to Make the Most Profit

The last aspect of micro that there's room to talk about is profit, which equals revenues minus costs. Since P is already taken for price, either write out the word "profit" or use the Greek letter π (pi), which is not 3.14 in this context, of course.

$$
\begin{array}{ccccc}
\text{Profit} & = & \text{Revenues} & - & \text{Costs} \\
\pi & = & TR & - & TC \\
& & \text{(total revenues)} & & \text{(total cost)}
\end{array}
$$

Like revenues and costs, profit is thought of as some function of quantity Q: if you produce 100 units, your profit will be $800 or whatever. You can imagine plotting total profit versus quantity:

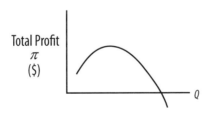

If that's your profit curve, how many units should you make and sell? Since you're a rational, self-interested profit maximizer, you'll make and sell the quantity corresponding to the biggest profit.

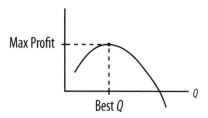

At lower quantities, you could make additional profit by producing additional units. In other words, your **marginal profit** (the extra profit from making and selling one more unit) is positive.

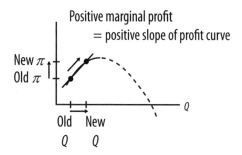

At high quantities, however, total profit is falling. Marginal profit is negative—you're actually losing money on each additional unit you make and sell.

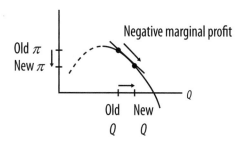

So, *at the maximum-profit point, the marginal profit is zero.* You can't make any additional profits by making more units, but you haven't lost money on any unit yet.[3]

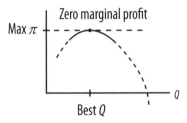

Putting this idea together with the profit equation, you get:

$$\text{Profit} \quad = \quad \text{Rev} \quad - \quad \text{Cost}$$
$$\text{Marginal Profit} \quad = \quad \underset{\text{(marginal revenue)}}{MR} \quad - \quad \underset{\text{(marginal cost)}}{MC}$$

Marginal revenue (MR) is the additional revenue you get by selling one more unit. In a competitive market, one in which you can't affect the market price yourself, MR is the market price:

$$MR = P \text{ (competitive market)}$$

Now, to maximize profits, you set marginal profit equal to zero.

Marginal profit $= 0$ (to maximize profits)

Marginal revenue $-$ Marginal Cost $= 0$

$$MR - MC = 0$$

$$\boxed{MR = MC} \text{ (to maximize profits)}$$

So now you know what quantity to make, if you know MR and MC. Just plot MC versus Q. If you're in a competitive market, $MR = P$, so draw a

---

3   If you've taken calculus, this idea should be familiar. The maximum of a curve shaped like this is located precisely where the slope of the curve is zero.

horizontal line corresponding to *P*. The profit-maximizing quantity is where *MC* and *P* cross:

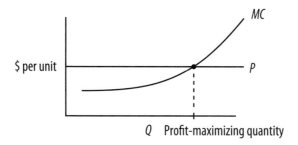

If you have a monopoly, you face the consumer demand curve completely on your own—there are no other producers. If you make more, you'll have to lower the price to unload all of your inventory, which cuts into your marginal revenue. Below, $MR = \$199 - \$100 = \$99$.

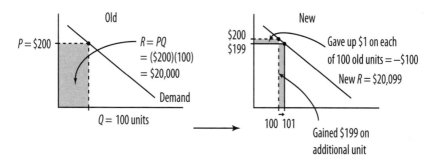

As you increase production, marginal revenue drops quickly. In fact, calculus tells us that *MR* falls twice as fast as demand:

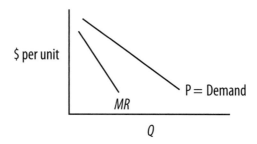

Since you're still a profit maximizer, whether you're a monopolist or not, you're going to produce the profit-maximizing quantity. This occurs where $MR = MC$.

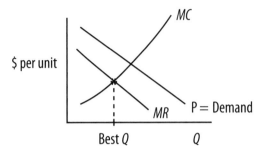

You'll wind up producing less and charging a higher price than in a competitive market:

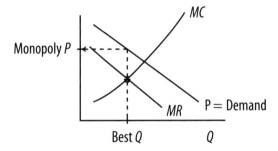

The MC curve can be seen as a supply curve, so under competitive conditions the market price and market-clearing quantity would be different:

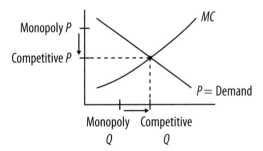

What Else is There in Micro

A couple of thoughts on remaining micro topics:

1) *Price discrimination* (different prices for different customers)

There are various legal and illegal ways to do this. You will make more money when you can price-discriminate, because you capture more of the *consumer surplus* (e.g., the $50 benefit that a customer gets when she pays $150 for something worth $200 to her). To price-discriminate legally, you can *version* your products (e.g., paperback vs. hardcover). You can also impose a *two-part tariff* (a fixed entrance fee to the park *plus* a per-ride charge). With a two-part tariff, you're effectively making different customers pay different amounts.

2) *Trade-offs and budgeting*

Economics is all about trading off costs and benefits. This came up earlier in the "$MR = MC$" condition for profit maximization: the marginal revenue from selling one more unit should equal the marginal cost of making that unit.

The principle of balancing marginal quantities applies more generally. Imagine you had $20 to spend on Snickers and M&M's. You buy $15 of Snickers and $5 of M&M's. If that's the right split for you, you would be just as happy spending a 21st dollar (one you just found on the floor) on Snickers as you would be if you spent it on M&M's. If that's *not* the case, then you misallocated the original $20. In economic terms, at $15 on Snickers and $5 on M&M's, your *marginal utility* for each type of candy is equal. A 16th dollar of Snickers would make you just as much happier as a 6th dollar of M&M's would.

If you are producing Snickers and M&M's, then you do the same thing. You adjust your production mix until the marginal revenue from spending one more dollar to make Snickers equals the marginal revenue from spending one more dollar to make M&M's.

Macroeconomics

Macroeconomics is concerned with the ***economies of entire countries***. "Macro" has a whole new set of concepts—and letters—but the core ideas of supply and demand developed in micro show up here as well.

Different macro schools of thought have been duking it out for years, and the current economic crisis has only intensified the debate. There are two main schools:

1) ***Neoclassical***
   - Makes the same assumptions as seen earlier in microeconomics
     – Firms and individuals are rational, self-interested, and profit-maximizing
     – Competition is perfect and information flows freely
   - Trusts *free markets* (the market mechanism unhindered by taxes, etc.) to do the best job of allocating resources efficiently and matching supply and demand
     – Market for labor
     – Market for capital (wealth to invest)
     – Market for money itself

2) ***Keynesian*** (pronounced "Kane-sian"), after economist John Maynard Keynes
   - Agrees with neoclassical economics in most respects
   - Argues that ***wages and prices are sticky***
     – Wages adjust slowly, so the labor market takes a "long time" to reach equilibrium (how long exactly is open to debate)
     – The government has a role in making up for this private-sector lag

- When private demand is low, the government should stimulate demand by spending money and by creating money
- When private demand is high, the government should restrain demand by taking in money (through taxes) and by destroying money
- In this way, according to Keynes, the government's *fiscal policy* (taxation and spending) and ***monetary policy*** (money creation and destruction) help smooth out the ***business cycle***—the ups and downs of economic activity observed in the world.

Although these two schools bitterly diagree about the proper role of government in the economy, they share many features. In b-school, you'll learn the neoclassical model primarily, since Keynes can be seen as a variation. Then you'll try to argue with your professors; good luck with that.

Circular Flow

"Macro" means "big," literally, so from the biggest point of view, here's what happens in a simplified national economy (one with no taxes, no savings or investment, and no outside trade):

1. People work for companies.
2. People buy stuff from companies.

That's it! When people work for companies, they provide labor and get paid wages:

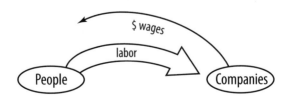

People can also sell materials or rent out their land or equipment. They are providing *factors of production* to companies, in return for money. As owners of companies, people can receive profits as well.

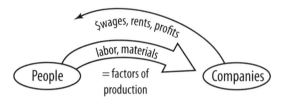

In turn, people buy goods and services from companies.

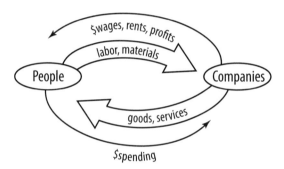

This way, there's a complete cycle of trade. Valuable stuff makes a full circle, and money also makes a full circle in the opposite direction. Imagine that over the course of a year, in a *very* tiny economy, people earn 1 million dollars for their work.

In this simplified view, there is no saving. People have nothing to do with their money but buy stuff from those same companies. How much stuff? Exactly $1 million worth.

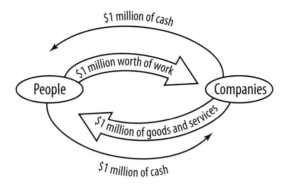

Notice that every flow on the diagram is worth $1 million. This $1 million of "economic activity" can be looked at in several different ways:

1) **Production** - the total value of goods and services produced. This is called **gross domestic product**, or **GDP**, or **output**.
   – Note that you exclude the value of any *intermediate* products bought and sold between companies. Alternatively, you can count them, but then you subtract their value from the *final* goods consumed by people, so that you're just counting **value added** at every step. Either way, you get $1 million.

2) **Income** - the money earned by people, whether as wages, rents, or profits. This is called **national income**, represented by the capital letter Y (don't ask us why).

3) **Consumption** - the money spent by people. This is given the letter C.

In this super-simplified economy with just people and companies (or households and firms, to use fancy names), there's a three-way **national income equation**.

$$\text{Production} = \text{Income} = \text{Consumption}$$
$$GDP = Y = C$$

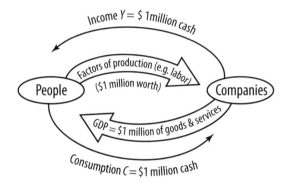

Other Players

To make the model more realistic, additional players can be added. These players will split the flows, but it'll all still form a circle.

Government

The government takes in taxes T and spends that money on goods and services. For simplicity, imagine that the government cannot run a **budget deficit** or a **budget surplus**—it must spend exactly what it takes in in taxes, no more and no less—and that the government imposes a 25% income tax on people only and provides an equal amount of benefits in return.

In a sense, all that happens is that the government gets inserted into the "bottom" flows on the simple picture above, as 25% of the money spent by consumers and 25% of the goods and services produced by companies are diverted through government hands.

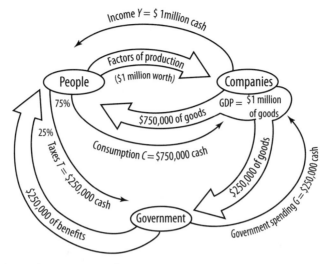

The adjusted equation is this:

$$\text{Production} = \text{Income} = \text{Expenditures}$$

$$GDP = Y = C + G$$

personal government
consumption spending

$$\$1 \text{ million} = \$1 \text{ million} = \$750,000 + \$250,000$$

Financial sector

Putting in a financial sector allows for savings and investment. If you assume that only people save 10% of their income and that the financial sector invests every dollar of savings, the picture looks similar to the previous one, with the financial sector in place of the government. That is, a fraction of the bottom flows of both money and goods/services move through the financial sector. In this case, these diverted flows are not taxes and government spending, but rather savings and investment.

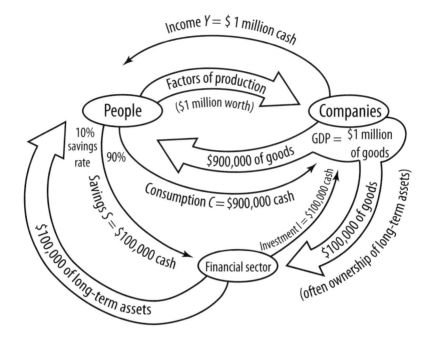

The national income equation adjusted for the financial sector is this:

$$\text{Production} = \text{Income} = \text{Expenditures}$$

$$GDP \;=\; Y \;=\; C \;+\; I$$

personal   investment
consumption

$$\$1 \text{ million} \;=\; \$1 \text{ million} \;=\; \$900{,}000 \;+\; \$100{,}000$$

The national income equation adjusted for *both* the financial sector and the government is this:

$$\text{Production} = \text{Income} = \text{Expenditures}$$

$$GDP \;=\; Y \;=\; C \;+\; G \;+\; I$$

personal   government   investment
consumption   spending

Note that I stands for investment, not income (which is Y).

Other Countries

Up to now, the picture has been of a **closed economy** with no international trade. An **open economy** interacts with those of other countries:

$X = $ **exports** $ = $ currently produced goods you sell to other
countries
$ = $ the money they pay you for those goods

$M = $ **imports** $ = $ currently produced goods other countries sell
to you
$ = $ the money you pay them for those goods

$NX = $ **net exports** $ = X - M$

So if you export $300,000 of goods and import $100,000 of goods, your $NX = \$300,000 - \$100,000 = \$200,000$. Here's the start of the picture with other countries added in:

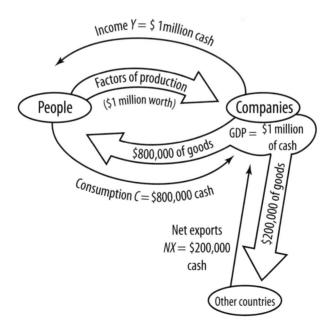

Notice that the flow is unbalanced. Where did those other countries get the $200,000 in cash to buy the exported goods? If you look around the diagram, you see that "People" on the left are earning $1 million but only spending $800,000 as current consumption. So your people (in your country) are $200,000 richer. To complete the flow, they give that $200,000 cash to other countries in exchange for *something*—but not currently produced goods or services, since those would be counted as *imports*, which are already included in the *NX* number of $200,000. In other words, *after* subtracting out imports, there's still a net outflow of goods to other countries; those goods must be paid for. (Pretend there is no borrowing or currency reserves lying around.) The only way for the other countries to get the extra $200,000 in cash to pay for the net exports is to sell *long-term assets* to your people, who are frankly saving that money—socking it away for the long term.

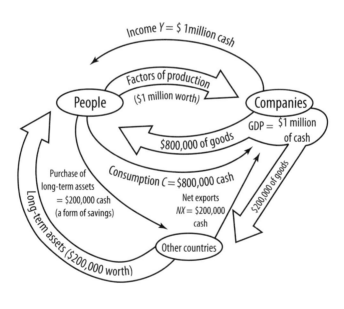

The national income equation adjusted for net exports is this:

$$\text{Production} = \text{Income} = \text{Expenditures}$$

Production =	Income =	Expenditures	
GDP =	Y =	C +	NX
		personal consumption	net exports
\$1 million =	\$1 million =	\$800,000 +	\$200,000

Putting all the expenditures together, you get the big kahuna equation:

$$\text{Production} = \text{Income} = \text{Expenditures}$$

GDP =	Y	= C +	I +	G +	NX
		personal consumption	investment	government spending	net exports

Letter Zoo

The capital letters don't stop there—macro is thoroughly infected with them. A complete rundown would take too many pages, but there are two more relationships you should know:

1) $CA + KA = 0$

This equation has to do with international trade. The **current account** CA tracks payments you receive from other countries for currently produced goods and services (minus what you pay other countries for *their* current goods). CA includes net exports NX, as well as **net factor payments** NFP (money that your people and companies are paid for work they do outside your country) and any gifts or foreign aid you receive. In the last diagram, you received \$200,000 in NX, so your CA was +\$200,000.

In contrast, the **capital account** KA tracks payments you receive as capital investments, in exchange for long-term assets (minus what you pay other countries for their long-term assets). In the diagram, you paid \$200,000 out to other countries for their long-term assets, so $KA = -\$200,000$. Notice that $CA + KA = 0$. This is always true.

By the way, K is used for "capital" in macro. Maybe this is the legacy of Karl Marx (*Das Kapital*)?

2) $S_{private} = I + (-S_{gov't}) + CA$

This equation lists the three **uses of private saving** $S_{private}$ (savings done by people or companies, not the government):

a) Provide investment I to companies, either directly or through financial institutions.

b) Offset government borrowing, which is negative saving $(-S_{gov't})$.

c) Allow foreigners to purchase your current products (CA), because you're buying long-term assets from those foreigners.

The Production Function

National income Y, also known as output, can be thought of as a *mathematical* output too. You feed it two inputs, and *voilà*—you have Y. The two inputs are **capital** K and **labor** N, where N = number of workers (some books use L for labor, but L shows up elsewhere).

Capital K, by the way, is generally the capital *stock* in the country: the machines, buildings, and others productive assets that help generate economic activity.

The magic transformation into Y can be written this way:

$$Y = A \cdot F(K, N)$$

where A is a constant known as **total factor productivity,** or *TFP*. Remember this number—it's like crack to macroeconomists. If you want to make an economy better, you've got to raise *TFP*. That is, you've got to make each worker and each dollar of capital turn more *effectively* into dollars of output Y. This is the key to building national wealth over the long term.

Meanwhile, $F(K, N)$, which you can call "F of K and N," is just some mathematical expression involving K and N. The key is that it should show **diminishing returns**—that is, another thousand workers should boost national income a lot more when you only have a few workers to begin with than when you already have zillions. The same holds true for capital investment: investing the first billion dollars does more to raise national income than the next billion, which does more than the next, and so on.

Thus, the relationship between Y and K or between Y and N should look like this:

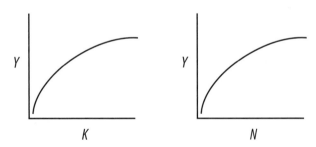

Flatter slopes out to the right mean diminishing returns. Here's a possible form of the production function:

$$Y = A \cdot K^{0.3} \cdot N^{0.7}$$

That's K to the 0.3 power and N to the 0.7 power. What do decimal exponents even mean? Well, $x^{0.5}$ is $x^{\frac{1}{2}}$, which is another way to write $\sqrt{x}$. The square root of x looks like this on a graph:

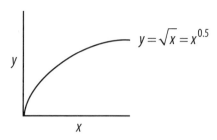

So those decimal exponents, like 0.3 on $K^{0.3}$, just create the diminishing returns we want.

The production function can also be written in terms of percent changes. You can derive this second form using calculus, or you can just remember that when you take percent changes, multiplication turns into addition, and exponents turn into multiplied coefficients.

1) $Y = A \cdot K^{0.3} \cdot N^{0.7}$

2) $\%\Delta Y = \%\Delta A + (0.3)(\%\Delta K) + (0.7)(\Delta\%N)$

This second form tells you that a 1 percent increase in A (total factor productivity) gives you a 1 percent increase in Y (income), but a 1 percent increase in K (capital) gives you only a 0.3% increase in Y.

Money Supply

There is only a certain amount of cash floating around; as Mom and Dad told you, it doesn't grow on trees. Macro cares about the **money supply**, because a country's economy can go haywire if adults aren't paying attention to how much cash is out there.

The most obvious form of money is physical **currency** (bills and coins), but many other things are "so money" (or at least "more or less money") because they have these characteristics.

- Measurable value
- Stable value
- Accepted in exchange for other assets $\Big\}$ high *liquidity*
- Convertible to currency

The money supply is referred to with even more letters and numbers. **M1** is the most liquid money aggregate and most narrowly defined. It includes not only the cash in your pocket but the cash in your checking account (***demand deposits***). **M2** is a broader aggregate, including all of M1 *and* the cash in your savings account and money market accounts. There are even broader aggregates, if you care to know. When you don't care exactly which money definition you're using, you just write plain old *M*.

Playing God with Money

The **Federal Reserve** is the central bank of the United States. It has the authority to print money—and to destroy money if it's being bad. When the Fed prints money, it doesn't airdrop Benjamins over Central Park (although one could argue that'd be pretty effective for some of the Fed's ultimate purposes). Rather, the Fed prints money and uses it to buy government bonds in the market. That's how the cash gets into circulation. The Fed doesn't always literally hand over bricks of printed greenbacks, but in theory that's what it's doing.

Moreover, a small purchase of government bonds can turn into a lot of circulating money through the ***money multiplier*** effect.

The Fed prints $100 and buys a government bond from Bank X. Bank X now is sitting on $100. Since banks are *theoretically* in the business of lending money, Bank X can now lend out this $100, or most of it anyway, keeping behind a certain percentage to comply with the Fed's ***reserve requirement***. Say the bank has to keep 10% on hand, or $10 in this case.

Then Bank *X* lends $90 to Company *Y*, which turns around and spends it on computers from Company *Z*. Company *Z* deposits the $90 with its bank, Bank *W*, which then turns around and lends $81 out...

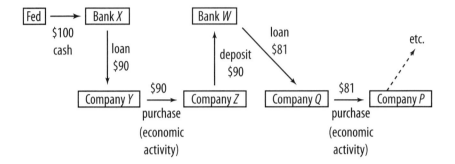

If banks are lending and companies aren't just sitting on their cash, that first $100 can turn into many hundreds of dollars of economic activity. This is how the Fed's $100 is multiplied through the economy.

Likewise, if the Fed *sells* a government bond to the public, money is pulled *out* of circulation, with a larger ripple effect at some multiple of the purchase.

Inflation

Your grandma kvetches that things cost more now than they did fifty years ago. She's right, sort of. **Inflation** is the rise in the **general price level** *P*. (Note: *P* here doesn't mean the price of any specific thing, as it did in micro. In macro, *P* tracks the overall rise in prices across the board.) *P* can be measured by something like the **consumer price index**, *CPI* (also known as the consumer **deflator**, which sounds like a rather specialized superhero, perhaps one who lets the air out of tires on getaway cars).

So, if the *GDP* of your little country is $1 million this year, and it was $900,000 last year, how much of that roughly 11% growth was *real* growth in the amount of goods and services your country makes—and how much was just inflation, just a rise in the overall prices of things?

Well, you've got to take these **nominal** dollar figures (the $900,000 last year and the $1 million this year), which represent the physical dollars moved around each year, and put them in **real** terms. That is, you choose a reference year—say, 2011—and put everything in terms of dollars from that year.

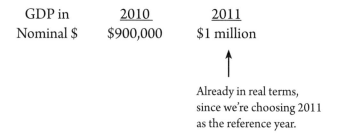

GDP in	2010	2011
Nominal $	$900,000	$1 million

Already in real terms, since we're choosing 2011 as the reference year.

How do you turn $900,000 of 2010 dollars into 2011 dollars? You increase that amount by the inflation rate. Say inflation was 3% from 2010 to 2011. Then you grow the $900,000 by 3%.

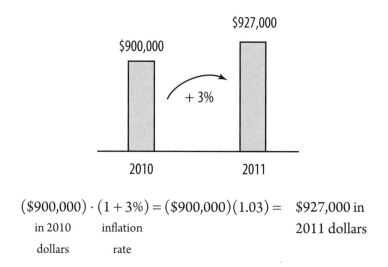

$$(\$900,000) \cdot (1 + 3\%) = (\$900,000)(1.03) = \ \$927,000 \text{ in}$$

in 2010   inflation   2011 dollars

dollars   rate

So now you can compare the *GDP*s in real terms, apples to apples:

	2010	2011
GDP in Real $ (2011 dollars)	$927,000	$1 million

The percent growth of the *GDP* in real terms is

$$\frac{\$1 \text{ million}}{\$927,000} - 1 \approx 0.0787 = 7.87\%. \ [4]$$

By the way, the percent growth in nominal terms was

$$\frac{\$1 \text{ million}}{\$900,000} - 1 \approx 0.1111 = 11.11\%.$$

This is *approximately* the real growth (7.87%) plus inflation (3%). The math doesn't let you simply add these percentages precisely, but as long as all the percents are small, you can get away with this approximation:

$$\begin{array}{ccccc} \text{Real Growth} & + & \text{Inflation} & \approx & \text{Nominal Growth} \\ (\%) & & (\%) & & (\%) \end{array}$$

Often, the reference year is somewhere in the past, and you bring both modern figures (2010 and 2011) back to 1987 or some other year when Huey Lewis was popular. You do this by dividing by a deflator calibrated to 1987 (that is, in 1987 the deflator equaled 1). As long as you bring all nominal amounts to the same "real" year, you'll get the same results in the end.

Inflation Bad, Deflation Bad

A high rate of inflation erodes savings and can even destroy economies. However, a low rate of inflation is actually okay: the Fed's unofficial target rate is 2%, not 0%. In fact, **deflation** (a fall in the general price leve) is really bad. You'd think it'd be fine, until you realize that it freezes economic activity. Cash becomes *more* valuable over time, so you don't spend it. Banks stop lending, businesses stop investing. For a little while, the falling prices seem great to you as a consumer, until your own wages get cut because your company's products are sold for less and less. Ugly.

---

4   This just uses the percent change formula: Percent Change = $\dfrac{\text{New Amount}}{\text{Old Amount}} - 1$, then express the decimal as a percent.

Let's avoid this over the next number of years—there's a real risk of deflation right now. So go out and spend wildly in da club. By purchasing bottles full o' bub, you're helping prevent a deflationary spiral.

Money Demand

The term "money demand" might seem obvious—everybody wants money. That's not what the macro concept of **money demand** is about. Rather, it's this: given that people and companies have, say, $1 billion in wealth, how much do they want to hold as money (currency, demand deposits) rather than in other non-monetary forms? Money's liquid (exchangeable), but it earns no interest (or very little—your checking account might pay a trivial rate), so there's a tradeoff between holding money and holding **nonmonetary assets** (stocks, bonds, real estate, etc.). Say that, out of $1 billion in total wealth, people and companies want to keep $100 million in the form of liquid money. You can write

$$M^d = \$100 \text{ million}$$

The little *d* stands for "demand."[5]

M^d is *nominal* money demand. To express this demand in *real* terms (factoring out inflation), you can write

$$\text{Real money demand} = \frac{M^d}{P}$$

where P is the general price level, as mentioned above. Real money demand is represented by the capital letter L, for *liquidity*. Two factors influence L.

---

5   It's not an exponent—macroeconomists should use subscripts instead and write M_d instead of M^d, but even economists don't always act rationally.

1) National income Y

The higher Y is, the more money is needed for transactions throughout the country. So money demand L goes up. This should make sense at an individual level too. Rich cats with a high income are the ones carrying the fat rolls of Benjamins.

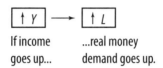

If income   ...real money
goes up...   demand goes up.

2) ***Real interest rate r*** on nonmonetary assets

Remember, people and companies have a choice about where they stash their wealth.

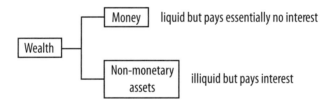

So if you keep $1,000 cash in your pocket at all times, you're choosing to give up the interest r you could earn on that $1,000 if you invested it in some non-monetary asset. Thus, you can think of r as the price of money—that's what it costs you to keep the $1,000 as liquid cash, earning zilch for interest.

As r goes up, the price of holding money (instead of investing it at r) goes up, so the demand for money (L) goes down. This is a typical demand curve.

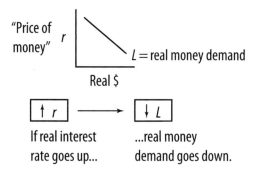

If you can invest wealth at 20%, you're more apt to stick the $1,000 in the 20%-paying investment (which is certainly not a monetary asset), because it's costing you $200 a year to carry around $1,000 in cash. On the other hand, if $r =$ only 1%, it's only costing you $10 a year to carry $1,000 in cash, so you're likely to keep more of your assets in cash or other monetary forms. An increase in the expected rate of inflation also decreases money demand, since nominal interest rates would be higher as well.

Money Supply and Money Demand

If real money demand looks like this—

does **real money supply (MS)** look like this?

The answer is no: the real money supply is essentially *fixed*:

At any interest rate, the real supply of money is essentially constant.

What about all that stuff earlier about the Fed creating and destroying money? That was all *nominal* money. In the short run, the Fed may be able to goose or stifle economic activity by creating or destroying nominal dollars, but people aren't stupid. Take an extreme example. One morning, to really jump-start the economy, the Fed makes a crazy announcement:

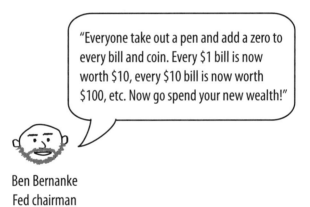

Ben Bernanke
Fed chairman

Yes, this is insane, but what would theoretically happen? Every business would add a zero to every price. The general price level *P* would jump by a factor of 10, but no one would *really* be wealthier, and the real money supply, for one thing, would remain the same. Maybe there'd be a short-term spurt as everyone tries to spend their newly inflated dollars, but prices would adjust pretty quickly in this scenario.

$$\text{Nominal money supply} \longrightarrow \frac{M}{P} = \text{Real money supply } MS \approx \text{constant}$$
$$\text{General price level} \longrightarrow$$

What neoclassical economists and Keynesian economists disagree about, among other things, is *how quickly* prices would adjust.

Neoclassical: *P* adjusts instantly

Keynesian: *P* takes time to adjust

But both sides agree that, in the long run, *P* adjusts to cancel out fluctuation in the nominal supply of money *M*.

So now you can put real money supply and real money demand on the same graph.

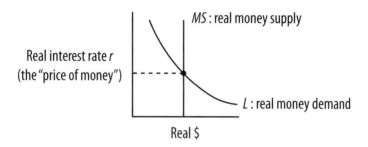

Where the two curves intersect determines the real interest rate in the economy.

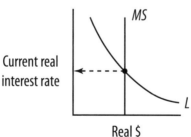

What's cool about this point is that it does two jobs at once. Most directly, it tells you where money supply equals money demand. That

$$\text{Monetary assets supplied} = \text{Monetary assets demanded}$$

at some magical interest rate *r*

But you get two for one. Every choice about where to keep your wealth is a choice between monetary and nonmonetary assets. (In fact, that "price of money" *r* is the interest you could earn on nonmonetary assets.) So if your economy matches up supply and demand on the *money* side, then it also matches up supply and demand on the *non-money* side.

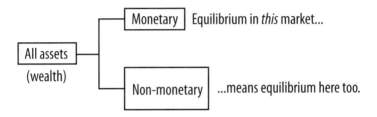

So, the point on the graph earlier gives you equilibrium in *both* asset markets. In fact, overall asset market equilibrium has been achieved.

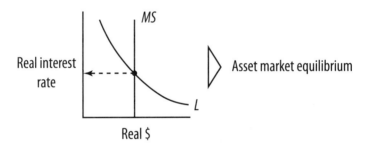

LM Curve

Almost there. What happens to the asset market if national income *Y* increases? Here's the simple chain of logic to remember.

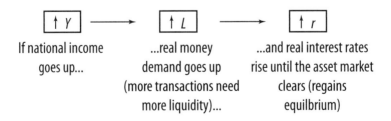

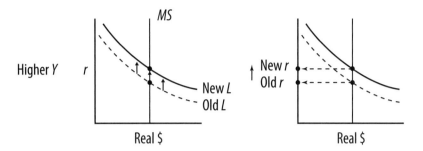

Notice that for any level of national income Y, there'll be a certain real interest rate r that clears the asset market—and the higher Y is, the higher the "asset-market clearing" r is. This relationship is called the **LM curve**. It goes up to the right.

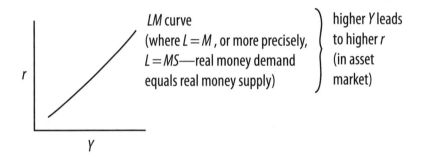

Investment and Savings

The real interest rate r is the master dial on the economic engine. It determines what happens throughout the economy, not just in the market for assets.

Take the market for investable dollars. Since r is the interest paid in general on investments, r is the "price of money" yet again—this time, the price of money for investments (not the literal price of holding cash, as it was earlier).

If you're a company and you can borrow money cheaply (at a low r), you'll do so and make more investments in your business. On the other hand, if you can't borrow money cheaply—if the cost of borrowing is high—then you'll borrow less and invest less. So the demand for investment I^d goes down when r goes up, and vice versa. This is a classic demand curve, sloping down to the right.

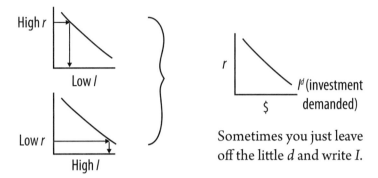

Sometimes you just leave off the little d and write I.

Where does the supply of investment money come from? From savings.

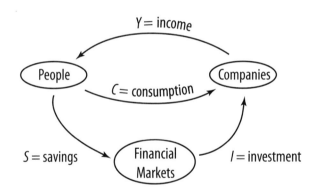

People will save more if they'll get a higher interest rate (a higher price for their saved money). This is a classic supply curve, sloping up to the right.

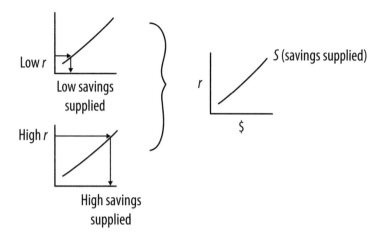

The intersection of these two curves determines the equilibrium in the market for investable dollars:

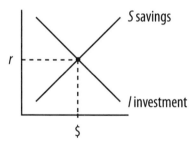

And...just as there was a two-fer before, this particular equilibrium gets you a bonus equilibrium as well. Before, equilibrium in the *money* asset market gave you equilibrium in the *non*-money asset market.

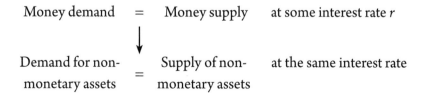

This is because every dollar of wealth is either monetary or non-monetary, and in the short run, wealth is constant. So if everyone allocates his or her wealth between money and "non-money" so that money equilibrium is reached, then "non-money" equilibrium is reached too.

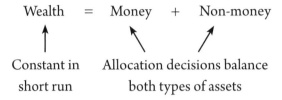

Likewise, people allocate their income between savings and consumption.

$$\text{Income} \quad = \quad \text{Savings} \quad + \quad \text{Consumption}$$
$$Y \qquad\qquad\quad S \qquad\qquad\qquad C$$

And if savings and investment reach equilibrium at some interest rate r, then consumption also reaches equilbrium. That is, the *demand* for consumption C becomes balanced with the supply of stuff to consume— that is, the goods and services companies sell to people. That's called the ***goods market equilibrium***.

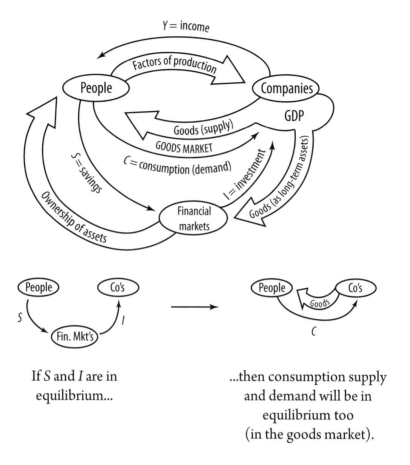

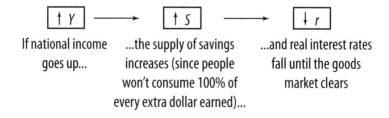

If S and I are in
equilibrium...

...then consumption supply
and demand will be in
equilibrium too
(in the goods market).

IS Curve

What happens to the goods market if national income Y increases? As
before, here's the simple logic to remember.

↑ Y	↑ S	↓ r
If national income goes up...	...the supply of savings increases (since people won't consume 100% of every extra dollar earned)...	...and real interest rates fall until the goods market clears

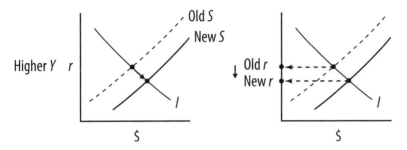

At any level of Y, there's a real interest rate r that clears the goods market—and the higher Y is, the lower the "goods-market-clearing" r is. This relationship is called the **IS curve**. It goes down to the right.

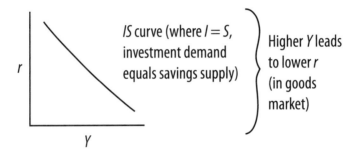

General Equilibrium: IS = LM (= FE!)

The big kahuna picture rolls this all together.

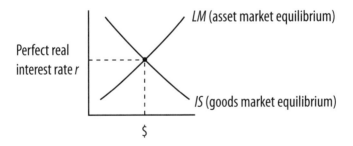

And since all the other parts of the circular economic diagram are in balance, humming along fine, the *top* part of the diagram must be in equilibrium too. This is where people work for companies, exchanging their labor and any other factors of production for wages, etc.

Thus, the economy must be at *full employment* (FE)—everyone who wants to work is working productively. So we can throw in one more line—the full employment line, which is fixed for any interest rate.

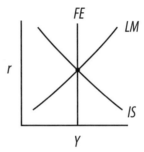

Of course, if achieving full employment were as easy as drawing a vertical line on a graph, the world would be a very different place.

At this stage, you'll start shifting the IS, LM and FE curves around in response to various "shocks," such as a sudden influx of workers into the labor market. These shocks will have an effect in the "short run"—one of those ill-defined terms that you can argue about all day long—and also a "long-run" effect ("long-run" being usefully defined either as longer than "short-run" or as the time frame in which we're all dead).

For instance, it can be argued that monetary policy—creating or destroying nominal dollars—only affects these curves in the short run, after which they return to their original equilibrium. But not all economists agree on this. Indeed, infinite are the arguments of macroeconomists, who can at times resemble the high priests of arcane sects rather than scientists. After all, one would think that the great natural experiment of the recent financial crisis would, if nothing else, provide reams of additional data and significant insights into the functioning of the global economy. Instead, the academic disputes seem to have only multiplied.

Macroeconomics attempts to order and explain the real world conceptually, but it often doesn't quite match up to reality—particularly where predictions are concerned. In response, there is a growing interest in behavioral economics, which posits that people often behave in idiosyncratic (not always perfectly rational) ways that influence market behavior. However, behavioral economics is not part of traditional b-school economics courses.

In macro, we each sometimes felt that we had to suppress our own thinking if we wanted to do well in the class. Unfortunately, the game to some extent was to figure out the professor's allegiances (e.g., to neoclassical or Keynesian economics) and then toe the political line. There can also be an element of handwaving in all these graphical maneuvers.[6]

Let's be honest—if you really wanted to go deep and hard into this stuff, you'd be getting a master's or a PhD. Figure out what really matters for your grade (e.g., increases in Total Factor Productivity seem to be the cure for almost any macroeconomic ill) and learn to parrot that back, Polly.

Game Theory

The final part of this giant chapter is about **game theory**. This is what Russell Crowe's *Beautiful Mind* gave birth to.[7] It's the study of specialized interactions called **games**, which have **players**. Each player makes a choice or choices, trying to win the most money (or something else good) and/or avoid penalties. This is known as **maximizing your payoff**.

---

6   We appreciate that macro has staggeringly complex objects of study (i.e., national economies).

7   Okay, it was actually John Nash, played by Russell Crowe, who is actually a Roman gladiator.

The key to all of game theory is to ask yourself one question, punk:

$$\boxed{\text{WWTOPD?}}$$

What Would The Other Player Do?

In other words, assume the other player is as smart and as motivated as you. Look at the game from his or her point of view. Think as far ahead as you can.

Mechanics of Game Theory

The first kind of game you'll study (in micro or some other course) is simple:

- *Two players* - you're player A, and player B is Bob.

- *Simultaneous* - you both *move* (make your choice) at once. Think Rock-Paper-Scissors. You don't have to literally move simultaneously—you could write down your moves on separate pieces of paper. The important thing is that neither of you knows anything about the other player's choice in advance.

- *Only two choices* - Each of you has a choice between just two possible moves. Rock-Paper-Scissors has three possible moves, so this simple game is even more basic than that.

- *One shot* - You play once, and then you're done, even if you "tie."

The way to represent such an exciting game is with a two-by-two matrix:

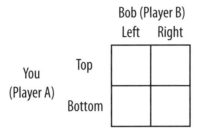

You choose top row or bottom row; Bob chooses left column or right column.

> You: "Are you ready, Bob?"
> Bob: "Ready as I'll ever be."
> You: "Okay, on the count of 3. One…two…—"
> You: "Bottom!" ——simultaneously—— Bob: "Right!"

In this scenario, the **outcome** of the game would be the bottom right box.

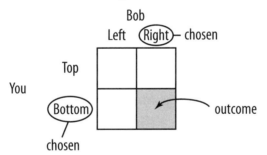

Now you look in that box to see what each player has won from some third party. (Obviously, you were able to see these rewards in advance.)

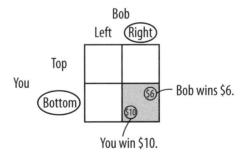

The rewards for you are in the bottom left corner of each little box. Here's a full set of your possible payoffs.

	Left	Right
Top	$16	$1
Bottom	$3	$10

(You)

For example, if "Top-Left" is the outcome you win $16.

The rewards for Bob are in the top right corner of each little box. Here's a full set of Bob's payoffs:

Bob

	Left	Right
Top	$7	$12
Bottom	$1	$6

And here's the full game:

Bob

	Left	Right
Top	$7 / $16	$12 / $1
Bottom	$1 / $3	$6 / $10

(You)

As you can see, the game is all about the pattern of payoffs. So what would you *really* do in this game? If you just study your own payoffs, you might be puzzled.

	Top	$16	$1
You			
	Bottom	$3	$10

You: "Hmm. If I go for top, I might win $16—but then again, I might only get $1. If I go for bottom, I only have an upside of $10, but my downside of $3 is better than $1 …

Stop! Remember you're not playing against a coin toss. You're playing against *another player*, someone just as smart and motivated as you.

WWTOPD?

What Would The Other Player Do?

Look at the game through Bob's eyes. What would Bob do?

Left	Right
$7	$12
$1	$6

Here's what Bob thinks, or ought to think:

> "Let's see. Right looks better at first glance. If A chooses Top row, then I should choose Right because $12 is bigger than $7. If, instead, A chooses Bottom row, then I should again choose Right because $6 is bigger than $1. Either way, Right's better for me, so I'm choosing Right."

Notice that Bob only compares his payoffs in the same row.

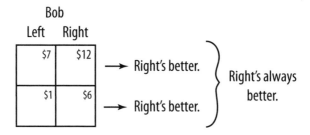

So for Bob, Right is a **dominant** strategy, because no matter what you do, Right is better for Bob than Left.[8]

Now come back to being player A. Knowing that Bob is going to choose Right, because that's his dominant strategy, what should *you* do? Look at *your* payoffs.

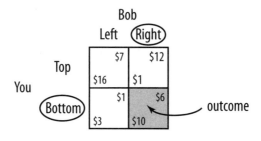

$10 is bigger than $1, so you should choose Bottom. Put away your wishful thinking—you aren't getting that $16.

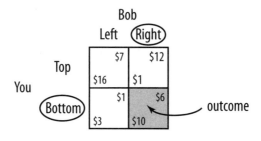

---

8   This concept of dominance shows up in Part IV, Chapter 26: Interviews and Offers. If some job is worse than another particular job on every dimension, the worse job is *dominated*. A *dominant* job is better than every other on every dimension.

This outcome is known as a ***Nash equilibrium***. Here's what defines a Nash equilibrium:

- You can't make yourself better off by making a different move by yourself. If you switch to Top, you're worse off.

- Likewise, Bob can't improve his payoff by *unilaterally* making a different move.

- You and Bob both understand this. Your expectations about each other's actions match reality.

What's interesting about this game is that there's a better outcome on the board—for *both* of you—but there's no way to get there.

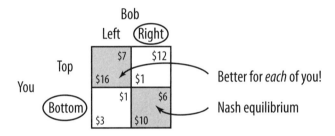

If only you and Bob could agree ahead of time! You want Bob to choose Left, and you'll choose Top. You'll make $16 instead of $10, and Bob will make $7 instead of $6 … maybe you even offer Bob a kickback ahead of time, since you're going to make a lot more, whereas the improvement's minor for Bob.

The problem is that this is a *one-shot* game. You and Bob have no history and no future. All the two of you have is this one moment. So Bob might promise all day long to go Left, but like Lucy pulling the football once Charlie Brown is running, Bob is strongly incented to make you choose Top (and then to choose Right and make $12 instead of $7). Knowing this, you should not believe Bob's assurances. You should go Bottom. Bob will go Right. And you're back at the Nash equilibrium.

The classic **Prisoner's Dilemma** game has slightly different payoffs but the same problem overall: The Nash equilbrium is not the best outcome on the board.

Prisoner B

	Cooperate	Defect
Cooperate	$6 / $6	$10 / $0
Defect	$0 / $10	$3 / $3

(Prisoner A on left: Cooperate, Defect)

For each prisoner, "Defecting" is the dominant strategy, so the Nash equilibrium is in the bottom right again. By the way, the names of the moves can be confusing. "Cooperate" means "cooperate *with each other* and stand strong against the authorities who are trying to get the prisoners to rat each other out." Likewise, "defect"means "defect from the coalition with the other prisoner," in other words, "betray the other prisoner by snitching."[9]

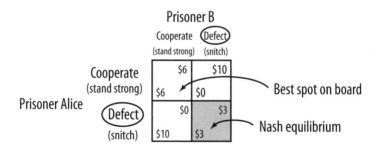

The Prisoner's Dilemma provides a good model of a cartel—and why cartels fail. Producers in a cartel have strong incentives to defect, so the arrangement falls apart unless enforced by other means.

---

9   To make matters more confusing, sometimes the Prisoner's Dilemma is written with *years of prison time* as the payoffs. Since you want *less* prison time, you have to make sure you're going for *low* numbers (not high ones, as you would with dollars).

The Prisoner's Dilemma also provides a counterexample to the **invisible hand**, Adam Smith's famous image of how the individually self-interested actions of buyers and sellers in a free market lead to the best outcome overall. In the Prisoner's Dilemma, each prisoner wisely acts in his or her own self-interest, but the result is not the best one possible.

A good way out of the Prisoner's Dilemma is to repeat the game for many rounds. In a **repeated game**, your reputation matters, and you'll cooperate more often (if only in your own self-interest). In real life, few games are truly one-shot. If you screw your partners on one deal, you might not see many other deals—or you might only find very suspicious partners in the future.

Be Unpredictable

The best strategy in a repeated game can be a **mixed strategy**, in which you change up your moves. The most important thing is to be unpredictable, because the other players will exploit any patterns in your moves.

Consider Rock-Paper-Scissors with the following payoff structure:

		Bob		
		Rock	Paper	Scissors
You	Rock	$0 / $0	$1 / −$1	−$1 / $1
	Paper	−$1 / $1	$0 / $0	$1 / −$1
	Scissors	$1 / −$1	−$1 / $1	$0 / $0

Every time you win, Bob pays you a dollar; when you lose, you pay him a dollar. This is an example of a **zero-sum game**: your gain is someone else's loss (and vice versa).

So what's your best opening move? If you don't know anything about Bob's past play, then you should roll dice and pick completely at random.

> Your chance of picking Rock: ⅓
> Your chance of picking Paper: ⅓
> Your chance of picking Scissors: ⅓

That's also Bob's best play, if he doesn't know anything about *your* history of playing Rock-Paper-Scissors. You and Bob will be evenly matched, and your expected winnings over time will be $0.

If Bob tends to throw Rock more often, then you can study the percentages and adjust your own probability accordingly (you'll throw Paper more often). This way, your expected winnings over time will be above $0.

By the way, to be truly unpredictable, actually roll dice, flip a coin, or use a random-number generator in Excel. Don't just make up what you think is a random string of moves. You're likely to flip flop too often. Truly random strings contain significant "runs" of just one move.

Even Be Irrational (Sometimes)

A counter-intuitive result of game theory is that it can be smart to be crazy. Take the game of **Chicken**, in which you drive a car straight at Bob, who's driving another car straight at you. Whoever swerves first loses and is a loser. It's not exactly a one-shot simultaneous game, but let's look at it that way for now:

		Bob	
		Go Straight	Swerve
You	**Go Straight**	Die (really bad) / Die (really bad)	Lose / Win
	Swerve	Win / Lose	Tie / Tie

Crazy to even play, right? Say that winning is worth $10 million. If you lose, you fork over half a million dollars. A tie is worth $0. And dying is still really bad. You might play just for the chance at that ten mill.

Here's how to win.

As quickly as you can, snap off your steering wheel, wave it out the window so Bob can see it, then throw it away.

You have now **strategically committed** to your course of action. You have removed your own fall back, play-it-safe option. Now here's what Bob faces:

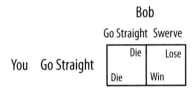

Bob now can only choose to lose or to die. Being rational, he will choose to lose, and you will win. You just have to make sure you break your steering wheel *before* Bob does—*not at the same time.*

This concept of **strategic commitment**—tying your own hands, cutting off your own escape routes, burning your own ships[10]—may seem utterly nuts. After all, isn't having choices good? Not always. By restricting your own choices, you can force Bob's hand. This even works when Bob is you as well—your future self, say. If you want to make sure you get up early tomorrow, set your alarm, but then take away the snooze button option. Place the alarm clock across the room. Or ask a sadistic roommate or two to wake you.[11] Your future sleepy self won't be able to betray your intentions.

---

10   As Hernán Cortés supposedly did after he landed on the shores of Mexico.

11   One of us did this once in undergrad. The roommates used ice, shaving cream and a compressed air horn, to impressive effect.

This is not to say that in every game, a preemptive, bold move is always the right thing to do. Sometimes "crazy like a fox" is just plain crazy. Some games are **sequential**, in which one player goes first, and it's not always the case that you should go first. Whether there's a *first-mover advantage* or a *second-mover advantage* depends on the game. The point is that you should really understand the game—its structure, its payoffs—in order to figure out your best play, which may or may not involve:

- *Seemingly irrational behavior,* such as cutting off your own options.

- *Random, unpredictable behavior,* such as choosing your next move by a coin flip.

Going Once, Going Twice...

Auctions are also an object of game-theoretic study. You probably already know about **English auctions**, in which bidders make higher and higher offers until there's only one bidder left. This is the kind of auction you run with a fast-talkin' auctioneer:

> "...I've got five hundred, five hundred from the little lady in the first row, do I hear six hundred, six hundred, going once, six hundred from the gentleman in the cowboy hat, six hundred for this fine oil painting of Elvis Presley's Bluetick hound, six hundred going once..."

So you bid $700 for this painting and *wham!* you won. You were the highest bidder, and now you pay $700. As you gaze at the sad-eyed Bluetick, you wonder, "No one else bid as high as me. Maybe it's not actually worth $700. Maybe I could have gotten it for $650..." This is known as the **winner's curse**. In an English auction, if you win, you tend to suspect you overpaid. There's also a lot of gamesmanship in an English auction—as a bidder, your best strategy depends not just on your own private valuation of the painting, but also on how many other bidders there are, how they behave, etc.

In contrast, a **second-price auction** (also known as a **Vickrey auction**) removes all the gamesmanship at a stroke. Every bidder submits one sealed bid. The highest bid wins—but that bidder only pays the *second* highest bid.

Amazingly, because of this change in the rules, your best strategy as a bidder is to submit your true valuation—your indifference point—or something just below it, so that you're *just* still willing to buy. You no longer care what the other bidders do.

Why does the second-price auction work so well? Let's say you really think that the painting is worth $675, or rather you'd just be willing to pay $675. You bid $675, and the next highest bid is $650. You win, and you pay $650. Should you have bid any lower than $675, say $655? No, because you'd still only pay $650. And it increases the chance that some *other* bidder could have bid lower than $675 *and win*, when you would have bought at $675. In a second-price auction, lowering your own bid to try to snag a bargain doesn't work, because it doesn't reduce the price you pay if you win. All it does is increase the chance that you lose the auction to a bidder who bid *less* than you were willing to pay. A similar argument explains why you wouldn't overbid either.

Second-price auctions, with modifications, have been adopted in various real-world scenarios, including the sale of Treasury bills. The initial public offering of Google was a kind of second-price auction.

I Call That a Bargain

You might take a whole elective course on bargaining and negotiations, but in case you encounter it within a first-year course, remember three things:

1) As in game theory, look at the situation through the other side's eyes. Assume they're as smart as you.

2) Figure out your own **BATNA**—the ***best alternative to negotiated agreement***. In other words, what's your best option if you can't reach agreement? By improving your own BATNA, you strengthen your hand in the negotiation.

1 + 2) Think about the other side's BATNA as well.

3) Never forget the ***larger game***—that of business school. If you win a classroom negotiation in a dirty way and become known as a giant jackass, you have lost points in that larger game. Of course, play to win, but always be a good sport.

Chapter 16:
Statistics

~~~~~~~~~~~~~~~~~~~~~~~~~~~~~~

Statistics is a rough but necessary subject. If you have a lot of quantitative information, stats help you boil it down to a few key numbers so you can make predictions and decisions. The word *statistics* can refer either to the subject ("Stats is fun!") or the key numbers themselves ("These performance statistics suck.").

There are five big areas of stats to cover:

1)	Descriptive Statistics	"The average salary is \$X …"
2)	Probability	"The chance of failure is 5% …"
3)	Distributions	Bell curve
4)	Sampling & Hypothesis Testing	"Given the sample of 100 customers we can conclude…"
5)	Correlation & Regression	"For every extra million dollars we spend on advertising, our market share increases by 3%..."

Descriptive Statistics

Say there are 500 people in your business-school class, and you want to think about the *number of years* each of you spent working between college graduation and business school.

Student	Years Since College	
You	4	
Alice Atwater	2	Each row is an *observation.*
Bill Burns	6	
... (497 more)	... (497 more)	

To make things simple, you'll probably round to the nearest whole number (instead of having data like 5.25 years, 7.8 years, etc.). Whole numbers are **discrete** (meaning "separated and countable"), so with this information, you can make a **histogram** to display the count in each category.

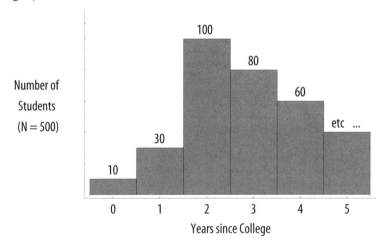

If you convert to percents, you can also show the same graph as a *frequency distribution*.

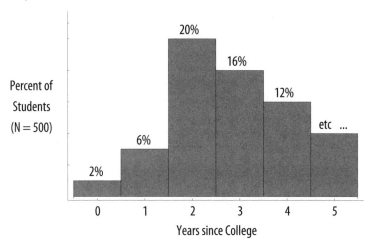

This pretty picture illustrates a link between statistics and *probability*. If you pick someone at random from your class, there's a 2% chance that he or she spent 0 years working, a 6% chance he or she spent 1 year, etc.

Now, what's the *average* amount of time your classmates have spent in the real world since college? There are three primary ways to answer this question:

1) Mean

2) Median   } Three types of average

3) Mode

The *mean* is most important. In fact, this is what Excel calls AVERAGE. Technically, this is the "arithmetic mean" (air-ith-MET-ik), but you'll never use the other means defined by statisticians, so you can just say "mean." You already know the formula from the GMAT or GRE:

$$\text{Mean} = \frac{\text{Sum}}{\text{Number}}$$

You add up everyone's "years since college" and divide that total by 500, the number of people in your class.

$$\text{Mean Years} = \frac{\text{Total Years}}{\text{Number of Students}}$$

$$3.36 = \frac{1,680}{500}$$

Here are some key symbols.

μ	Greek letter *mu* ("myoo") which is an "m"	Mean of a whole population (like your class)
N	Number	Size of a population
Σ	Capital Greek letter *sigma*, which is a capital "S"	Process of adding numbers to get a sum

Since Σ represents a process, you have to tell it what to do. First, to label the different values you want to add up, use *subscripts* (like the 1 in x_1).

Student	**Years Since College**	
You	4	$= x_1$
Alice Atwater	2	$= x_2$
Bill Burns	6	$= x_3$
...	...	...

So now you can write the Total Years this way:

$$\text{Total Years} = x_1 + x_2 + x_3 + \ldots + x_{500}$$

But that's really annoying. Instead, use Σ to indicate that you're summing all the x's up from x_1 through x_{500}.

$$x_1 + x_2 + x_3 + \ldots + x_{500} = \sum_{i=1}^{500} x_i \quad \longleftarrow \quad \text{dummy subscript}$$

A curly i or j is a typical "dummy" subscript in the expression.

$\sum_{i=1}^{500} x_i$ means "add up all the x's, starting at x_1 and going up to and including x_{500}." The $i = 1$ on the bottom means "start with x_1." The 500 on top means "finish with x_{500}."

Once it's all Greeked up and generalized, the mean equation looks like:

$$\mu = \frac{\sum_{i=1}^{N} x_i}{N}$$

But even in a toga, this equation is still just:

$$\text{Mean} = \frac{\text{Sum}}{\text{Number}}$$

You can compute the mean "years since college" another way. Since a lot of the numbers are repeated, it makes sense to add them up in groups.

Add ten 0's
thirty 1's,
a hundred 2's,
eighty 3's,
sixty 4's, etc...

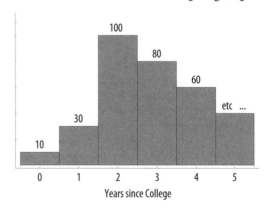

Ten 0's is ten times zero. Rewriting, you get:

$$\text{Mean} = \frac{10 \cdot 0 + 30 \cdot 1 + 100 \cdot 2 + 80 \cdot 3 + \ldots}{500}$$

Now split up the numerator:

$$\text{Mean} = \frac{10}{500} \cdot 0 + \frac{30}{500} \cdot 1 + \frac{100}{500} \cdot 2 + \frac{80}{500} \cdot 3 + \ldots$$

$$= 2\% \cdot 0 + 6\% \cdot 1 + 20\% \cdot 2 + 16\% \cdot 3$$

Notice that the percents you just calculated are the same as those on the frequency distribution.

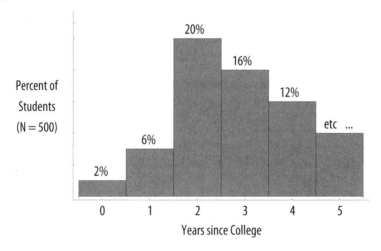

To find the mean, consider the *frequencies* as percents or decimals. Multiply each observation by its frequency, and add the results up. You'll get the mean. In toga form, the equation looks like:

$$\text{Mean} = \Sigma x \cdot p(x)$$

where $p(x)$ is the percent frequency of x occurring in the population—in other words, $p(x)$ is the *probability* of picking someone at random with x years since college. Include every possible value of x in your sum.

Written this way, the mean is also called the ***expected value*** of x. It's the "average" value you'd expect if you pulled a lot of people at random and averaged their x's (years since college). Expected value is not the value you'd expect from any one person necessarily. It's like when the census reports that the average US family has 2.2 children. We've never met 0.2 of a child, but 2.2 is still the expected value considering the country as a whole.

The ***median*** is the middle number, or the 50th percentile: half the people have more years since college (or the same number), and half have fewer years (or the same number). You can read the median from the percent histogram—just add from the left until you hit 50%.

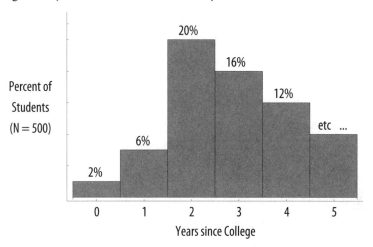

Years since College (at least)		Cumulative Percent
0		2%
1	+ 6% =	8%
2	+ 20% =	28%
3	+ 16% =	44%
4	+ 12% =	56% STOP!

This means that the median is 4 years. The ***mode*** is the observation that shows up most often, corresponding to the highest frequency on the histogram. If none of the years to the right of 4 have more than 20% of the population, then the histogram's peak is 20%, and the mode is 2 years.

Gimme The Spread

Mean, median, and mode are all "central" measures—they answer the question "where's the center of all the data?" But often, you want to know how spread out the data is.

The crudest measure of spread is ***range***, which is just the largest value minus the smallest value. While this is easy to calculate, it's susceptible to ***outliers***—oddball observations that, rightly or wrongly, lie far away from most of the others. For example, if one person in your program is in her 70s and has been out of school for 50 years, then your range of "years since college" would be huge because of that one outlier. Outliers are sometimes erroneous data (someone typed in 55 instead of 5), so you should always look closely at outliers to see whether they're legit.

A better measure of spread is ***standard deviation***. It's a pain to calculate by hand, but it's got nice mathematical properties, and now everyone just crunches it in Excel. If your computer's stranded on an island without you, you calculate standard deviations this way:

1) Figure out the mean.

Student	Years Since College
You	4
Alice Atwater	2
Bill Burns	6
...	...

Mean $\mu = 3.36$

2) Subtract the mean from each observation and square those differences, also known as **deviations**.

Student	Years Since College	Minus the Mean	Deviation	Squared Deviation
You	4	− 3.36	= 0.64	$(0.64)^2 = 0.4096$
Alice A.	2	− 3.36	= −1.36	$(-1.36)^2 = 1.8496$
Bill B.	6	− 3.36	= 2.64	$(2.64)^2 = 6.9696$
...	...	...	...	...

3) Take the mean of all those squared deviations. That is, add them all up and divide by the number of observations, in this case 500.

$$\frac{0.4096 + 1.8496 + 6.9696 + \ldots}{500} = 7.672$$

This result is known as the *variance*. Why? It just is, son.

4) Finally, take the square root of the variance.

$$\sqrt{7.672} \approx 2.77 = standard\ deviation\ (SD)$$

What the hell does that result of 2.77 mean? Roughly, SD indicates how far on average a data point is from the mean, whether above or below (which would be average distance). That's not the precise mathematical definition of SD, but it's close enough—and average distance is much easier to grasp.

To get average distance, you would measure each point's distance from the mean, ignoring direction. Then you'd take the mean of all those distances (add 'em up and divide by the number of points). Again, although the average distance and standard deviation are not exactly the same thing, they behave in much the same way mathematically, and they're close enough for government work.

Consider a few cases with the same mean, but different spreads.

Case 1: Every observation = 4

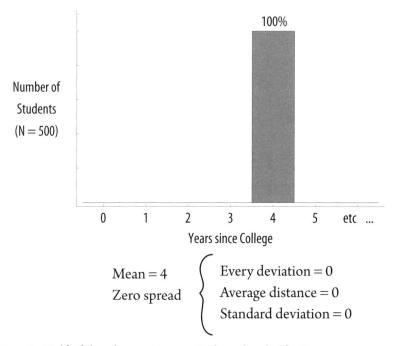

Mean = 4   Every deviation = 0
Zero spread   Average distance = 0
              Standard deviation = 0

Case 2: Half of the observations = 5, the other half = 3

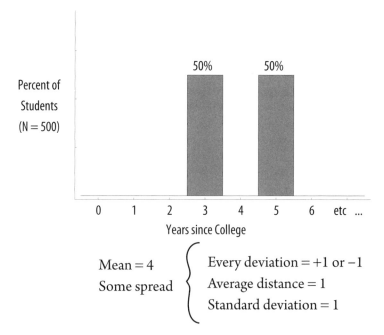

Mean = 4   Every deviation = +1 or −1
Some spread   Average distance = 1
              Standard deviation = 1

Case 3: Realistic spread

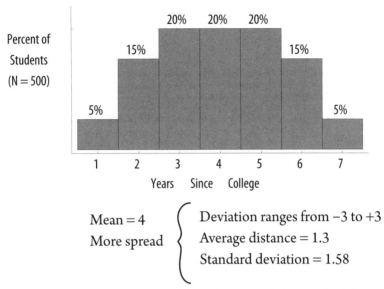

Mean = 4
More spread

{ Deviation ranges from −3 to +3
Average distance = 1.3
Standard deviation = 1.58

Here, the average distance of every point from 4 and the standard deviation (defined by the weird procedure earlier) are not exactly the same,
but they are pretty close. Notice that in the last case, the numbers are
not "4 plus or minus 1.58." Usually there's a significant amount of data
more than a standard deviation away from the mean. But it can be shown
that at least 3/4 of the data is always within two standard deviations
of the mean, and when the histogram is **bell-shaped** (with one central
hump and two little *tails* like a bell seen from the side), you can make
even tighter claims:

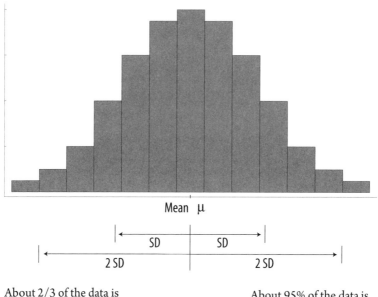

Mean μ

| SD | SD |
| 2 SD | 2 SD |

About 2/3 of the data is
within 1 SD of the mean

About 95% of the data is
within 2 SD's of the mean

If the mean is 4 and the SD is 1.2 for some bell-shaped data, then at least 19 of every 20 observations (95%) are between 1.6 $(= 4 - 2 \times 1.2)$ and 6.4 $(= 4 + 2 \times 1.2)$.

Standard deviation is incredibly important in other subjects you'll encounter in business school. In finance, standard deviation is a typical way to measure the **risk** or **volatility** of an investment. You measure the daily percent changes (**returns**) of Apple stock, say, then you compute the standard deviation of a whole bunch of those daily returns. The higher the standard deviation, the more volatile the stock is and the riskier it's considered, generally speaking.

In operations and manufacturing, standard deviation is used in **process control**. For instance, if you're making lug nuts for nuclear missiles, you'll have tight specifications to meet. The more the lug nuts vary in size, the less likely it is that they'll be acceptable to the government (your client). So you'll have to measure and try to reduce the standard deviation of the width, the thickness, etc., of the batches of lug nuts.

The symbol for standard deviation is σ, a lowercase Greek letter *sigma*. Don't confuse this with big sigma (Σ), which means summation. By the way, σ is the sigma in the term **Six Sigma**, a famous process improvement methodology.[1]

Now, what's been assumed so far is that you've been working with the entire population you care about—the 500 people in your b-school class. Often, though, you can't get data from everyone. Maybe you can only get a sample of 50 people, but you'll want to extrapolate your results to all 500.

This difference between **samples** and **populations** turns out to be so important that the symbols for the statistics themselves are different in each case.

	Population	**Sample**
Size	N	n
Mean	μ	$\bar{x}$
Standard Deviation	σ	s
Variance	σ^2	s^2

The bar over the x means the average of the x's.

---

1   Experts in this methodology are called Six Sigma Black Belts, the goofiest martial artists known to man. If you encounter such a nerdy ninja in a dark alley, fear not.

For a sample, the statistics aren't written with Greek letters. You compute the **sample mean** $\bar{x}$ ("the mean of a sample set of data") the same way as you do a population mean μ:

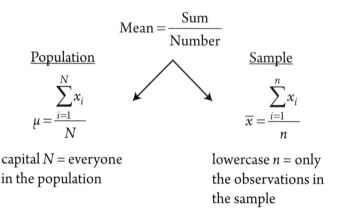

$$\text{Mean} = \frac{\text{Sum}}{\text{Number}}$$

Population   Sample

$$\mu = \frac{\sum_{i=1}^{N} x_i}{N} \qquad \bar{x} = \frac{\sum_{i=1}^{n} x_i}{n}$$

capital N = everyone in the population

lowercase n = only the observations in the sample

Weirdly, you compute variance and standard deviation slightly differently in each case.

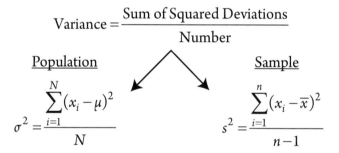

$$\text{Variance} = \frac{\text{Sum of Squared Deviations}}{\text{Number}}$$

Population   Sample

$$\sigma^2 = \frac{\sum_{i=1}^{N} (x_i - \mu)^2}{N} \qquad s^2 = \frac{\sum_{i=1}^{n} (x_i - \bar{x})^2}{n-1}$$

You divide by $n - 1$ on the right, rather than by n (the number of observations in the sample) as you'd expect. The reason is technical, but the rationale is simple: you always use *sample statistics* to estimate *population statistics*. You never care about the sample itself—you compute the sample stats so you can learn about the whole population. And it turns out that, mathematically, dividing by $n - 1$ makes s^2 a better **estimator** of σ^2 then dividing by n. Why? It just does.

You turn variance into standard deviation the same way for both sides—by taking the square root.

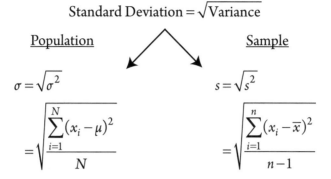

$$\text{Standard Deviation} = \sqrt{\text{Variance}}$$

Population

$$\sigma = \sqrt{\sigma^2}$$

$$= \sqrt{\frac{\sum\limits_{i=1}^{N}(x_i - \mu)^2}{N}}$$

Sample

$$s = \sqrt{s^2}$$

$$= \sqrt{\frac{\sum\limits_{i=1}^{n}(x_i - \overline{x})^2}{n-1}}$$

Mean and standard deviation are the two most important statistics to compute about any data set. There are ways to measure **skew** (lack of symmetry around the mean) and other aspects of the data, but don't worry about those for now.

Probability

You already know that:

$$\text{probability of success} = \frac{\text{Number of successful possible outcomes}}{\text{Total number of possible outcomes}}$$

You encountered this on the GMAT or GRE: "What's the probability of rolling an odd number with a fair 6-sided die?"

Answer: You could roll any of three odd numbers $(1, 3, \text{or } 5)$, and there are six total possible outcomes $(1, 2, 3, 4, 5, \text{or } 6)$. So the probability is $\frac{3}{6} = \frac{1}{2}$. In math symbols, you write $P(\text{Odd}) = \frac{1}{2}$ or $P(X = \text{odd}) = \frac{1}{2}$.

The "P" can be upper or lower case. X is a **random variable**—in this case the roll of the die.

Probabilities range from 0 (impossible) to 1 (completely certain). You can't have less than 0 success, and you can't be more successful than 100% of the time. This is not like high school, when you might have been able to swing a GPA above 4.0.

Of course, you assume that the die is fair—that all the possible outcomes are equally weighted. That's not always the case in reality. When various outcomes have different likelihoods of occurring, think of probability as a long-run average. If $P(\text{Heads}) = \dfrac{3}{5}$ for a weighted coin, then you expect 3,000 heads if you flip the coin 5,000 times (3 out of 5).

Probabilities are often written as decimals or percents.

$$P(\text{Heads}) = \frac{3}{5} = 0.60 = 60\%$$

Decimals are the least intuitive. Get used to them; they show up. Also be ready and able to switch to percents or fractions, rephrasing as a long-run average rate.

$$P(\text{Heads}) = 0.60 \quad \longrightarrow \quad P(\text{Heads}) = 60\% = \frac{60}{100} = \frac{3}{5}$$

"60% of the time, I get heads. 3 flips out of 5, I get heads."

By making the probabilities concrete in this way, you'll make more sense of them.

A Medical Example

The complexities of probability are often illustrated through some story about a dread disease that's very hard to detect in its early stages. As the patient, you either have this disease or you don't; there is no middle ground. In techier terms, your true disease state is Sick or Okay.

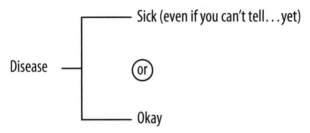

Now, along comes a new test for this disease. If you take this test, you get either a **positive** result (supposedly indicating that you have the disease) or a **negative** result (supposedly indicating that you don't have the disease).

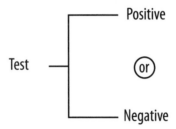

Note that positive in this context is bad, while negative is good.

No test is perfect. There are two kinds of *false* (= untrue) results.

- A *false positive* is a positive result for someone who *doesn't* actually have the disease.

- A *false negative* is a negative result for someone who actually *does* have the disease.

False positives are scary, but false negatives kill people, so if you have to choose just one to reduce, you'd want to reduce false negatives.

You can see all the results in a 2×2 table:

		Test	
		Positive	**Negative**
Disease	**Sick**	True positives	False negatives
	Okay	False positives	True negatives

Think through each of these four boxes. One way people mess all this stuff up is by not clearly distinguishing the disease itself from the *test* results. Never use the same labels for the actual disease and for the test. Stick with more descriptive labels, such as the four above (Sick/Okay and Positive/Negative).

You can also total each row and column.

		Test		
		Positive	**Negative**	**Total**
Disease	**Sick**	True positives	False negatives	All sick
	Okay	False positives	True negatives	All okay
	Total	All positive	All negative	Everyone

Something called the **false positive rate** has a very counter-intuitive definition. People screw this up all the time[2], so be careful. The false positive rate is the *number of false positives divided by the total number of Okays*, not the total number of positives. So, if the false positive rate is 3% on this test, the table will look like this:

		Test		
		Positive	**Negative**	**Total**
	Sick			
Disease	**Okay**	3 (false pos)	97 (true neg)	100 (all okay)
	Total			

Out of 100 people truly without the disease, 97 people get *true negative* test results, and 3 people get *false positive* results.

$$\text{False positive rate} = \frac{\text{False Positives}}{\text{All Okays}} = \frac{\text{False Positives}}{\text{False Positives} + \text{True Negatives}}$$

It's easy to think that true positives go in the denominator, but that's wrong—true *negatives* go there, because they combine with false positives to give you the total disease-free population.

---

2   In 1999, the New England Journal of Medicine published a letter revealing that, out of 63 published stories mentioning "false positive rate" in a two-year period, *nearly half* had miscalculated the number. Maybe you should give this chapter to your friends in med school, or at least half of them.

Likewise, a *false negative rate* of 2% means that 2% of all sick people get false negative results, while 98% get true positive results.

		Test		
		Positive	**Negative**	**Total**
Disease	**Sick**	98 (true pos)	2 (false neg)	100 (all sick)
	Okay			
	Total			

$$\text{False negative rate} = \frac{\text{False Negatives}}{\text{All Sick}} = \frac{\text{False Negatives}}{\text{False Negatives} + \text{True Positives}}$$

Let's say that 1% of all people have the disease. This is called the **base rate**—the natural rate of occurrence of the disease.

Now you have the test done, and the lab results come back:

> *Dreadful Disease:* **Positive**
> *Have a nice day!*
>
> *– Dr. Nick*

What's the chance that you *actually* have the disease?

To review, you know three things:

> False positive rate = 3%
>
> False negative rate = 2%
>
> Base rate = 1%

To answer the question, you can fill in the grid. The key is to pick smart numbers—large whole numbers that allow you to avoid decimals. For the big total population, you might think that 100 is good. In fact, 10,000 is way better (you'll avoid decimals this way).

Test

	Positive	Negative	Total
Sick			
Okay			
Total			10,000

Disease (labels rows Sick and Okay)

Now use the base rate. 1% of all people actually have the disease. 1% of 10,000 = 100. That means 9,900 people are Okay.

Test

	Positive	Negative	Total
Sick			100
Okay			9,900
Total			10,000

Disease (labels rows Sick and Okay)

Next, use the false positive rate. 3% of Okay people get false positives; the other 97% of Okay people get the negatives. 3% of 9,900 is 297, while 97% of 9,900 is 9,603.

	Positive	Negative	Total
Sick			100
Okay	297	9,603	9,900
Total			10,000

The false negative rate states that 2% of Sick people get false negatives, while the other 98% get true positives.

	Positive	Negative	Total
Sick	98	2	100
Okay	297	9,603	9,900
Total			10,000

Finally, you can sum up the number of positive tests you'll get out of 10,000 people and the number of negative tests.

	Positive	Negative	Total
Sick	98	2	100
Okay	297	9,603	9,900
Total	395	9,605	10,000

Out of the 395 positive test results, only 98 people are *actually* Sick. This means that even if you get a positive test result, you only have a $\frac{98}{395} \approx$ 25% chance of having this dreadful disease. Phew. That's probably much lower than you thought.

This surprising result is an effect of the low base rate 1%. Such a small number of people actually have the disease that the false positives are relatively more numerous. This is why, if you test positive for some rare disease, you shouldn't necessarily freak out. Just get retested, while you explain the relevant principles of probability to your physician. You almost certainly understand them better.

The Language of Probability

	Positive	Negative	Total
Sick	98	2	100
Okay	297	9,603	9,900
Total	395	9,605	10,000

Sick, Okay, Pos, and Neg are known as **events**. Even if you think of being Sick as a state, *picking* someone Sick out of a group is an event.

Sick is the opposite of Okay. The technical term is **complement**, because together, the two events cover everybody.

$$\text{Sick} = \text{NOT Okay} = \sim\!\text{Okay} = \overline{\text{Okay}}$$

Those last two symbols for NOT (the squiggle and the bar over the top) are kind of evil. It's especially annoying that the bar is used over variables (like $\bar{x}$) to mean "*average*," but over events (like Okay) to mean "not." And the squiggle doesn't mean "approximately" here—it means "not." Huh? Yeah.

Since Sick and Okay cover everybody and they don't overlap as labels —no one is ever both Sick and Okay in this world—this set of events {Sick, Okay} is said to be **MECE** ("mee-see"):

- *Mutually Exclusive:* no one is both Sick and Okay.

- *Collectively Exhaustive:* everyone is either Sick or Okay.

{Pos, Neg} is also MECE: there are no gaps and no overlaps. Consultants love to throw around this acronym. While it's good to break down important issues in a MECE way, it's also good not to sound like a jackass, so use the term sparingly in civilian conversation.

Looking again at the grid, you can read off some probabilities.

	Positive	Negative	Total
Sick	98	2	100
Okay	297	9,603	9,900
Total	395	9,605	10,000

$P(\text{Neg})$ = "The probability of getting a negative test result."

$= \dfrac{9,605}{10,000} = 0.9605$

$= 96.05\%$

$P(\sim\text{Sick})$ = "The probability of picking someone who's *not* Sick out of the whole group."

$= \dfrac{9,900}{10,000} = 0.99$

$= 99\%$

AND and OR

What's the probability of picking someone who is both Okay and Negative? Find the box at the intersection of Okay and Negative:

	Positive	Negative	Total
Sick			
Okay		9,603	
Total			

There are 9,603 people who are both Okay and Negative.

Then divide by the total population (10,000).

$$P(\text{Okay AND Neg}) = \dfrac{9,603}{10,000} = 0.9603 = 96.03\%$$

This can also be written as $P(\text{Okay} \cap \text{Neg})$. The $\cap$ symbol is called an *intersection*, and $P(\text{Okay} \cap \text{Neg})$ is the *joint probability*. Each of the four boxes in the original 2×2 table represents an intersection.

	__Positive__	__Negative__
__Sick__	Sick ∩ Pos	Sick ∩ Neg
__Okay__	Okay ∩ Pos	Okay ∩ Neg

Notice that the number of people who are Okay AND Negative is less than the total number of people who are Okay. It's also less than the total number of people who are Negative.

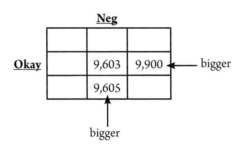

"AND" does not mean addition. You're applying the AND to the *condition* (you want people who are both Okay AND Negative), making the condition more stringent. This restricts the number of people who meet an AND condition. Think of it this way: how many folks have won the lottery? How many folks have been hit by lightning? Okay, how many folks have both won the lottery AND been hit by lightning? The answer to the last question is the smallest number.

In contrast, if you want to find people who are Okay **OR** Negative, you're relaxing the condition. People can be either Okay OR Negative (or both), so three of the four boxes in the 2×2 meet the condition:

	__Pos__	__Neg__
__Sick__	✕	2
__Okay__	297	9,603

$$\longrightarrow \quad 2 + 297 + 9{,}603 = 9{,}902$$

Only the 98 people who are both Sick and Positive are left out.

$$P(\text{Okay OR Neg}) = \frac{9{,}902}{10{,}000} = 0.9902 = 99.02\%$$

This can also be written as $P(\text{Okay} \cup \text{Neg})$. The $\cup$ symbol is called a *union*.

You might know that you can add probabilities to get an OR probability. If you do this addition, remember to subtract off the overlap, or you'll end up double-counting it.

Okay OR Neg　=　All Okay　+　All Neg　−　Okay AND Neg

9,902	9,900	9,605	9,603

Conditional Probability

What is the probability of a positive test result GIVEN that you are Sick?

In other words, you're not just one of the 10,000 any more. You're one of the 100 sick people.

	Positive	Negative	Total
Sick			100
Okay			~~9,900~~
Total			~~10,000~~

Given this *condition*, what's the chance you get a positive test result?

	Positive	Negative	Total
Sick	98	2	100
Okay			~~9,900~~
Total			~~10,000~~

You're in the Sick row. 98 out of 100 sick people test positive. So the probability we want is $\dfrac{98}{100} = 0.98 = 98\%$.

This kind of probability is called **conditional**. It's written with a vertical bar that means "given":

$$P(\text{Pos} \mid \text{Sick}) = \quad \text{"the probability of testing positive,}$$
$$\uparrow \qquad\qquad \text{GIVEN that you're Sick."}$$
$$\text{"given"}$$

Notice the difference:

	Positive	**Negative**	**Total**
Sick	98		100
Okay			✕
Total			✕

$$P(\text{Pos} \mid \text{Sick}) = \frac{98}{100}$$

	Positive	**Negative**	**Total**
Sick	98		
Okay			
Total			10,000

$$P(\text{Pos} \cap \text{Sick}) = \frac{98}{10,000}$$

All that's different is what you divide the 98 by—but that makes all the difference. You can relate the probabilities to each other:

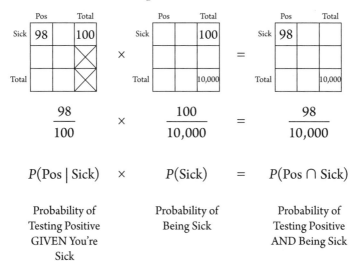

$$\frac{98}{100} \quad \times \quad \frac{100}{10,000} \quad = \quad \frac{98}{10,000}$$

$$P(\text{Pos} \mid \text{Sick}) \quad \times \quad P(\text{Sick}) \quad = \quad P(\text{Pos} \cap \text{Sick})$$

Probability of Testing Positive GIVEN You're Sick   ×   Probability of Being Sick   =   Probability of Testing Positive AND Being Sick

This formula can be rearranged:

$$P(\text{Pos} \mid \text{Sick}) = \frac{P(\text{Pos} \cap \text{Sick})}{P(\text{Sick})}$$

Intersections are the same regardless of order:

$$P(\text{Pos} \cap \text{Sick}) = P(\text{Sick} \cap \text{Pos}) = \frac{98}{10,000}$$

In contrast, conditionals most definitely depend on order:

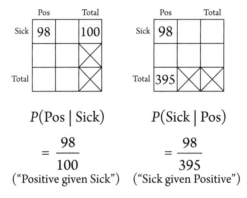

$$P(\text{Pos} \mid \text{Sick})$$
$$= \frac{98}{100}$$
("Positive given Sick")

$$P(\text{Sick} \mid \text{Pos})$$
$$= \frac{98}{395}$$
("Sick given Positive")

In each case, you use the 98 people who are both Sick and Positive, but the denominators are different. Be sure to divide by the correct "given" group, which comes second in the expression. As a shortcut, think of the vertical slash (|) like a diagonal slash (/) meaning "divided by." This is some deep stuff here, worth chewing on.

Again, in class you might see all these numbers as decimals. Switch to whole numbers if you can, but don't let the decimals freak you out.

	Pos	Neg	Total			Pos	Neg	Total
Sick	0.0098	0.0002	0.01		**Sick**	98	2	100
Okay	0.0297	0.9603	0.99	=	**Okay**	297	9,603	9,900
Total	0.0395	0.9605	1.00		**Total**	395	9,605	10,000

Bayes' Rule

The original big question—what's the probability that you're actually sick, given a positive test result—can now be written in probability-speak.

$$P(\text{Pos} \mid \text{Okay}) = 3\% \text{ (false positive rate)}$$

$$P(\text{Neg} \mid \text{Sick}) = 2\% \text{ (false negative rate)}$$

$$P(\text{Sick}) = 1\% \text{ (base rate of illness)}$$

What is $P(\text{Sick} \mid \text{Pos})$?

Bayes' Rule is a complicated formula used to compute the answer. We've chosen to omit this formula, because it's downright sadistic. Good news: you already computed the answer using the grid.

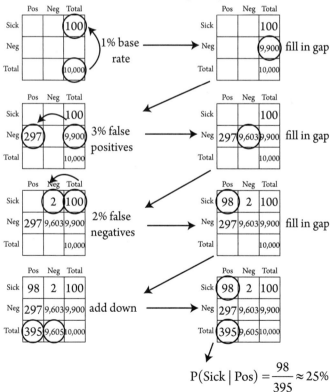

$$P(\text{Sick} \mid \text{Pos}) = \frac{98}{395} \approx 25\%$$

If you can, avoid the Bayes' Rule formula. Either use the grid above or a probability tree described below.

Probability Trees

If you're not a fan of grids, you can represent the situation with a ***probability tree*** instead. As the tree branches out to the right, it subdivides the original group further and further.

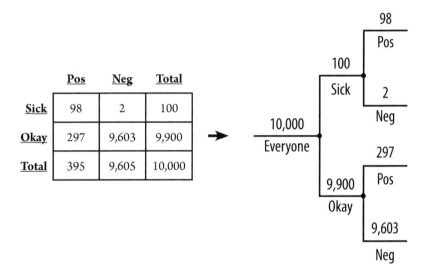

You can imagine starting on the left and moving to the right. At each junction—each dot—you make a choice about which path to take according to the probabilities shown.

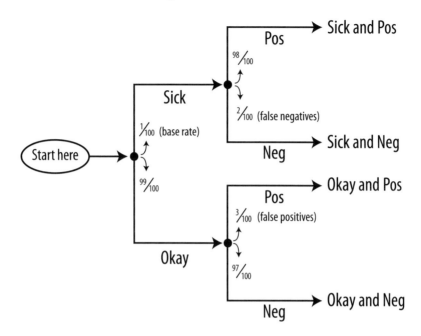

Make sure that the branches at each junction are MECE and that the probabilities at each junction add up to 1 (100%). In comparison to the grid, the big disadvantage of trees is that you only see *one* set of subtotals (e.g., the total number of Sick people = 100 and the total number of Okay people = 9,900). However, you need the subtotals of Positive and Negative test results as well. The key to doing Bayes' Rule with trees is to set up the tree one way, fill in all the numbers, then rearrange to get the other subtotals:

Set-up   Rearranged

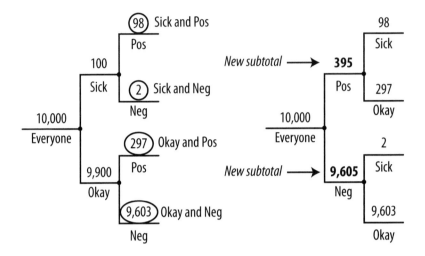

Notice how the four numbers on the ends of the tree (the "leaves") are the same as before, but they've been shuffled to allow the middle tier of the tree to show the positive/negative subtotals (395 and 9,605). The 395 is necessary to figure out $P(\text{Sick} \mid \text{Pos}) = \dfrac{98}{395} \approx 25\%$.

Long story short: you can do Bayes' Rule with a tree, but be ready to draw two of them. The grid is easier overall, but b-school has a thing for trees, so you should become familiar with them.

Independence Day

The last probability topic is **independence** (along with its opposite, **dependence**). The question is:

> Does knowing whether one outcome happened *change your expectations* regarding another outcome?

If so, then the two outcomes are called **dependent**. Careful: this doesn't mean that one outcome literally *depends* on the other. All it means is that knowing about one of them *influences your thinking* about the other one. If you know whether A happened, would you change your bet about whether B happened? If yes, then A and B are dependent. If not, then A and B are *independent*.

A classic case of independence is a coin toss and a roll of a die. Frank secretly flips a coin and rolls a die. Before Frank shows you the coin, he shows you the die: it's a 3. Would you change your bet on the coin? Of course not. That's independence.

In contrast, the medical test is deliberately NOT independent of the disease. If you test positive for the disease, your expectations about truly having the disease rise from the 1% base rate to roughly 25%. $P(\text{Sick})$ and $P(\text{Sick} \mid \text{Pos})$ are not at all the same. That's dependence.

With a coin flip and a roll of the die, you have this grid (filled in with 120 as the smart number of total experiments):

Die

		1	2	3	4	5	6	Total
	Heads	10	10	10	10	10	10	60
Coin	Tails	10	10	10	10	10	10	60
	Total	20	20	20	20	20	20	120

$P(\text{Heads} \mid 3) =$ "probability of flipping Heads, given that you rolled a 3" $= 10/20 = 1/2.$

$P(\text{Heads}) = 60/120 = 1/2.$

Since these two probabilities are the same, the outcome "Heads" and the outcome "3" are independent.

The other test for independence is to see whether the joint probability
—the chance that both outcomes occur—equals the product of each
separate unconditional probability.

$$P(\text{Heads AND 3}) \overset{?}{=} P(\text{Heads}) \cdot P(3)$$

flip heads and roll a 3   flip heads   roll a 3

$$\frac{10}{120} \overset{?}{=} \frac{1}{2} \cdot \frac{1}{6}$$

$$\frac{1}{12} \underset{\text{true}}{\overset{\checkmark}{=}} \frac{1}{2} \cdot \frac{1}{6}$$

Since this is true, Heads and 3 are independent. In contrast, Sick and
Positive are *not* independent (they are dependent), because this equation doesn't hold.

	Pos	Neg	Total
Sick	98	2	100
Okay	297	9,603	9,900
Total	395	9,605	10,000

$$P(\text{Sick AND Pos}) \overset{?}{=} P(\text{Sick}) \cdot P(\text{Pos})$$

$$\frac{98}{10,000} \overset{?}{=} \frac{100}{10,000} \cdot \frac{395}{10,000}$$

$$\frac{98}{10,000} \overset{?}{=} \frac{395}{1,000,000}$$

✗

Not true

Decision Trees

You can represent probabilities with trees:

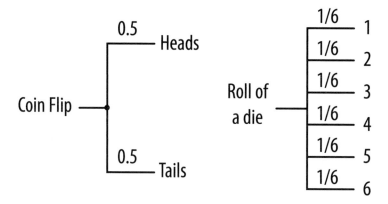

Label each branch with its probability.

You can also represent payoffs on each branch and calculate the expected value of a tree, which would be the average payoff if you played the game a lot of times.

Game: Heads = you win $5. Tails = you lose $3

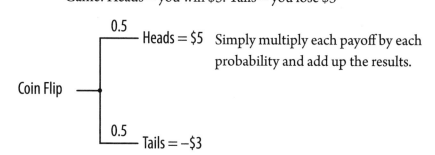

Simply multiply each payoff by each probability and add up the results.

Expected value of a coin flip

$$E(\text{flip}) = \left(\begin{array}{c} \text{Chance} \\ \text{of Heads} \end{array}\right)\left(\begin{array}{c} \text{Payoff} \\ \text{of Heads} \end{array}\right) + \left(\begin{array}{c} \text{Chance} \\ \text{of Tails} \end{array}\right)\left(\begin{array}{c} \text{Payoff} \\ \text{of Tails} \end{array}\right)$$

$$= (0.5)(\$5) + (0.5)(-\$3)$$

$$= \$2.50 - \$1.50$$

$$= \boxed{\$1.00}$$

This $1 means that if you did 100 coin flips, you'd expect to earn $100 total, or an average of $1 per flip. Of course, on no actual flip can you earn precisely $1, but that's what you'd expect as a long-run average, so if your pockets were deep enough to handle occasional runs of $3 losses, you'd want to play this game over and over. Like a casino, you'd come out ahead in the end.

Finally, you can represent choices or **decisions** with trees. For instance, you might have a choice between the coin flip game and receiving $0.90 for sure. To distinguish choices from random events, you use different symbols—a box for choice and a circle for a random event.

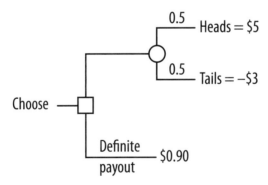

The expected value of the coin flip is $1.00, so if you can stand the risk of losing $3 or if you can play the game over and over (taking the risk of losses along the way)—you'd probably choose coin flip. But if the numbers get much larger, armchair psychology says that you'll become more **risk-averse** and will likely choose the certain payout.

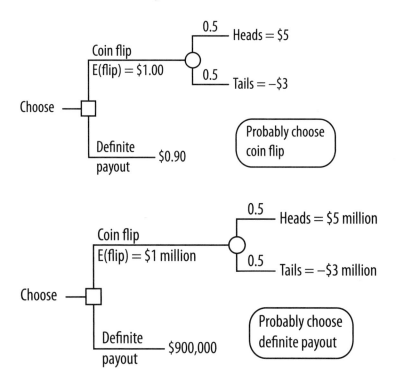

Distributions

Distributions are essentially histograms.

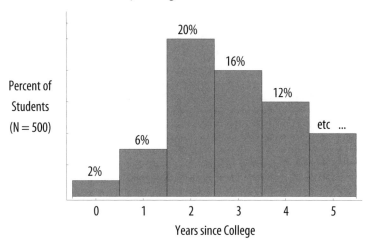

You use percents in order to show probabilities. The previous distribution is equivalent to this list:

$$P(0 \text{ years}) = 2\% = 0.02$$

$$P(1 \text{ year}) = 6\% = 0.06$$

$$P(2 \text{ years}) = 20\% = 0.20$$

The distribution reflects the actual frequency of "years since college" you observe in your b-school class.

Three "classic" distributions appear all the time in statistics. These don't correspond exactly to reality, but they're used all the time to simulate the world, like three classic soap operas.

To help you keep the distributions straight, we've created three simple stories or scenarios, one for each distribution. Memorize these, and you'll be a hop, skip, and a jump ahead.

	Distribution	**Scenario**	**Typical Question**
1)	*Binomial*	A bunch of coin flips	How likely am I to get exactly 6 heads in 10 flips?
2)	*Poisson* ("pwah-son")	Customers coming into a store	How likely is it that exactly 7 customers come in this hour?
3)	*Normal*	Weights in a population	How likely is it that a random person weighs between 100 pounds and 130 pounds?

The Binomial Distribution

This scenario involves a bunch of coin flips.

- You flip a coin a certain number of times. The number of flips is n. Each flip is independent of every other flip.

- Each flip has two possible outcomes

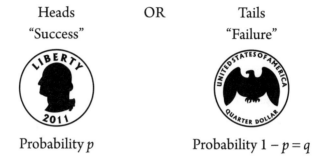

Heads	OR	Tails
"Success"		"Failure"
Probability p		Probability $1 - p = q$

Lowercase p is always used for the probability of success. The probability of failure is $q = 1 - p$.

- The coin doesn't have to be fair, although it could be.

$$P(\text{Heads}) = p = 0.50 \qquad \text{Fair coin}$$

$$P(\text{Heads}) = p = 0.75 \qquad \text{Heads more probable}$$

$$P(\text{Heads}) = p = 0.30 \qquad \text{Tails more probable}$$

- Whatever p is, it stays the same for all flips. Use the same coin throughout.

- The binomial distribution tells you the probability of any particular total number of Heads.

Say you flip a weighted coin 4 times. The coin is weighted so that on any given flip, the probability of Heads is 70%. The binomial distribution fills in the blanks below:

Chance of	4 Heads	in 4 flips	$= P(x=4)$	= _____
"	3 Heads	in 4 flips	$= P(x=3)$	= _____
"	2 Heads	in 4 flips	$= P(x=2)$	= _____
"	1 Heads	in 4 flips	$= P(x=1)$	= _____
"	0 Heads	in 4 flips	$= P(x=0)$	= _____

You know enough from the GMAT or GRE to fill in the first blank. Since each flip is independent, and $P(\text{Heads}) = 0.70 = 70\%$, then the probability of 4 Heads in a row is this:

4 Heads = Heads Heads Heads Heads

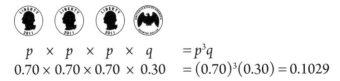

$$p \times p \times p \times p \qquad = p^4$$
$$0.70 \times 0.70 \times 0.70 \times 0.70 \quad = (0.70)^4 = 0.2401 \approx 24\%$$

For 3 Heads, the situation is a little different. First of all, you've got 1 Tails mixed in, since you've got 4 flips and no other options besides Heads and Tails.

3 Heads = Heads Heads Heads Tails

$$p \times p \times p \times q \qquad = p^3 q$$
$$0.70 \times 0.70 \times 0.70 \times 0.30 \quad = (0.70)^3(0.30) = 0.1029$$

The other complication is that there's more than one sequence of flips that gives you exactly 3 Heads and 1 Tails. It turns out there are 4 such sequences:

1)	H	H	H	T
2)	H	H	T	H
3)	H	T	H	H
4)	T	H	H	H

} 4 different ways

If you remember the combinations formula from the GMAT or GRE, here it is again, rearing its ugly head ...

$$\frac{\text{Flips!}}{\text{Heads! Tails!}} = \frac{4!}{3! \; 1!} = 4 \text{ different ways}$$

Those exclamation points are **factorials**. 4-factorial (written as "4!") is $4 \times 3 \times 2 \times 1 = 24$. 3-factorial is $3 \times 2 \times 1 = 6$. All in, the probability of 3 Heads (and 1 Tails) is this:

Probability of 1 arrangement	$\times$	Number of arrangements	$=$	$P(3 \text{ Heads})$
H H H T		$\dfrac{\text{Flips!}}{\text{Heads! Tails!}}$		
$p \cdot p \cdot p \cdot q$	$\times$	$\dfrac{4!}{3! \; 1!}$	$=$	$4p^3 q$
$(0.70)(0.70)(0.70)(0.30)$	$\times$	4	$=$	0.4116 $\approx 41\% \text{ chance}$

For 2 heads (and 2 tails), the same calculation works out this way:

Probability of 1 arrangement	$\times$	Number of arrangements	$=$	$P(2 \text{ heads})$
H H T T		$\dfrac{\text{Flips!}}{\text{Heads! Tails!}}$		
$p \cdot p \cdot q \cdot q$	$\times$	$\dfrac{4!}{2! \; 2!}$	$=$	$6p^2 q^2$
$(0.70)(0.70)(0.30)(0.30)$	$\times$	6	$=$	0.2646 $\approx 26\% \text{ chance}$

1 heads and 3 tails:

Probability of 1 arrangement	$\times$	Number of arrangements	=	$P(1 \text{ heads})$
H T T T		$\dfrac{\text{Flips!}}{\text{Heads! Tails!}}$		
$p \cdot q \cdot q \cdot q$	$\times$	$\dfrac{4!}{1! \; 3!}$	=	$4pq^3$
$(0.70)(0.30)(0.30)(0.30)$	$\times$	4	=	0.0756 $\approx 7.6\%$ chance

0 heads and 4 tails:

Probability of 1 arrangement	$\times$	Number of arrangements	=	$P(0 \text{ heads})$
T T T T		$\dfrac{\text{Flips!}}{\text{Heads! Tails!}}$		
$q \cdot q \cdot q \cdot q$	$\times$	$\dfrac{4!}{0! \; 4!}$	=	$4pq^3$
$(0.30)(0.30)(0.30)(0.30)$	$\times$	1	=	0.0081 $\approx 0.8\%$ chance

By the way, 0-factorial, or 0!, equals 1.

The graph of all these outcomes looks like this:

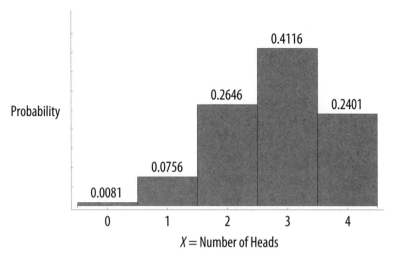

Binomial distribution for 4 flips $(n = 4)$
with 70% chance of heads $(p = 0.70)$

The binomial distribution depends on the total number of flips ($n = 4$ in this case) and the weighting of the coin ($p = 0.70$ in this case). For other values of n and p, you'll get a different set of probabilities.

The general formula for the binomial distribution with a given n and p (and with $q = 1 - p$) is:

$$P(x = \text{number of Heads}) = \frac{n!}{x!(n-x)!} p^x q^{n-x}$$

Compare to the earlier case.

$$
\begin{array}{l}
n = 4 \\
p = 0.70 \\
q = 0.30
\end{array}
\left\{
\begin{array}{|c|c|c|c|c|}
\hline
P(x = 4) & = & 1 & p^4 & = 0.2401 \\
\hline
P(x = 3) & = & 4 & p^3 q & = 0.4116 \\
\hline
P(x = 2) & = & 6 & p^2 q^2 & = 0.2646 \\
\hline
P(x = 1) & = & 4 & p q^3 & = 0.0756 \\
\hline
P(x = 0) & = & 1 & q^4 & = 0.0081 \\
\hline
\end{array}
\right.
$$

The mean, variance, and standard deviation of the binomial distribution have simple formulas.

Mean $\mu = np$

$\mu = (4)(0.70) = 2.8 = $ mean number of Heads

This formula should make sense. If $n = 100$ flips and $p = 0.60$ (60% chance of Heads), then you'd expect 60 Heads, on average, in those 100 flips.

$$np = \mu$$

$$(100)(0.60) = 60 \text{ Heads}$$

Variance $\sigma^2 = npq = np(1-p)$

$$\sigma^2 = \longleftarrow (4)(0.70)(0.30) = 0.84$$

This formula just "is." Sorry.

Standard Deviation $\sigma = \sqrt{\sigma^2} = \sqrt{npq} = \sqrt{np(1-p)}$

$$\sigma = \sqrt{0.84} \approx 0.92$$

If p is exactly 0.5, the binomial distribution is symmetrically hump-shaped:

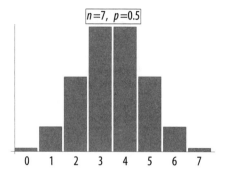

The closer p is to 1 or to 0, the more skewed the distribution from one end to the other.

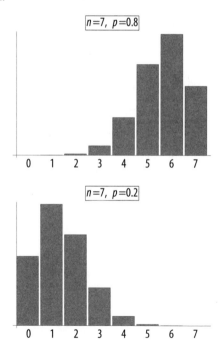

Since you'll encounter problems that aren't literal coin flips, you will need to draw analogies. To use the binomial distribution, you have to be able to map the given problem to *a fixed number of coin flips*. Here's an example. How many people in your company have January birthdays?

Fixed number n	Number of flips	Number of people in your company
Independent events	Flips	Birthdays
Success	Heads	Birthday in January
Probability p of success	$p = P(\text{Heads})$	$p = P(\text{Birthday in Jan.})$ $\approx 1/12$
Constant p?	p stays same for all flips	p stays same for all people
Failure	Tails	Birthday in another month
Probability q of failure	$q = 1 - p = P(\text{Tails})$	$q = P(\text{Birthday in another month})$ $\approx 11/12$
Random variable X	How many heads?	How many people with Jan. birthdays?

Do this kind of clear mapping to the coin flips scenario, and you won't go wrong. If the mapping fails, the situation doesn't fit. For instance, if you don't have a fixed number of trials (coin flips), then you can't use the binomial distribution.

The Poisson Distribution

The scenario is customers coming into a store. On average, they arrive at some set rate (say, 3 per hour—this store isn't doing so hot). But the customers also arrive totally independently of each other, at random, so sometimes you get more than 3 an hour and other times less:

Long run average: 3 customers per hour

9am   10am   11am   12pm   1pm   2pm   3pm

These customer arrivals can then be modeled as a so-called **Poisson process**, and the number of customers you actually do get in any given hour obeys the **Poisson distribution**.

The formula for this distribution is a little ugly. First, you need to know that the letter **e** in math is a special number around 2.72 that's almost as important as π. Go math! You might have known and loved e way back when as the base of the natural logarithm (which is not an a cappella algebra group). This number e can be raised to a power; you can do this with the (e^x) button on your calculator or EXP() function in Excel. It's better than bad; it's good.

If your average arrival rate is 3 customers per hour, then the chance that x customers actually arrive in a particular hour is given by $P(x) = \dfrac{e^{-3} \cdot 3^x}{x!}$.

Let's see how that works. The chance that you get exactly *zero* customers in that hour is:

$$P(x=0) = \frac{e^{-3} \cdot 3^0}{0!} = \frac{e^{-3} \cdot 1}{1} \approx 0.0498$$

↑
Particular number
of customers this
hour   Chance of exactly zero customers $\approx$ 4.98%

Check out the probabilities for other particular numbers of customers arriving in that hour. Think about the shape of the distribution.

$$P(x=1) = \frac{e^{-3} \cdot 3^1}{1!} = \frac{e^{-3} \cdot 3}{1} \approx 0.1494$$

Chance of exactly 1 customer arriving $\approx$ 14.94%

$$P(x=2) = \frac{e^{-3} \cdot 3^2}{2!} = \frac{e^{-3} \cdot 9}{2} \approx 0.2240$$

Chance of exactly 2 customers arriving $\approx$ 22.40%

$$P(x=3) = \frac{e^{-3} \cdot 3^3}{3!} = \frac{e^{-3} \cdot 27}{6} \approx 0.2240 \text{ again}$$

Chance of exactly 3 customers arriving $\approx$ 22.40%

$$P(x=4) = \frac{e^{-3} \cdot 3^4}{4!} = \frac{e^{-3} \cdot 81}{24} \approx 0.1680$$

Chance of exactly 4 customers arriving $\approx$ 16.80%

$$P(x=5) = \frac{e^{-3} \cdot 3^5}{5!} = \frac{e^{-3} \cdot 243}{120} \approx 0.1008$$

Chance of exactly 5 customers arriving $\approx$ 10.08%

$$P(x=6) = \frac{e^{-3} \cdot 3^6}{6!} = \frac{e^{-3} \cdot 729}{720} \approx 0.0504$$

Chance of exactly 6 customers arriving $\approx$ 5.04%

$$P(x=7) = \frac{e^{-3} \cdot 3^7}{7!} = \frac{e^{-3} \cdot 2,187}{5,040} \approx 0.0216$$

Chance of exactly 7 customers arriving $\approx$ 2.16%

This distribution technically goes on forever, but the values get tinier and tinier. In other words, it's not *impossible* for 20 customers to show up in a single hour—it's just very, very unlikely (about 7 chances in 100 billion).

The graph looks like this:

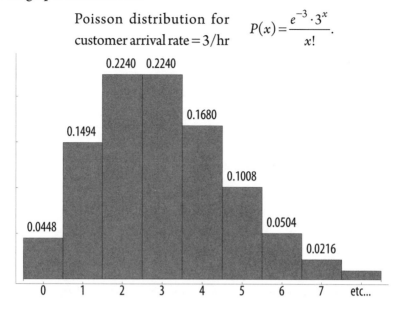

Poisson distribution for customer arrival rate = 3/hr

$$P(x) = \frac{e^{-3} \cdot 3^x}{x!}.$$

The average number of customers is 3, as you'd expect—that was specified at the beginning. Magically, the variance also turns out to be 3, so the standard deviation is $\sqrt{3}$. For Poisson distributions, the mean always equals the variance. How about that?

Mean $\mu = 3$ customers

Variance $\sigma^2 = 3$

Standard deviation $\sigma = \sqrt{3} \approx 1.7$ customers

In general, the arrival rate is given the Greek letter *lambda*, which looks like λ. This is the most general formula:

Poisson distribution with a customer arrival rate $= \lambda$ per hour

$$P(x) = \frac{e^{-\lambda} \cdot \lambda^x}{x!}$$

Mean $\mu = \lambda$

Variance $\sigma^2 = \lambda$

Standard Deviation $= \sqrt{\lambda}$

The Poisson distribution can substitute for the binomial distribution when n is large (say, over 50) and p is very small (say, less than 0.1). This can be useful because the binomial gets computationally annoying as n gets larger and larger.

The big reason they teach you the Poisson distribution in business school is that lots of things a manager might want to keep track of are Poisson processes, or approximately so:

- Customers arriving at a store

- Jobs arriving at a computer server

- Errors occurring on an assembly line

- The slamming of porta-potty doors, when your RV is parked near a whole bank of them and you are camping out for Duke basketball tickets with a few thousand other grad students.

- You get the idea.

Continuous vs. Discrete

Pardon the interruption—a digression is necessary before we get to the third distribution (the so-called normal distribution). Up to now, the questions have all been about **discrete random variables**—whole number outcomes.

- How many heads do I get in 10 coin flips, with $p = 0.6$ (60% chance of heads on each flip)?
- How many customers arrive this hour, if the average arrival rate is 3 customers per hour?

The possible answers are 0, 1, 2, 3, etc.—only whole numbers.

The distributions so far have told you how likely each of those outcomes is. Each outcome is discrete, so you draw histograms. Each discrete value on the x-axis has its own hash mark and column of probability.

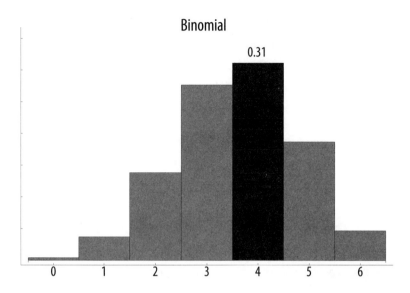

$$P(x = 4) = 0.31$$

The probability that $x = 4$ is 31%.

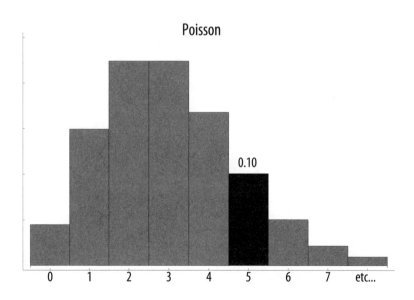

$$P(x = 5) = 0.10$$

The probability that $x = 5$ is 10%.

Things change when there are continuous outcomes. What if you want to measure a weight that could take on *any* value, including ones with decimals, like 103.732 pounds? That kind of outcome is called a ***continuous random variable***—it can be any real number in some range. You assume you can measure the weight with infinite precision.

In this case, you no longer talk about the probability of *some particular number* as an outcome. Why? Because it's too improbable that someone's weight is exactly equal to some random, infinitely long decimal.

exact

Probability that my brother-in-law weighs *exactly* 216.271381545992... (don't stop!) pounds is zero.

What you do instead is talk about a ***range*** of weights. You can sensibly measure the probability of a weight being in a range.

Probability that my brother-in-law weighs **between** 200 and 250 pounds is 0.36 (36%).

To represent this sort of probability, you use something *similar to* a histogram—a ***continuous probability distribution.***

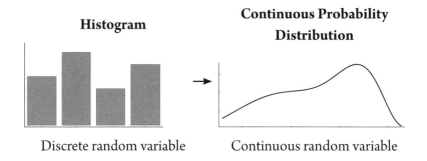

Histogram	Continuous Probability Distribution
Discrete random variable	Continuous random variable

The mathematical difference is in the way you indicate a probability. For a discrete random variable, the *height* of the column is the probability itself:

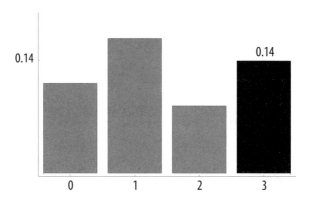

$$P(x = 3) = 0.14.$$
The probability that x is 3 is 14%.

On a continuous probability distribution, the *area under the curve* and between two end points is the probability.

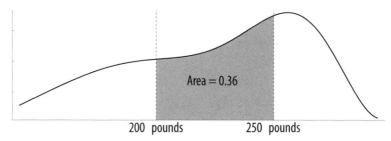

$$P(200 < x < 250) = 0.36.$$
The probability that the weight is between 200 and 250 pounds is 36%.

The total area under any continuous distribution is 1 (100%), since the maximum probability is always 1 (nothing can be more than 100% likely to occur).

The Normal Distribution

The most important distribution in all of statistics is the ***normal distribution.*** This is the continuous distribution known as the ***bell curve***:

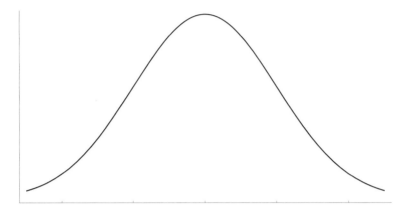

The curve never actually touches the *x*-axis, but it gets very close as it goes on forever in both directions.

Fortunately, you can ignore the function that defines this curve because you never care about the actual *height* of the curve. You only care about the *area under the curve*, or under parts of the curve. And to find that area, you have to use a pre-printed table of values or a special Excel function, so the formula for the shape would do you no good anyway.

Every normal distribution has essentially the same shape: a central hump with two long, symmetrical tails on either side.

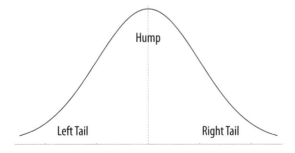

The peak of the hump is centered over the mean. So if some population of people has a mean weight of 150 pounds, and that weight is "normally distributed," then the distribution looks like this:

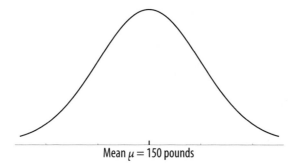

Mean $\mu = 150$ pounds

The curve is completely symmetrical around the mean.

The other thing you have to specify about a normal distribution is how spread out it is.

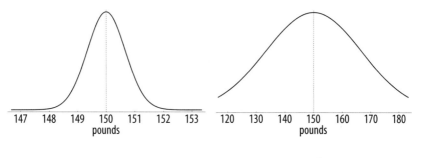

Very narrow   Broader

Small standard deviation   Bigger standard deviation

The standard deviation σ provides a great yardstick for these normal curves. The area under the curve from the mean to a point exactly one standard deviation away from the mean is always 0.3413 (~34%).

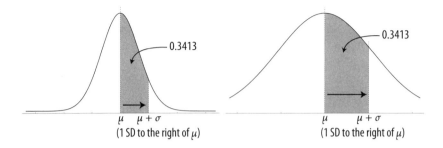

The area is the same, no matter how skinny or wide the normal curve is (how big the standard deviation is in units). In probability terms, 34% of a normally distributed population will lie between the mean and one standard deviation above the mean.

For instance, if the mean $\mu = 150$ pounds and the standard deviation $\sigma = 1$ pound, then 34.13% of the population weighs between 150 and 151 pounds:

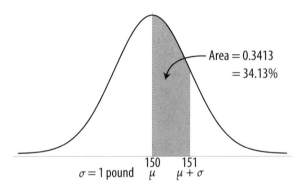

If the standard deviation σ is instead 12 pounds, then 34.13% of the population weighs between 150 and 162 pounds:

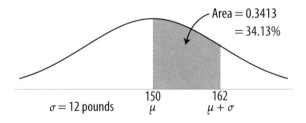

For the normal distribution, the following guidelines are always true. ~68% of the population is within 1 standard deviation of the mean.

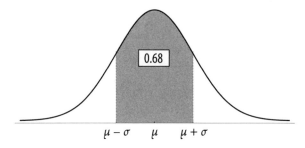

~95% of the population is within 2 standard deviations of the mean.

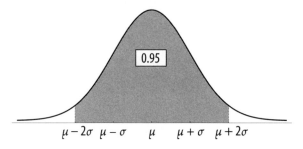

~99.7% of the population is within 3 standard deviations of the mean.

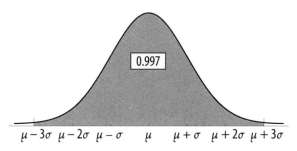

Remember, the total area under the whole curve from $-\infty$ to $+\infty$ is exactly 1, so you approach 100% but never get there.

Ultimately, what you always want to do is express the range you care about in terms of standard deviations from the mean. Imagine the following Socratic dialogue:

Socrates:	"What percent of the population weighs between 144 and 155 pounds, if the weight is normally distributed?"
You:	"What's the mean? What's the standard deviation?"
Socrates:	"The mean μ is 150 pounds, and the standard deviation is 2 pounds."
You:	"Okay. The curve is centered on 150 pounds, and the yardstick is 2 pounds."

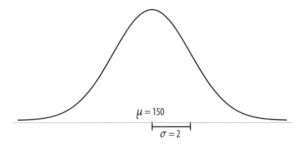

$\mu = 150$

$\sigma = 2$

You again:	"All right. How many yardsticks away from 150 are each of the endpoints of the range I care about?"

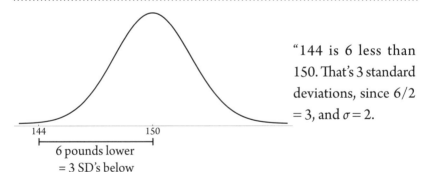

144   150

6 pounds lower
= 3 SD's below

"144 is 6 less than 150. That's 3 standard deviations, since 6/2 = 3, and $\sigma = 2$.

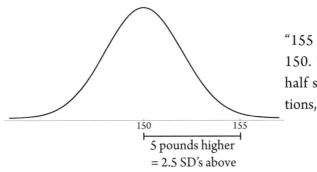

"155 is 5 more than 150. That's 2 and a half standard deviations, since $5/2 = 2.5$.

5 pounds higher
$= 2.5$ SD's above

These "counts of standard deviations" are called **Z-scores**.

Low end: 144 pounds $= 3$ SD's below the mean $\longrightarrow Z = -3$

High end: 155 pounds $= 2.5$ SD's above the mean $\longrightarrow Z = +2.5$

The Z-score of the mean μ itself is 0 (since it's no distance away from itself), and the Z-score of $\mu + \sigma$ is 1 (that's 1 SD above the mean). In a sense, what you're doing is changing over to "Z-score land," a happy place that is home to the **standard normal curve**, where the Z mean is always zero and the Z standard deviation is always one. Computing a Z-score is called **standardizing**.

Original Curve:

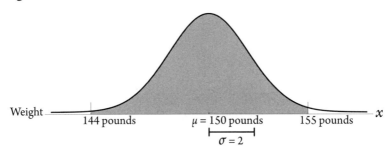

Standard Normal:

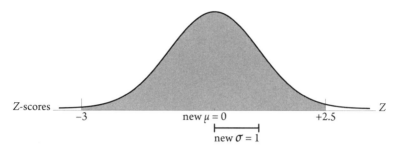

Remember, a Z-score just tells you how many standard deviations away from the mean some number is. Here's the formula:

Endpoint	−	Mean	=	Z-score	.	SD
x	−	μ	=	Z	.	σ

Rearranging, you get this:

$$\frac{x - \mu}{\sigma} = Z$$

Now what? You have this:

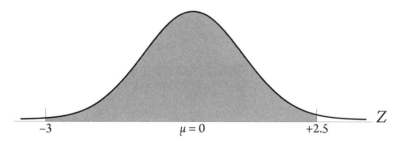

Now you look up the area in the back of your textbook, where you'll find a fancy-dancy table that lays out hundreds of Z-scores and areas. Or you can compute the area in Excel.

If you use a table, it's a two-step process because of the way the tables are always laid out—they only do half of the curve.

Step 1: Right half

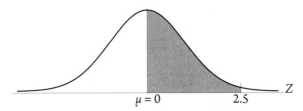

You want the area under the curve between $Z = 0$ and $Z = 2.5$. Many tables go to the hundredth's value, so 2.50 is the number you look up.

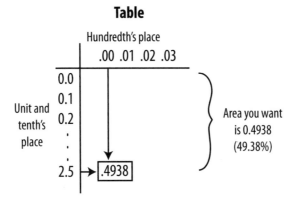

Step 2: Left half

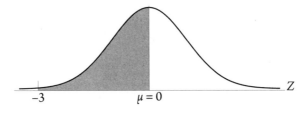

You want the area under the curve between $Z = -3$ and $Z = 0$. You don't need another table for negative values—the area is the same to the left and to the right of the mean. Again, look up the endpoint to the hundredth's place (3.00).

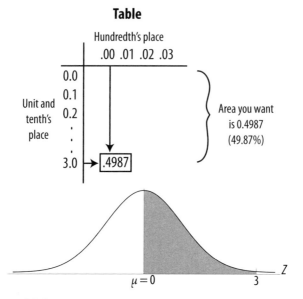

Finally, you add the two areas up.

Area between	=	Area between	+	Area between
$Z = -3$ and		$Z = 0$ and		$Z = -3$ and
$Z = 2.5$		$Z = 2.5$		$Z = 0$
				(same as area
				between 0 and 3)
	=	0.4938	+	0.4987
	=	0.9925 (99.25%)		

> You: "99.25% of the population weighs between 144 and 155 pounds, if the weight is normally distributed with a mean of 150 pounds and a standard deviation of 2 pounds."

Whew! Socrates had better not kill himself now.

With Excel, it's still two steps, but the formulas work a little differently than the table does. The Excel function NORMSDIST gives you the **cumulative** area up to some Z-score, all the way from minus infinity $(-\infty)$ on the far left. For example, NORMSDIST(1.2) computes the following area as 0.8849:

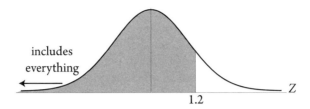

Say you want to find the area between $Z = -0.3$ and $Z = 1.2$. Compute the NORMSDIST value for the upper end of the range (1.2), then subtract the NORMSDIST value for the lower end of the range (-0.3). Don't flip the curve, as you would when working with a table. Keep the Z-scores negative.

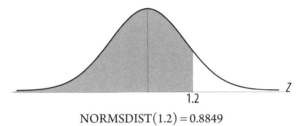

NORMSDIST$(1.2) = 0.8849$

MINUS

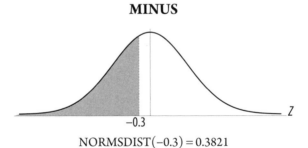

NORMSDIST$(-0.3) = 0.3821$

EQUALS

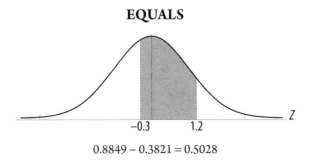

$0.8849 - 0.3821 = 0.5028$

You can use the normal distribution to approximate the binomial distribution if n is large and p is near 0.5. Again, the binomial distribution is a pain to calculate for large n (the factorials in the formula get ginormous), so the normal can substitute when p is close to ½.

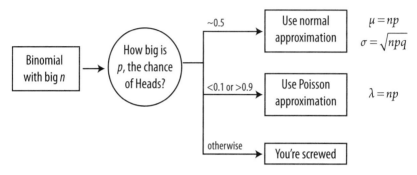

Sampling & Hypothesis Testing

Earlier we made a big deal out of the difference between a whole population and a sample taken from that population. That's because you usually can't survey the whole population you're interested in (all potential consumers, all eligible voters, etc.), so you have to make do with a smaller sample and extrapolate to the population.

		Sample $(n = 50)$		Population $(N = \text{millions})$
Mean	$\bar{x}$	gives you a guess at	μ	(unknown)
Standard Deviation	s	gives you a guess at	σ	(unknown)

Your single best guess at the population mean μ is the sample mean $\bar{x}$, called a **point estimator** (a single best guess) for μ.

Consider the "years since college" scenario again, with $N = 500$ people in your class. You take a **random sample** of 25 classmates $(n = 25)$, in which you pick the 25 classmates totally at random. Everyone has to have an equal chance of being picked. In the real world, truly random samples are difficult to generate, but they're crucial for accurate results—if the sample isn't random, all bets are off. This is one reason why pharmaceutical drug trials are extremely costly to run.

If the true (but unknown) population mean μ is 3.0 years, then the expected value of the sample mean will be—surprise!—3.0 years as well. That is, you'd properly expect your sample mean to be 3.0 years.

$$E(\bar{x}) \qquad = \qquad \mu$$

Expected value of   Population
sample mean   mean

Imagine you did 100 different experiments and took 100 different random samples, each one with 25 people. Measure the sample mean $\bar{x}$ for each of these samples.

Sample 1	$\bar{x} = 3.2$	Average should be 3.0,
Sample 2	$\bar{x} = 2.7$	the real mean of the
Sample 3	$\bar{x} = 2.9$	population.
...	$\bar{x}$...	
Sample 100	$\bar{x} = 3.4$	$\mu_{\bar{x}} = \mu_{pop}$

How spread out would those 100 sample means be? That is, what would their standard deviation be? The answer depends on two factors.

1) The *standard deviation of the population* you're taking the samples from. This is the raw source of any spread in the sample means.

If the population contains widely varying data, then the samples extracted from that population will have widely varying means.

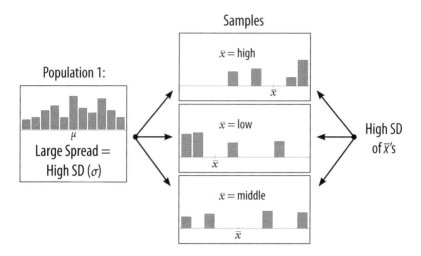

On the other hand, if the population numbers are all packed in tightly, then you simply can't generate samples very far apart from each other, so the sample means will have a low standard deviation.

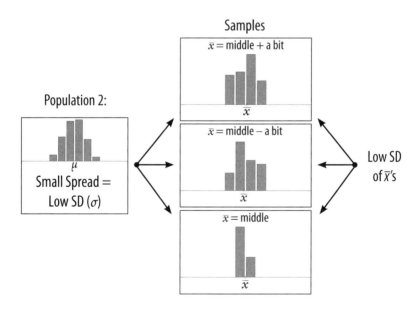

2) *The value of* n *for each sample*—how big each sample is. The larger *n* is, the tighter the $\bar{x}$'s will bunch around the population mean. That's because the more data you have *in each sample*, the more likely you are to draw from all parts of the population. Each additional data point makes a sample more representative of the population.

If you take small samples, say with $n = 7$, then there's a good chance that within any given group of 7 points, you pick a bunch from one end or the other of the population, causing the mean to be skewed. Thus the sample means will be highly variable.

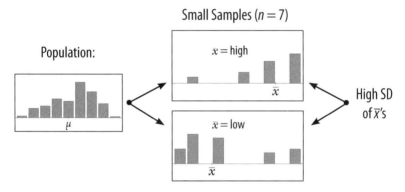

In contrast, if you take large samples, say with $n = 50$, then each sample is more likely to represent the whole population and therefore to have a mean close to the true population mean. The sample means will be bunched tightly together.

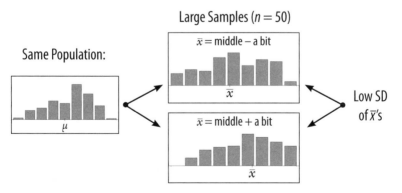

The standard deviation of the sample means is determined by the SD of the population and the size of the sample. The precise mathematical relationship is:

$$\sigma_{\text{sample means}} = \frac{\sigma_{\text{population}}}{\sqrt{n}}$$

$$\sigma_{\overline{x}} = \frac{\sigma_{\text{pop}}}{\sqrt{n}}$$

Remember that $\sigma_{\text{sample means}}$ is *not* the standard deviation within any one sample. Rather, you grab a whole bunch of samples. You calculate the sample mean $(\overline{x})$ of each sample. The $\sigma_{\text{sample means}}$ is the standard deviation of all those means.

Since usually you don't know σ_{pop}, you approximate it with s, the standard deviation of a single sample. In reality, you probably only took one sample. Why waste your time with multiple small samples when you can combine them into one large sample, which will be more useful anyway? Approximating σ_{pop} with s is fine, so long as n is large enough (> 25 or so). The definition of "large enough," vague as it may seem, doesn't depend on the size of the original population. A sample of 25 data points works for a population of 500 or of 5 billion. (What makes the second case hard is making sure that the 25 points are truly randomly chosen out of all 5 billion possibilities.)

The **Central Limit Theorem** goes further. The **CLT** says that these sample means are distributed in an approximately *normal* way (meaning the normal distribution), no matter what the underlying population is like, as long as n is big enough (again, > 25 or so).

Say you have a weirdly distributed population. Take a bunch of random good-sized samples from that population, and plot all the sample means. Magically, that plot will look like a normal distribution. This is why it's so "normal."

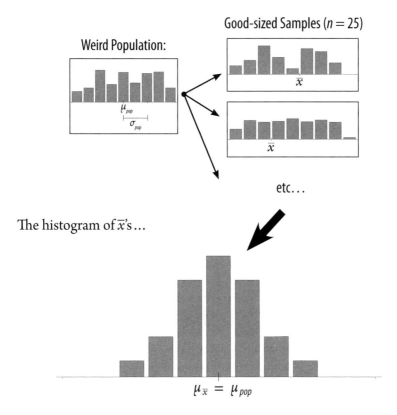

The histogram of $\bar{x}$'s …

$$\mu_{\bar{x}} = \mu_{pop}$$

… fits a normal distribution.

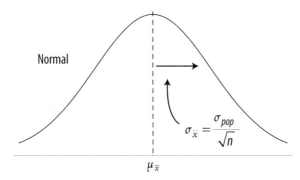

Why does all this matter?

Because it lets you take just one good-sized random sample and do two things:

1) Estimate the population mean.

Sample mean $\bar{x} = 3.2$ years ⟶ You: "I think the mean μ for the whole class is 3.2 years"

2) Give a reasonable **confidence interval** for that point estimate. A confidence interval is exactly what it sounds like—it is a range of values that you have a certain degree of confidence in.

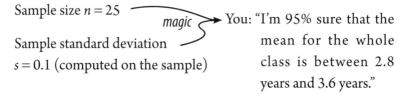

Sample size $n = 25$

magic

Sample standard deviation $s = 0.1$ (computed on the sample)

You: "I'm 95% sure that the mean for the whole class is between 2.8 years and 3.6 years."

We'll show you how to do this magic—hang tight.

The mean of your particular random sample lives in a normal distribution: the distribution of $\bar{x}$'s (the sample means).

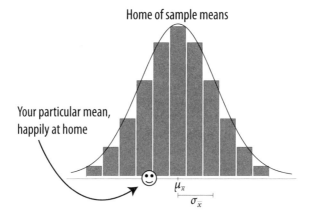

Home of sample means

Your particular mean, happily at home

$\mu_{\bar{x}}$

$\sigma_{\bar{x}}$

The mean of all the $\bar{x}$'s is the population mean, and the standard deviation of all the $\bar{x}$'s (which is also known as the **standard error**, or **SE**, so that you don't confuse it with the population standard deviation) is given by that formula from earlier:

$$\sigma_{\bar{x}} = \text{SE} = \frac{\sigma_{\text{pop}}}{\sqrt{n}}$$

All the nice properties of the normal distribution can be applied here.

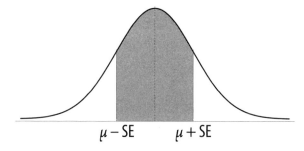

~68% of sample means will be within 1 standard error of the population mean $(-1 \leq Z \leq 1)$.

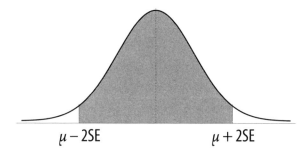

~95% of sample means will be within 2 standard errors of the population mean $(-2 \leq Z \leq 2)$.

You can flip around this thinking and say this:

- If you just know a single sample mean, 95% of the time, the population mean will be within 2 standard errors of it.

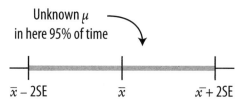

All you have to do is compute the standard error, then we can set up the confidence interval.

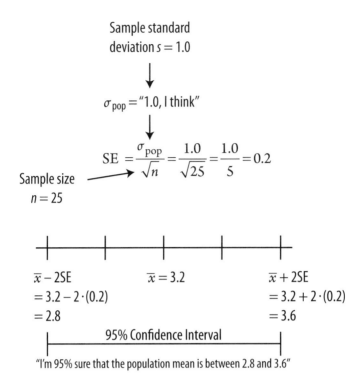

Sample standard
deviation $s = 1.0$

$\downarrow$

$\sigma_{pop} = $ "1.0, I think"

$\downarrow$

$$SE = \frac{\sigma_{pop}}{\sqrt{n}} = \frac{1.0}{\sqrt{25}} = \frac{1.0}{5} = 0.2$$

Sample size
$n = 25$

$\bar{x} - 2SE$	$\bar{x} = 3.2$	$\bar{x} + 2SE$
$= 3.2 - 2 \cdot (0.2)$		$= 3.2 + 2 \cdot (0.2)$
$= 2.8$		$= 3.6$

95% Confidence Interval

"I'm 95% sure that the population mean is between 2.8 and 3.6"

By the way, 1.96 is often used instead of 2 for the Z-score corresponding to a 95%-confidence level, since 1.96 is a little more accurate.

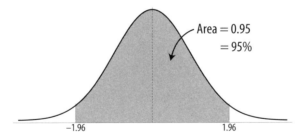

Area $= 0.95$
$= 95\%$

-1.96　　　1.96

If you want a higher level of confidence, you need a higher Z-score (more "standard errors" away from the mean), which means a wider interval. For instance, a range of ±3 for Z encloses 99.7% of the area under a normal curve, so ±3 SE's gives you a 99.7% confidence interval.

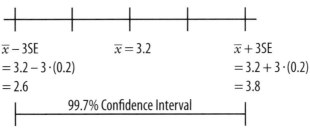

$\bar{x} - 3SE$ $\bar{x} = 3.2$ $\bar{x} + 3SE$
$= 3.2 - 3 \cdot (0.2)$ $= 3.2 + 3 \cdot (0.2)$
$= 2.6$ $= 3.8$

99.7% Confidence Interval

"I'm 99.7% sure that the population mean is between 2.6 and 3.8"

Small Sample

If n is small and you don't know the population σ (which you almost never do), you're up a creek—unless you know or have reason to assume that the underlying population is normally distributed. If so, the sample means for small samples follow something called a **t *distribution*,** which is a lot like the normal distribution, except it's got bigger, fatter tails. The t distribution you use depends on the exact sample size, too—the smaller n is, the flatter and more spread out t is.

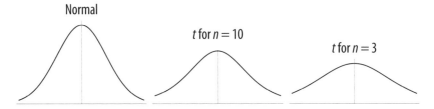

You look up and use t scores the same way you use Z scores—to find a confidence interval for your estimate of the population mean.

Hypothesis Testing

The 95% confidence interval in the earlier example was 2.8–3.6, meaning that you're 95% sure that the real population mean is somewhere between 2.8 and 3.6.

If you had the prior hypothesis that the population mean was 2.2, then you could **reject** that hypothesis with 95% certainty. The prior hypothesis, a kind of default position, is known as the **null hypothesis** or H_0. You typically want to reject this uninteresting hypothesis.

$$H_0 : \mu = 2.2$$

null hypothesis

"I reject thee with 95% certainty, because my 95%-confidence interval does not include thee. I am 95% sure that μ is between 2.8 and 3.6."

You might not be able to reject a different null hypothesis, though.

$$H_0 : \mu = 3.0$$

another null
hypothesis

"I would like to reject thee, since my $\bar{x} = 3.2$; however, since my 95%-confidence interval includes thee, I cannot be sure enough that you are *not* true. Drat!"

Notice that you are not *accepting* the null hypothesis that $\mu = 3.0$—you are "***failing to reject***" the null hypothesis. "Failing to reject" is like when you reluctantly agree to a second date with a none-too-promising prospect, but you go along with it because you have nothing better to do.

There is also an **alternative hypothesis**, H_a, which is what you wish to support instead of the null. Say H_0 proposes that $\mu = 3.0$. Then H_a could simply be that μ *doesn't equal* 3.0. If that's the case, you need a **two-tailed test**, which allows you to reject the null if the result is *either* a lot larger than 3.0 *or* a lot smaller than 3.0.

In contrast, you have a **one-tailed test** if your H_a proposes only that μ is *greater than* 3.0. For some reason, you won't be able to reject the null if

μ winds up being extremely low. Similarly, you have a one-tailed test if your H_a proposes specifically that μ *is less than* 3.0.

This issue may seem tricky, but which kind of test to use should be apparent in the wording of the problem. Just think about whether you'd like to "prove" that the mean is different from a specified number (two-tailed test) or only that it falls to a particular side of that number (one-tailed test).

$H_0 : \mu = 3.0$	Type of Test	Tails
$H_a : \mu \neq 3.0$	Two-tailed	
$H_a : \mu > 3.0$	One-tailed	
$H_a : \mu < 3.0$	One-tailed	

To test a hypothesis:

1) Define H_0 and H_a first. Usually the problem specifies an assumed mean, μ_0, and also indicates whether you need a two-tailed or a one-tailed test.

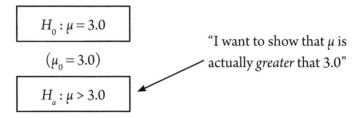

$$H_0 : \mu = 3.0$$

$$(\mu_0 = 3.0)$$

$$H_a : \mu > 3.0$$

"I want to show that μ is actually *greater* that 3.0"

2) Take your random sample of size n and calculate $\bar{x}$ and s. Say you get these results:

$$\bar{x} = 3.3 \qquad s = 1.0 \qquad n = 100$$

3) Figure out how many standard errors (SE) the $\bar{x}$ is away from your assumed null mean μ_0. This tells you how "close" or "far" $\bar{x}$ is.

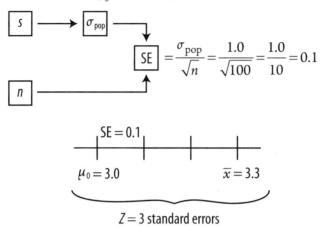

$$SE = \frac{\sigma_{pop}}{\sqrt{n}} = \frac{1.0}{\sqrt{100}} = \frac{1.0}{10} = 0.1$$

The one-step formula is:

$$Z = \frac{\bar{x} - \mu_0}{SE} = \frac{\bar{x} - \mu_0}{\sigma_{pop} / \sqrt{n}} = \frac{\bar{x} - \mu_0}{s / \sqrt{n}}$$

4) Now, for a one-tailed test, look up how much area would lie further away from 0 on a standard normal distribution than that Z-score.

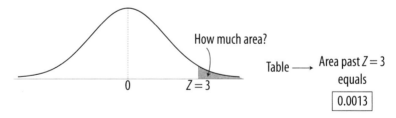

That 0.0013 is known as the **p-value** of this test. (No connection to the little p from earlier, with the binomial.) If $p = 0.0013$ for this test, it means that there's only a 0.0013 chance (0.13%) that the following situation has occurred: the null hypothesis is true (i.e., μ is really 3.0) *and* you get $\bar{x} = 3.3$ with your sample, together with the other stats. 3.3 might not seem all that much bigger than 3.0, but since the standard error is so

small (only 0.1), that 3.3 is a full 3 standard errors above the null mean. That's very unlikely *unless* the null hypothesis is wrong. So now you can take the final step, figuring out where you stand on the null hypothesis.

5) Decide on a confidence level and either reject H_0 or "fail to reject" H_0.

- Wanna be 90% sure? Okay—reject.

    90% sure = 10% chance of error is okay for you. This acceptable error level is *a*, the Greek letter alpha.

    Since $p < a$, you can safely reject it. $0.0013 < 0.10$

- Wanna be 99% sure? Okay—reject.

    $a =$ only 0.01, but p is still smaller.

- Wanna be 99.9% sure? Hmm—sorry! You can't be that sure with the results of this experiment. Z is large (good), so p is small (good), but not small enough for your finicky tastes. If you have a very small a (here, $a = 0.001$), then you'll need an even smaller p-value in order to reject the null hypothesis.

Long story short, there are two ways a hypothesis test can shake out, given a particular confidence level.

1) Good enough to reject H_0 ($\overline{x}$ is "far" away from μ_0 as measured by the SE yardstick).

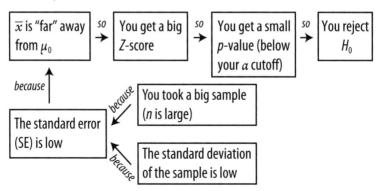

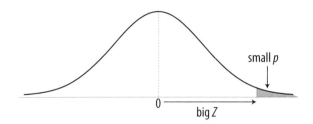

2) Not good enough to reject H_0 ($\bar{x}$ is "close" to μ_0 as measured by the
    SE yardstick).

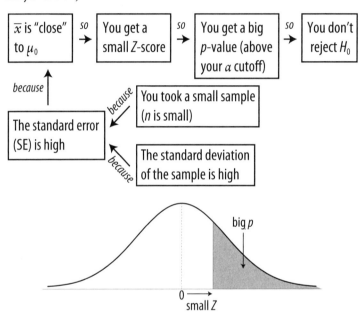

If you can reject H_0, then your results are ***statistically significant*** (with
p = whatever small level you found). For instance, if $p = 0.0013$, then
your results are "significant" at the 90th, 95th, 99th, and even 99.8th percent confidence level. (Only you know whether you have this level of
confidence in your *significant* other; we hope that he or she has a big
enough Z and a small enough p for you.)

Correlation and Regression

Up to now, everything has had to do with one variable—one measurement, one kind of data.

Student	Years since College
You	4
Alice Atwater	2
Bill Burns	6
...	...

One variable for each observation.

What if you get *two* pieces of data about each person? Now you can look at patterns.

Example 1: Years since College and Height

Student	Years since College	Height
You	4	5 feet 7 inches
Alice Atwater	2	5 feet 10 inches
Bill Burns	6	5 feet 2 inches
...	...	...

To look for a pattern, you put all these observations on a scatterplot:

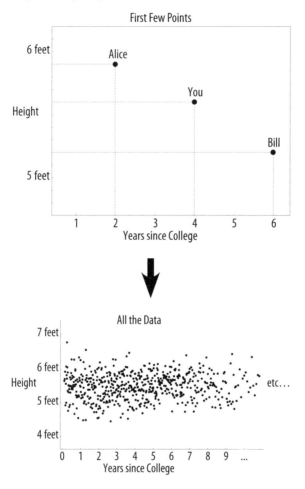

The second graph would almost certainly reveal no overall pattern. The "shotgun blast" shows that the two variables, Years since College and Height, are basically **uncorrelated**.

Example 2: Years since College and Age

In contrast, if you plot Years since College versus Age, you'll get a pattern.

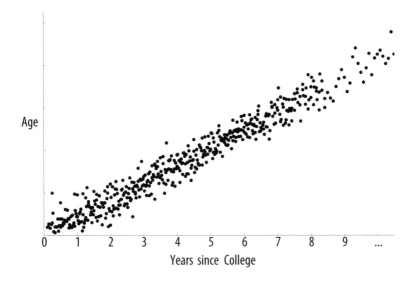

Age

Years since College

Most people are either high on both scales or low on both scales. You don't run into many Doogie Howsers (young age but many years since college) or Rodney Dangerfields[3] (old age but few years since college). This means that Years since College and Age are highly **correlated**.

You can measure the degree of correlation with **r**, the **correlation coefficient**. Don't worry about how to crunch r—Excel will do it for you with the CORREL function. The important thing is to understand what r tells you.

---

3   As Thornton Melon in the movie *Back to School.*

Range of *r*	Correlation	Pattern	
1 (max)	Perfect positive	All points lie on a line of positive slope	
0.*something*	Positive	Points cluster around a line of positive slope	
0	None	No pattern (shotgun blast) *or* a non-linear pattern	
−0.*something*	Negative	Points cluster around a line of negative slope	
−1 (min)	Perfect negative	All points lie on a line of negative slope	

Notice that *r* doesn't tell you the *slope* of the line. What *r* tells you is the *sign* of that slope, and more importantly *how tightly the points cluster* around a line of positive or negative slope.

Here's another way to think about correlation. Say you pick John Johnson out of the population, and John Johnson has a relatively *low* number of Years since College (below the mean). What would you expect for the levels of his other stats—Low, High, or No Idea?

Age: Positive Correlation ($r > 0$)

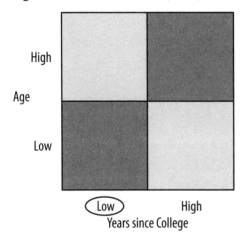

If you plot everyone on a two-by-two grid, you see large concentrations in the darker areas. So you expect John to have a Low age (that is, he's young). The higher *r* is, the higher the probability that he's Low on Age.

Height: Zero Correlation ($r = 0$)

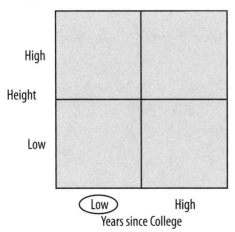

On this grid, there's no pattern. You have No Idea what to predict for John's height. Knowing his Years since College tells you zilch about his height.

Familiarity with Facebook (FwF): Negative Correlation ($r < 0$)

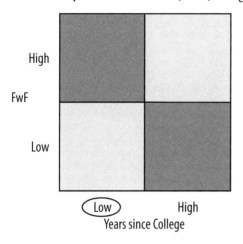

This plot shows lots of High-Low matchups. Since John is Low on Years, you expect him to be High on Facebook (so to speak). The closer r is to -1, the higher the probability is that his FwF is High.

Regression

The name *regression* is a historical accident—it has nothing to do with reliving high school (or past lives). In the context of statistics, "doing a linear regression" means finding the ***best-fit line*** through a scatterplot.

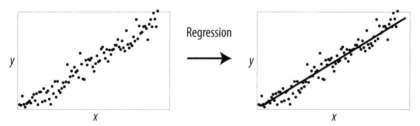

You do this so you can describe the relationship between x and y more precisely and even predict values of y given values of x.

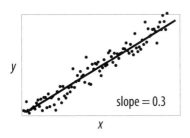 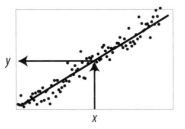

"If *x* increases by 1, *y* goes up   "If *x* = 30, I predict
by 0.3 on average."   that *y* = 50."

A few questions pop up right away:

- *Which variable should be* x, *and which should be* y?

  On a plain old scatterplot, it doesn't matter much, but when you regress, you want to make *x* the **independent** variable (the input or the **predictor** variable). Then *y* is the **dependent** variable (the output or the **predicted** variable). This could reflect that *x* somehow causes *y*, or it could simply mean that *x* is the easier thing to measure or control in the real world, while *y* represents the ultimate phenomenon that you care about and want to explain in terms of *x*. For instance, if you have Sales and Price as variables, you'd make Price your *x* variable and Sales your *y* variable. Sales of a product are a function of the Price of that product, and you want to explain Sales in terms of Price.

- *What does "best fit" mean?*

  The best-fit line minimizes the overall distance, in some sense, between the points and the line.

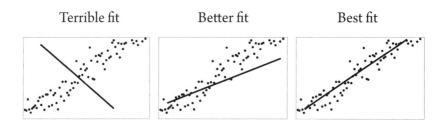

Terrible fit   Better fit   Best fit

In standard linear regression, you measure the overall distance between the points and the line this way:

1) Measure each deviation or error: the vertical distance to the line

2) Square each of those errors and add them all up

$$(-0.5)^2 = 0.25$$

$$(0.3)^2 = 0.09$$

$$(-0.2)^2 = 0.04$$

$$\ldots$$

$$= \boxed{9.83}$$

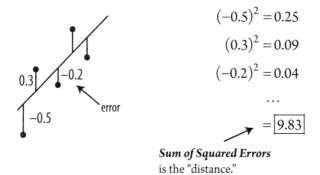

Sum of Squared Errors is the "distance."

The best-fit line has the smallest possible "sum of squared errors." This is why this line is often referred to as the **best squares** line.

• *What does it mean to "find" a line?*

The general equation of a line is $y = mx + b$, as you recall from the GMAT or GRE. The letter m represents the **slope** of the line, while b represents the **y-intercept**, where the line crosses the y-axis.

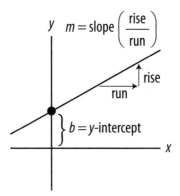

A line with equation $y = 3x - 2$ intercepts the y-axis at $(0, -2)$, and if x increases by 1, y increases by 3:

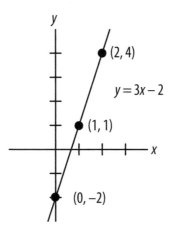

Finding the line means finding the values for the slope m and the y-intercept b. In "Statistics Land," different letters are often used, unfortunately:

Instead of $y = mx + b$

you have $y = \beta_1 x + \beta_0$ or $y = \beta_0 + \beta_1 x$

β is the Greek letter **beta** (also used in finance, with a related but distinct meaning). So β_0 (beta-zero) is the y-intercept, while β_1 (beta-one) is the slope. These are collectively known as the **coefficients** of the regression line.

- *How do you actually find the coefficients?*

    Not to worry—computers do all the computations. In Excel, you call up a Regression procedure from a Data Analysis "toolpak" (an add-on package), and this procedure spits out not only the coefficients but also other information you need to tell whether those coefficients are *significant*.

    After all, the procedure can only *estimate* those coefficients from the data you give it—it assumes you're giving it a *sample*, not the whole population. (This should make sense—the "whole population" would include all future data or missing values you're trying to predict, and so if you knew the whole population, you wouldn't need to do a regression—in fact, you'd be God.)

    The regression procedure basically says, "Here's the best-fit line *based on* the particular data you supplied, but you should check whether this line is truly meaningful and would apply to the broader population. So here's each coefficient, plus a *standard error* of that coefficient, plus a *t-statistic* for testing whether that coefficient is significantly different from zero, plus the associated *p-value*—now think about that!"

In Excel, a table with sample entries would look like this:

	Coefficients	*Standard Error*	*t Stat*	*P-value*	*Lower 95%*	*Upper 95%*
Intercept	1.158	0.472	2.455	0.036	0.091	2.225
X Variable	0.964	0.080	12.088	7.24E-07	0.784	1.144

The columns tell you lots of juicy tidbits:

Coefficients: The best-fit line is $y = 0.964x + 1.158$. The second row contains the slope information, which is usually much more important than the intercept info.

Standard Error: The slope 0.964 is just an estimate of the "true" slope of the best-fit line *for the whole population,* so the standard error tells you how good your estimate is. The smaller the standard error relative to the coefficient itself, the better the estimate. In this case, the standard error (0.080) is very small relative to the estimated slope (0.964), so the estimate is excellent.

t-stat: This tells you how many standard errors the coefficient is away from zero. The null hypothesis is *always* that each coefficient is zero. A high t-score is good (meaning that you'll be able to reject the null hypothesis and claim that the coefficient is significant). For instance, the t-stat for β_0 is 2.455, since 1.158 is 2.455 standard errors above zero.

p-value: This is the *p*-value associated with the t-statistic in the previous column, if you do a two-tailed test on each coefficient:

β_0 intercept

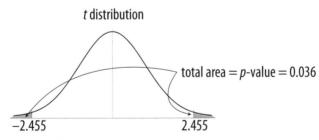

t distribution

total area $= p$-value $= 0.036$

−2.455   2.455

3.6% chance of being wrong
if you reject the null hypothesis for β_0.

β_1 slope

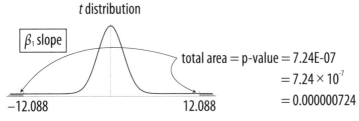

0.0000724% chance of being wrong
if you reject the null hypothesis for β_1.

With these results, you can claim that the slope of the best fit line is *not* zero with very high certainty (100% minus 0.0000724%, in fact!). You can claim that the intercept is not zero with reasonably high certainty, too (100% minus 3.6%, or 96.4%).

Long story short—look for *tiny* p-*values*, such as 0.036 or 0.000000724. Those tell you that the coefficients you found are good.

Note: Output such as 7.24E−07 is very tiny. Convert to powers of 10 or decimals to see it clearly.

$$7.24\text{E} - 07 = 7.27 \times 10^{-7}$$
$$= 7.24 \times 0.0000001$$
$$= 0.000000724$$

Sometimes in a regression, you find that the *y*-intercept isn't significant (*p*-value's too big) but the slope *is* significant. Pay attention to the slope—that's often all you really care about, since you might just want to know the *increase* in sales for every dollar of additional marketing spend.

Estimation vs. Prediction

So now that you have your beautiful line, you're all ready to use it.

$$y = 0.964x + 1.158$$

If $x = 20$, you predict… $y = 0.964(20) + 1.158$
$$= 20.438$$

What you should recognize is that this specific **prediction** has two sources of error built into it:

1) Estimation error

   The coefficients of the line were only estimated from a sample, so the real best fit line for the whole population might not be this exact line.

2) Additional random error

   Even around the theoretical best-fit line, there will be "noise," random deviation between the points and the line.

Here's another way to think about the issue.

Estimation: When $x = 20$, what do you expect the average value of y to be across the whole population?

$$E(y \mid x = 20) = 0.964\,(20) + 1.158$$

Expected value of y, given $x = 20$, is 20.438.

Prediction: If you pluck <u>one</u> observation with $x = 20$ out of the whole population, what do you predict y to be? You can't help it—you use the same equation:

Predicted $y = 0.964\,(20) + 1.158 = 20.438$.

The predicted single value of *y* and the estimated mean value of *y* (for a whole lot of observations) are the same number. But the error built into each is different.

Estimated mean value of *y* = 20.438 ± smaller error
                               (*only* the error that your line isn't quite right for the whole population)

Predicted specific value of *y* = 20.438 ± larger error
                                (estimation error plus random error, since the data doesn't all fall on even the best line)

Residuals

Residual is another name for error or deviation—it's the vertical distance between some data point and the best fit line.

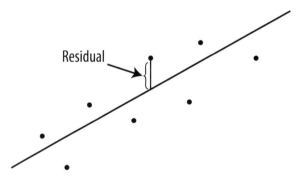

A residual can be positive or negative.

When you stress-test a regression to verify how robust it is, you look at the residuals. You want to make sure that they don't show a pattern:

- They should be independent of each other.

- They should be randomly scattered around zero, with more "small" residuals than "large" (ideally, they should form a normal distribution around zero).

- They shouldn't change in general size from one end of the plot to the other. For instance, the errors on the right side shouldn't be twice as big as those on the left side.

That last issue is more serious than it seems. If you run into it, you might have to rescale a variable to equalize errors. You'll learn a few tricks in class about how to rescale appropriately.

Multiple Regression

Finally, you can have more than one predictor variable. For instance, you might try to predict sales of winter coats using both marketing spend and average temperature.

$$y = \beta_0 + \beta_1 x_1 + \beta_2 x_2 \quad \left\{ \begin{array}{l} x_1 \text{ \& } x_2 \text{ are both predictor variables.} \\ \text{You still have just one } y. \end{array} \right.$$

This is where art and science meet in real life—how many predictors to use, how they should be rescaled or combined. Remember a couple of key points about multiple regression, which is often the last topic in your first stats class (we say "first" because we know you're coming back for more):

1) Fewer Predictors = Usually Better

    You might think, "The more the merrier." In fact, the more x's you throw in, the greater the chance that one of them gums up the whole works. Stick with fewer predictors, and your model will be cleaner and your life will be easier.

2) Independent Predictors = Always Better

    You don't want the predictors to be correlated. Here's the ideal scenario with two predictor variables:

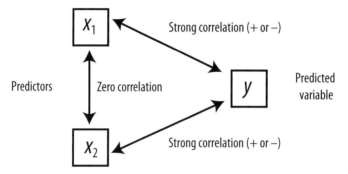

    If two predictor variables are strongly correlated, drop one of them or combine them sensibly somehow into a single index (add them, multiply them, or something). Then do your regression.

CHAPTER 17:
ACCOUNTING

The Big Picture of Accounting

Accounting is the standard way of keeping track of money in the business world. Accountants seem hard-wired to enjoy this stuff, even when they look haggard at tax time. So long as we get our refunds, we're happy to let them do the work.

Whether the subject is a regular business, a non-profit, or even a single person (you), accounting answers these questions:

- Where is the money coming from and where is it going?

- How much do you own and how much do you owe? (Notice the difference a single letter makes between *own* and *owe*.)

- How are you doing financially *right now*?

- How is that financial picture changing over time?

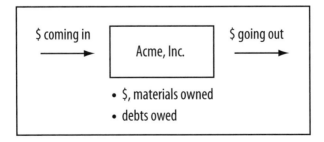

There are three types of accounting:

1. **Financial accounting** answers questions for outside investors and creditors. Standards are mandated by the government and are pretty complicated as a result.

2. **Managerial accounting** is for internal use. It builds off of financial accounting, adding customized metrics to help managers do their job well.

3. **Tax accounting** is for the IRS. Think April 15.

In b-school, you'll focus on types 1 and 2.

The Big Three Financial Statements

1. The **balance sheet** takes a *snapshot* on a particular date.

- How much do I *own?*
- How much do I *owe?*   } as of June 10, 2011
- How much is left *over?*

2. The **income statement** records *changes* to that picture over time.

- How much did I *make?*
- How much did I *spend?*
- How much was left *over?*   between Jan 1, 2011 and Dec 31, 2011
- What happened to what I *own* and *owe?*

3. The **statement of cash flows** keeps track of (you guessed it) cash.

- Where did the *cash come from?*   between Jan 1, 2011
- Where did the *cash go?*   and Dec 31, 2011

Balance Sheet (which has the terrible abbreviation "B/S")

Let's start with the balance sheet, a very personal balance sheet: yours. Imagine that all you have in the world is $100 sitting in a checking account—and you borrowed $90 of that $100 from your Uncle Joey.

What you *own* = ***Assets*** (A) = $100 in the checking account

What you *owe* = ***Liabilities*** (L) = $90 loan from Uncle Joey
            (also known as debt)

What's *left over* = ***Shareholders' Equity*** (SE) = $10 that's yours
            (net worth)

What you *own* minus what you *owe* is what's left over:

$$A - L = SE$$

This fundamental equation drives the balance sheet.

Conceptually, this equation often gets rearranged a little. Think of *assets* as *resources* …

Assets	
Checking Account	$100
[There to help you operate]	

and think of *liabilities* and *shareholders' equity* as *claims* on the assets.

Liabilities	
Loan from Uncle Joey	$90
[His claim on your assets]	
Shareholders' Equity	$10
[Your residual claim on the assets, as you are the "shareholder" of you]	

The claims ($90 and $10) are different. Uncle Joey has the *primary claim*. If your $100 goes down to $50 or up to $200, you still owe him $90. You, as the shareholder, have a *residual* or *secondary claim*. If your $100 goes down to $50, you're suddenly under water with $40 of "negative equity" (like all too many homeowners recently), but if the $100 goes to $200, your $10 of equity becomes $110. Shareholders take more risk than debtholders and get more potential upside as a result. That's the basic risk-reward tradeoff.

Since both liabilities and shareholders' equity are claims, go ahead and group them together on one side of the balance sheet.

$$A - L = SE \quad \rightarrow \quad A = L + SE$$

Now your balance sheet might look like this:

Balance Sheet as of Today		
Assets Checking Account		$100
Total Assets		**$100**
Liabilities Loan from Uncle Joey		$90
Total Liabilities		$90
Shareholders' Equity		$10
Total Liabilities & Share. Equity		**$100**

There are many different kinds of assets, liabilities, and shareholders' equity. You'll keep track of them in separate **accounts** with different names. Some of these accounts apply to a company more easily than to a person.

Asset Accounts

- *Cash* - Money in any kind of bank account.

- *Marketable securities* - Stocks and bonds you happen to have.

- *Accounts receivable* - Money that customers legally owe you.

- *Inventory* - Stuff you have to sell.

- *Advances to landlord* - If you prepaid your rent, then that's an asset from your point of view—you have squatter's rights for a while. That's worth something.

- *Other prepaid expenses*

All of the above are called **current assets**—they're already equivalent to cash (the most liquid asset) or will be converted to cash within a year.

Non-current assets turn into cash much more slowly:

- *Land*

- *Buildings*

- *Equipment*

  } Generally worth less now than when you bought them. That decline in value is called depreciation.

- *Intangible* (but measurable) *assets* - Patents and brands are examples of intangible assets. To count patents as assets, you must have bought them from another company. Otherwise, they're not measurable (in dollars) from an accounting point of view. This is one of the limitations of accounting. A homegrown intangible asset that's never been bought or sold, such as the Coca-Cola brand, does not show up "on the books."

Liability Accounts

- *Accounts payable* - Money that you legally owe to someone.

- *Salaries payable* - Money that you legally owe to your employees.

Both of the above are examples of **current liabilities**—debts you need to pay off within a year.

As you'd expect, there are also **non-current liabilities**:

- *Long-term bonds* - Mortgages or other long-term debts.

Shareholders' Equity Accounts

These accounts apply better to a company than to a person.

- *Common stock* - The original *paid-in capital* by shareholders. In other words, this is the money the business got directly in exchange for shares of stock. It is *not* the current value of that stock in the market.

- *Retained earnings* - All the cumulative profits (or earnings) of the company that were left (or retained) in the company. The shareholders have rightful claim on the company's profits. They can either be paid those profits—as *dividends*—or they can leave them in the company as a kind of reinvestment. These reinvested profits are retained earnings. (Typically, management decides how much of the profits to pay out as dividends.)

Retained earnings is the account that balances the books—in other words, it makes $A = L + SE$ true. So compute everything else first. Once you know every other A, L, and SE account, you can solve for retained earnings.

Income Statement *("I/S")*

Unlike a balance sheet, which is a snapshot, the income statement is a movie. It records changes over time.

Here's a picture of the pitcher

$10

The movie you want to picture in your head is super-exciting: a pitcher of water filling up (good) or draining (bad). The following case is slightly simplified, but it captures the essence of the income statement.

1. Start of the movie: Jan 1.

The very first frame of the movie is a snapshot. This snapshot is the shareholders' equity on that day. Forget about whether this is $10 of assets, with no liabilities, or $100 of assets, with $90 owed to Uncle Joey.

2. Good changes through the year.

Over the year, you pour $50 into the pitcher. These $50 are called ***revenues***.

The water level rises.

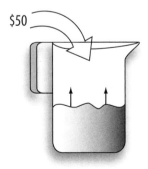

$50

3. Bad changes through the year.

During the same period, you also spend $35 from the pitcher. These $35 are called **expenses**.

The water level falls.

4. End of the movie: Dec 31.

How much is in the pitcher? Figure this out before you go on.

The math is straightforward:

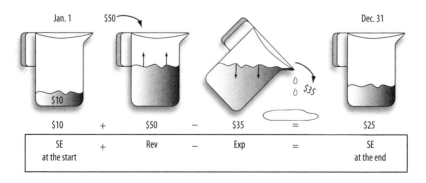

You often rearrange this to put revenues minus expenses on one side of the equation.

$$\$50 - \$35 = \$15$$

$$\text{Rev} - \text{Exp} = \text{Net Income (NI), or Earnings, or Profits}$$

That $15 is how much shareholders' equity (SE) changed (from $10 up to $25).

Now you have:

$$\text{Rev} - \text{Exp} = \text{NI} = \text{Change in SE}$$
$$\text{SE}_{end} - \text{SE}_{start}$$

$$\$50 - \$35 = \$15 = \$25 - \$10$$

This fundamental relationship drives the income statement. There are still a few questions to address.

Question 1: **What time period is covered?** (How long is the movie?)

Answer 1: **A year or a quarter, usually.** However, the year might not start on January 1. The *fiscal year* might start on July 1 or some other date.

Question 2: **When do you "recognize" revenue?** (When does a sale hit the income statement?)

Answer 2-a: **When you get paid, fool.**

If you get paid $50 in cash today, then you "book" the revenue today. This method is called **cash accounting**. This is how the IRS expects us to book our personal revenue (salary) when we pay our taxes for the year. What's the date on the check?

This method has attractive simplicity. However, it is also easy to manipulate, if you're a business.

Answer 2-b: **When you finish most or all of the job and you get an asset** (e.g., an IOU) **in return.**

This method is called **accrual accounting**. It means that you book the revenue when you do the work or deliver the goods—and the customer is obligated to pay you. It doesn't matter if that customer takes 30 days or 90 days to actually pay you. This is how all major public companies in the US track their revenue.

In the long run, cash accounting and accrual accounting are equivalent, since they only differ with respect to timing. Did GM book a particular sale in 1967 or 1968? It doesn't matter now. We're just glad they sold something.

Question 3: **When do you recognize expenses?**

You have the same two possible answers:

Answer 3-a, cash accounting: **When you pay the bill, fool.**

Answer 3-b, accrual accounting: **When the related revenue is booked** (matching principle) **or when you get the benefits** (period expense).

Say you're Wal-Mart. If you sell a TV and book the sale now, you book the expense of purchasing that TV wholesale now (as "cost of goods sold" or COGS), even if you actually purchased that TV six months ago. That's called the matching principle. You "match" the sale to the expenditure. It works well when a sale and a related expense can be tied together.

Alternatively, some expenses (like rent) are not tied to particular revenues. In that case, you just spread the expense evenly over the period. If you prepay two years of rent for some reason, you book a chunk of that rent every quarter for the next two years.

By the way, we slightly simplified the income statement. We pretended that shareholders reinvested all the profits, but they might have gotten some dividends. If that's the case, then net income is not equal to the change in retained earnings exactly; you also have to add in the dividends to get net income.

$$\underset{\text{(All Profits)}}{\text{Net Income}} \quad = \quad \underset{\substack{\text{(Profits distributed to}\\\text{shareholders)}}}{\text{Dividends}} \quad + \quad \underset{\substack{\text{(Profits reinvested in the}\\\text{company)}}}{\substack{\text{Change in Retained}\\\text{Earnings (in SE)}}}$$

Equivalently, you could write that net income minus dividends equals the change in retained earnings.

From Revenues to Net Income

An income statement from a real company tells a story. The exact details differ among industries and companies, but the overall gist is the same: you usually don't subtract off all the expenses in one fell swoop. Instead, you often subtract them off of revenues bit by bit, starting with the costs you can most directly attribute to the revenues, so that investors can understand the dynamics of the business better. Various intermediate steps in this "multiple-step income statement" are often computed on the road from revenues to net income. If nothing else, several big buckets of expenses are broken out on a single-step income statement so that investors can calculate those intermediate steps themselves and have some clue about how the business functions.

Here's a typical pathway, somewhat simplified:

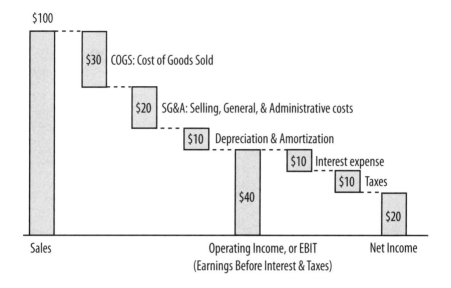

Revenues and expenses from **going concerns** and discontinued opera-tions are generally separated from each other, as well as any unusual rev-enues or expenses—either one-time or from non-operational activities, however those are defined. Often these unusual items are expressed as net *gains* or *losses* on the road to net income.

The Big Picture In Pictures

Here's the balance sheet:

Assets	$100
Liabilities	$90
+ SE	$10

Top = Bottom

A = L + SE

Like a pitcher of water, the balance sheet changes as revenue pours in and expenses pour out.

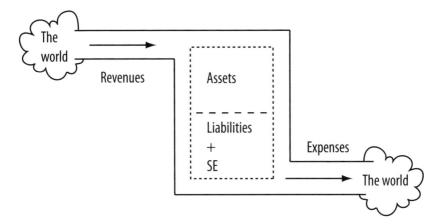

The income statement records those changes:

Rev	–	Exp	=	NI	=	Div	+	Change in RE
				Profit		Dividends		Retained Earnings $(RE_{end} - RE_{start})$
$50	–	$35	=	$15	=	0	+	$(\$25 - \$10)$

Be sure to grasp these relationships with simple numbers first. No matter how many zeros are tacked on, the concepts remain the same.

Transactions

A transaction in accounting world is just a flow of money from one "place" to another.

The places in question are accounts within any of the five big categories: Assets, Liabilities, Shareholders' Equity, Revenues, and Expenses. Just as before, an asset account tracks a specific kind of asset, a liability account tracks a specific kind of liability, and so on.

So a transaction is like a pipe that sucks some money out of one account and dumps it into another.

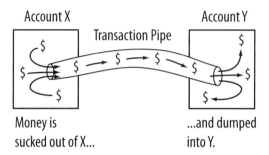

Account X   Account Y

Transaction Pipe

Money is   ...and dumped
sucked out of X...   into Y.

Money is never created or destroyed—it's just moved from one place to another. However much was sucked *out* of X has to equal the amount dumped *into* Y.

In other words:

$$\frac{\text{Outflow}}{\text{out of X}} = \frac{\text{Inflow}}{\text{into Y}}$$

In your personal life, you deal with this all the time. When you transfer $100 from checking to savings, you have an outflow of $100 from your checking account and an inflow of $100 into your savings account. Every pipe has two ends. When you withdraw $200 from the ATM, you have an outflow of $200 from some bank account and an inflow of $200 into your "cash in your pocket" account. Always look at outflows and inflows from the point of view of the accounts, not the pipe itself. $200 flowed *out* of the bank account and *into* your pocket.

Occasionally, one or both ends of the pipe splits, but the total outflows from one set of accounts still have to equal the inflows into the other set of accounts:

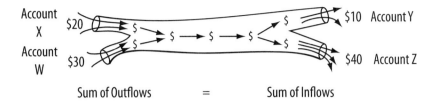

Account
X $20

Account
W $30

$10   Account Y

$40   Account Z

Sum of Outflows   =   Sum of Inflows

Take a look again at your original balance sheet. You have $100 in cash and you still owe Uncle Joey $90, so you have $10 in shareholders' equity. It's the start of the accounting period, so all revenue accounts (such as Salary) and expense accounts (such as Lunch) have been reset to $0. All that means is that so far this quarter or year, you haven't received any salary yet, and you haven't bought lunch yet.

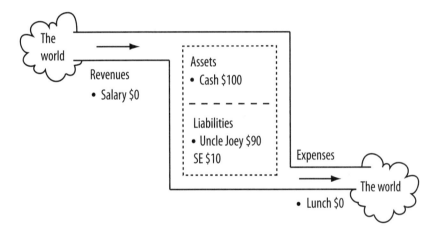

The world

Revenues
• Salary $0

Assets
• Cash $100

Liabilities
• Uncle Joey $90
  SE $10

Expenses

The world
• Lunch $0

Now visualize some transactions.

1. You get paid $50 (cash) in salary.

The inflow is easy: $50 flowed *into* your cash account. Where did it come from? From a revenue account called Salary. So from the Salary account's point of view, that's an *outflow*.

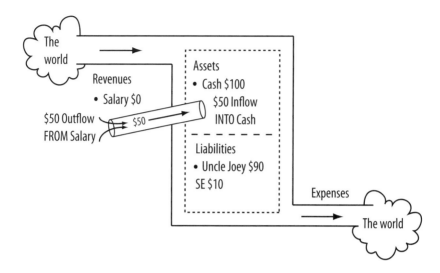

If that's confusing, think of the Salary account as your *employer's* bank account. The $50 got sucked *out* of that account, so we call that an outflow. Of course, there's a matching inflow: $50 flowed into *your* cash account.

Every transaction pipe must have two ends: where the money's getting sucked out of, and where the money's getting dumped into. The fact that there are two ends to the pipe is reflected in the name **double-entry accounting**, which is the basis of all modern accounting. Every transaction is recorded in two places: where the transaction pulls money from, and where the transaction spits the money out.

Now, take some of your cash and do something with it. You're hungry but you're a little physically scared as well. So you'll do two more transactions to take care of your physical and psychological needs.

2. Pay $30 to your uncle. This calms you down.

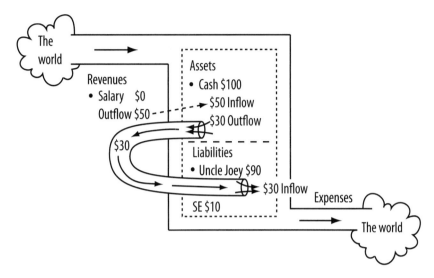

3. Spend $35 on lunch to assuage your hunger. Given your uncle's propensity toward violence, this may not be the wisest use of funds, but you must record the transaction properly nonetheless:

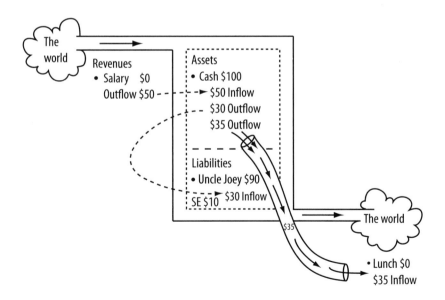

Notice that *revenue* accounts typically have *out*flows (from *their* point of view). These outflows are matched by *in*flows into other accounts, usually assets such as cash. Meanwhile, *expense* accounts typically have *in*flows (again, from *their* point of view). To the restaurant, your $35 went *into* some account. That inflow into an expense is matched by an outflow from some other account, usually an asset or a liability.

It's important to keep the changes straight.

Start with the cash account, which is an asset account. The **beginning balance**, or BB, was $100. After all these transactions, what's the **ending balance**, or EB?

Assets	• Cash	$100	BB
		$50	Inflow
		$30	Outflow
		$35	Outflow
		$?	EB?

You do the math exactly as you'd expect. You add inflows and subtract outflows.

Assets	• Cash	$100	BB
		+ $50	Inflow
		− $30	Outflow
		− $35	Outflow
		$85	EB

For this purpose, you don't care where the inflows came from or where the outflows went. You're just looking at what happened to *your* cash balance. All asset accounts work the same way. Inflows increase the balance, while outflows decrease the balance.

What about the Uncle Joey liability? You originally owed him $90. What do you owe him now?

Liability	• Uncle Joey	$90	BB
		$30	Inflow
		$?	EB?

Think of any liability as a credit card. What happens to your balance when you pay some money to your issuer? Your balance goes *down*.

Liability	• Uncle Joey	$90	BB
		− $30	Inflow
		$60	EB

If you like, you can think of liabilities as "negative money." In fact, accounting predates the theory of negative numbers, and some of the first mathematical explanations of negative numbers referred to positive numbers as fortunes (assets) and to negative numbers as debts.

When you put $30 of normal, positive money against negative $90, you get negative $60. You're bringing the debt closer to zero:

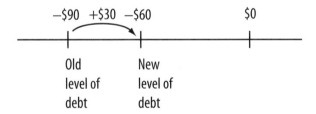

It's probably easiest, though, just to think of what happens to your credit card bill. Inflows of money *decrease* the balance of any liability. Outflows of money (using your credit card) *increase* the balance. As you'd expect, this is the exact opposite of what happens with assets.

How about revenues and expenses?

Since revenue accounts usually just have outflows, that's what we total up over any period of time. By the way, an inflow back into a revenue account would not be impossible, but it would indicate something weird:

your boss overpaid you and you have to return some of the money. In a business context, a refund to a customer would fall into this category.

Conversely, expense accounts usually just have inflows into them. An outflow back upstream from an expense account indicates something weird: a refund paid back to you from a vendor, for instance.

The Evil Language of Accounting

Unfortunately for all of us, the accounting world refers to outflows and inflows by crazy, counter-intuitive terms. In fact, these terms mean *precisely the opposite* in accounting from what they mean in your everyday life.

Let's say you have an inflow of $50 into your checking account. What would you call that, a credit or a debit?

You'd *think* it was a credit, right? But no, in accounting land, that's called a **debit.** If you *debit* a cash account $50, you are putting $50 *into* it!

It's insane, but true.

Likewise, if you **credit** an account in accounting world, you are sucking money *out* of that account! This language is a historical accident that we all have to live with.

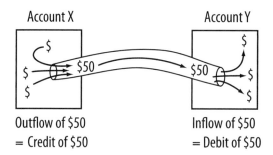

Amazingly, accounting textbooks and professors seem to ignore or gloss over the fact that this terminology is completely bass-ackwards. What some of them do, instead, is tell you to forget what these terms *mean*, and just memorize a bunch of rules about what credits and debits *do to* different types of accounts.

That's a bad strategy.

A much better strategy is to think in terms of actual movements of money, as you've been doing, and just accept the fact that the ends of the pipe have been misnamed in "accounting Latin."

An *outflow* of money out of an account is always a *credit*.

> Outflow = Credit

An *inflow* of money into an account is always a *debit*.

> Inflow = Debit

If you just memorize these reversed terms, then you can actually use your common sense to figure out what's happening in the language of credits and debits. Just remember: "*credit out, debit in.*"

Look again at the three transactions in the big picture, replacing the language.

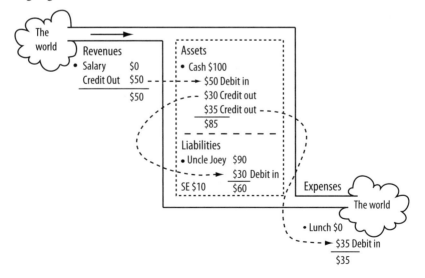

If you just consider the $30 payment to Joey, you can see a couple of key accounting tools in action.

Journal Entry

Think of the journal as a diary: an entry records a transaction in a very standardized way. The pattern is always as follows:

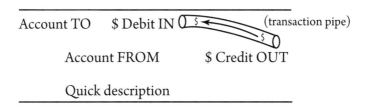

Account TO	$ Debit IN	(transaction pipe)
Account FROM	$ Credit OUT	
	Quick description	

Why they always put the destination before the starting point of the money is another mystery. Plus, you have to imagine the money flowing left. But you can deal. Here's the Joey payment as a journal entry:

Joey's loan	$30
Cash	$30
Paid Joey $30 out of cash on 12/15/11.	

T-Accounts

These keep track of credits and debits for an individual account. Again, consider the $30 Joey payment.

Cash		Any Asset Account	
$100		Beginning Balance	
	$30	Debits (if any)	Credits (if any)
$70		Ending Balance	

You add debits and subtract credits.

It would be easier if we just wrote:

Asset	
Beginning Balance	
Inflows	Outflows
Ending Balance	

You add inflows and subtract outflows. This is what you're actually doing with debits and credits—don't lose sight of that.

Balances for liabilities go on the right:

Uncle Joey		Any liability account	
	$90		Beginning balance
$30		Debits (if any)	Credits (if any)
	$60		Ending Balance

For liabilities, you add credits (outflows) and subtract debits (inflows). After all, you want your liabilities to go down.

In all cases, credits go on the right and debits go on the left. This is frequently cited as if it were something truly deep and explanatory. Yes, it's good to know, but it's no substitute for knowing what credits and debits actually are (outflow and inflows). Of course, sometimes you'll solve a simple problem mechanically. However, unless you understand that a credit is an outflow of money from an account, while a debit is an inflow of money to an account, you'll never be able to reason through a complicated scenario correctly.

We harp on this point because this is where your accounting professor will typically fail to grasp the difficulty. Again, accountants are a special breed, whom we must love just as they are.

Tying Revenues and Expenses into the Balance Sheet

Consider the $50 salary payment for a minute.

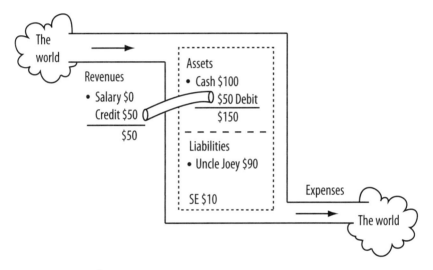

Is it now true that

Assets	=	Liabilities	+	SE?
$150	=	$90	+	$10?

Nope! ~~$150 = $100~~

Something's definitely wrong with this picture. Here's what's going on: you now have $150 in cash. And you still only owe $90 to Uncle Joey. So you must have $150 − $90 = $60 in shareholders' equity, not $10.

This means that this revenue account, which now shows $50, must actually be a *Shareholders' Equity* account for A = L + SE to still work.

Assets		
• Cash	$100	
	$50	After the transaction,
	$150	A = $150
Liabilities		
• Uncle Joey	$90	L = $90
SE		
• Retained Earnings	$10	
• Salary	$50	SE = $60
Total SE =	$60	L + SE = $150

The same thing is true of expense accounts. Technically both revenues and expenses are "temporary" shareholders' equity accounts.

At the end of any accounting period, you have to zero out every revenue or expense account's balance by moving money to or from that catch-all SE account, retained earnings—the one that captures all reinvested profits of the company since it was founded.

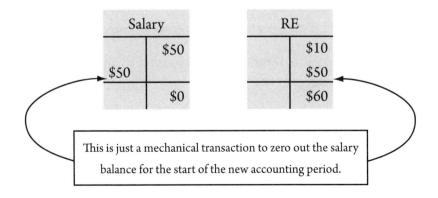

This is just a mechanical transaction to zero out the salary balance for the start of the new accounting period.

Final Thoughts on Financial Accounting

1) The Statement of Cash Flows is a beautiful thing. Really? Yes.

You'll learn how to build and interpret the SoCF in your accounting class. If you've understood the previous material, you'll be fine. Just realize that the SoCF sheds wonderful light on the movement of cash. In fact, the content of the SoCF overlaps significantly with that of the B/S and the I/S. In theory, with sufficiently detailed B/S's and I/S's, the SoCF is redundant. However, that's not the point. The purpose of the SoCF is to reveal how cash is flowing to and from three principal sorts of activities:

1. Operations (cash from customers, less cash paid to suppliers, employees, etc.)

2. Investing (purchase and sale of long-term assets)

3. Financing (cash to and from investors, either shareholders or bondholders)

Without a careful handle on these cashflows, a firm might look good on its balance sheet and income statement but run out of dough mid-year.

When you're doing an accounting case, you're often doing *forensics*: what the heck happened to this company over the last six months? Word to the wise—look at the SoCF. The other good place to look for buried treasure is in the "Notes to the Financial Statements." Companies love to bury bad news and inconvenient truths in these footnotes. That's where you'll find good clues to a company's well-being, or lack thereof.

2) Learn typical journal entries and T-account maneuvers for complicated transactions.

The way to make sure you know how to account for "the sale of machinery at a loss" or any other procedure is to write out a sample transaction with small, easily grasped numbers. Make a well-labeled journal entry on your review sheet, whether you can take such a sheet into your exam or not. Likewise, create sample T-accounts for funky accounts.

For example, Allowance for Uncollectibles is a "contra-asset" account, a kind of liability account attached directly to Accounts Receivable to track money you won't ever collect from your deadbeat customers. Here is the notation on the review sheet one of us was able to create and use on the final:

Allow for Unc (XA)	
	BB
write off	Bad Debt Expense
	EB

The important thing is not that you know what these terms mean right now. Rather, just remember to come up with meaningful notations for typical credits and debits in tricky accounts. This way, you'll know how to use those accounts.

A Few Points on Managerial Accounting

Managerial accounting (also known as cost accounting) is a separate subject from financial accounting, which is what has been covered so far. It is not as quantitatively or conceptually hard, thank goodness, so we'll say much less about it here.

A couple of the key questions in this field:

1. How do you properly allocate costs to different product lines, so you can compare profitability?

2. How do you track performance against a budget?

To address the first question, you first have to distinguish *variable costs* from *fixed costs*. Variable costs change with the level of production. For instance, the **direct cost** of the materials out of which a product is made is a variable cost. Some **overhead costs** are also variable. In contrast, a *fixed cost* doesn't vary over wide ranges of production. For example, the CEO's salary is a fixed cost, at least in the short run.

The interesting issue is how to allocate these fixed costs and other costs that aren't natually attributed to different product lines. In theory, you go to town with **activity-based costing** and track everyone's activities as they relate to your various products. There will always be some residual fixed costs , though. The typical approach is to compute a **contribution margin** for each product.

Revenues from sales	$100 M
Variable Cost of Goods Sold	− $40 M
Contribution Margin	$60 M

The contribution margin then "contributes" to covering the fixed costs. Contribution margins are very proprietary pieces of information because, together with fixed costs, you can compute the **breakeven point**, the number of units sold below which the firm is losing money and above which it's making money. At this point, the firm "breaks even" with zero profit.

Say that a particular product sells for $200. The variable COGS is $80, so the contribution margin per unit is $120. This means that every unit sold contributes $120 toward covering whatever fixed costs this product is responsible for. Say those fixed costs are $12 million. Then the company must sell x units to break even, where x satisfies:

$$(120)\underbrace{(x\,\text{units})}_{\text{total contribution margin}} = \underbrace{\$12\,\text{million}}_{\text{fixed costs}}$$

$$x = \frac{12\,\text{million}}{\$120} = 100{,}000\,\text{units}$$

More generally, the breakeven point (BE) is given by:

$$BE = \frac{\text{Fixed Costs}}{\text{Contribution Margin per unit}}$$

Graphically, the relationship between profit and units sold can be seen this way:

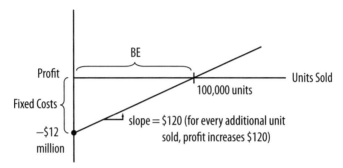

As for managing performance against a budget, the game is all about computing **variances**—not in the statistical sense, but in the more general sense of "differences." The idea is this: if you sell $150,000 more than you predicted, how much of that difference was because you sold more or fewer *units* and how much was because you sold at a different *price* than you predicted? Likewise, if your costs are not what you budgeted, which department should be blamed—if at all?

The computations are not difficult; it's just a matter of learning the terms and keeping good track.

CHAPTER 18:
FINANCE

~~~~~~~~~~~~~~~~~~~~~~

Whether it's "FIGH-nance" or "fi-NANCE," this stuff is at the heart of business. Learn it well (or at least well enough to get through exams).

Bird in the Hand

The most fundamental finance concept is the ***time value of money***. Here it is, in a nutshell:

$$\frac{\$100}{\text{Today}} = \frac{\text{More than } \$100}{\text{Tomorrow}}$$

Why is this true? Two main reasons:

1. **Delayed gratification.** Say you owe Jill $100. If you pay her right now, she can spend that $100 right away, so if you're going to make her wait till tomorrow, you need to give her a little more than $100.

2. **Risk**. What if between today and tomorrow, you take off for Austria, leaving Jill high and dry? She trusts you, but she still needs a little extra incentive to wait and take the risk you might leave town. Plus, because of inflation, a dollar might not buy as much tomorrow as it does today.

Together, delayed gratification and risk mean that you have a choice: pay Jill $100 now or pay her more than $100 later.

A way to visualize this equivalence is with column charts:

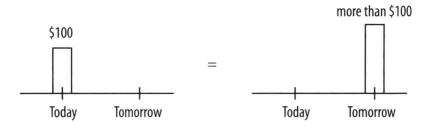

As you move a column of money (called a **cash flow**) to the right and thus into the future, it has to grow to stay equivalent. That growth is the **interest** you have to pay Jill to accept the delay and to take the risk that you might not pay her.

Now try slightly larger specific numbers and change the time frame to a year:

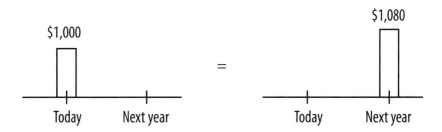

In words, here's the situation: you owe Jill $1,000 today. She tells you that you can either pay her the grand right now, or you can pay her $1,080 in exactly one year.

You took either the GMAT or the GRE, so you know something about the math here. By asking for $1,080 next year, Jill is charging you an 8% annual **interest rate**.

$$\$1,080 = \$1,000 + 8\% \text{ of } \$1,000$$

$$\text{(the \textbf{principal})} \quad \text{(the \textit{interest})}$$

$$= \$1,000 + (0.08)(1,000)$$

$$\left(\text{since } 8\% = \frac{8}{100} = 0.08\right)$$

To go even further, you could pull out the $1,000 "common factor" on the right, which leaves behind a 1 and a 0.08.

$$\$1,080 = \$1,000 + (0.08)(\$1,000)$$

$$= \$1,000(1 + 0.08) = \$1,000(1.08)$$

Here's a key bit of math to get comfortable with:

Adding 8% to some amount of money	$=$	Multiplying that amount of money by 1.08

Likewise, adding 13% to some amount is the same as multiplying that amount by 1.13. You can generalize if you've expressed the interest rate as a decimal r (like 0.08 or 0.13) and you have $1,000 today:

Next year's equivalent amount of cash	$=$	$\$1,000\,(1+r)$

If you like percents better, then there's just a slight difference in the formula. If you write the interest rate as x percent ($x\%$), then just write in $\dfrac{x}{100}$:

Next year's equivalent amount of cash	$=$	$\$1,000\left(1 + \dfrac{x}{100}\right)$

After all, 1.08 can be written as $1 + 8/100$. Just keep track of whether your variable is already a decimal (like *r* above). If the variable isn't a decimal already, you need to divide it by 100 (like *x* above).

If *P* is today's principal and *r* is the annual interest rate (as a decimal), you can see the column equivalence this way:

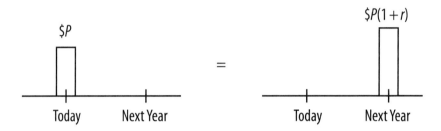

As a shorthand, put these pictures together:

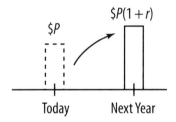

The way this picture is drawn indicates the way we've been thinking: today's money earns interest and becomes a bigger amount of money next year.

The Power of Compounding

What if you let the money sit for *two* years? Then you have something called **compounding**. You earn "interest on the interest," so in the second year, you earn a little more interest than in the first year.

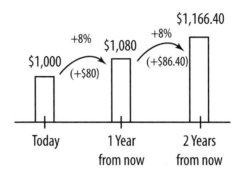

Notice that you're not *adding* the same amount of money each year. However, you are doing the same multiplication each year: both times, you're multiplying by 1.08.

This means that you can write the final amount this way:

$$\begin{aligned}
\$1,166.40 &= \$1,080(1.08) \\
&= \$1,000(1.08)(1.08) \\
&= \$1,000(1.08)^2
\end{aligned}$$

Compounding over several years is the same as multiplying by a number bigger than 1 several times:

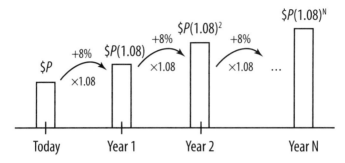

If you have to compound over shorter periods, the concept works similarly. Say you'd like to find the *future value* of $1,000 after one year of monthly compounding at a *nominal annual rate* of 6%. Then you don't have just one period of a year—your period is 1 month, so you have 12 periods in that year.

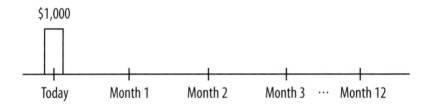

The period interest rate is the nominal interest rate (6%) divided by the number of periods in a year (in this case, 12). $60 \div 12 = 0.5\%$, or 0.005 as a decimal. So you get 12 periods of half a percent interest:

This is slightly better than waiting till the end of the year and getting 6% all at once, since that non-compounded 6% is only calculated on the $1,000 principal. In contrast, when you're compounding along the way, you're getting little bits of interest on the interest, yielding you an extra $1.68 in this case. This is not a lot of money, but imagine a principal of $1 million. Or $1 billion. Then compound interest becomes real money you care about.

A nominal annual interest rate of 6%, compounded monthly, is equivalent to an *effective annual interest rate* of 6.168%. Your credit card company knows all about this, of course.

Bring It Back

So far, we've been thinking about the growth of money *into the future*. For instance, $1,000 today turns into $1,080 next year, at an annual interest rate of 8% (a *simple* rate, not compounded).

Now let's flip the script.

If $1,000 today is equivalent to $1,080 next year, doesn't that also mean that $1,080 next year is equivalent to $1,000 today?

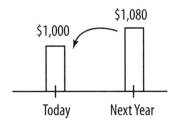

The rule is simple. To go forward in time, you multiply by 1.08. So to go back in time, you divide by 1.08.

$$\text{Today} \qquad\qquad\qquad \text{Next Year}$$

$$\$1,000 \xrightarrow{\times 1.08} \$1,080 = \$1,000(1.08)$$

$$\$1,000 \xleftarrow{\div 1.08} \$1,080$$

$$\$1,000 = \frac{\$1,080}{1.08}$$

In finance, you are often pulling a future cash flow back in time to the present, in order to figure out what it's worth today. To do this pull-back, you *divide* the cash flow by $1 + r$, where *r* is called the **discount rate**.

For instance, a cash flow of $500 one year from now, discounted at 10%, is only worth $454.54 today:

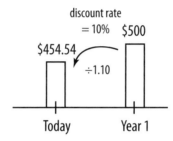

The word "discount" can be misleading. In the retail world, if you discount the price of a sweater by 10%, you subtract 10% from the original price, which is the same thing as multiplying that price by 90% or 0.9. Contrast that with the finance world. If you bring back a future cash flow at a discount rate of 10%, you *don't* subtract 10%. Instead, you divide the cash flow by 1.10.

Your aim is to solve this puzzle—what is the *current* dollar figure that, if you added 10% to *it*, would give you $500 (or whatever the future cash flow is)? The answer is $\frac{\$500}{1.1} = \$454.54$.

If you pull a future cash flow back in time across multiple periods, you do the reverse of compounding. Rather than multiply repeatedly, you divide repeatedly.

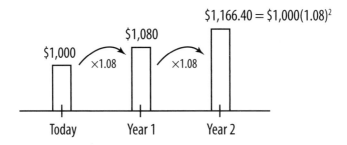

Risk and Reward

The *higher* the discount rate, the *less* some promised future cash flow is worth today.

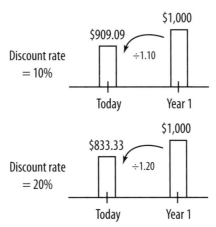

These different **present values** reflect a difference in perceived risk. The higher the discount rate, the riskier the investment. A low-risk investment has a low discount rate—in other words, it pays a low effective rate of interest. For instance, a stable bank with deposits insured by the U.S. government is very low-risk, and so that bank's promise to pay $1,000 in a year is worth very close to $1,000 now.

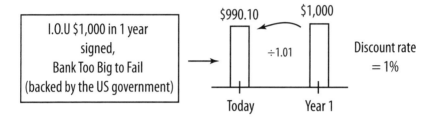

You won't be rewarded with a lot of interest for taking such a low-risk gamble.

The Name's Bond...

If the I.O.U. is traded publicly on Wall Street, you can "impute" or figure out the effective discount rate from the marketplace. This kind of I.O.U. is often called a **bond**.

The lower the current **price** of a bond, the higher its **yield**, a.k.a. effective interest rate, a.k.a. discount rate. A company might sell some I.O.U.'s to the public, but since the risk on those is generally higher than that of the bank bond, the discount will be greater. The I.O.U.'s will be worth less right now, so they'll be cheaper to buy.

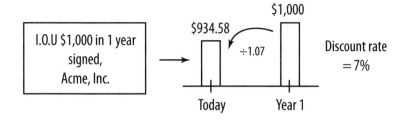

Borrower/Issuer	Current Value of 1-Year $1,000 Bond	Discount Rate, or Yield
Bank Too Big To Fail	$990.10	1%
Acme, Inc.	$934.58	7%
Uncle Joey	$833.33	20%

The riskier the borrower, the greater return you'll demand on your money, so the yield goes up. You hand over less right now to that risky borrower in return for the promise of $1,000 in a year.

Multiple Cash Flows

If an investment promises you more than one cash flow at different points in time, then you bring each one back to today by discounting, then add up all the results. Say that Uncle Joey has an "investment vehicle" to tell you about:

"This thing can't miss! You'll get paid $1,000 next year, then another $1,000 every year after that for a total of 5 years. You want in?"

What would you offer to pay him right now? Well, it depends on how risky you think the investment is (and how much or little you trust Uncle Joey). Just realize that every offer—every present value of that investment—corresponds to an effective discount rate, and the lower your offer, the higher the rate you're demanding.

Let's say that you think that this investment ought to be paying you 15% all the way through. Here's how to figure out your offer.

1.   Draw a picture of the proposed future cash flows.

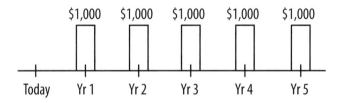

2.   Bring each cash flow back to today. Since the discount rate is 15%, we need to divide by 1.15 ($= 1 + r$, where $r = 15\% = \dfrac{15}{100} = 0.15$).

   We have to divide by 1.15 for every year between now and the future cash flow. That's the same as squaring, cubing, etc. 1.15 and dividing by the result.

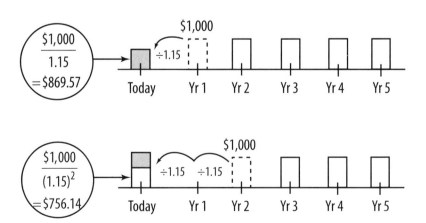

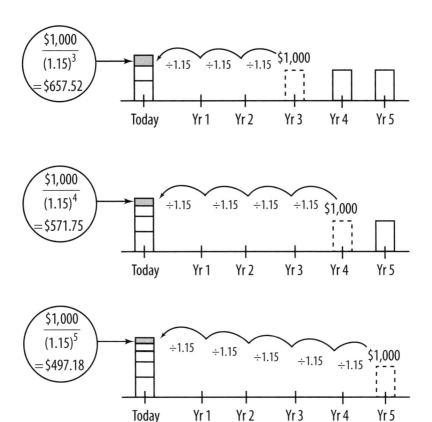

3. Now add up all those present values to get the *net present value*, or *NPV* of the investment.

$$NPV = \frac{\$1,000}{1.15} = \frac{\$1,000}{(1.15)^2} + \frac{\$1,000}{(1.15)^3} + \frac{\$1,000}{(1.15)^4} + \frac{\$1,000}{(1.15)^5}$$

$$= \$869.57 + \$756.14 + \$657.52 + \$571.75 + \$497.15$$

$$= \$3,352.16$$

This is what Uncle Joey's investment is worth to you right now, if you use a discount rate of 15%.

This kind of analysis, also known as a ***discounted cash flow*** or ***DCF***, is perfect for a spreadsheet. Make that computer do jumping jacks.

	A	B	C	D	
1					
2		Discount Rate	15%		
3					
4	Year	Cash Flow	Divide by	Discounted Cash Flow	The "divide by"
5	0	0	1.000	$0	column is 1.15
6	1	$1,000	1.150	$869.57	raised to the
7	2	$1,000	1.323	$756.14	
8	3	$1,000	1.521	$657.52	relevant power:
9	4	$1,000	1.749	$571.75	$1.15, (1.15)^2,$
10	5	$1,000	2.011	$497.18	$(1.15)^3,$ etc.
11					
12			NPV	$3,352.16	

Here's the same sheet with formulas shown.

	A	B	C	D	
1					
2		Discount Rate	15%		
3					
4	Year	Cash Flow	Divide by	Discounted Cash Flow	After you type in
5	0	0	=(1+$C$2)^A5	=B5/C5	the formulas in
6	1	$1,000	=(1+$C$2)^A6	=B6/C6	C5 and D5, you
7	2	$1,000	=(1+$C$2)^A7	=B7/C7	
8	3	$1,000	=(1+$C$2)^A8	=B8/C8	can just copy
9	4	$1,000	=(1+$C$2)^A9	=B9/C9	them down.
10	5	$1,000	=(1+$C$2)^A10	=B10/C10	They'll adjust
11					on their own.
12			NPV	=SUM(D5:D10)	

If you build this worksheet in Excel, try playing with the discount rate and see what happens to the NPV. As you lower the rate, the NPV goes up. If the discount rate drops all the way to 0%, then the NPV reaches the theoretical maximum of $5,000, because every future dollar is worth exactly $1 today. If you increase the discount rate, the NPV decreases, since future dollars are worth less in today's dollars.

Deal or No Deal

Should you take Uncle Joey's deal? It all depends on the cost to buy in. You've already figured out that if you discount at 15%, all the future cash flows are worth $3,352.16 to you right now. Say you've compared this deal to other investments with various rates of return, and you're comfortable with applying a 15% discount rate in this case.

Then your decision is easy: if Uncle Joey offers you the deal for anything less than $3,352.16, you should jump on it. For instance, if he wants to charge you $3,000, then things look good from your point of view. You'll spend three grand right now and get $3,352.16 in present value. Your "instant" profit is $352.16, so you're overjoyed.

On the other hand, say Uncle Joey won't take a penny less than $4,000, because he says the deal is "practically a sure thing." Who cares what he says or thinks? *You* think that the project is risky enough (and that Uncle Joey himself is risky enough) to merit a 15% discount rate, and so you're losing money if you spend $4,000 to get $3,352.16 in present value. Leave the deal on the table at that price, even if he is your godfather.

People often calculate the NPV of an investment including not just the future cash flows but the initial outlay as well. In that case, represent that initial outlay as a negative cashflow.

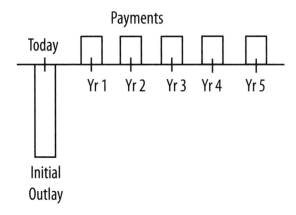

If you run the numbers with the initial outlay included, then the decision rule is simply this: take the deal if the NPV is greater than zero, and reject it if not. The NPV is essentially your instant profit on the deal, and you only want positive profits.

For instance, if Uncle Joey insists on a $4,000 upfront investment, then your NPV is $3,352.16 − $4,000 = −$647.84. Notice that the four grand is not discounted at all, because it's already in today's dollars. Since the NPV is negative, you reject the offer.

Your uncle sputters, "But I'm only asking for four grand, and you're going to get five back!"

Since you're taking finance, you use charts and graphs to explain to him the time value of money and net present value.

Uncle Joey scratches his prominent ears and says, "Hmm. If you choose a lower discount rate, the future cash flows will be worth more today, right? So let me ask you this. What rate would you have to use to make this deal worth your while?"

Your uncle has an interesting point. After all, if the discount rate were 0% (which is unrealistic, but just for giggles), then the $5,000 of future cash flows would be worth exactly $5,000 today, so you'd take the deal for a price of $4,000 and pocket a positive NPV of $1,000. Meanwhile, at 15%, the NPV is negative. Thus there must be some discount rate between 15% and 0% that *leaves you indifferent* between taking the deal and not taking it. That indifference point is called the **internal rate of return**, or **IRR**. It's the "just-right" discount rate that makes the NPV of all the cash flows equal to zero.

You can use the HP 10b11 financial calculator to figure out the IRR. Input all the cash flows above, making sure to put in *negative* $4,000 for the first cash flow in Year 0, then click the IRR button. The calculator runs and spits out 7.93%.

This means that if you apply a discount rate between 0% and 7.93% to Uncle Joey's project, you'll get a positive NPV and take the deal. Conversely, if you apply a rate higher than 7.93%, as you did before, you'll get a negative NPV and pass on the deal.

Putting this another way, you compare the IRR of 7.93% to the discount rate you apply to similar investments. This comparison rate is called the **hurdle rate** or the **opportunity cost of capital**. If the IRR is higher than the hurdle rate, then take the deal; otherwise, don't. For instance, you had decided earlier that the hurdle rate for this investment ought to be 15%. Since the IRR came in at only 7.93%, it didn't "clear the hurdle" of 15% that you had set, so you tell Uncle Joey no.

Incidentally, you can also figure out the IRR using the Excel spreadsheet from earlier. Just try different numbers in the discount rate cell till you get as close as you want to $4,000 for the NPV of just the future cash flows (since that spreadsheet didn't include the initial outlay). Or, as is described in Chapter 14, use the Goal Seek tool in Excel. On the Data ribbon, choose What-If Analysis, choose Goal Seek, then ask Excel to *set cell* D12 *to value* $4,000 *by changing cell* C2. *Voilà!* The answer is 7.93%, to a couple of decimal places.

For various technical reasons, the IRR rule isn't as good as the NPV rule ("take deals with positive NPV"), so stick to the latter. However, IRR is alive and well in industry, so you need to know how to find it and use it.

... *James Bond*

Many bonds (the formal I.O.U.'s that companies and governments sell) have a periodic constant payment called a **coupon**. These coupon payments end when the bond reaches **maturity** and dies. At the end of the bond's life, the **principal** or **face value** of the bond is typically paid back as well, whether or not the bond was actually purchased for that face value.

Take a $1,000 face-value bond with a 5% coupon paid every year for 3 years, at which point the bond matures. First, note that the 5% is *not* necessarily the discount rate you should apply! It's just a way of expressing the coupon as a percent of the face value of the bond:

$$\text{Coupon} = 5\% \times \$1,000 = \$50$$

You can lay out the cash flows you'd get, if you happened to own this bond.

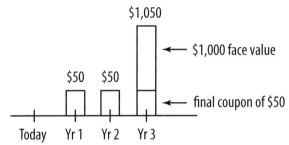

If you discount these cash flows at say 7%, you'll get an NPV of $947.51.

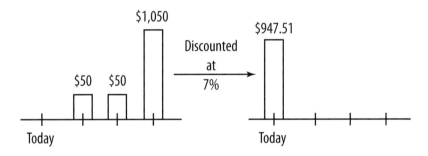

If you discount at only 3%, the NPV is $1,056.57.

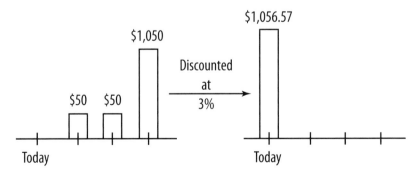

And if you discount at exactly 5%, which happens to be the coupon rate, then the NPV is exactly $1,000, the face value. Ta da!

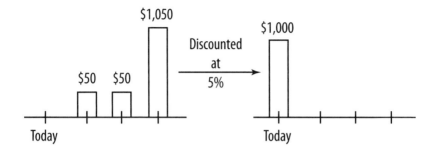

That's no accident. Something that pays you $50 a year like clockwork, then gives you an extra $1,000 at the end, is worth exactly $1,000 to you right now if the interest rate you're demanding is exactly 5%. Then the coupon is paying you the perfect amount of interest each year to keep you happy, and at the end you're also given your money back.

If, however, these cash flows are regarded in the marketplace (and by you) as riskier than comparable investments that pay 5%, then you and the other market participants will demand a discount bigger than 5%, and the current price of the bond falls below the face value (known as *par*) of $1,000.

Likewise, if you and everyone else start to consider these cash flows *less* risky than comparable investments that pay 5%, the price will rise above par, and the yield of the bond (the applicable discount rate) will drop below 5%.

Finally, there are **zero-coupon bonds** that don't pay a coupon at all, but only return one payment at maturity. That payment could be the face value of the bond or the face value plus compounded interest. "Zeros" have a current price below the dollar amount of the final payment, unless something very weird's going on in the bond market.

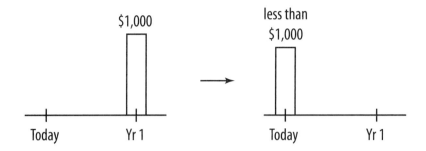

US Treasury bills, or **T-bills**, are short-term zero-coupon bonds issued by the US government, with maturities up to a year. The US government also issues bonds with much longer maturities (up to 30 years). The yields on US government bonds with different maturities are usually not the same, a fact known as the **term structure of interest rates**.

If you plot the interest rates of the various bonds, you get the **yield curve**. Normally, this curve slopes upwards, because longer-term bonds typically pay higher interest than short-term bonds do. When the yield curve "inverts" or "flips," look for dragons flying out of the sky, because Armageddon (or at least a recession) is probably approaching.

Forever's A Long Time

It may seem strange, but you can measure the NPV of an *infinite* stream of payments:

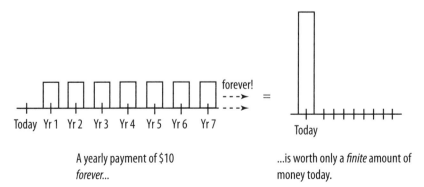

A yearly payment of $10 forever...

...is worth only a *finite* amount of money today.

The reason this is possible is that the present value of payments in the distant future shrinks exponentially (in a very literal sense), as long as there's a positive discount rate. So this infinite set adds up to a finite number. It's just like saying that:

$$\frac{1}{2} + \frac{1}{4} + \frac{1}{8} + \frac{1}{16} + \frac{1}{32} + \frac{\text{forever!}}{\cdots} = 1$$

If you go halfway across the room, then halfway again, then halfway again, and again, *forever*—you reach the other side.

Whoa. Deep.

Okay, so how do you do this infinite sum? Say you've got this promise of a yearly payment of $10 forever. You trust the issuer of this **perpetuity** a great deal, so you'll apply the relatively low discount rate of 5%.

You could set up an infinite spreadsheet, with an endless number of rows...

Discount Rate | 5%

Year	Cash Flow	Divide By	DCF
0	0	1.000	0
1	$10	1.050	$9.52
2	$10	1.103	$9.07
3	$10	1.158	$8.64
⋮			

till   kingdom   come

...but that's not very practical. Or you could do a complicated mathematical derivation (cool but also impractical), or you could learn a simple formula.

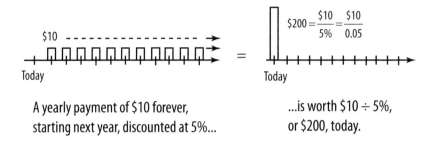

A yearly payment of $10 forever, starting next year, discounted at 5%...

...is worth $10 ÷ 5%, or $200, today.

Amazing. That infinite set of discounted cash flows adds up to exactly $200. More generally, here's the formula:

$$\frac{\text{NPV of a}}{\text{perpetuity}} = \frac{\text{Payment}}{\text{Discount Rate}}$$

$$\$200 = \frac{\$10}{0.05}$$

A little thought can reveal why this must be the case. This investment is going to pay you $10 a year indefinitely. If 5% is the discount rate you apply to this investment, then a $10 annual payment must represent 5% of the value of the investment.

$$\$10 = 5\% \text{ of the value}$$

$$\$10 = (0.05)(\text{Value})$$

$$\frac{\$10}{0.05} = \text{Value} = \$200$$

Notice how big a multiplier this is: 20 times the annual payment of $10 is the NPV ($200). That 20 is just 1 divided by the discount rate:

$$20 = \frac{1}{0.05} = \frac{1}{5\%}$$

The smaller the discount rate, the bigger the multiple, because future cash flows don't get discounted as much. So the whole stack is worth (relatively speaking) a lot today.

Discount Rate $= 2\%$ ▷ Multiplier $= \frac{1}{0.02} = 50$ ▷ A yearly payment of $10 forever is worth $10 \times 50 = 500 today, if you discount at 2%.

Conversely, the larger the discount rate, the smaller the multiple, because future cash flows get discounted a lot. So the whole stack is not worth very much today.

Discount Rate $= 15\%$ ▷ Multiplier $= \frac{1}{0.15} = 6.667$ ▷ A yearly payment of $10 forever is worth $10 \times 6.667 = 66.67 today, if you discount at 15%.

Notice *how sensitive* the NPV of a perpetuity is to the discount rate, especially when the discount rate is small. This is one way to fudge numbers to make them come out the way you want.

A key point to remember when you value a perpetuity is that the first payment always starts *next* year, in Year 1; today is Year 0. In fact, in any DCF (discounted cash flow) analysis, today is Time 0.

A Growing Stream

What if that infinite stream of payments is itself getting larger over time? How much are they worth now?

Let's say that next year, you'll get a $10 payment, and then every payment after that will be larger than the previous by 3%.

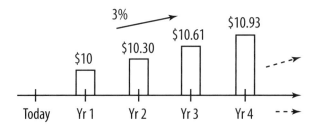

All you have to do is pick a discount rate that exceeds this growth rate. (To be conservative, pick small growth rates and large discount rates for perpetuities.) Say the discount rate $r = 8\%$. Then the math turns out to be easy.

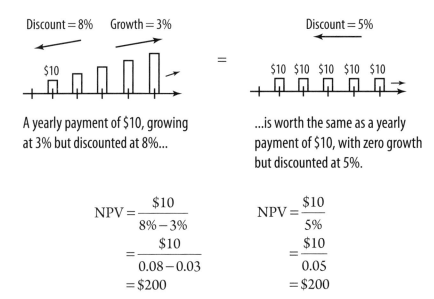

Discount = 8%   Growth = 3%

A yearly payment of $10, growing at 3% but discounted at 8%...

$$\text{NPV} = \frac{\$10}{8\% - 3\%}$$
$$= \frac{\$10}{0.08 - 0.03}$$
$$= \$200$$

Discount = 5%

...is worth the same as a yearly payment of $10, with zero growth but discounted at 5%.

$$\text{NPV} = \frac{\$10}{5\%}$$
$$= \frac{\$10}{0.05}$$
$$= \$200$$

In general, if the growth rate is g and the discount rate is r, then:

$$\text{NPV of a growing perpetuity} = \frac{\text{Payment (next year)}}{r - g}$$

This is why you pick large r's and small g's. To avoid dividing by zero or a negative number, you must make r bigger than g.

Stock Valuation

Why all this focus on perpetuities? For one thing, because owning a share of stock in a dividend-paying company gives you the right to an endless stream of dividends (unless the company goes bankrupt, gets acquired, cuts its dividend, or whatever). And in theory, *the current value of the stock is the net present value of all expected future dividends*, discounted back at an appropriate rate—even if the company does not currently pay dividends! (If a company declares it will *never* pay dividends, then it's telling its owners they can *never* take any profits out directly. Bad news.)

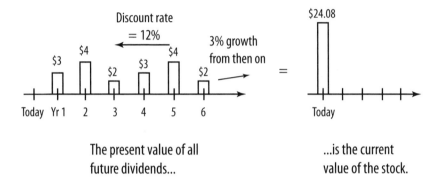

The present value of all future dividends...   ...is the current value of the stock.

Here's how the process goes.

1. Estimate future dividends both in the near term and in the long term.

    At some point, you'll have to pick a final dividend and then estimate a continuing growth rate. Be careful—that final dividend ($2 in Year 6) and growth rate (3%) wind up contributing over half of the NPV of $24.

2. Compute the present value of all but the final dividend.

$$\text{PV of Years 1–5} = \frac{\$3}{1.12} + \frac{\$4}{(1.12)^2} + \frac{\$2}{(1.12)^3} + \frac{\$3}{(1.12)^4} + \frac{\$4}{(1.12)^5}$$
$$= \$11.47$$

3. Compute the present value of Year 6 and later dividends in two steps:

    a) Bring the growing perpetuity back to a Year 5 value. Remember that perpetuities are valued using "next year's" payment as the first payment, so if Year 6 is "next year" for the moment, then Year 5 is "this year."

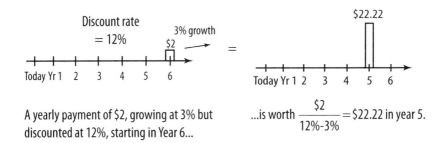

A yearly payment of $2, growing at 3% but discounted at 12%, starting in Year 6...

...is worth $\dfrac{\$2}{12\%-3\%}=\$22.22$ in year 5.

$$\text{Value in Year 5}=\frac{\text{Payment in Year 6}}{r-g}$$

This $22.22 is known as the **terminal value**.

    b) Now bring that $22.22 in Year 5 back to today, by discounting at 12% over 5 years.

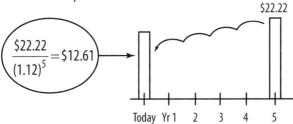

$$\frac{\$22.22}{(1.12)^5}=\$12.61$$

4. Add up the two large present values:

$11.47	+	$12.61	=	$24.08
PV of		PV of		
Years 1–5		Years 6–Infinity		

Alternatively, you might use something called *free cash flow* (*FCF*) to value a company.

Free cash flow (FCF)	=	Cash flow from operations (money thrown off by the operating activities of the company)	−	Capital expenditures (big investments by the company in equipment, etc.)

Free cash flow is the cash available to pay back investors (both debthold-ers and shareholders). The current value of a company, including both debt and equity, is the net present value of all predicted FCF's. It is hard to game these FCF numbers on accounting statements, and they provide better insight into companies that don't pay dividends currently or have never done so. You do the same kind of DCF analysis on free cash flows as you do on dividends.

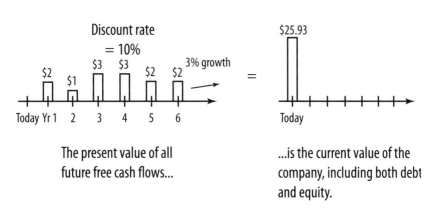

The present value of all future free cash flows...

...is the current value of the company, including both debt and equity.

There are other ways to value stocks besides fundamental analysis of cash flows. Most importantly, you can compare the company to others in its industry. For instance, you might simply look at the *P/E ratios* (the ratio of stock price to earnings per share) of a number of competi-tors. Then you can determine whether Company X is expensive or not. The P/E tells you how many dollars you need to spend right now to buy a dollar of earnings, so a higher P/E means more expensive earnings.

When you think about this kind of ratio, however, don't abandon your knowledge of discounted cash flows. The P/E ratio works like a multiplier on a perpetuity. That is, a P/E of 20 times earnings means that profits represent only 5% (= 1/20) of its stock price. A higher P/E means a lower percent return in this sense.

What Discount Rate Should You Use?

The key principle in picking an r for a set of future cash flows is this:

> Consider those cash flows as promises—as an investment you can buy into. Apply the same discount rate as you would to similar investments with similar risks.

Go back to the idea of risk and return. Riskier investments need to promise a higher expected rate of return, in order to attract money. Lower-risk investments do not need to pay as much.

This begs the question: how do you measure risk?

Risk = Volatility

A low risk investment changes value in a relatively smooth, predictable way. If you plot how much that investment is worth at any point in time, you see a smooth curve:

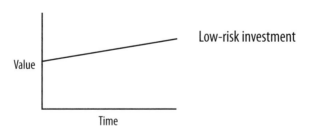

In contrast, a high-risk investment changes value in a jagged, unpredictable way:

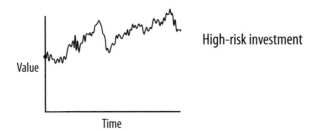

You can quantify this contrast. Gather up all the daily **returns** on each investment—the daily percent changes in the value of each.

| | Daily Return | |
Date	Low-risk	High-risk
March 1	+0.07%	+0.7%
March 2	+0.07%	+0.02%
March 3	+0.08%	−0.87%
March 4	+0.07%	+1.28%
March 5	+0.06%	−0.56%

The low-risk returns are very steady, with low volatility, while the high-risk returns are all over the map—they're highly volatile.

Statistics rides to the rescue. As discussed in Chapter 16, the **standard deviation** of each set of returns provides a convenient measure of volatility over the relevant time period.

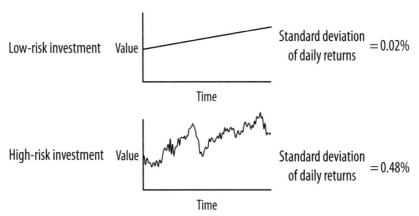

However, this approach doesn't go far enough. Standard deviation on its own just tells you about the risk of this one investment, as if it were the only investment in the world. But your risk also depends on every *other* investment you hold. Adding an inherently risky investment to your **portfolio** of investments can actually *reduce* your overall risk. This happens most clearly if this new investment tends to move opposite to everything else you hold:

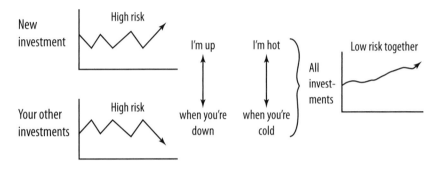

Katy Perry in "Hot 'N' Cold" is really singing about **negative correlation**. A new investment that's negatively correlated with your other investments is a great thing, because you can raise your expected return while lowering your overall risk. This is the basic principle behind hedge funds, which theoretically try to hedge their bets.

You don't have to have negative correlation to win. A group of **uncorrelated** investments that move randomly relative to each other, or even investments with imperfect positive correlation, give you the benefits of **diversification**.

Eggs in Many Baskets

According to the principle of diversification, you're better off with your eggs in many different baskets than with your eggs in just one basket, as long as the baskets are at least somewhat independent.[1] Be careful—in

---

1　　　This is assuming you're a financial investor with little direct control over the companies and

times of market stress, previously uncorrelated values can become very correlated. No one thought that real estate prices in 20 different US cities would all decline at once—but they did. Lots of baskets got into one big handbasket and then all went to hell together.

The Capital Asset Pricing Model, or CAPM

Back to the big question—what discount rate should you use to evaluate some potential investment, say the stock of some company?

The CAPM (pronounced "Cap-Em") gives you a process. To calculate the right discount rate for the stock, you need three pieces of information:

1. The *"risk-free" rate of return*, r_f

   This is the return you could get from a theoretically riskless investment. Sadly, there is no such riskless thing in reality. Short-term US government debt (Treasury bills) is taken as the proxy. (If the US government ever defaults on T-bills, get ready for a wild ride, Mad-Max style.) Depending on your time frame, you might take $r_f = 5\%$ to 7%. Recently, the risk-free rate has been much lower.

2. The *market rate of return*, r_m

   This is what you'd earn by holding a basket of claims on every possible asset in the world. Sadly, a complete *market basket* also doesn't exist. The return on the *S&P 500*, a basket[2] of common stocks of the 500 largest publicly held US companies, is often taken as the proxy. Alternatively, you can take the *market risk premium* (conveniently defined as $r_m - r_f$), which historically has been around 8%, and add it to your value for r_f to get r_m.

---

other assets you invest in. A game theorist might counsel you in some situations (in which you have direct control) to put all your eggs in one basket and guard that basket with your life. This is known as **strategic commitment.** Whatever you do, don't count your eggs before they hatch.

2   It is a mystery why finance folks like baskets, whereas consultants prefer buckets.

3. The **beta** (Greek letter β) of the stock

    Beta is a number that answers this question:

    If the whole stock market twitches upwards 1%, what do you expect this particular stock to do, on average?

    High-beta stocks tend to twitch upward more than 1%—say 2% or even 3%. Tech stocks typically have high betas.

    Low-beta stocks don't tend to twitch upward as much as 1%. Maybe they'd tend to go up only 0.5%, or not move at all (zero beta), or even go negative, although that's really rare. Utilities have low betas.

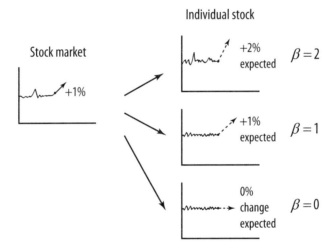

Like standard deviation, beta measures risk, but in a different way. Standard deviation measures the risk of an investment in isolation. Beta tells you what happens to your overall risk when you add some new investment to your portfolio. Beta is a measure of **nondiversifiable risk**—the risk you can't simply get rid of by holding a bunch of different assets. By the way, you're generally presumed to be holding a portfolio consisting of some blend of the whole market basket and the risk-free asset. In theory, that's always supposed to be the best you can do.[3]

Anyway, the beta of stock X is itself the product of two numbers:

a) The correlation between the price of stock X and the overall level of the market.

b) The relative volatility of stock X, compared to the average volatility of the market. This is expressed as a ratio of standard deviations.

A high beta can come from a high correlation between the individual stock and the market (they tend to move together).

A highly volatile asset, though, could be completely uncorrelated with the overall market. In that case, the zero correlation would cause the asset to have a zero beta.

Once you have a beta for the stock (sometimes you just look it up or average the betas of comparable companies), you make a graph, with beta along the x-axis and return along the y-axis.

Return

Beta

You put two points on the graph. One is for the risk-free investment. Since the risk-free asset has no risk, its volatility is zero, and its beta is also zero. However, it has some positive return, the risk-free rate r_f.

---

3   Warren Buffett, Steve Cohen, and other billionaire investors would say otherwise, of course. Buffett and Cohen follow very different investing philosophies, but there's nothing odd about what they primarily invest in—the common stock of US companies—and they both have beaten the market handily, year after year.

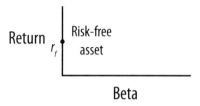

The other point is for the market basket. This asset has a return of r_m and a beta of 1, by definition. (Beta measures *correlation with* and *volatility relative to* the market. The market is always perfectly correlated with itself and is as volatile as itself, so the market beta = 1.)

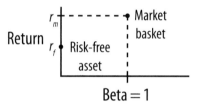

Draw a line between the two points. The expected return of any stock—what we've been looking for—lies on that *security market line*. You tell us the beta (on the *x*-axis), and we'll tell you the expected return (on the *y*-axis).

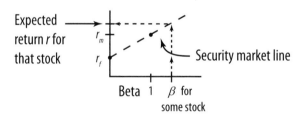

This is the heart of CAPM. As a formula, the security market line looks like the formula for a line.

$$y \quad = \quad mx \quad + \quad b$$

vertical axis · slope · horizontal axis · y-intercept

$$r \quad = \quad (r_m - r_f)\beta \quad + \quad r_f$$

Conceptually, CAPM is a fancy way of expressing the typical risk-return tradeoff:

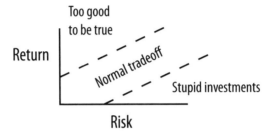

What Else Is There in First-Year Finance?

1. *Efficient Market Hypothesis (EMH)*

This says that big capital markets, such as that for **large-cap US equities** (the common stock of big US companies), are very competitive places. Everyone else in the game is probably as smart as you are. So if you've spotted what you think is a mispricing on some stock, the EMH would say you're wrong—**the price is right,** as Bob Barker might say, because it already incorporates all the information and insights anyone could have.

The battle is on between efficient-market theorists and proponents of the new field of behavioral finance, which seeks to account for market bubbles and panics rather than command them to hide or not to exist in the first place. You won't do more than give a head nod to the existence of behavioral finance in an introductory course, though, so don't get all excited.

2. *Capital Structure*

Is your company funded more by debt (liabilities) or equity (stock ownership)? This is the question of capital structure. In a perfect world, the **MM** theorists (Miller & Modigliani, who never had a tiger show in Vegas) would argue that it doesn't matter. In the real world, or at least in the US, debt financing gets a tax break—companies don't get taxed on interest payments, but profits due to equity shareholders are taxed first at the corporate level. So the **weighted average cost of capital**, or WACC, blends the cost of debt and the cost of equity together with that debt tax break.

In general, finance class reminds you constantly that capital—money to invest—isn't free. Your investors demand a return on that capital. And what you choose to do with that capital, as a manager in a company, should always be considered relative to what *else* your investors could do with their money. If you don't have a good project to invest in, one that has a positive NPV (meaning it beats out industry-standard projects), you should give your investors their money back, or sleep with one eye open.

3. *Options*

A financial **option** is the right to buy or sell some asset at a certain price. For instance, a **call option** on stock X with a **strike price** of $10 is the right to *buy* the stock at $10, either at some future date or up until then. (A **put option** is the right to *sell* the stock. Think *call*—you can *call* it to you when you want. *Put*—you *put* it to someone else when you want.) Options are side bets on the direction you expect a stock price to go. Two key points to remember about options:

> a) **Put-call parity**: the prices of calls and puts are linked together with the price of the underlying stock and the risk-free rate at which you can borrow money. If you know three of these num-

bers (price of a call, price of a put, price of the stock, and the risk-free rate), you can figure out the fourth.

b) **Volatility**: the higher the volatility of the underlying stock, the more valuable the option. That may seem counter intuitive, until you realize that holding an option has *no downside* (except for the cost of the option in the first place). If you've got a call option with a strike of $10, you're betting the price of the stock will go up (that way, when you *exercise* the option and buy the stock at $10, you can resell it right away for more). So, if the price goes up, that's what you do, and you make money. But if the price goes down, so what? You let the option expire unexercised. So you *like* volatility in the stock, because you don't care that that means more potential downside for equity holders (you're not one of them). You've taken a one-sided bet, and the more extreme the possible upside, the better for you.

CHAPTER 19: MARKETING

This chapter is deliberately short, since the typical first-year course doesn't contain too much quantitative content (the focus of this academic section). However, it's worth introducing a few key concepts and tools.

What Is Marketing?

Marketing likes to consider itself distinct from "sales," which has a hard, pushy connotation. Marketing is all about ***customer needs***—figuring out those needs, whether they're explicit or not, and then meeting those needs in a profitable way. In other words, the ***value*** of your product to your customer must be higher than its price to him or her. Meanwhile, the sale price has to more than cover *your* costs, so that you can make a profit.

As a subject of study and as a profession, marketing is not soft and fuzzy. It's *very* quantitative and data driven. You might think that marketers are "creatives" dreaming up funny new ad campaigns. Yes, marketers need to be creative, but they are squarely on the business side of things—and no, it's not their job to come up with funny ads. That's what Mad Men are for.

What Do Marketers Do?

STP: Segment, Target, Position

Marketers cut up large groups of customers into smaller, more homogeneous **segments**. Then they **target** certain higher-priority segments and **position** products to appeal to those segments.

Marketing Mix: the Four P's

The way marketers position the company's offerings is by adjusting elements of the **marketing mix**, the levers available to marketers. These levers are commonly labeled the Four P's[1]:

1. **Product**: its actual features.
2. **Price**: not only the direct price but also discounts, etc.
3. **Place**: where the product is available, or the **channels** from you to the customer.
4. **Promotion**: advertising, public relations, etc.

Both Rational And Non-rational Appeals

Good marketing works on every level. It takes into proper account the rational drives of consumer behavior—for instance, the fact that price cuts typically lead to increased demand. However, marketing also seeks to understand how real consumers are not perfect "utility-maximizers" and to capitalize on that understanding. In this regard, marketing has a lot in common with social psychology and behavioral economics. Ultimately, whether by rational or by non-rational means, marketers want customers to "sign on the line that is dotted," as Alec Baldwin's character proclaims in *Glengarry Glen Ross*, an astounding film and play about real estate salesmen.

---

1   Developed by Jerome McCarthy. So simple; so brilliant. Our competing model "The 13 X's" has not caught on as well.

Glengarry also provides two marketing-related acronyms:

A	Always
B	Be
C	Closing

ABC expresses what you always gotta be doing.

A	Attention
I	Interest
D	Decision
A	Action

The AIDA model was actually published in 1925 by E. K. Strong, although the D stood for Desire. Either way, AIDA is actually a useful little mnemonic for the stages of the buying process: first, you need the customer's *attention*, then you pique his or her *interest* and awaken *desire*, until the customer makes the *decision* and takes *action*. Of course, Alec Baldwin delivers this with more oomph.

Defining and Sizing a Market

The word **market** has different meanings in different fields.

- In finance, it's never "a" market—it's always "the" market or "the" markets, meaning the financial markets, where financial securities are bought and sold. In the same way, to Wall Streeters, "the city" only means one city: New York (unless you're in London, in which case it's The City).

- In economics, a market is a collection of both buyers and sellers, buying and selling something.

- In marketing, the term **market** usually refers just to the buyers— the **current or potential customers of a product** or set of products.

This immediately brings up a question of scope:

- How broad is the geographic range you care about?
- How broad is the product definition?

<u>Narrow</u>   ————————▶   <u>Broad</u>

The market for   The market for
children's DVDs   children's entertainment
in Atlanta.   in the Southeast.

Once you've decided on a geographic and product scope, you can **size** the market:

- How many customers are there or could there be? (Less common)
- How much money do those customers spend annually or could they spend annually? (More common)

So you'll hear these kinds of remarks:

"The market for children's DVDs in Atlanta is $X million."

How do you get to $X million? By multiplication:

$$
\begin{pmatrix} \text{Market for} \\ \text{children's DVDs} \\ \text{in Atlanta} \end{pmatrix} = \begin{pmatrix} \text{Number of} \\ \text{customers in} \\ \text{Atlanta} \end{pmatrix} \times \begin{pmatrix} \text{Annual spending on} \\ \text{children's DVDs,} \\ \text{per customer} \end{pmatrix}
$$

You can break up the factors on the right further. **Households (HH)** are often a convenient "customer" to think about.

$$
\begin{pmatrix} \text{Number of} \\ \text{customers in} \\ \text{Atlanta} \end{pmatrix} = \begin{pmatrix} \text{Population} \\ \text{of Atlanta} \end{pmatrix} \times \begin{pmatrix} \dfrac{1\ \text{Household}}{\#\ \text{of People}} \end{pmatrix} \times \begin{pmatrix} \%\ \text{of HH with} \\ \text{young children} \end{pmatrix} \times \begin{pmatrix} \%\ \text{of those} \\ \text{HH that buy} \end{pmatrix}
$$

Each of these terms on the right of the equation can be either looked up or estimated.

Try an estimation:

$$\left(\begin{array}{c} 3 \text{ million people} \\ \text{in Atlanta} \end{array} \right) \times \left(\dfrac{1 \text{ Household}}{3 \text{ People}} \right) \times \left(25\% \right) \times \left(80\% \right)$$

| Making this up | Also making this up | Assuming children between 2 and 15, about 1/4 of the population | High (but not 100%) **penetration** of DVD players |

$$= 200{,}000 \text{ households in the market}$$

Now break up the annual spending per household:

$$\begin{array}{c} \text{Annual spending on} \\ \text{children's DVDs} \\ \text{per customer} \end{array} = \left(\begin{array}{c} \text{Number of purchases} \\ \text{per year} \end{array} \right) \times \left(\text{\$ per purchase} \right)$$

$$= \left(10 \text{ DVDs} \right) \times \left(\$15 \right)$$

| Maybe estimated too high | Average retail, estimated |

$$= \$150 \text{ per household}$$

So this is what you get from this back-of-the-envelope calculation:

$$\left(\begin{array}{c} \text{Market for} \\ \text{children's} \\ \text{DVDs in Atlanta} \end{array} \right) = \left(\begin{array}{c} \text{Number of} \\ \text{customers} \\ \text{in Atlanta} \end{array} \right) \times \left(\begin{array}{c} \text{Annual spending on} \\ \text{children's DVDs} \\ \text{per customer} \end{array} \right)$$

$$= \left(200{,}000 \text{ HH} \right) \times \left(\$150 / \text{HH} \right)$$

$$= \$30 \text{ million}$$

If you want to do that math in your head, borrow a 0 from the $150 to make 2,000,000 on the left, then multiply:

$$200,000 \quad \times \quad \$150$$

$$2,000,000 \times \$15$$

$$2 \text{ million} \quad \times \quad \$15$$

$$= \$30 \text{ million}$$

If your **market share** is 10%, then you're selling $3 million of the children's DVDs to the Atlanta market. In real life, you do all these estimates and calculations much more precisely. But you have to be able to scribble something on the back of any envelope.

Quant in Marketing

Although the typical first marketing course isn't that quant-heavy, a number of quantitative tools are used by working marketers. You could say that marketing is an arena in which many quant tools born in other subjects come out to play.

1. Economics and Marketing

Marketers often try to figure out the actual **demand curve** for their products and/or for the industry. One way to do this is with little experiments with discounts. The information about price elasticity of demand is well worth the cost.

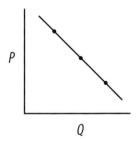

Marketers may also try to find the customer **utility function**, which measures the typical customer's utility or happiness as a factor of various product attributes. In other words, you have a mathematical representation of customer preferences.

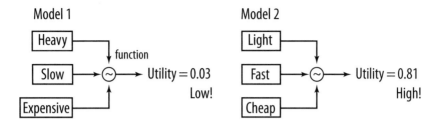

Model 1 is obviously worse (= has lower utility) than Model 2; you don't need a utility function to know that. But what about a heavy, cheap model vs. a light, expensive model? (Think laptops.) Now the utility function gets interesting. Using such a function to represent consumer preferences can shed light on tough decisions, such as trading off weight and cost.

Finally, a quant concept frequently used in economics is that of **marginal benefit** and **marginal cost**. In marketing, theoretically you'd want to optimize your marketing mix by equalizing the marginal benefit of the last dollar you spent on each part of the mix:

Marginal Benefit (MB) of final $1 spent to improve Product attributes		MB of final $1 spent on Pricing elements (e.g. discounts)		MB of final $1 spent on Place elements (e.g. channel incentives)		MB of final $1 spent on Promotion (e.g. advertising)
	=		=		=	

It might be difficult to measure all these marginal benefits, but the thinking exercise is worthwhile anyway.

2. Accounting, Finance, and Marketing

To measure progress and success, marketers use metrics defined in accounting and finance, such as **contribution margin** (price minus variable cost) and **return on investment** (profit divided by investment, to simplify matters radically). For instance, you might use the contribution margin and a product's fixed costs (FC) to do a quick **breakeven analysis**. Say that you can sell the product for $100, while the variable cost is $60. Then the contribution margin is $100 − $60 = $40, which is the amount each sale contributes to cover fixed costs and ultimately to provide profit. The breakeven (BE) is the number of units you must sell to cover the fixed cost exactly. If FC = $400,000, and each unit contributes $40 to cover that cost, then your BE is $400,000/$40 per unit = 10,000 units. You can visualize this situation on a graph, as was shown in the Managerial Accounting section of Chapter 17:

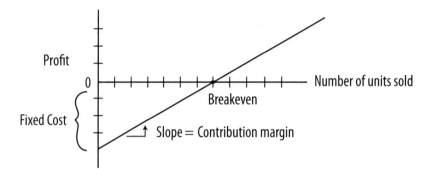

Accounting is the language of business, they say, and marketers must speak that language. Finance provides a means of evaluating possible future cash flows from projects such as a potential new product launch. For instance, if your analysis of this launch shows a positive *net present value*, after you discount future cash flows at an appropriate rate, then finance says you should pull the trigger and launch the product. As you monitor the launch, you would study *sales variance* reports to examine how reality matched your forecasts.

3. Statistics and Marketing

Statistical tools are of extreme importance in marketing. The first tool shows up in first-year stats class:

a) **Regression analysis** permits you to forecast demand and predict the sales response to various marketing levers you might pull, such as increased spending on promotions.

The next few tools probably won't be covered in your stats course, but you should understand what they are used to do.

b) ***Factor analysis*** (or principal components analysis) reduces a very complex picture of your customers to a simpler one. Say you know 50 separate pieces of information about each of your customers. That's a 50-dimensional space—way too hard to conceptualize. Factor analysis can help you reduce the number of variables, maybe down to three or four. Moreover, those three or four variables might have meaningful interpretations themselves, shedding light on your customer base.

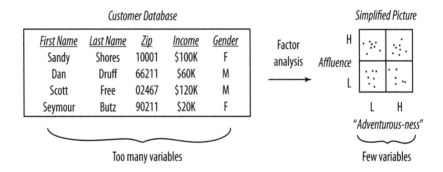

c) ***Cluster analysis*** does what it says—it helps you separate data into natural clusters.

These clusters might correspond to market segments. Customers within a segment are similar to each other but different from customers in other segments. Clusters can provide the appropriate grouping.

d) *Conjoint analysis* lets you efficiently uncover customer preferences, as expressed through utility functions. You ask customers to pick between various models of a product. Those models embody different possible attributes, such as price, speed, color, etc. The nice thing is that you don't have to ask about every possible combination of attributes (which would take way too long). You can discover customer preferences with just a few well-chosen questions.

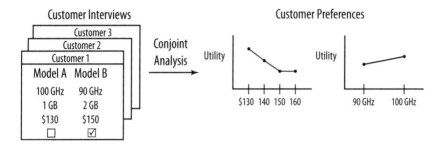

Chapter 20:
Operations & Supply Chain

~~~~~~~~~~~~~~~~~~~~

If you like the "business = factory" metaphor that we discussed at the beginning of Part III, you've come to the right place. Operations and Supply Chain Management are all about making the factory sing with efficiency.

"Ops" is a very broad subject, but this chapter focuses on three core quantitative topics:

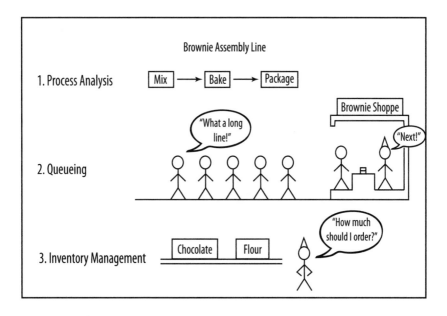

Process Analysis

Processes are recipes or assembly lines with stages. Say you're making a lot of brownies to sell.

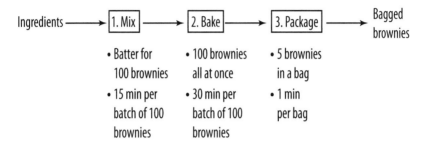

Lay out what happens at each stage and how much time it takes—the *cycle time*, or **CT**, for that stage. For instance, the cycle time for the Mix is 15 minutes per batch of 100 brownies. You can leave it like that, or you can convert to a "per brownie" time in either minutes (min) or seconds (sec):

$$15 \text{ min} \times \frac{60 \text{ sec}}{\text{min}} = 900 \text{ seconds}$$

$$900 \text{ sec} \div 100 \text{ brownies} = 9 \text{ seconds per brownie}$$

You just have to remember that the Mix stage is a **batch process**—a single dollop of brownie batter doesn't literally come out every 9 seconds.

To compare cycle times, express them all with the same denominator—per brownie, or per batch of 100 brownies. Just pick one. Batches are often more intuitive when the stages actually involve them (as in baking examples), but the most important thing is to be consistent.

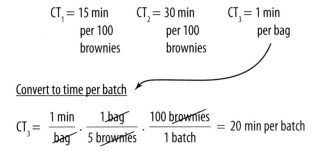

$$CT_1 = 15 \text{ min per 100 brownies} \quad CT_2 = 30 \text{ min per 100 brownies} \quad CT_3 = 1 \text{ min per bag}$$

Convert to time per batch

$$CT_3 = \frac{1 \text{ min}}{\text{bag}} \cdot \frac{1 \text{ bag}}{5 \text{ brownies}} \cdot \frac{100 \text{ brownies}}{1 \text{ batch}} = 20 \text{ min per batch}$$

How fast can this assembly line crank out a batch? How much time does one batch of brownies take?

First, you have to clarify what you mean, since there are two possibilities.

1) Is the question "How long does a particular batch take *from start to finish?*"

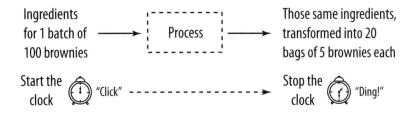

Ingredients for 1 batch of 100 brownies → Process → Those same ingredients, transformed into 20 bags of 5 brownies each

Start the clock "Click" ⤍ Stop the clock "Ding!"

This is called the **manufacturer's lead time, MLT**, or just **lead time**. And no, this isn't necessarily the sum of all the cycle times. This isn't a special run on Saturday for the CEO's birthday party, *when no other brownies are in the system.* Lead time tells you how long it takes one set of ingredients to go all the way through *when the factory is running normally*—and there's a difference. More on this later.

2) The question could also be "How often does a full batch of brownies come out of the system?" In other words, what's the cycle time for the whole process?

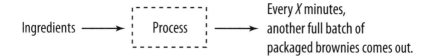

Look at the second question first:

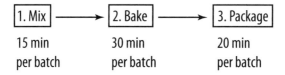

If the stages have different cycle times, then the overall pace is set by the **slowest** stage, which in this case is the Bake stage. If the mixers work constantly, they'll just pile up unbaked batter next to the ovens. And the packagers can't work continuously either—a new batch of brownies comes out of the oven every half-hour, so the packagers do their thing for 20 minutes, finish the job, then sit around for 10 minutes of **idle time** as they wait for more brownies to be baked.

Here's the work schedule:

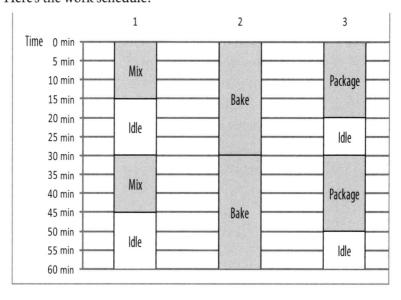

So the ***overall cycle time*** of the process is 30 minutes per batch, meaning that every 30 minutes, another full batch of packaged brownies emerges from the factory.

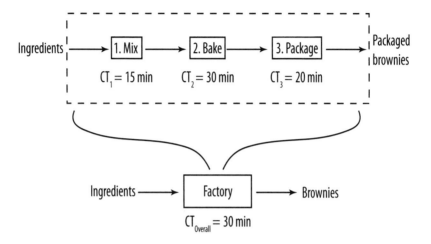

The Bake stage is what constrains your operation—it's your ***rate-limiting step*** or ***bottleneck***. If you owned the brownie factory, where should you spend more money?

- Hire more mixers and buy bigger mixing bowls?

- Buy a second oven, doubling your baking capacity?

- Hire more packagers?

Of course, you'd buy another oven. Spending more money on the other steps only increases the idle time. On the other hand, with another oven, you can't bake a single brownie any faster, but you can double the batch size at that step—so your effective cycle time for the Bake stage would be cut in half, from 30 minutes to 15 minutes. In that case, the Bake stage would no longer be the bottleneck. Instead, the slowest step would be Packaging ($CT = 20$ min).

The idea that the slowest stage sets the pace for the whole process was the point of an odd novel about operations that we were both assigned in school. This novel is called "The Goal," and years later we both easily recall the somewhat offensive image of Herbie, the overweight kid on the Boy Scout hike who slows the whole group down:

Slow
Herbie

The group winds up putting Herbie at the front, where everyone else can "encourage" (i.e., berate) him. Eventually they relieve him of his backpack, lightening his load so they can all walk faster. All that's left behind is Herbie's dignity:

Herbie,
faster but
sadder

Neither of us likes this example, but at least it's memorable. If you want to speed up a process, find the Herbie—the bottleneck—and put all your efforts into making that part of the process go faster.

Back to brownies. Assume you haven't bought a second oven, so the process still looks like this:

Ingredients ⟶ 1. Mix ⟶ 2. Bake ⟶ 3. Package ⟶ Packaged Brownies

$$CT_1 = 15 \text{ min} \qquad CT_2 = 30 \text{ min} \qquad CT_3 = 20 \text{ min}$$
$$(\text{bottleneck})$$

The overall cycle time is 30 minutes per batch. You can also say that the overall **throughput time** (**TPT**) is 1 batch per 30 minutes.

$$\frac{\text{Cycle time}}{CT} = \frac{30 \text{ min}}{1 \text{ batch}} \qquad\qquad \frac{\text{Throughput}}{TPT} = \frac{1 \text{ batch}}{30 \text{ min}}$$

Throughput is a rate of *stuff per time* (stuff/time), say batches/min. In contrast, cycle time is *time per stuff* (eg. 30 min/batch). Cycle time and throughput are just reciprocals of each other.

$$CT = \frac{1}{TPT} \qquad\qquad TPT = \frac{1}{CT}$$

How long will it take a *particular* set of ingredients to get through the system under normal conditions? This is a different question: the question of lead time. Remember that all three stages, including idle time for the first stage, have to take 30 minutes per batch. However, you can chop off the last 10 minutes.

Ingredients ⟶ 1. Mix ⟶ 2. Bake ⟶ 3. Package ⟶ Packaged Brownies

	1. Mix	2. Bake	3. Package	
	CT = 15 min	CT = 30 min	CT = 20 min	
	+ Idle = 15 min		No idle time	
	Total = 30 min			

$$\text{MLT} \quad = \quad 30 \quad + \quad 30 \quad + \quad 20 \quad = \quad \boxed{80 \text{ min}}$$

You don't count the 10 minutes of idle time in packaging because the batch is through that final step in 20 minutes.

So 80 minutes is the manufacturer's lead time. Imagine that there are partially-finished brownies at every stage in the assembly line. Now you decide to make a special batch of brownies with nuts.[1] If you add the nuts to the very next batch, how long will it take for that batch to get made? 80 minutes is the answer. Notice that you have to add in the first step's idle time to get the correct overall lead time because the special batch with nuts has to wait for the ovens to free up.

Be sure to keep the cycle time CT and the manufacturer's lead time MLT straight:

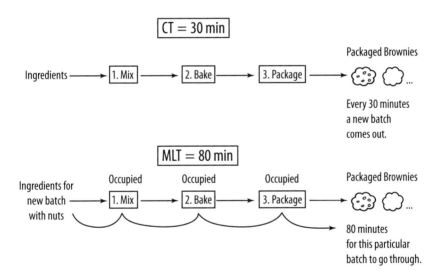

CT and MLT have a simple relationship:

$$\begin{array}{ccccc} \text{MLT} & = & 2\frac{2}{3} & \times & \text{CT} \\ 80 & = & 2\frac{2}{3} & \times & 30 \end{array}$$

---

1   Or whatever your preferred additive is for brownies.

This 2⅔ is almost the same thing as 3, the number of stages. One way to think of MLT is to multiply CT by the number of stages (3), then shave off the idle time from the final stage (10 minutes). That's why the number is slightly below 3.

In fact, 2⅔ is the **average number of batches in the system** at any one time. The ⅔ comes from the fact that the last stage only takes 20 minutes (out of 30 for a cycle), so there's only a batch there ⅔ of the time. The batch is "gone" during the 10 minutes of idle packaging time, so we count just ⅔ of a batch in our average.

The 2⅔ batches being mixed, baked, and packaged are also known as **Work in Process**, or **WIP** (pronounced "whip"). It's a form of unfinished inventory. The general formula is this:

Manufacturer's Lead Time	=	Work in Process	×	Cycle Time
80 min	=	2⅔ batches	×	30 min per batch
for 1 batch to travel through from start to finish		the average amount of stuff being worked on at all stages		the time between two batches coming off the line

If a new batch comes out every 30 minutes, and it takes 80 minutes to go all the way through, there must be $80/30 = 2⅔$ batches in the system. This relationship is known as **Little's Law**. It works even when there's fluctuation in the system and the numbers are just averages. You can rewrite Little's Law in terms of throughput TPT, which equals $1/CT$:

$$\text{MLT} = \text{WIP} \times \frac{1}{TPT}$$

$$\text{TPT} \times \text{MLT} = \text{WIP}$$

$$\left(\frac{1 \text{ batch}}{30 \text{ min}}\right) \cdot (80 \text{ min}) = 2⅔ \text{ batches}$$

Queueing

Queueing theory is all about *waiting in line*. The next time you're at the DMV, just think: you can ponder this theory over and over and over again as you wait for your number to be called.

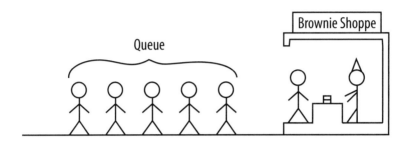

In the picture, there are 5 people in the **queue** (the line, to us Americans) and 1 person being served by the **server** behind the computer.

Little's Law shows up here too, if you think of the queue itself as a process. The people in the queue are like a Work in Process: unfinished inventory.

Say there are 5 customers on average in the queue—in other words, the **mean queue length L_q** = 5. Also say the **mean wait W_q** in the queue is 20 minutes (that's just like lead time, the time for 1 batch to get all the way through the factory). What's the equivalent of cycle time? In other words, if someone is served every X minutes, what is X? Or rather, how often do you get to yell, "You got served!"?

Process version of Little's Law:

$$\text{Manufacturer's Lead Time} = \text{Work In Process} \times \text{Cycle Time}$$
$$MLT = WIP \times CT$$

Queueing version of Little's Law:

$$\begin{array}{ccccc} \text{Mean Wait} & = & \text{Mean Length} & \times & \text{Mean Service Interval} \\ \text{in Queue} & & \text{of Queue} & & \text{Between Customers} \\ W_Q & = & L_Q & \times & X \\ 20\text{ min} & = & 5\text{ customers} & \times & X \end{array}$$

$$X = \frac{20\text{ min}}{5\text{ customers}} = 4\text{ min per customer}$$

This is often rewritten using a ***mean throughput rate R,*** which would be 1 customer every 4 minutes in this case.

$$\begin{array}{ccccc} \text{Mean Length} & & \text{Mean Wait} & \times & \text{Mean Throughput} \\ \text{of Queue} & & \text{in Queue} & & \text{Rate} \\ L_Q & = & W_q & \times & R \\ 5\text{ customers} & = & 20\text{ min} & \times & \dfrac{1\text{ customer}}{4\text{ min}} \end{array}$$

This says that if you can serve 1 customer every 4 minutes and there are 5 customers in the queue on average, then each customer will wait a total of $4 \times 5 = 20$ minutes, on average.

This also works if you include the person being served:

Mean Total People in System	=	Mean Wait in System	×	Mean Throughput Rate
L	=	W	×	R
6 customers	=	24 min	×	$\dfrac{1\ \text{customer}}{4\ \text{min}}$

There are a few other symbols to know:

- **Mean arrival rate λ** (Greek lambda) = number of customers arriving every hour (or every minute, every day, or whatever time period you choose)

- **Mean service rate μ** (Greek mu) = number of customers being served every hour (or other time period)

Think of λ as the mean rate of flow *into* the queue, while μ is the mean rate of flow *out of* the system.

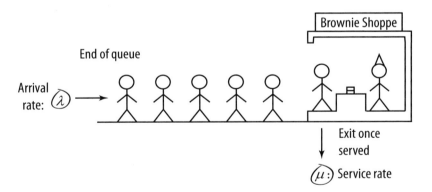

If the arrival rate and the service rate are the same and perfectly constant over time, then the line will be perfectly constant in length.

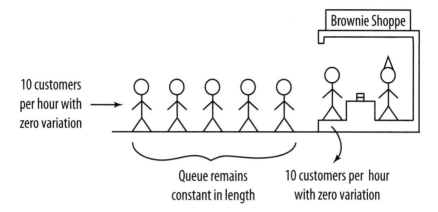

10 customers per hour with zero variation →

Queue remains constant in length

10 customers per hour with zero variation

Notice, however, that *any* queue length works equally well here. You could have a constant queue length of 2 customers—or 20, or 200, and if the arrival rate and service rate are perfectly constant and perfectly matched, those queues won't change in length. But obviously, from the point of view of the shop, it's better to have a short queue than a long queue—you have happier customers when they wait less. No one wants to smell fresh-baked brownies they can't eat.

So how do you shorten the queue length? You need to have the service rate exceed the arrival rate.

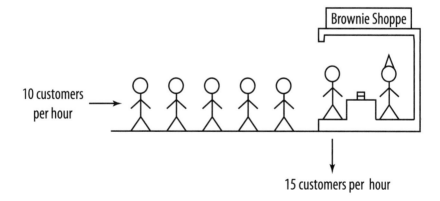

10 customers per hour →

15 customers per hour

Logically, you'd think that this would drive the queue length to zero—it's like draining the tank faster than you're refilling it. You'd be right if the arrival rate and service rate were perfectly constant. But they're typically not. In fact, the arrivals and departures are usually modeled as Poisson processes (see Chapter 16: Statistics), in which the customers act randomly and independently. This means that arrivals sometimes happen close together…

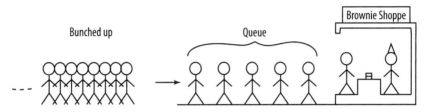

…and sometimes they're spread far apart.

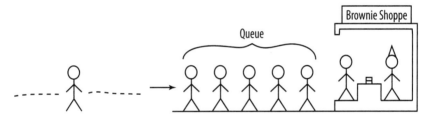

Departures (services) are similarly bunched—sometimes the order is quick, and sometimes it's slow.[2] Consider all the possible combinations:

		Service	
		Fast	Slow
Arrival	Fast	Balance: queue remains same length	Faster arrival: queue grows
	Slow	Faster service: queue shrinks **but** **cannot go below zero**	Balance: queue remains same length

---

2   Ever been to a Starbucks? Of course you have. What ever happened to ordering plain coffee? The guy in front of you has to have his grande soy extra-dry mocha latte with Splenda. That takes a fatiguing amount of time—both to order and to make.

You already know what happens when arrival and service are in balance—nothing. The queue stays the same length. When customers arrive faster than they're served, the line grows, and when customers are served faster than they arrive, the line shrinks. All that should make sense. Here's the key asymmetry, though—the queue can never get shorter than zero customers long. There's no such thing as a negative queue. What this means is that some of the *slow arrival + fast service* situations result in zero-length queues, and the server is idle. Unfortunately, you can't bank that idle time for the rush hours, when you have *fast arrival + slow service*, so the line tends to grow. Even if the arrival rate λ equals the service rate μ, any queue length from zero to infinity is equally likely if the arrivals and departures are randomly spaced. Over time, the queue length will explode.

This is very counter-intuitive. It turns out that if you want a short queue, on average, then you'll want to have your service rate μ be *significantly faster* than the arrival rate λ.

$$\text{Good situation: } \lambda = \frac{10 \text{ customers}}{\text{hour}} \qquad \mu = \frac{15 \text{ customers}}{\text{hour}}$$

The so-called **traffic intensity** (symbolized by the Greek letter ρ, or rho) is the ratio $\dfrac{\lambda}{\mu} = \dfrac{10}{15} = \dfrac{2}{3}$, in this case. You can also express this intensity in terms of the mean time between arrivals and the mean service time.

Arrivals	Service
$\lambda = \dfrac{10 \text{ customers}}{\text{hr}}$	$\mu = \dfrac{15 \text{ customers}}{\text{hr}}$
$\dfrac{1}{\lambda} = \dfrac{1}{10}$ hr per customer	$\dfrac{1}{\mu} = \dfrac{1}{15}$ hr per customer
Mean time between customers = 6 min $\left(\frac{1}{10} \text{ hour}\right)$	Mean service time = 4 min $\left(\frac{1}{15} \text{ hour}\right)$

$$\rho = \frac{\text{Mean service time}}{\text{Mean time between customers}}$$

$$\text{Traffic intensity } \rho = \frac{4 \text{ min}}{6 \text{ min}} = \frac{2}{3}$$

Unfortunately, the math on this shows a couple of troubling results.

1) The average **utilization** of your single server is equal to ρ.

   Joe behind the counter is only busy serving customers ⅔ of the time $(\rho = \tfrac{2}{3})$.

2) The average queue length L_q is equal to $\dfrac{\rho^2}{1-\rho}$.

   In this case, L_q works out to $\dfrac{\left(\tfrac{2}{3}\right)^2}{1-\tfrac{2}{3}} = \dfrac{\tfrac{4}{9}}{\tfrac{1}{3}} = \dfrac{4}{3}$.

   The line will be, on average, 1.33 customers long.

What if you want to reduce the fraction of time your server is idle from ⅓ to ⅕, so that $\rho = \tfrac{4}{5}$? Then the average queue length becomes:

$$L_q = \frac{\rho^2}{1-\rho} = \frac{\left(\tfrac{4}{5}\right)^2}{1-\tfrac{4}{5}} = \frac{\tfrac{16}{25}}{\tfrac{1}{5}} = \frac{16}{5} = 3.2 \text{ customers in line}$$

That's letting your server be idle 20% of the time. What if it still drives you nuts to see him or her standing around? Say you only can tolerate 10% idle time. Then you'd need $\rho = \tfrac{9}{10}$, and you'd have

$$L_q = \frac{\rho^2}{1-\rho} = \frac{\left(\tfrac{4}{10}\right)^2}{1-\tfrac{9}{10}} = \frac{\tfrac{81}{100}}{\tfrac{1}{10}} = 8.1 \text{ customers in line}$$

And that's **average** line length—you'd often have many more waiting.

Long story short—if you want short queues for your customers, you need to have substantial "idle" time for your servers. They can of course be doing other things for you during that idle time, but don't expect them to be talking to customers. Queue length and server idle time are in tension, and you must trade them off against each other.

A couple of last things on queues—if you have multiple servers, it's generally better to **pool the queues** into one long line.

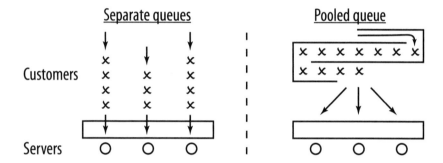

All kinds of businesses have caught on to this principle. Not only does it seem fairer to customers and reduce their stress of choosing the right line, a pooled queue often has shorter average waiting times, with less variance in those times as well.

However, the other principle is that a **priority scheme** for "quick" customers can help reduce average wait times for everyone. An express checkout line is good for you even if you aren't using it—it siphons off the quick-to-serve customers and reduces wait times for all.

Inventory Management

Congratulations, you've optimized your brownie-making process and your customer queue.

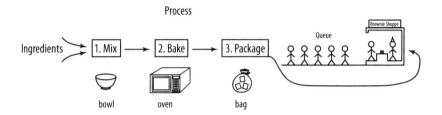

Now that business is hoppin', how much chocolate should you order? How should you manage your inventory of ingredients? Not surprisingly, inventory is subject to Little's Law as well.

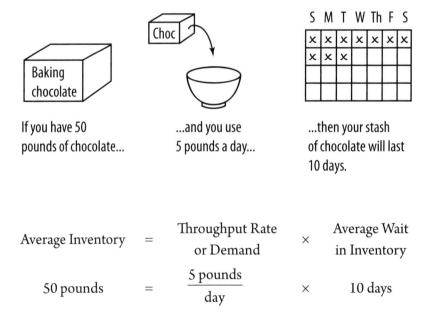

If you have 50 pounds of chocolate...

...and you use 5 pounds a day...

...then your stash of chocolate will last 10 days.

$$\text{Average Inventory} = \frac{\text{Throughput Rate}}{\text{or Demand}} \times \frac{\text{Average Wait}}{\text{in Inventory}}$$

$$50 \text{ pounds} = \frac{5 \text{ pounds}}{\text{day}} \times 10 \text{ days}$$

This section covers two fundamental models of inventory management. Both are simplified (like every other model in the world), but they provide important starting points.

1. Economic Order Quantity (EOQ)
    –   Use when demand is perfectly constant over time

2. Newsvendor
    –   Use when demand is uncertain, and you only have one chance, in advance, to order inventory

Economic Order Quantity

Say you use 5 pounds of chocolate a day in your brownie shop—day in, day out. From now until the end of time you will use 5 pounds of chocolate every day. (This demand, or throughput, is labeled *d*.)

There are two competing principles when it comes to figuring out your chocolate supply:

a) Order A Big Amount

This way, you save on the **ordering cost**. This is *not* the cost of the chocolate itself. Every time you place an order, you incur a separate cost of, say, $45 between shipping, handling, receiving, and even placing the order itself. This **per-order cost** is usually labeled *a*. You don't want to pay this cost too frequently, so you want to place fewer but larger orders.

b) Order A Small Amount

This way, you save on the **storage cost** (usually labeled *h*, for holding). This cost includes rent on the storage facility, electricity for the refrigerator to keep the chocolate cold, and even spoilage of some fraction. All in, say this cost is $2 per pound per day, for every pound of chocolate you hold in inventory. This cost leads you to want to place frequent, small orders.

Conveniently, the minimum total cost comes when these two principles are in balance—that is, when the ordering cost and the storage cost equal each other over the course of time.

$$
\begin{array}{ccc}
\text{Ordering Cost} & = & \text{Storage Cost Over} \\
\text{Over Time} & & \text{Time}
\end{array}
$$

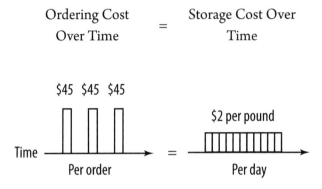

There is a "right size" for every order that balances these two costs. This right size is labeled Q (for quantity). To really grasp the principles at work, take two extreme examples:

Example 1: Order Once Every 30 Days

To meet the demand of 5 pounds of chocolate a day, you need to order $5 \times 30 = 150$ pounds each time. Over the course of 30 days, that drops steadily to zero, at a rate of 5 pounds a day:

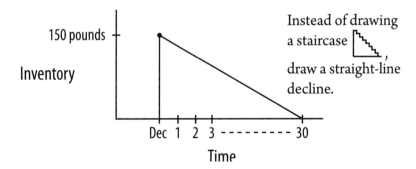

On December 30th, just as stocks reach zero, your next order of 150 pounds arrives. (Either your supplier can instantly meet your needs, like a genie, or you time your order perfectly in advance.) Another 30 days go by, the chocolate inventory falls steadily to zero, and the cycle repeats:

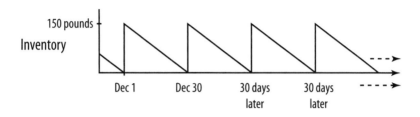

This sawtooth shape is typical of this sort of inventory model.

What are your costs over time (besides the cost of the chocolate itself, which will always be 5 pounds per day, times the price per pound)? In other words, what are your average daily costs of ordering and storing the chocolate?

a) **Daily Ordering Cost = Low** (because you're ordering infrequently)

$45 per order every 30 days gives you a daily cost of $45 ÷ 30 = $1.50.

You can write this using unit cancelation:

$$\frac{\$45}{\text{order}} \cdot \frac{1\ \text{order}}{30\ \text{days}} = \frac{45}{30}\ \text{dollars}\Big/\text{day} = \$1.50 \text{ per day}$$

b) **Daily Storage Cost = High** (because you're keeping a lot around)

Your inventory changes every day, but smoothly. You go from 150 pounds to zero at a steady rate, so you can just take the **average inventory** as $\dfrac{150+0}{2} = 75$ pounds.

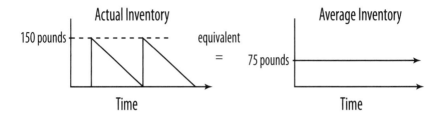

The average daily storage cost is $2 per pound per day, times 75 pounds = $150 per day. This is way more than the daily ordering cost of $1.50, and the total daily cost of $1.50 + $150 = $151.50 per day is too big.

Example 2: Order Once a Day

The other extreme is to order 5 pounds each day (since you use exactly 5 pounds per day).

a) ***Daily Ordering Cost = High*** (because you're ordering often)

$$\frac{\$45}{\text{order}} \cdot \frac{1 \text{ order}}{1 \text{ day}} = \$45 \text{ per day}$$

b) ***Daily Storage Cost = Low*** (because you're keeping very little around)

The average inventory is ½ of the order amount, so the average inventory is only ½ × 5 pounds = 2.5 pounds.

$2 per pound per day × 2.5 pounds = $5 per day

The total daily cost is lower than before ($45 + $5 = $50), but you can go still lower when the two costs equal each other.

Take a look at the symbols again:

$$d \quad = \quad \frac{\text{demand,}}{\text{in pounds per day}} \quad = \quad \text{5 pounds per day}$$

$$a \quad = \quad \frac{\text{ordering cost,}}{\text{per order}} \quad = \quad \text{\$45 per order}$$

$$h \quad = \quad \frac{\text{storage cost,}}{\text{per pound per day}} \quad = \quad \text{\$2 to store 1 pound for 1 day}$$

$$Q \quad = \quad \frac{\text{order quantity}}{\text{in pounds}} \quad = \quad \text{how much to order each time}$$

Use t for the days between orders. In the first case, t was 30 days, and Q was $5 \times 30 = 150$ pounds. The general formula is a rate-time-work relationship:

$$Q \quad = \quad d \quad \times \quad t$$

$$\text{amount} \quad = \quad \text{demand} \times \quad \text{time}$$

$$150 \text{ pounds} \quad = \quad \frac{5 \text{ pounds}}{\text{day}} \quad \times \quad 30 \text{ days}$$

The daily ordering cost is the per-order cost (a, or \$45) divided by the days between orders.

$$\text{Daily Ordering Cost} = \frac{a}{t}$$

Since $Q = d \cdot t$, you can solve for t and substitute:

$$t = \frac{Q}{d} \rightarrow \text{Daily Ordering Cost} = \frac{a}{Q/d} = \frac{ad}{Q}$$

The daily storage cost is the "per-pound-per-day" cost, which is h, times the average inventory, which is $Q/2$.

$$\text{Daily Storage Cost} = h \times \frac{Q}{2} = \frac{hQ}{2}$$

Now set the daily ordering cost and the daily storage cost equal to each other, and lo—you'll get Q in terms of the other numbers.

Daily Ordering Cost		Daily Storage Cost
	=	
$\dfrac{ad}{Q}$	=	$\dfrac{hQ}{2}$
$2ad$	=	hQ^2
$\dfrac{2ad}{h}$	=	Q^2

$$\boxed{\sqrt{\frac{2ad}{h}} = Q}$$

In this case, we get $\sqrt{\dfrac{2(\$45)(5)}{(\$2)}} = 15$ pounds.

This is the **Economic Order Quantity**, or **EOQ**. You should order 15 pounds at a time, which means you'll need to order every 3 days.

Test this quantity and see that you get the smallest total cost, compared to the total cost for any other order quantity.

$$\text{Daily Ordering Cost} = \frac{ad}{Q} = \frac{\$45 \cdot 5 \text{ pounds/day}}{15 \text{ pounds}} = \$15\big/\text{day}$$

$$\text{Daily Storage Cost} = \frac{hQ}{2} = \frac{(\$2 \text{ per pound})(15 \text{ pounds})}{2} = \$15\big/\text{day}$$

Total Daily Cost $= \$15 + \$15 = \$30$

With calculus, you can prove that this is the smallest possible cost—or you can just take our word for it. The principle that the costs should be the *same* to you both ways is rather deep, though—it's another aspect of the indifference principle. The best result often comes when you are indifferent between two options, or in this case, two costs.

At the end of the day, if you have constant, predictable demand on your inventory, then use this model. Figure out your per-order cost and storage cost, plug into the EOQ formula, and that's how much to order every time.

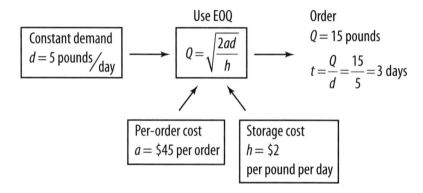

Newsvendor Model

The other fundamental inventory model involves very different assumptions.

1. Demand is now *random*. You don't know what it's going to be. All you know is that it will follow some *probability distribution.*[3]

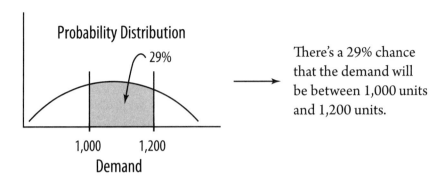

There's a 29% chance that the demand will be between 1,000 units and 1,200 units.

- That 29% was just completely made up as the area under the curve between 1,000 units and 1,200 units. The total area under the curve is always 100% (= 1). You usually take the distribution to be continuous  rather than discrete because it makes the math easier.

2. You have one shot at ordering—you can only do it once, and in advance.

The model is called "newsvendor" because selling newspapers is the perfect scenario. Say that you decide to sell the Sunday *New York Times* from your brownie shop.

Brownie Shoppe

You have to order the newspapers the night before, but you don't know exactly how many you'll sell the next day—and you can't place a second order.

Some numbers can help make things more concrete:

- Cost per paper $c = \$2$

- Sale price of paper $s = \$5$
  (Ops folks use s rather than p, which could indicate probability.)

- Profit per paper $= s - c = \$3$

For now, assume that the papers are worthless if you don't sell them by the end of the day. In other words, the salvage value $v = \$0$.

There is a probability distribution for the demand, but you don't need to know the distribution's exact shape right now.

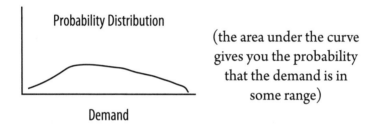

(the area under the curve gives you the probability that the demand is in some range)

How many papers should you order on Saturday night? Imagine that you're already decided to order 40 papers, which happens to be way on the left side of the distribution:

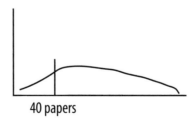

What's the chance that actual demand will be less than 40 papers? It depends on the shape of the distribution; say the answer is 15%.

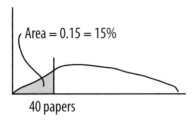

Then the chance that demand will be at least 40 papers is 85%.

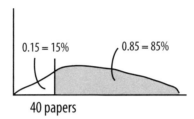

Remember, the total area under the curve is 1. (Also, it doesn't really matter what you do with the possibility of demand being *exactly* 40. The chance that demand is exactly any *particular* number is usually very small.) So, do you order the 41st paper? To consider the possible outcomes, you can look at a probability tree. Again, see Chapter 16: Statistics for a refresher.

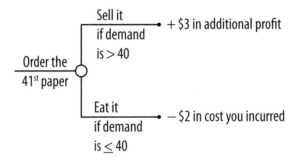

The $3 on the top branch equals $s - c$. It also has another name: ***under-age cost*** (pronounced "UN-der-ij," not "under-AGE," which can result in different kinds of costs altogether). Underage cost, or C_u, is the *cost of underestimating* demand by one paper. In this case, if you underestimate demand and you *could* have sold one more paper, you'd miss out on $3 of profit, so $C_u = \$3$. Likewise, ***overage cost*** ("OH-ver-ij"), or C_o, is the *cost of overestimating* demand and "eating" one of your newspapers. Since the paper cost you $2 and you get nothing for it ($0 salvage value), $C_o = \$2$.

What are the probabilities down each branch? Look at your distribution. Again, ignore what happens at exactly 40 papers.

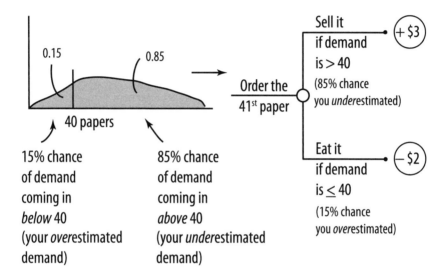

Would you take that bet? You have an 85% chance of winning $3 or a 15% chance of losing $2. So the expected value of the tree is:

$$
\begin{aligned}
\begin{matrix} \text{Expected} \\ \text{Value} \end{matrix} &= \begin{pmatrix} \text{Probability} \\ \text{of Top} \\ \text{Branch} \end{pmatrix} \times \begin{pmatrix} \text{Value} \\ \text{of Top} \\ \text{Branch} \end{pmatrix} + \begin{pmatrix} \text{Probability} \\ \text{of Bottom} \\ \text{Branch} \end{pmatrix} \times \begin{pmatrix} \text{Value} \\ \text{of Bottom} \\ \text{Branch} \end{pmatrix} \\[2ex]
&= \quad (0.85) \quad\times\quad (\$3) \;+\; (0.15) \quad\times\quad (-\$2) \\
&= \quad \$2.55 \qquad\qquad\quad\;\; +\; (-\$0.30) \\
&= \quad \$2.25
\end{aligned}
$$

The expected value is positive, so you should take that bet and order the 41st paper, and likewise the 42nd, and the 43rd ... Each one has a positive expected value to you, meaning that on average, you'd make money ordering that paper.

As you decide to order more and more papers, though, you move to the right on the distribution, and the probabilities of each branch shift. The chance of the top, *good* branch falls, while the chance of the bottom, *bad* branch rises.

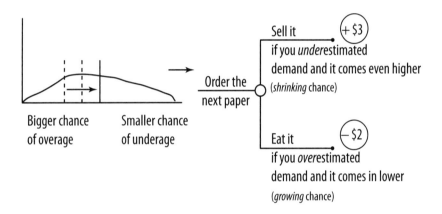

So the expected value of each additional paper is smaller and smaller, although still positive (so you decide to order it). At a certain point, though, the expected value of the next paper hits zero. At this magic number Q, the top branch's expected value (*EV*) cancels out that of the bottom branch.

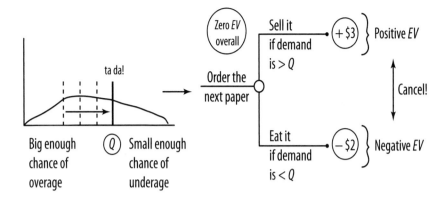

Beyond that point, additional papers *lose* you money—the trees have negative expected values. The chance of loss is too great.

So where is that magic Q? The answer lies in the probabilities:

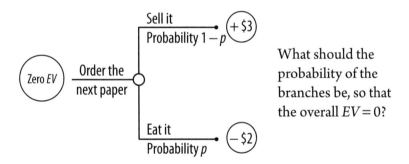

What should the probability of the branches be, so that the overall $EV = 0$?

First, notice that if the bottom branch has probability p, then the top branch has probability $1 - p$. Now plug into the equation for the overall expected value:

$$
\begin{array}{ccccc}
\text{Expected} \\
\text{Value}
\end{array}
=
\left(
\begin{array}{c}
\text{Probability} \\
\text{of Top} \\
\text{Branch}
\end{array}
\right)
\left(
\begin{array}{c}
\text{Value} \\
\text{of Top} \\
\text{Branch}
\end{array}
\right)
=
\left(
\begin{array}{c}
\text{Probability} \\
\text{of Bottom} \\
\text{Branch}
\end{array}
\right)
\left(
\begin{array}{c}
\text{Value} \\
\text{of Bottom} \\
\text{Branch}
\end{array}
\right)
$$

$$
0 \quad = \quad (1-p) \quad (\$3) \quad + \quad (p) \quad (-\$2)
$$

Solve for p.

$$0 = (1-p)3 - 2p$$
$$0 = 3 - 3p - 2p$$
$$0 = 3 - 5p$$
$$3 = 5p$$

$$\boxed{3/5 = p}$$ so $p = 0.6 = 60\%$

Put this on the tree:

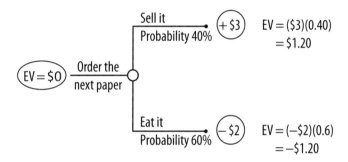

You are indifferent about ordering the next paper at this point. The *marginal profit*[4] is zero, and you've reached the maximum expected profit. Another way to look at the situation is on the distribution curve:

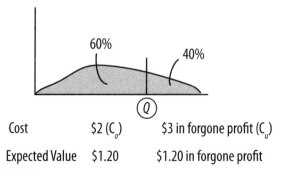

	Cost	$2 (C_o)$	$3 in forgone profit (C_u)$
	Expected Value	$1.20	$1.20 in forgone profit

The probability of overage p (= 60%) is related to the overage and underage costs in the following way, putting in C_u for $3 and C_o for $2:

$$\text{Expected Value} = \left(\begin{array}{c}\text{Probability}\\\text{of Top}\\\text{Branch}\end{array}\right)\left(\begin{array}{c}\text{Value}\\\text{of Top}\\\text{Branch}\end{array}\right) = \left(\begin{array}{c}\text{Probability}\\\text{of Bottom}\\\text{Branch}\end{array}\right)\left(\begin{array}{c}\text{Value}\\\text{of Bottom}\\\text{Branch}\end{array}\right)$$

$$0 = (1-p) \quad C_u \quad + \quad (p) \quad -C_o$$

$$0 = C_u - pC_u - pC_o$$

$$0 = C_u - p(C_u + C_o)$$

$$p(C_u - C_o) = C_u$$

$$\boxed{p = \frac{Cu}{Cu + Co}} = \frac{\$3}{\$3 + \$2} = 60\%$$

This ratio $\dfrac{Cu}{Cu + Co}$ is called the **critical ratio**. The magic order quantity Q is uncovered by finding the point on the demand distribution at which the cumulative probability up to that point equals the critical ratio.

To recap, imagine that you have these costs in a newsvendor situation:

Underage cost (missed profit) = $3 = C_u

Overage cost (unsold profit) = $2 = C_o

What's the right order quantity?

a) *Draw the demand distribution.*

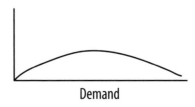

Demand

b) *Calculate the critical ratio.*

$$\frac{C_u}{C_u + C_o} = \frac{\$3}{\$3 + \$2} + \frac{\$3}{\$5} = 0.60 = 60\%$$

c) *Figure out the magic point Q where you've got 60% of the area on the left.*

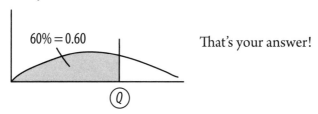

That's your answer!

If the C_u, the cost of being under the real demand, gets huge, then the critical ratio grows toward 100%. What if you could sell each paper for $20? Then you'd order lots and lots of papers.

$$s = \text{sale price} \quad = \$20$$
$$c = \text{cost} \quad\quad\quad = \$2 \quad = C_o$$
$$s - c = \text{profit} \quad\quad = \$18 \quad = C_u$$

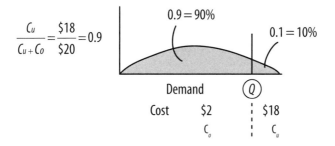

$$\frac{C_u}{C_u + C_o} = \frac{\$18}{\$20} = 0.9$$

But if you could only sell each paper for $2.50, you'd order many, many fewer:

$$s = \text{sale price} \qquad\qquad = \$2.50$$
$$c = \text{cost} \qquad = \$2 \qquad = C_o$$
$$s - c = \text{profit} \qquad = \$0.50 \quad = C_u$$

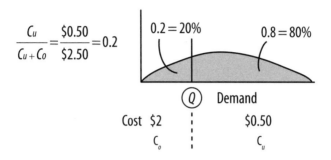

$$\frac{C_u}{C_u + C_o} = \frac{\$0.50}{\$2.50} = 0.2$$

Lastly, if your goods have salvage value, you trim your overage cost. If you order too many papers, you won't end up losing as much money. So go ahead, order a bunch. Newspaper publishers will thank you.

CHAPTER 21:
COMMON THREADS

As you go through the first year of school, people occasionally try to weave everything together for you—in a capstone strategy course, in an interdisciplinary business simulation, etc. However, you may still be left with the feeling that you've learned a lot of disconnected stuff.

This brief wrap-up will not completely eliminate that feeling. After all, you *do* learn a lot of disconnected stuff in business school. Still, it's worth highlighting a number of simple, repeated themes.

Seven Common Threads

The first three threads relate to the **marketplace**. The fourth thread has to do with **scale effects**, and the last three are about **uncertain outcomes**.

> *Thread #1:*   **Trade can benefit both sides of an exchange. The more different the two sides are, the more benefit they can extract from trade.**
>
> *Economics, Decision Analysis, Strategy, Negotiations*

Differences are what "grow the pie." If Ahmed really loves crust and you really love filling, then the two of you should figure this out and split the pie up so that he gets more crust and you get more filling. Granted, you aren't literally expanding the pie, but you're both happier than you would have been otherwise. This is why economists love trade: it can be so beneficial.

Differences in preferences (e.g., for the components of pie) and in endowments create opportunities for trade. But differences in *forecasts* or in risk tolerances can also create value. Every day, people happily take different sides of bets, whether in Vegas or on Wall Street. The reason is that people simply don't predict the same outcomes with the same likelihoods.

In fact, if a negotiation stalls, you might be able to break the logjam by adding in a bet. If you think your Widget 2012 is going to fly off the shelves, but Suzie Retailer won't stock it because she thinks it won't sell, then try to make the deal low-risk to Suzie on the front end. Consider paying her to stock the widgets; in return, ask for a bigger cut of any profits on the back end. This way, you're each putting your money where your mouth is. If the widgets don't sell, then Suzie makes out because she got cash up front. On the other hand, if the widgets sell like proverbial hotcakes, you get a bigger profit per unit than otherwise. In essence, you've taken on some of Suzie's risk for a greater possible upside.

As Mark Twain said, "It is difference of opinion that makes horse races."

> *Thread #2:* **Competition in a marketplace forces down profits, because alternatives become easy to choose.**
>
>   *Economics, Finance, Marketing, Negotiations*

In the classic model of a perfect market, supply and demand interact to create a market price with zero "abnormal" profits. This model is introduced in microeconomics but shows up in practically every other subject. When you study a company's financial statements, for instance, you need to question abnormally high margins: why is this particular company able to earn such unusual profits? Was competition artificially restrained in some way? Are there large barriers to entry blocking potential new competitors? Is the product unique, so that the company functions somewhat like a monopoly?

Even when you aren't operating in a market, remember what competition does: it forces competition. In a one-on-one negotiation, improving your BATNA (*Best Alternative To Negotiated Agreement*) gives you more leverage. Your improved BATNA competes better with the other side's offer, and it becomes easier for you to walk away.

Thread #3:   **Your competitor is as smart and as hard-working as you.**

Economics, Finance, Strategy, Negotiations

Even though you try not to underestimate the other side, you probably will—it's very hard to overcome the relevant cognitive biases. Small, active investors play the stock market thinking that they're smarter than average. But every time they buy or sell, someone who's probably more knowledgeable is on the other side of the transaction. In the long run, those active little traders tend to lose out, in some cases perfectly timing the market to buy high and sell low.

Consider taking systematic measures to give proper weight to the other side's point of view. For instance, set up a formal "devil's advocate" role on your team. A football team gets better when its practice squad effectively simulates the next opponent's strategy.

One of the best ways to learn to respect your competitor is to have your butt kicked a few times when the stakes are not so high. This is why simulations can be so useful. At the end of the day, there's no teacher like experience.

> *Thread #4:*   **When you double a recipe, not everything about the recipe exactly doubles.**
>
> *Economics, Operations, Accounting, Marketing*

You don't bake two cakes for twice as long as you would bake one cake. Some elements of the recipe, such as baking time, increase by less than 100%—if they increase at all. When costs increase by less than 100%, you have *economies of scale*.

However, if you eat both cakes in one sitting, you don't enjoy the second one as much as the first one. In fancy terms, the marginal benefit of the second cake is less than that of the first cake. This situation is known as *diminishing returns*, decreasing returns to scale—or indigestion.

In both cases, the slope of the curve diminishes as you go out to the right:

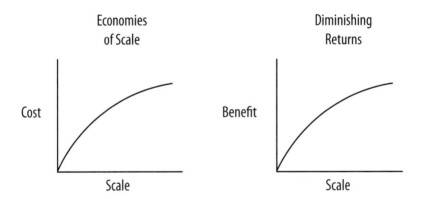

On the other hand, some parts of the recipe double exactly. For instance, you need twice as many eggs for two cakes as you do for one. Such components increase linearly with the scale of the project.

Finally, certain costs might suddenly jump as you increase the recipe. Maybe you want to start selling cakes as a business. You can't just multiply your recipe by twenty and buy twenty times as many eggs. You need a new kitchen, a delivery truck, several Keebler elves, etc. Costs that go up more than linearly are called *diseconomies of scale*.

On the other hand, you might encounter *increasing returns*. Perhaps now that you can guarantee a regular supply of cakes, you can sell them through Magnolia Bakery (which has all the bomb frostings), and you'll make much more per cake than ever before.

In both cases, the slope of the curve increases as you go out to the right.

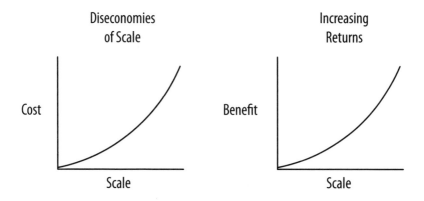

As you consider how an operation can be rescaled or what happens when more or fewer products are sold, think about what happens to important components—whether they change linearly or not, and if not, which way the curve bends and why.

Thread #5: **You can assess the attractiveness of small bets with expected value.**

Economics, Statistics, Decision Analysis, Finance

Here's a bet: you have a 70% chance of winning $5 and a 30% chance of losing $10. Should you take this bet? Yes, since the expected value is $(0.70)(\$5) + (0.30)(-\$10) = \$3.50 - \$3.00 = \$0.50$. In other words, if you take this bet over and over, you'll average a $0.50 profit per bet. Take this bet as often as you can (or let us do it).

Expected value is a great way to combine probabilities and outcomes into a single number. It's most appropriate as a criterion when the bet is small—in other words, when the worst case won't break you financially (assuming you're not allowed to declare bankruptcy and walk away).

Thread #6: **You can assess the risk of a bet by considering the uncertainty and variability of the potential outcomes, as well as the correlation to other bets you've taken.**

Statistics, Decision Analysis, Finance, Strategy

One aspect of risk is *uncertainty*: the fact that an outcome is not perfectly guaranteed. Uncertainty can be quantified with probability, which varies between 0% (impossible) and 100% (guaranteed). In finance, the discount rate is often used to capture uncertainty—an uncertain future cash flow is assigned a higher discount rate than a guaranteed future cash flow. (As an aside, the guaranteed future cash flow would not have a discount rate of zero, but rather some positive "risk-free rate." The discount rate captures not only the uncertainty but also the delayed gratification of a future cash flow.)

In addition to uncertainty, another aspect of risk is the *variability* of possible outcomes. Two bets can have the same expected value but have vastly different variability:

Bet #1	Bet #2
50% chance of winning $5	50% chance of winning $5 million
50% chance of losing $4	50% chance of losing $4,999,999
Expected value: $0.50	Expected value: $0.50

The second bet has a much greater variability, and you'd be much less likely to take it than Bet #1 (again, assuming that you can't declare bankruptcy). You can quantify this variability with standard deviation. The first bet has a standard deviation of $4.50, whereas the second bet has a standard deviation of nearly $5 million. For more complicated bets, you might separately consider the worst-case scenario before placing your chips.

Finally, you can assess the riskiness of a bet by considering how the outcomes are *correlated* with the outcomes of other bets you have already taken. For instance, insurance is a bet you take to reduce your overall risk. Your insurance policy offsets other bets that you take in life—simply by owning a house or being alive, say. You purchase fire insurance so that it pays you when the outcome of your "owning a house" bet is bad (that is, fire destroys your house). Notice that these outcomes are negatively correlated: you get a good result from the insurance bet when the house bet goes south.

In other cases, you might decide to increase your risk by taking on a bet that is positively correlated with your other bets. This kind of *speculation* is similar to doubling down at the blackjack table (you add to your bet when your hand is strong and the dealer is showing a crummy card).

Thread #7:   **You should demand a higher expected return for taking on higher risk.**

Economics, Stats, Decision Analysis, Finance, Strategy

If you are asked to take on risk, you should ask to be compensated for it. A higher risk demands a higher expected return. Likewise, if you reduce your risk, say by sharing the investment with a partner, you should expect to share any upside as well. Of course, you can take dumb risks that no one will compensate you for, such as sticking your face in a fan, but that's obvious.

The connection between risk and return is hammered home throughout the b-school curriculum. What's often not emphasized enough is how you actually measure return (generally, by expected value or expected utility) and risk (generally, by assessing uncertainty, variability, and correlation with other bets).

Two Key Tensions

Key Tension #1: **How rationally can you expect people to behave?**

There are two camps on this issue, which is a never-ending source of debate.

Camp A: **People are basically rational when money's on the line.**

This is the position of neoclassical economics. In fact, *homo economicus* is the abstract person in standard economic models who pursues his or her own self-interest perfectly and maximizes his or her own utility at all times. According to the Camp A view, markets generally work efficiently if left to their own devices. Camp A includes not only neoclassical economics but also standard finance theory, decision analysis, and so on.

Camp B: **Even when supposedly acting in their own self-interest, people are not as rational as Camp A thinks.**

The fields of social psychology, cognitive science and organizational behavior have all contributed to this position, which identifies systematic, persistent biases in the way people perceive, decide, and act. According to this view, markets do not work as efficiently as Camp A imagines. Camp B thinking has given rise to the newer fields of behavioral economics and behavioral finance. Some Camp B folks simply resist the reduction of human behavior to utility maximization.

Key Tension #2:   **How much should people spread their bets?**

This is a narrower debate academically than the first, but it affects your life directly. Again, there are two schools of thought.

School 1: **Spread your bets. Don't put all your eggs in one basket.**

This is the idea of a *portfolio play*. Pick lots of offsetting bets, and you'll ride safely through the storms. According to this view, options (both in stocks and in life) are always worth something, so you keep your options open. You see this position a lot in traditional economics and finance.

School 2: **Concentrate your bets. "Put all your eggs in the one basket and—*watch that basket.*"** (Mark Twain)

This is the idea of *strategic commitment.* You can sometimes change the game for the better by putting all of your chips on one number. In this view, options can actually have negative value, so under certain circumstances you preemptively close them off. You see this position in game theory, where it has been developed the most.

Schools 1 and 2 can be reconciled, perhaps, if the scenarios are spelled out. It's often best to spread your bets when you don't have control over the outcomes—you're entrusting your baskets to lots of other people. On the other hand, when you have control and you want to bind your future self to a course of action, it may be better to commit yourself to a single basket. Some decisions are all-or-nothing, at least in a sequential sense (e.g., the choice of an MBA program, a job, or a mate). With these decisions, you are forced to put all your eggs in one basket, so you may as well commit to that basket wholeheartedly.

Capstone Comments

Fortunately, you don't have to pass a general exam before they hand you a diploma. Unfortunately, that means no one will demand that you really pull together everything you've learned. Broad strategy courses aim to paint the big picture, but they often fall short of synthesizing the full range of topics encountered in business school. Part of the reason is that Strategy has its own particular material to cover. Moreover, as a generally less quantitative field, Strategy glosses over mathematical insights from other parts of the canon.

We think it's useful to consider how all the subjects in the b-school curriculum interact, as well as what they tell you about yourself. For instance, relative to the key tensions above, where do you stand? Which threads are most apparent to you? And what are the implications for your career choices?

On that note, continue reading into Part IV.

PART IV:
LANDING THE PERFECT JOB

So here you are, hundreds of pages into this book. Maybe you've started your MBA program; maybe you're still waiting for orientation. Either way, we know you've completely sorted out what you want to do when you're all done with school.

What do you mean, you still aren't sure?

In truth, most of us enter the hallowed halls of business school only about 50% certain of what we want to do. If we know the industry, we may not know the function…or maybe we know the function, but we don't know the industry. We may have target companies, but it's up to them to hire us. Plus, with the ups and downs of today's economy, it is hard to know where you'll find employment 21 months (give or take) down the road. It's pretty easy to understand why folks might be open to a variety of career paths.

But enter indecisively at your own peril. Too many options can leave you stretched too thin, popping off half-hearted cover letters to dozens of possible employers and running breathless from one recruiting event to another.

So what is an open-minded business school student to do?

First thing is to start winnowing down your options.[1] To do that, you need information. Ask a lot of questions and keep noodling over what's going to make you happy, both in the short term and in the longer term. After that, you need to come up with a (feasible) plan of attack. And then, it's all about execution. Lesson learned: tiny crab cakes are harder to eat than you think. And watch out for that dab of tartar sauce just to the left of your lip. No, your other left. Now…up…up…a little more. There. Got it.

---

1   And, by the way, this section is a misnomer; there is no such thing as "The Perfect Job." It's as mythical as Bigfoot, the Loch Ness Monster, and Santa Claus.

CHAPTER 22:
WHEN I GROW UP...

~~~~~~

Let's review.

Q: Why do people go to medical school?
A: *To become doctors.*

Q: Why do people go to law school?
A: *To become lawyers.*

Q: Why do people go to business school?
A: *To become, umm...*

It's not that there's no reason to go to business school, but an MBA isn't a license to practice some profession.[1] Nor, for that matter, do you need an MBA to do any of the things that MBAs typically do. You can be a banker, consultant, marketer, entrepreneur, or executive without a business degree. Related jobs that do require certifications (i.e., CPAs, brokers, etc.) don't care whether you have an MBA, so long as you have passed the requisite licensing exams.

What does this all mean? Your MBA does not have to define you or your career path. You don't have to go after one of those "typical" MBA jobs if you don't want to; there are myriad applications for your newly-formed

---

1   We know, we know—MD and JD degrees don't automatically admit you to professions either: you have to pass the boards or the bar. But these degrees are required for their respective career paths, and that's what we're trying to get at. Sheesh...if you were going to get snippy, maybe you should have thought more about going to law school.

skill set. You just might have to think creatively and work hard to make your case to those who might not be particularly familiar with the degree.

The flip side of this "lack of a license" is that, just because you have or are in the process of getting that piece of paper, you do not automatically merit any particular job/industry/salary. Jettison any subconscious sense that you deserve a certain kind of position in return for your two-year investment. The world already stereotypes us MBAs as entitled, and you need to bend over backwards to counter that impression.

Yes, we understand: you need and want something worthwhile to do when your time at business school is up. You need an internship for that first summer and a decently compensated full-time gig for after graduation, so that you can pay off those astronomical loans. (Ugh.)

However, you don't necessarily have to jump at the first offer or scramble after every possible chance at employment. Most likely, you're pursuing your MBA because you want to have a long and successful career doing *something*. Now is the time to launch (or re-launch) yourself down that path. But which path is right for you?

You may already be 100% certain, or you may still be tossing a bunch of ideas around in your head. Regardless, you need to take a stand on a few of the "lifestyle and personality" issues related to your career decision and your immediate job hunt.

The Touchy-Feely Stuff

Career discussions around the b-school water fountain largely focus on companies and compensation. If you're new to finance, you'll be trying to decipher whether "Morgan" is a reference to JP or Stanley. But what does your career choice say about your life, not just your future earnings potential?

It is often taken for granted that most post-MBA jobs require more than your typical 40-hour workweek. But will you work 50, 70, 90 or more hours a week? Will you work downtown, in your home office, or on the road? Will yours be a career that allows you to take time off, either for a few days at a time or for longer stretches? What sort of "off ramps" are there, should you decide you want to go in a different direction down the line? How much flexibility is there within the career path, as well as with particular potential employers?

On your own, do an informal but thorough assessment of what is actually important to you in your working life. Spend some time chewing over the big issues as they relate to your life at different intervals—at graduation, in five years, in ten years, and even further into the future.[2]

Consider the following list of questions:

1) What level and structure of compensation are you looking for? What mix of guaranteed salary, bonuses, commissions, stock options, etc. would you prefer?

2) How much and how hard do you want to work? Do you want regular hours with occasional overtime, or are you okay with a highly demanding and/or less predictable schedule?

> *Your most valuable resource is your classmates. If you want to go into consulting, meet as many ex-consultants as you can and learn their birthdays because they'll be able to help you. Build relationships playing dodgeball, carrying them home from a party, whatever. Institutional resources are good but classmates are key.*
>
> *-- Chike, Wharton '12 (U Penn)*

---

2   If, like Biff in *Back to the Future II*, you have access to a future year's almanac, we should talk.

3) What is your appetite or tolerance for risk? What sort of uncertainty in your life can you stand—and what sort drives you up the wall?

4) How predictable would you like your career path to be? Do you desire a ladder with clearly defined rungs, or do you anticipate bouncing around?

5) Are you someone who needs frequent change and new challenges, or are you looking for something more typically routine?

6) How much do you want to compete with your colleagues at work? How sharply does the path narrow as you climb, and what do people do who don't stay on that path?

7) To what degree will you need/want to take time off to care for children or other family members, and will the career track support this?

8) How much travel are you willing to do, month after month? How open are you to living in different cities or moving throughout the course of your career?

9) What mix of daily activities do you prefer? How much talking on the phone, meeting people face to face, speaking in front of groups? How much managing, planning, number-crunching, researching, writing, editing, negotiating, decision-making?

10) What sorts of accomplishments do you crave each day, week, month, year? How do you want your success to be measured and recognized?

11) Who do you want to be responsible to and for? Who is your ideal client, customer, boss, direct report, colleague?

A simple model of the sweet spot you're aiming for is this three-circle Venn diagram:

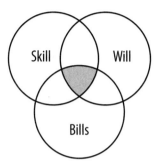

Figure out what you've got the *skill* for, what you've got the *will* for—and how you're gonna pay the *bills*. That covers it all. Like Gym-Tan-Laundry, you can guide your life by Skill-Will-Bills.

A Special Note to Career Switchers

A number of students go back to school because, earlier in life, they got on a different track than the one they want to be on now. This group sees business school as an opportunity to reboot and try all over again, starting down a different, perhaps more focused, path.

It can be much more difficult to make a huge career leap than to get a higher-level job in an industry or field in which you already have years of experience. Tackling an internship in your desired area demonstrates that you have the chops to cut it in a full-time position, but even landing such an internship can be hard. A Catch-22 often applies: you need experience to get experience. How do you break in?

As a career switcher, you have to start executing your very focused plan immediately. What field are you pursuing? What additional training do you need? How can you explain your existing skill set in a way that will make sense to potential employers, who may not really understand your previous industry?

For example, a former journalist who wants to be a consultant might encounter skepticism about her fit for the job. But she can counter that her training as a journalist goes beyond "communications skills" and is more directly relevant to consulting than one might think.

Every day on the beat, the journalist had to go find the story. She assessed whatever information she had, dug tenaciously to fill in the blanks, and constructed a convincing summary for folks with no access to all of the source material. The only difference, really, was the end result: an article rather than a PowerPoint deck.

How's that for spin?

CHAPTER 23:
THE BIG BUCKETS OF MBA JOBS

~~~~~~~~~~~~~~~~~~~~~~~~~~~~~~~~~~

To describe the most common MBA roles, it seems only fitting to use consultant-speak. While it's a mystery why things besides sand and dirt are put into buckets, we recognize that an orderly categorization of careers is essential to making an informed, farsighted decision.

What follows is a high-level breakdown of major industries and common roles that b-school students tend to gravitate toward. As particulars jump out at you, do more research on your own. Talk to your classmates, colleagues, friends, relatives, professors, guest speakers, and anyone else willing to offer insight.

Chapter 24 describes how to procure informational interviews and how to make use of professional clubs to enhance your knowledge base. You may also want to flip back to Chapter 5: Firm Up Your Career Knowledge for additional tips.

A word to the wise: even if landing a job is *just one* of the reasons you are pursuing your MBA, it will often feel like the dominant one. The buzz around careers pervades campus like background radiation, and it's easy to get caught up in all of the craziness. When that happens, remind yourself of all of the things you were certain of when you entered school—your interests, priorities, and values—and make sure that you're still acting in concert with them.

You will get a job. You will not *be* that job. And it won't be the last job you ever get. So have another crab cake.

Round Pegs, Square Holes

What if you're no longer sure about any of these buckets? What if, after a few months in b-school, you're wondering whether you're in the right sandbox altogether?

We empathize with problem children. One of us walked into the career services office early in the first term, sat down with an advisor, and with crossed arms promptly announced, "I don't want to be a consultant or a banker."

This may resonate with you. If so, pat yourself on the back once. It's good to realize what you don't want, and kudos for bucking trends. Don't stop there, though. Examine why you don't want such-and-such a career, and use those insights to figure out what you do want. This process will take time, and not everyone is going to understand or be sympathetic.

It helps to find kindred spirits, so that you're not the only fish swimming against the herd. As one of our friends put it, "At business school, I felt like a tiger in Antarctica." But there are other tigers around; you just have to seek them out. Find professors or other mentors who have taken roads less traveled. And more of your classmates than you might think are in the same boat, or at least paddling nearby. To switch up the metaphor yet again, even the squarest pegs have some rounded edges.

The Career Matrix

Mama Bear: "I want to work in marketing."
Papa Bear: "I want to work in high-tech."
Baby Bear: "I want to work in marketing for a high-tech company!"

The first two career dimensions that MBAs typically think about are *function* (e.g., marketing) and *industry* (e.g., high-tech). There may be an ideal intersection of the two for you (e.g., high-tech marketing), but most students, if they had to choose between industry and function, clearly lean one way or the other.

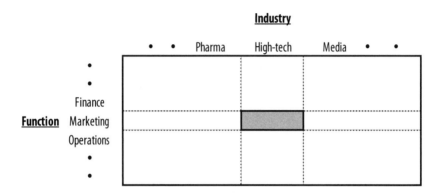

Your industry and function preferences will broadly dictate many other features of your career path, such as compensation, responsibilities, geography, and lifestyle. For instance, high-tech marketing and pharmaceutical operations may command different salary ranges.

Say that you're Baby Bear, with a hankering for high-tech marketing. Within that target industry and function, you'll have more specific preferences to take into account as you examine particular employers. For instance, you may have geographic proclivities (Silicon Valley or Shanghai?) and lifestyle considerations (raise a family or rock the single life?). You may or may not be motivated by certain causes (e.g., green energy) that you want to incorporate into your career. Each employer will offer a different mix of strengths and weaknesses across these dimensions.

While you may very well find a job at the perfect intersection of Industry Street and Function Avenue, you also want to know your second-choice corners. If your priority is function, look at other industries that offer similar marketing experiences (e.g., consumer packaged goods, media, commercial banks, etc.). If, on the other hand, all you've ever wanted is to work for a high-tech company, what other non-marketing roles would interest you there?

Wall Streeters need to refine their sweet spot among particular finance roles and players. For instance, you might fancy doing sell-side equity analysis at a large investment bank (more on what this means in a few pages). However, you'll need to keep thinking about the broad grid of industries and functions. Which sectors are you passionate about covering as an equity analyst? You may or may not have the luxury of choice right away, but in order to succeed, you will eventually need some degree of specialization. Prospective consultants face similar considerations: they need to examine the specifics of the consulting microcosm (e.g., large vs. small strategy firms) while developing their interests on the primary industry/function matrix. You can't just be a "banker" or a "consultant"; you need to have a clientele in the wider world of business, and that clientele will be specialized to some degree.

The good news—the big takeaway here—is that there are probably a lot more acceptable options than you may have initially thought, more roles that will lead you down the right path and open doors along the way.

At the same time, you might also wonder what it really means when it comes down to the nitty-gritty of actually doing these jobs. For the most complete information, start with the well-known career guides, then talk to people. You can't understand a horse's life without hanging out a lot at the stable.

In the pages that follow, you'll find a quick overview of various career tracks, so that you can begin the thought process.

Sectors and Specializations

Before any professional club presidents cry foul, we want to make it clear that the following descriptions have much more to do with functions than with industries. Real estate, media, healthcare, and other popular industries are often treated as separate areas within business school but, in truth, they tend to offer many of the same functional career choices. You can be in real estate finance or media marketing, hospital administration or retail operations.

If your devotion is to a particular industry, the general career track is to progress to positions of higher responsibility within the same functional category, often moving between competitive firms. However, there are plenty of other options. If your goal is to don the CEO hat one day for real, check out where current CEOs started. For example, many retail companies are led by folks who came up through the marketing ranks, while a quick look at real estate firms reveals a preference for finance veterans. Again, these are great topics for conversations with those who are already established in the field.

And, of course, you can always try to start your own company, in which case it's much easier to lay claim to the CEO cap. You're knitting it yourself.

Finance

Whether you carried *The Wall Street Journal* to kindergarten or you still believe that stock is for soup and bonds are for the bedroom, business school will expose you to a variety of finance-related careers that you may never have thought of before. Popular with the MBA set, finance tracks often come with platinum paychecks and clear (if up-and-down) career trajectories. However, the finance umbrella is broad, and telling your advisor that you want "to be in finance" isn't exactly helpful.

To see the big picture of Wall Street, flip the page. The first diagram gives the bird's eye view from however many thousand feet up you like; the second diagram outlines important roles.

A Bird's Eye View of Wall Street

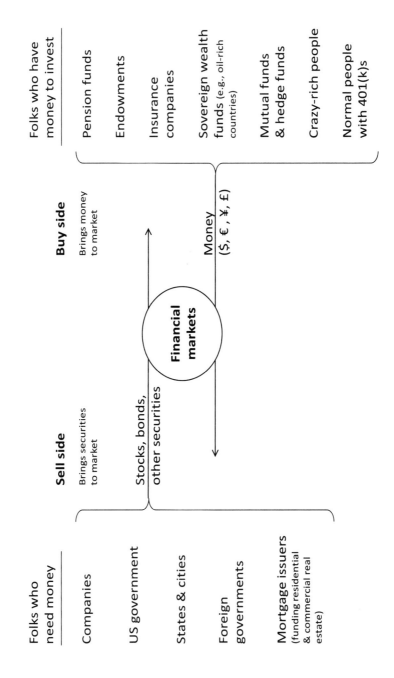

Sell side
Brings securities to market

Buy side
Brings money to market

Stocks, bonds, other securities

Money ($, €, ¥, £)

Financial markets

Folks who need money

Companies

US government

States & cities

Foreign governments

Mortgage issuers (funding residential & commercial real estate)

Folks who have money to invest

Pension funds

Endowments

Insurance companies

Sovereign wealth funds (e.g., oil-rich countries)

Mutual funds & hedge funds

Crazy-rich people

Normal people with 401(k)s

A More Detailed View of Roles on the Street*

Sell side

- Investment banking (a.k.a. "corporate finance" *within* an i-bank)
  - Underwrite securities (bring stocks and bonds to market)
  - Advise on mergers and acquisitions
  - Bundle loans for resale (e.g., mortgage-backed securities)
  - Structure new derivative products
- Corporate finance (within large companies)
  - Interface with i-bankers
- Equity research
  - Publish reports

Financial markets

- Stock exchanges (shares of public co's)
- Bond markets (long-term debt)
- Money markets (short-term debt)
- Derivatives markets (e.g., options)
- Commodities markets (e.g., wheat)
- Futures markets (e.g., next year's wheat)
- Foreign exchange markets (e.g., £, ¥)

- Sales & trading
  - Execute client orders (make markets as needed)
  - Trade on bank's own behalf
- Prime brokerage
  - Lend securities to hedge funds
  - Keep securities in safe custody
- Ratings agencies

Buy side

- Asset/portfolio management
  - Divisions of i-banks
  - Independent mutual funds
  - Hedge funds
- Private wealth management

- Investment advisory (a.k.a. stockbrokers)
- Venture capital funds (invest directly in young private companies)
- Other private equity funds (e.g., leveraged buyouts, distressed securities)

* Banks often play more than one role

There is a key difference between the *sell side* and the *buy side*. Financial markets provide a way for invested capital to get where it needs to go. Working with the people who need money, the sell side creates securities and sells them into the financial markets. Conversely, the buy side works with investors to direct their money into the securities created on the sell side.

Roles on the Sell Side

Investment Banking – Investment bankers are the kings and queens of the deal. Their clients are companies looking to buy a company, sell a division, or raise money through stock or bond offerings underwritten by the bank. Bankers act as advisors and brokers for these deals—and you can jump right into the mix, provided you don't value sleep very highly. At the junior level, investment banking associates are concerned with creating models to evaluate and price a transaction. These models, as well as the rest of the argument for why a company should undertake one course of action or another, are put together as "pitch books," also known as the bane of the junior investment banker's 4 am existence. But if a deal is to be struck, it all starts with the pitch.

Bankers can be involved in securitization—bundling loans into products for resale, such as mortgage-backed securities or CDOs, which you might have heard about as many have blown up recently. Investment bankers may also help develop and sell other "structured products," coming up with more ways for investors to place wagers in the marketplace. These exotic securities may demand more intricate quantitative skills than plain-vanilla stocks and bonds.

Success as an investment banker requires good hunting—you eat what you kill, because the bank only gets paid its 7% fee if the deal goes through or the new securities sell. As you move to higher rungs, you cut back on the killer hours and interact more with existing or potential clients to win business. Big bonuses make these jobs lucrative but compensation ebbs and flows, so if you like high risk paired with high rewards, you're in luck.

Corporate Finance – At *Fortune* 500 companies, "corp fin" is an internal role primarily concerned with the capital markets. As such, corporate finance folks at, say, IBM work closely with investment bankers on issuing new securities, negotiating acquisitions or spin-offs, and the like. Much of the day-to-day work is similar to that of an investment banker; only this time, you're the client.

Fresh out of school, you will work on an internal team, shuttling from project to project. You'll attempt to gain more responsibility over time and, eventually, a CFO title. Want to leave? No worries. Your skill set will allow you to transfer to a similar role at a different company or to an investment bank on the other side of the deal. In fact, that's what the "investment banking" part of a big bank is actually called: the corporate finance division. You'll fit right in.

Equity Research – Equity research is all about trying to understand how a public company will be valued over the coming weeks/months/years, using a variety of quantitative tools as well as qualitative approaches to make your predictions. Have a passion for grasping the movements of energy stocks or blue chip retailers? You can focus your expertise on one area. As a junior analyst, you'll start out working under someone more established, who publishes regular reports. Eventually, you will start adding your name to these reports and then strike out on your own with the primary byline. One day you might even be *the* expert on the Street. If there's a bit of the cool nerd or closet academic about you, equity research could be up your alley.

Equity research is technically walled off from the corporate finance divisions of investment banks, since equity analysts are supposed to take unbiased views of the companies they cover. Possible conflicts of interest abound: a company may decide not to bring the bank its corporate finance business if its stock is rated poorly by the bank's analyst. Beyond normal political jockeying, you'll need to juggle a variety of such real conflicts as you move up the ranks.

Roles on the Buy Side

Many activities on the buy side are similar to those on the sell side. For instance, a junior analyst evaluating a company's prospects would run the same kind of models, wherever he or she sits. The difference is that on the buy side, there's only one client for that information: your boss, representing the fund that you work for. In contrast, on the sell side you have numerous clients.

As a result, the traditional career flow has often been for b-school graduates to start on the sell side, then move to the buy side after a number of years. Potential buy-side employers typically want you to cut your teeth with multiple clients on the sell side before hiring you and becoming your single client, so to speak.

Asset/Portfolio Management – Asset managers gather capital and deploy it in the markets on behalf of their clients. Large investment banks have asset management divisions (separated from both the investment bankers and sell-side equity research because of more possible conflicts of interest). Other asset managers include large mutual-fund companies, such as Fidelity and Vanguard, as well as hedge funds.

A junior role in asset management can share many characteristics with sell-side equity research: you're building models and analyzing what a company will be worth in the future. Expect to present your findings to upper management, as opposed to writing out reports designed for publication. Over time, your responsibilities will grow to encompass the management of more and more investment positions within the fund. Eventually, you'll manage a whole portfolio and raise capital from investors.

Hedge funds do not usually invest in shrubbery, as one of us once thought. Historically, the "hedge" part did mean that the fund was supposed to hedge its positions against general market movements, but now hedge funds kind of do whatever they want to, including placing large directional bets. For instance, hedge fund manager John Paulson wagered heavily against subprime mortgages in 2008, resulting that year in a personal payday of $2 billion (that's billion, not million). The strategies that hedge funds employ may be more or less arcane quantitatively, but either way, you will need to be completely comfortable with numbers to run with the hedge-fund dogs.

Private Wealth Management – What's your golf handicap? Private wealth management is perhaps the most relationship-driven of all popular finance roles. As a private wealth manager (PWM) at an investment bank, private bank or family office, you advise the affluent on all matters related to keeping and growing their wealth, such as investments, estate planning, tax strategy, etc. The relationship becomes very personal; each one takes years to cultivate but just seconds to blow up.

As an associate, you support an existing PWM, creating models, learning investment strategies, interfacing with existing clients, etc. Eventually, you will be tasked with going out and getting your own clients. This may involve hundreds or even thousands of cold calls, or you may be given some starter clients. Either way, this sort of finance job is not for wall-flowers. You have to be able to sell yourself, as well as your institution.

As with other finance tracks, after a while you might move to a smaller shop and do the same thing for a more limited number of clients. Or you might shift to a fundraising position, either for asset managers or even outside of the finance industry. If you've built a career getting people to turn their money over to you, a number of different sorts of organizations can capitalize on your skill set.

Investment Advisory – Investment advisors do the same thing as private wealth managers, just for somewhat less affluent clients. "Registered reps" are not just stock jockeys; they help their investors plan for their retirements and meet their other financial goals. As an investment advisor, you'll typically work in teams. All the same, you'll need to bring a great deal of hustle to the table to build a client base.

Private Equity – Had enough of the DJIA and NASDAQ? Want to be able to have more control over a particular company? Why not just buy it, get involved in management, and reap the rewards when the company skyrockets in value? Private equity funds do exactly this: they invest in companies "privately" (outside of the public financial markets) with the hopes of hitting a home run to more than compensate for frequent strikeouts.

Venture capital funds make their investments in early-stage companies, looking for the next Google, Facebook or Groupon to take public in an IPO or to sell to a top-dollar-paying acquirer. Other kinds of private equity shops focus on financial maneuvers such as leveraged buyouts (buying a public company with cheap bank debt, then running the company so as to juice its value when you take it public again in a few years). There are even vulture funds that pick over the dead or dying carcasses of distressed companies.

From a career perspective, PE firms have typical buy-side needs. Of course, they require the Excel monkeys and research analysts that pervade other areas of finance. They also need fundraisers, the salespeople who will go after the big dollars from pension funds, institutional investors, high net-worth individuals, and others. Then there are those that have to set the strategy, think about which companies to acquire, and actually structure the deal, using many of the same skills that someone in underwriting or mergers and acquisitions might use.

Private equity firms also need folks with significant general management skills and/or industry knowledge, in order to run or advise their portfolio companies. Finally, PE/VC folks need to have the "swing for the fences" mindset. The gig is not for the faint of heart.

Roles in the Middle

Sales and Trading – Traders are responsible for rapidly buying and selling every sort of security in the financial markets. They are the neurons of the hive-mind of Wall Street, firing their synapses in dizzying alternation. Sales folks pass orders to traders, trying to find the best price for their clients. If you live and breathe the ticker between 9:30 and 4:00 Eastern, sales and trading may be for you. Be ready to drink the essence of competition, distilled on a daily basis.

Traders sometimes must "make markets" in securities they are responsible for, providing liquidity when no one else wants to buy or sell. Proprietary traders take this idea one big step further; they trade on the bank's own account. In recent years, the largest source of profits for investment banks has in fact been proprietary trading, but there are looming financial regulations that may forbid certain types of banks from this activity. Regardless, too much money is at stake for the practice to end entirely—it just may be outsourced to other players on the Street.

Prime Brokerage – Many large investment banks provide prime brokerage services to outside asset managers, making their lives easier. For instance, a bank might lend a hedge fund thousands of shares of stock in order to execute a complicated transaction. Prime brokerage is one of the numerous behind-the-scenes functions that keep the wheels of the financial world turning.

Excellent relationship management and seamless execution are crucial to winning and maintaining prime brokerage business. You must understand and stay ahead of the needs of your clients. If you want to move to the buy side eventually, prime brokerage could be a pathway.

Ratings Agencies – Moody's, S&P, and Fitch are the key players in the business of rating bonds as to their quality. The importance of this role in the financial universe cannot be overstated. Recently, shudders passed through global halls of power when Moody's and S&P whispered that they just might have to consider, years from now, downgrading the unblemished triple-A rating of US government debt. If this sort of influence appeals to you, and you love number-crunching, the agencies may have a place for you.

Marketing

Those who have never dabbled in marketing often have a much "softer" view of the field; they think that marketing is about coming up with a creative slogan, attractive packaging, and incentives for both stores and shoppers. The real truth? All of those activities are based on hard numbers.

For all of the "soft and fuzzy" associations, marketing is a highly quantitative field. Brand managers must rigorously assess everything, including consumer behaviors, distribution channels, marketing creative, product placement, competitive environment, and much, much more. Analysis is driven by data, both numerical and qualitative.

MBA recruiting for marketing positions tends to be dominated by consumer packaged goods (CPG) companies—the guys who make the products we use on a regular basis. Think companies like Procter & Gamble, Johnson & Johnson, Kraft, Unilever, and Revlon. While these may be the big guns, nearly every company requires marketers. If you have an industry preference, exercise it here. American Express, Citibank, and Chase all have huge consumer products divisions; just think about all of the credit card offers you got in the mail within the last week. Think that health insurance policy just sells itself? Someone's running marketing for Blue Cross/Blue Shield and all of its competitors. And don't forget about marketing in industries such as media, entertainment and sports. Smaller companies may not come to campus to recruit or have as defined career paths, but they still have marketing needs.

Brand Management – Do you have a passion for Planters peanuts? Have you always thought about ways to increase Mr. Peanut's market share? Do you dream about shelf space and peanut packaging options? Do you long to take business away from those non-monocle-wearing peanut producers? Do you want to manage a P&L? If so, consider a career in brand management.

Brand managers (and their assistants, which is what most MBAs start out as[1]), work with a whole slew of departments to set the overall strategy for a particular brand or sub-brand (e.g., cashews). Assistant brand managers may be responsible for a segment of the market (e.g., grocery store sales, discount clubs, online retailers, etc.) or tasked with growing market share amongst a defined group of consumers. They work with retail partners, production and distribution, market research, sales, research and development, creative, etc. to position the brand appropriately.

Brand managers generally get to see the whole picture when it comes to their product. This often gives them a lot of clout (particularly when the brand is doing well). So, it's not surprising that people rising through the ranks of brand management are handed more prestigious and valuable brands as they prove themselves. In the end, they may find themselves at the helm of huge divisions or even the entire corporation.

Advertising – If you have sat through a marketing course, you've probably already figured out that "marketing" and "advertising" are not the same thing. Advertising is one very small area of an overall marketing strategy. As opposed to brand management, advertising tends to be dominated by creative types and not MBAs (which isn't to say that MBAs aren't creative, but it's not exactly what you're known for out in the world).

At the same time, advertising agencies are currently increasing the number of MBAs they have on staff as they broaden their strategic offer-

---

[1]   That is, assistant brand managers, not assistants to the brand managers.

ings. How should a company spend its dollars between direct marketing, various social media and other online platforms, and more traditional media outlets? What should the messaging strategy be? And how does this align with other elements of the brand's growth strategy?

Agencies are not the types of employers who generally recruit on campus, so going after such a job requires a bit more leg work on your part. But how much fun will you have telling your classmates that you're going to be one of the next "Mad Men"?

Consulting

A college senior we know was contemplating a consulting gig when she encountered a very wise man. "You haven't even graduated college yet; you're 22 years old. Outside of pop culture, what could you possibly consult on?"

It was a good question—and one that echoes the even bigger challenge: *What does a consultant do?*

Basically, consultants are rented brains. Companies bring them in to look at particular areas of trouble or interest, recognizing that top consultants have good investigative skills, a structured approach to problem-solving, and a useful outside perspective. What consultants actually do varies from firm to firm, client to client, and consultant to consultant. Which is why no one can define the job.

Management Consulting – Owners of perhaps the vaguest titles in the field of consulting, management consultants are brought in to work on all manner of management issues. They can be requested to do due diligence on a proposed action, initiate a study on market expansion, figure out how to integrate companies after a merger, or develop a strategic plan for a particular aspect of a business. Or just about anything else under the sun. Sometimes, it's even to diagnose an ill-defined company illness.

Seen the movie *Office Space*? Yes, consultants can be the bad guys who come in and figure out ways to save money, whether by cutting jobs or by realigning resources. But they can also be great saviors, creating a roadmap to increased profits or greater efficiency.

Management consultants tend to work in small teams, often at the client site, which might be around the corner or on the other side of the world. Lower-level consultants tend to do more of the grunt work—creating models, doing interviews, preparing presentation decks, etc. Consultants, like their friends in finance, tend to work long hours and be rather attached to their smartphones and laptops. Projects may last weeks or months, depending upon the scope of work.

Those who move up in the consulting ranks start to manage projects, build fruitful client relationships, and become "thought leaders." As you advance in your career, you will develop expertise in particular industries and functions. You will also be responsible for generating work. Partners in the top firms are trusted advisors for those in power positions at other companies. They are in regular contact, looking for ways to grow those relationships and plant the seeds for new projects.

Those who leave consulting often get hired away by a past client or find a functional role in their area of expertise. Given the breadth of exposure, a lot of MBAs view a few years spent as a consultant as almost a second master's degree—only this one actually pays a salary. Like a medical school rotation, consulting work can provide a range of experiences across industries and functions. But with a lot less blood.

Internally, your life in a consulting firm will be more entrepreneurial than you might think. The game is to land your next project early, while you're still pulling 70 hours a week on your current gig. Be ready to network and find mentors higher up the hierarchy.

Specialized Consulting – Brand consulting, IT consulting, project implementation…they're all consulting and operate in similar fashion to diversified management consulting. These niche companies are great homes for those who have a passion for and/or experience with functional areas or industries.

Internal Consulting – While most major companies higher consulting firms at some point, a lot also keep their own staff of consultants on hand. These groups, often with some form of the word "strategy" in their title, get farmed out to tackle various issues in all departments. Such roles are a great way to get to know a particular company from top to bottom, inside and out—which can be a great asset if you hope to move into senior management.

One nice thing about being an internal consultant is that the lifestyle tends to be way better; you won't travel nearly as much. However, you often need outside experience first because, when you only have your employer as your client, you have to know what you're doing. This is similiar to starting on the sell side and moving to the buy side in the finance world.

General Management

Every company needs someone to be in charge, so why not you? General management is most often associated with larger, so-called blue chip companies. These corporations—e.g., General Electric, General Motors, etc.—take MBAs into rotational programs that involve stints in various areas of the company. The upside is that you will get a lot of exposure to a company and its various facets; the downside is that you will be moving around quite a bit during your initial tenure. Multinational corporations often suggest or require at least one rotation outside of your home country, which may be a plus or minus in your book.

Career-wise, you're looking to be a manager and, eventually, an executive. Depending upon where you land post-rotation, you may be in a particular business or functional role that could have a lasting impact on your career trajectory. However, general managers build skill sets that allow them to move to similar positions at other companies, both within and outside their industry. If you crave P&L responsibility and like to manage people, general management is in your future.

Entrepreneurship

It's the one job that will never come calling; it's the one you create for yourself. Many MBAs dream of starting their own business, whether right after school or down the line. It ain't easy but, for some, it's the only career that will be fulfilling.

The key to being a successful entrepreneur (in addition to having a good idea and a lot of luck) is temperament. Entrepreneurs are passionate, dedicated, and driven. They are self-disciplined and organized. They are confident and resourceful, creative and resilient. They must be like Weebles, the toy that wobbles but doesn't fall down. They're not solo operators; they ask for help and leverage their networks all of the time.

MBAs who launch companies straight out of school often have to contend with one very stark reality that their peers don't: no one is paying them a salary or providing them with benefits. Such a situation can definitely add to one's stress—but it will be a motivating factor to getting the business off the ground. The good news is that, while your friends are all complaining about the ridiculous demands being placed on them by their managing directors and supervisors, you get to smile and nod. Ridiculous demands may be placed on you by your clients, customers, and investors, but none of them are your boss. And that makes all the difference.

If you're not ready to take this plunge right out of school, don't worry— you didn't miss out on on-campus recruiting. Years down the road, the possibility will still be there for you to strike out on your own.

Other Possibilities

Jobs in other functions and industries are also wide open to you. Numerous sectors, such as health care management, media, and real estate, have particular roles that may not be replicated in other industries. Be sure to check these kinds of positions out if you are fonder of a particular industry than of a specific function. Yup, this means it's time to go back to the informational interview and find out all you can about the roles and responsibilities that are out there.

Operations – If you're interested in a manufacturing-based business, operations and logistics are key. After all, how is the stuff getting made? How is it getting to consumers? What parts do you need and how are they sourced? MBAs are often hired into roles as logistics managers and planners, forecasting needs and placing orders to keep everything up and running. Are you a bottleneck breaker? Then you may have found your perfect home. Ex-military are often called to this duty. Fortunately for them, the path to ultimate greatness and the executive suite at places such as Wal-Mart and UPS goes through the warehouse.

Human Resources – Whereas most of us think of HR as dealing primarily with tax forms, employee benefits, and time sheets, HR is really about a company's most important resource: its people. Those who have an interest in organizational development and psychology, executive leadership, compensation, and other people-management issues will find that they are needed by all kinds of employers. And if you can explain the ins and outs of a complex benefits plan, you're all that much more valuable. Senior HR folks act as trusted counselors to top management and get involved in the toughest personnel (and personal) crises. Like to help people figure out their place in the world, even if you haven't quite figured out yours? HR could be for you.

Non-Profit Management/Government – The salaries aren't the same as at a bank and the goal isn't money-making, but the skills involved at a non-profit organization or government agency are very much the same as at any for-profit. If anything, these organizations require their professionals to be more creative in their use of resources, as they try to operate on lean budgets. Associations, charities, and think-tanks are all in need of researchers, marketers, fund raisers, and general managers. And while the perks may not be quite on par, careers in these areas often lend themselves to a better work/life balance than many of the more traditional MBA paths. If you value a particular cause or enjoy ending your work day while the sun's still shining, look at the opportunities available to you in your preferred field.

With the rise of social enterprise, some MBAs are having their cake and eating it, too. That is, they work in the private sector but in a cause-driven company, division, or function. Possibilities range from a large corporate foundation (AT&T) to a traditional "crunchy" employer (Ben & Jerry's) to old-school businesses adopting new ways (a utility building a wind farm). You might even join a "green" energy start-up—or finance it through your socially responsible venture capital fund.

It's Only for Now

There's a lot of pressure put on finding the perfect job for after school. But here's the thing—there's no "perfect job." And even if you do think you've landed something great, MBAs average only 18 months at their first post-school job. That's less time than you were in school! So, good or bad, wherever you end up is most likely a temp job, in a sense.

And don't just take our word for it. To quote the great musical *Avenue Q*:

Don't stress,
Relax,
Let life roll off your backs
Except for death and paying taxes,
Everything in life is only for now!

CHAPTER 24:
THE PROFESSIONAL
NETWORK

If you've been a good reader, you'll remember that we touched on how to gather career-related information back in Chapter 5, when we suggested that you start to feel out some possible careers prior to showing up on campus. On the off chance that you don't have perfect recall on minimal sleep, the highlights are below, along with a few new tips especially for now, when you're a student:

1) **Read the rags.** We're talking *The Wall Street Journal, Financial Times, BusinessWeek,* etc. What stories are you drawn to and which stories do you skip right over? This should be very telling of your own interests.

2) **Read the guides.** This little book is hardly exhaustive on the career side. So pick up the *Vault, WetFeet,* and any other guide to whatever tracks pique your interest.

3) **Talk to your career management office.** If you are interested in the sort of job that recruits on campus, these guys are a prime resource. Make an appointment to speak with a counselor—particularly one who specializes in an area that intrigues you—and pick his or her brain thoroughly. Inquire about any resources the office has relating to either your chosen career path or specific companies.

4) **Join the career clubs.** Going after a consulting gig? The consulting club is great for giving the inside scoop on the recruiting process,

the key companies, and interview tips. Get involved in as many prep activities as you can, and definitely turn to second years for advice. After all, these guys just went through the same process. Moreover, they *want* to see you succeed, since they're branded with the same cattle iron as you. Yippee ki-yay—you've got coaches in your corner.

5) **Talk to your fellow students.** One of the really cool parts of business school is that you've got this massive population of people who have all sorts of previous experiences, some relevant to you, some not so much, some good, and some bad. Talk to those who have dabbled in the areas that you're interested in. Are they going back or making a run for the hills? Why or why not? You can usually get the unvarnished truth from these folks, so keep chatting them up.

6) **Contact alumni.** Maybe your career service office can direct you to some specific folks, or your marketing club has a list of alums who want to be contacted. Now is a great time to talk to people in the field. And who better than those who came from the same starting spot? Go through the alumni database and send a few warm emails; you'll be amazed at the response.

7) **Attend conferences and fairs.** It doesn't matter if you're straight, white, and male, you can attend any of the minority-oriented career conferences and fairs out there. The National Black MBA Association, National Society of Hispanic MBAs, and Reaching Out host some of the more popular ones.

Reach Out and Touch Someone (but not literally—that's harassment)

Years ago, before most of us can remember, your "network" largely consisted of the people you saw on a daily basis: your friends and family. Then, as you got older, it was the people who you could call or write, largely because you knew their telephone numbers or addresses. Then it became the people whose email addresses you had. And then, there was Facebook.[1] (Cue the harps!)

The notion of "networking" has grown over the past few years, as social and professional networks have proliferated and people from all walks of life have jumped aboard the bandwagon. What once seemed like distant relationships are now constantly updated, and long-lost friends are now easily found. It is not unusual for any of us to suddenly hear from people we haven't thought about in decades.

From a business school student's perspective, this is excellent news. It means that (1) your network has expanded exponentially from what it used to be and (2) you should be more comfortable with the notion of approaching people from "out of the blue."

> *Classes are not a good way to learn about careers.*
>
> *-- Nick, Marshall '12 (USC)*

For most, the hardest thing about networking is not finding the people to network with, but making the actual contact. Even in writing or with a personal introduction from a mutual friend, asking someone to give you his or her time when you can offer nothing in return is a hard request for most of us to make. (And if you don't see what the big deal is, clearly

---

1   Ok, fine. So first there was MySpace and Friendster and the precursors to Facebook and all of that. But you get the idea. We all have profiles now. Even this book. So go out and friend us!

you do not have enough demands on your time.) But the majority of those who receive polite requests are happy to help; and if they are not, they will simply turn you down.

Moreover, as email has taken root as the preferred method of business communication, reaching out to former colleagues or even perfect strangers has become easier for even the shyest of people. No longer must you pick up a phone and endure that awkward moment where you try, as fast as you can, to explain who you are and why you are calling, all while being apologetic for potentially having interrupted something actually important. Email allows the recipient to respond in his or her own time (which can leave you, the sender, gnawing your nails down to the quick) and is thus less imposing.

> *If you're not building your network, you're cutting the value of your MBA in half.*
>
> *-- David Cooley,*
> *Associate Director,*
> *External Relations and*
> *Career Counselor,*
> *Anderson (UCLA)*

So don't be afraid to go through your contacts and to ask your friends and family to pool their resources as you explore career options and companies. If you exhibit an honest desire to learn from someone's experience, respect for his or her time, and a genuine appreciation for any efforts put forth on your behalf, you will end up making friends for life. And if you do try to contact someone and get rebuffed, so what? You are in no worse of a position than you were before you started.

Footloose, but not Fancy Free

To use yet another b-school buzzword, you want to be *strategic* in your approach to networking. You need a plan of attack: start with your safest and best bets before moving on to more difficult targets. Along the way, you'll build a strong foundation of both interview skills and industry knowledge, giving you the confidence to approach those who fall outside of your immediate circles.

First, evaluate your network. Think Kevin Bacon: it's all about degrees of separation. Then, you'll be ready to kick off your Sunday shoes and begin the informational interview dance.

1) **Personal acquaintances (one degree).** These are the easiest to access and the most likely to help you out, whether you are seeking broad career information or specific contacts. They're also the least intimidating—you can expect that they will be enthusiastic about your request and will help you in as many ways as possible.

   Start your networking here. Send an email, make a phone call, or mention in a casual conversation that you would love to sit down over a cup of coffee/lunch/drinks and talk about whatever the specific topic is. The more you can make it appear that your target's experience or particular knowledge is relevant to your personal search, the better. It should go without saying that you want to be deferential to the other person's schedule and commitments (and at least try to pick up the tab if there is one when you meet).

   > *There's a lot of power in networking. I didn't realize how much happens behind closed doors.*
   >
   > *-- Sharon, CBS '11 (Columbia)*

2) **Alums, friends of friends, and others you don't actually know (two or three degrees).** A huge part of why you chose your school was its reputation and the reputation(s) of its alumni. You wanted the network and now you've got it—so take advantage. As awkward as it may be, alumni expect that they will hear from both current and former attendees of their alma mater. Again, you're in luck— email is usually an easy way to reach out to these folks, and you can

probably get their addresses from your university. In your initial message, explain clearly what the connection is, why you are seeking advice, and what you are asking for. Then sit back and wait. No one likes a stalker.

3) **Random strangers (six degrees).** It is a different type of "cold call" than what you have grown accustomed to in your capital markets class, but you can always try writing a letter or calling someone you want to speak with, even if there is no connection. Stories abound of people who write letters to CEOs and celebrities and actually get a response. It is a long shot, but if you honestly think that someone will be useful in your job search, it is not a lot of skin off your back (or time spent) to write a letter. Be sure to triple spell-check.

> *Students have this perception that alums understand the current student experience but they don't. Some sort of context setting is very important when you reach out to them.*
>
> *-- Erin Gasch, Director, Alumni Relations, Fuqua (Duke)*

A note on letters in general: studies have shown that letters with the word "you" tend to have higher positive response rates than those without. We all have a tendency to talk a lot about "I" in cover letters and these sorts of networking solicitations, but make it about the other person and you'll actually wind up with better results.

Still not too sure how to go about this? Check out the following samples of interview requests.

Letter to a Friend of a Friend

Dear Mr. George Lucas:

Please allow me to introduce myself. My name is Luke Skywalker and I was given your name by my friend, Han Solo. Han thought you might be willing to speak with me about a career directing feature films. I spent the past few years working on my uncle's farm but am now enrolled at your alma mater, the University of Southern California.

Over the years, I have had a bit of success creating short films and submitting them to festivals in galaxies far, far away. I have always found your work and career path to be inspirational.

If possible, I would love twenty minutes of your time to discuss how you have come to be a director, what you have found most rewarding and most difficult, and any advice you might have for someone considering this career path. I am happy to meet over the phone or at your favorite lunch spot at your convenience.

Many thanks in advance for your time. I believe your insights will be invaluable to formulating my future plans.

Sincerely,
Luke Skywalker

Letter to a Professional Deity

Dear Mr. Warren Buffett:

As a future fellow alum of Columbia Business School, I hope that I may ask you for a bit of advice. I have long dreamed of becoming a world-class investor and thought you might be able to shed some light on how to achieve this goal. I know that your status has been many years in the making; I am curious as to how you would map out a career, if you were starting over now.

While I have been working as an investment analyst for the past two years, I realize I have much to learn. As such, I am thrilled to be pursuing my MBA this fall. I know the classroom education will be phenomenal but, at this point, I would love to gain some personal insight as to how I can best fulfill my dreams.

I will be in the Omaha area in the coming weeks and would love to grab just a few minutes of your time for a cup of coffee whenever is most convenient. I truly appreciate your willingness to take this on and look forward to speaking with you.

Sincerely,
Every MBA in America

P.S. I have attached my resumé to give you a better understanding of my background. Again, many thanks.

Getting the Most Out of an Informational Interview

Congratulations on landing an interview! Now you must prepare. The onus is on you to lead the discussion and to get your questions answered. Thus, you should arrive with questions either in mind or on paper.

Think about what your goals are for your conversation. If you're speaking with one of your "one-degree" connections, you can afford to be more casual and ask the "dumb" questions that you really need to get answered. Since these people already know you and like you, ask them for honest critiques of your performance afterwards. For instance, what questions did you fail to ask or where might you have shown a lack of preparation? Be gracious and accept the feedback humbly.

As you move up the power ladder and reach further out in your network, take care to reduce your ignorance. Never go into an informational interview with anyone who could theoretically offer you a job without knowing a good deal from earlier conversations and other background research. You could do yourself damage by appearing unserious or lazy.

Furthermore, take time to learn the interviewee's public bio. Don't just rattle this off (it could be quite unnerving for the person sitting across from you); rather, ask about particular transitions that interest you and that reveal the character and motives of the other person.

> *We're all here to search for a viable career path but you want to know what a particular career path actually means. What is the lifestyle over the next two years and what's it like after that?*
>
> *-- Arvind, Anderson '12 (UCLA)*

To ensure a strong first impression, come with a clear understanding of what makes your interviewee's company, industry, or personal background special. Check for any recent news or press releases that might be relevant to your discussion, and have a few insightful questions prepared.

Once you have a sense of who this person is, figure out what specific information you want to get out of your meeting. To that end, prepare an opening to the conversation in which you explain why you approached the other person, why you are interested in this particular field, and what long-term goals you are considering. It's also worth asserting that you are hoping to get a true "insider's" perspective. Being deferential and respectful will earn you brownie points—and it's the right thing to do.

Not sure what questions to ask? Try these on for size.

Top Questions for Informational Interviews

1) What drew you to this field?

2) What do you enjoy most about your job?

3) What do you find the most difficult or challenging? Is that something particular to this firm or role, or do you see it as applicable to the industry?

4) What makes you stay in the industry?

5) Where do you see yourself next year? In five years? Fifteen?

6) What would be the most surprising misconception about your position or industry?

7) How has the field been evolving in response to (something you have read about recently)?

8) What is a little known, but very real, frustration with this job?

9) Can you describe your daily workload or talk about how you balance your job with any outside responsibilities or interests?

10) If you were starting your career today, what would you do the same? What would you do differently?

11) What else would you consider doing if you weren't in this role but were still in this industry?

12) How much opportunity do you see within your field?

13) What personalities are most successful in this sort of position? Why?

14) What qualities do you look for when hiring someone into your company?

15) Are there other ways I can explore this field?

16) Who else would you suggest I speak with?

17) Is there any specific advice you have for me, given my background and goals?

Of course, make your mother proud and send follow-up thank-you notes and/or emails. As you link up with other folks that you are referred to, always circle back to the person who was your initial contact. A few quick keystrokes can go a long way toward solidifying your name in their memory and making a positive impression.

Keep in mind, though, that an informational interview may not lead to a job. It's *informational* for a reason.

> *I always thought that somehow, an informational interview was supposed to magically lead to a job. Like, you have the interview, something happens, and then, poof! Job! But you have to be realistic that an informational is just that—and won't necessarily lead to an offer.*
>
> *-- Rachel, Haas '11 (Berkeley)*

The Multiplier Effect

The real key to networking is that you don't want your network to stop with one person; you want that one person to offer to introduce you to three more, and for each of those people to introduce you to three others, and... Essentially, you want to create your own pyramid scheme (albeit, a respectable one), where you are the beneficiary at the top. Doing this requires deft skill. You want every person you meet with to walk away confident that he or she could put you in front of another one of their colleagues or friends and that you would make a good impression. If someone fears that you will be a bumbling idiot, you won't get a lot of referrals. Thus, you want to always demonstrate that you are polite, intelligent, respectful, and an all-around good Boy or Girl Scout.

If you can make such an impression, then most of your conversations will turn, at some point, to next steps in your process. If a particular person or company was mentioned earlier in the conversation, it is perfectly appropriate for you to return to that topic:

Me: You mentioned Oprah Winfrey earlier as someone I should speak with.[2] How might you suggest I contact her or anyone else who might be appropriate?

Person Whose Connections I Covet: I do think she'd be a great person for you to sit down with. I'll give her a call and see what I can do.

Me: That would be great. I know you already have my resumé, but please let me know if there is anything else I can provide— maybe a short summary of what I am looking for or anything else that might shed some light on what I am trying to do.

If the conversation does not make it to that point but you still have a positive vibe, you can revisit the subject of other contacts when you send your thank-you note. In addition to expressing gratitude, you should also mention a particular part of the conversation that struck you or something that you found insightful. Following that, you can ask for assistance or referrals.

Sample Thank-you Note

Dear Person Whose Connections I Covet,

I just wanted to drop you a note to thank you for your time this afternoon. It was incredibly helpful for me to hear about your experiences in the plastics industry. While I had always envisioned myself in the real estate sector, my interest in plastics was piqued by the stories you told about the challenges of injection molding.

I would love to continue my exploration of the plastics industry and was hoping you might be willing to introduce me to Bob or Sally, both of whom you spoke so highly of today. If either of them would be willing to sit down with me as you have, I am sure I would benefit from hearing about their experiences and career paths.

---

2   Lest you think this is a made-up example, one of us actually had this conversation.

Again, many thanks for your time and effort; I truly appreciate it. I will also be sure to keep you posted on my progress.

All the best,
Me

You get the basic idea. Now go forth and write your own thank-you notes. Er, after you've had some meetings.

.

CHAPTER 25:
FOR WHOM THE RECRUITING BELL TOLLS

By now, discussions of your future plans are most likely dominating your life. And if they're not, you're probably not spending much time on campus or talking with your family.

Depending upon your chosen career path, formal recruiting will take up a significant portion of your calendar. Key seasons and dates differ greatly across industries. Companies that traditionally do more extensive hiring jump in first, while companies with less formalized processes wait until later in the school year to begin hiring conversations in earnest. The following two pages contain rough calendars for first- and second-year recruiting. Obviously, this is another thing that schools differ on; be sure to find out the particulars that will impact you.

Does this mean that if you're committed to one of those later career groups, you get to sit around during the fall and twiddle your thumbs? Absolutely not. Your recruiting season isn't just later; it's longer. You have months in which you can be networking, conducting informational interviews, shadowing individuals, and researching specific companies so that you're already in the mix by the time the gates open up. If you wait until the spring to begin any conversations, you're going to lag behind your more ambitious classmates. You're ambitious too, so go get what you want.

First Year Recruiting Calendar

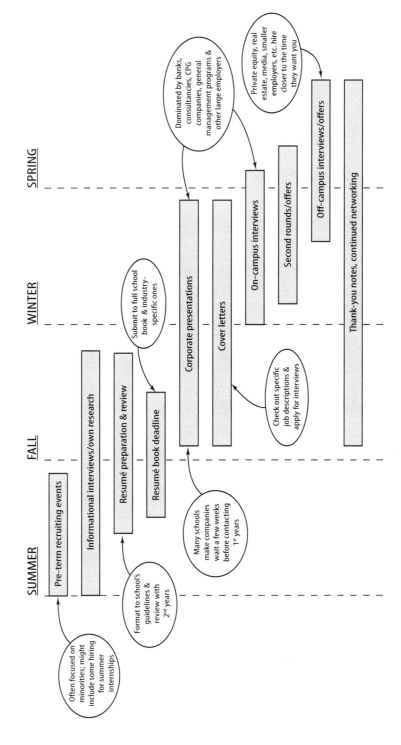

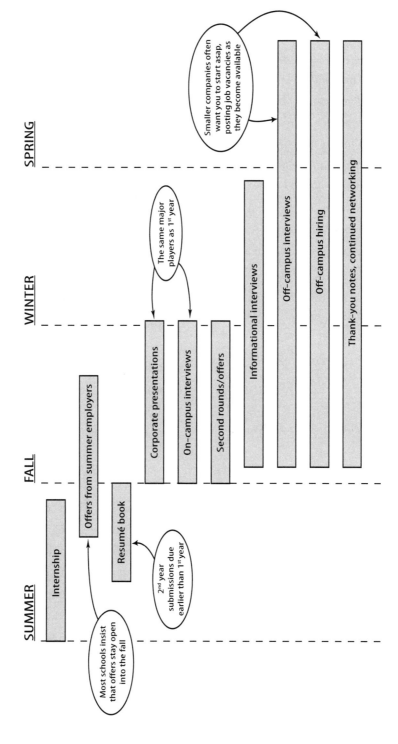

Second Year Recruiting Calendar

Whose Job Search Is It Anyway?

> *I am amazed by the power of conformity at business school, the number of people who are pursing similar career paths without a lot of thought behind it. As soon as you get into the whole recruiting thing, you're done because you invest time and emotion into it and you start to identify with those particular jobs. So don't start recruiting if you don't want to [go down that path].*
>
> *-- Ari, HBS '11 (Harvard)*

In a word: yours. It's not your mother's, it's not your father's, it's not your friend's, and it is *definitely* not your career services representative's. After all, he or she already has a job. It's you who needs one.

Some students view the MBA experience as transactional. You write a big check, show up, do some work, and leave with a piece of paper, a job, and a salary with a number of zeros tacked on the end. We hope that, by now, you've come to realize that this is not the case, both because you should be giving more to the experience and because jobs aren't simply handed out like free t-shirts. As with every other aspect of b-school, you will get out of your job search what you put into it, assisted a bit by luck and market conditions.

MBA career centers are not job placement offices. They do not have a set of positions that they slot students into; the role of career services is to *service* your career, not define it. These offices provide numerous valuable resources, from industry and company profiles to databases of alums who are willing to be contacted. They organize company visits and strive to attract potential employers. You can often find career coaches who will give you direction if you are struggling to define your passion, or who can help you with your "elevator pitch." At the end of the day, it's still up to you to prepare for interviews and meetings. They're the coaches; you're the player. They can't actually join you on the court or on the field (i.e., the pitch, if you're from a Commonwealth country) or in the Octagon (if you're an ultimate fighter).

> *Your career counselor is not going to put you in a job. It's not our job to edit your cover letters or tell you what to wear. We are here to teach life-long skills and partner with you, the student.*
>
> *-- Jennifer Chow Bevan, Associate Director,*
> *Career Services, Anderson (UCLA)*

You, On Paper

You remember the three "Rs" of grammar school, right? Well, the three "Rs" of business school might as well be Readin', wRitin', and Resumés. Each school has its own resumé format; yours must conform to your school's specifications if you want it to be included in the resumé book.

What's a resumé book, you ask? Why, that's where your career services office bundles your resumé with those of your classmates and presents them to companies looking to hire upstanding, accomplished folks like yourself. Unless you have *absolutely* no interest in getting a company to solicit you for a job, submit your resumé for the school-wide book, as well as for any smaller, more focused books compiled by the professional clubs to which you belong.

> *For banking and finance, you really have to signal the market [that you're interested in being recruited] by joining the professional club.*
>
> *-- Debbie Berechman, Executive Director,*
> *MBA Program, Sloan (MIT)*

Don't think that you can simply add "MBA" to your education section and reconfigure your margins before handing this in. Nonononono. Your resumé is most often the first impression a future employer will have of you; you need to make sure that it is the best representation of you, your accomplishments, and your skills, particularly as they relate to your desired industry.

There are a million books out there on how to write resumés, but the best resources are sitting right next to you: second years who have had success in the field you're hoping to enter. Take advantage of "resumé review" sessions and pay attention to the advice you get; your second-year mentors can tell you when a line is too full of jargon or otherwise underwhelming. They will also likely know the key words or traits that employers home in on. If you are applying to positions in different industries, you may need to prepare multiple resumés that focus on different skill sets or experiences. Annoying? Yes. But you do want a job, right?

Whatever you do, allow a lot more time for resumé preparation than you think you'll need. It always takes longer than you anticipate and you don't want to make *any* mistakes.

On-Campus vs. Off-Campus Recruiting

If you grew up watching *Sesame Street*, you probably remember the time that Grover, the loveable, furry blue monster, explained the difference between "near" and "far" by running to and from the camera until he passed out from exhaustion.[1] Recruiting often involves running back and forth between companies that are "near" (on-campus) and "far" (off-campus).

As Grover illustrated, it takes a lot of energy to run from near to far and back again, which is why many students often prefer to focus their efforts, at least initially, on the industries and particular companies that come

---

1   If you don't remember it, look for it on YouTube. It's well worth it.

to campus. However, this often means overlooking other employment options, so weigh this decision carefully. Both forms of recruiting can be extremely time-intensive processes but require different approaches and techniques.

On-campus recruiting refers to those companies that travel to your school, make some sort of presentation over lunch or cocktails, and return for a first round of interviews. Interview slots take one of two forms: open or closed. An open interview slot is one anyone can sign up for, in theory. In contrast, the employer decides who gets closed interview slots. To get one yourself, you must submit a resumé and maybe a cover letter or formal application.

> *It pays to be focused; your "backup" plan is someone else's first choice.*
>
> *-- Tripp, Ross '11 (Michigan)*

Making it onto a "closed list" is a good thing—you survived the initial cut. However, if you aren't on the closed list, don't be dismayed. Companies hire students they meet in open interviews, so bid for the slots you want. Yes, that's right—there is an auction set for your future job. Schools differ in their polices, but the basic idea is that students are allocated a certain number of bid points ahead of time. During the recruiting season, you use your points to bid for interview slots. Check with your career services office and second years for more information, such as the typical market-clearing price for hot employers.

If on-campus recruiting is "near," off-campus is "far." Off-campus recruiting isn't really "recruiting" because the companies in question aren't really recruiting you; you're recruiting them. You have to apply through their websites, contact the HR departments, and network with current employees and connected alumni. Industries that do not traditionally take on large numbers of business school students are generally only accessed through off-campus channels. Media, sports, and other smaller companies rarely send teams of recruiters out to find the one or two MBAs that they will hire that year, so you have to reach out to them. This does not mean that these companies are any less interested in speaking to you than the banks or the consulting firms; they just tend not to have as formalized a process for recruiting or starting a particular "class" of associates.

> *The MBA machine tends to focus on only a few jobs, but we all came in idealistic about finding something we love. It helps to talk to students who interned at esoteric jobs that might not have a presence on-campus.*
>
> *-- Lisa, Booth '12 (Chicago)*

Channels for accessing off-campus recruiting are also much more mysterious and variable. The onus will be on you, but the payoff can be great.

Whether you focus on on-campus or off-campus recruiting, the whole "looking for a job" thing is at least the equivalent of another class. However you put in the hours every week—attending presentations, doing informational interviews, scouring websites for job postings, reading industry journals—most every b-school student will be doing substantial work to find … well … work. This makes sense: your time at business school is primarily about where you will be for all of the time that comes *after* business school.

> *The smartest students often limit themselves by targeting particular companies. It's better to think about what kind of work will make you happy.*
>
> *-- Peter Giulioni, Jr., Assistant Dean & Executive Director, MBA Career Services, Marshall (USC)*

The Funny Psychology of Timing

It has always struck us as interesting that certain careers with more fixed paths follow more fixed recruiting practices. Large companies, banks, and consultancies that hire MBAs every year have the game down and thus tend to follow a pretty standard lineup of events and interviews, usually early in the recruiting season. Smaller companies and industries (e.g., media, real estate, private equity, etc.) that are less focused on MBAs operate on a later calendar, often opting for just-in-time[1] hiring late in the season.

There's natural selection at work here. Those who are able to let the early recruiting cycle pass without feeling as though they've missed the boat are the ones who have the temperament to survive in those less predictable industries. Furthermore, those are the sorts of industries that are less inclined to come to campus, meaning that those who are gunning for such jobs have to take initiative and show passion for what they are interested in.

Think of it this way: Two students think that they want summer internships in real estate, but one of them starts to waiver and attends a bunch of consulting presentations in the fall, not because he has any interest in becoming a consultant but because of the appeal of having his summer internship locked up sooner rather than later. The other student doesn't give the presentations a passing glance; she knows what she wants and would rather spend the time in the fall building her real estate network. At the end of the day, the guy who wants the certainty of a job will do better in consulting, where the paths and processes are more defined. The girl who can handle the ambiguity? She'll ride the waves of the real estate market just fine.

---

1   "Just-in-time" is a term stolen from your operations course. It means just what you think it does.

So Many Events, So Little Time

Most schools impose a moratorium on would-be employers coming to campus until at least a month into your first year. But when the flood-gates open, expect to be deluged like never before. We're talking lunch presentations, wine and cheese events, and more swag than you can shake a custom-printed stick at.

There is no way you can do it all. Nor should you try.

However, it is very important to go to the events sponsored by any company that you would like to be employed by. The recruiting processes is like a courtship—and each party needs to express a fair amount of interest if things are ever going to proceed beyond cocktails. Companies care a great deal about those who show them love: there will be sign-in sheets so that the host can contact you and also verify that you were willing to give up two hours of your Thursday evening to mingle with employees of the company.

> *Trying to go to all of the events is just suicide.*
>
> *-- Mike, CBS '11 (Columbia)*

Wine and cheese hours provide a window into how a particular firm or company sees itself. As you stand around talking to people who were probably in your shoes only two or three years prior, pay specific attention to highlighted aspects of the culture and lifestyle, noting words used to describe the work environment. While small to the outside world, these subtle language differences among otherwise similar companies are well known within the industry and to each company's recruiters. When you sit down to interview, you're going to want to earn all of the brownie points you

> *By the time the interviews roll around for the "traditional path" jobs, [the companies] have pretty much already figured out who they want to hire.*
>
> *-- Kristen, Booth '12 (Chicago)*

can by knowing the appropriate buzzwords and ways in which the company differentiates itself.[2]

> *Learn to network by going to the presentations of companies you don't really care about so that you're not as nervous when you do have to face the ones you're interested in.*
>
> *-- Kevin, Ross '12 (Michigan)*

What Not to Wear

Are you the guy who goes to Accounting in sweats? Are you the woman who dashes around campus in skinny jeans and stilettos? We have no problem with you—unless you try to get away with said outfit at a recruiting event.

As much as you may enjoy expressing your personal style through your clothing, most recruiters want to see you conform to traditional business dress. What this means may differ across industries and geographies, but you should always err on the side of being more formal than need be and more conservative than you would like to be. Banking, consulting, and most other *Fortune 500*-type companies will expect to see you in nice business casual attire at on-campus events and in suits at off-campus events and interviews. Tailored, pressed, and in a dark color. No Canadian tuxedos or wrinkled Dockers for this one.

While you should definitely have at least one suit in your wardrobe (and, ladies, you should probably have a skirt, as well as pants), talk to second-year students before you rush out and open a charge account at Barney's. Find out what the protocol is for your industry, both in terms of dress and the number of events you can expect to have with each potential employer. You don't want to be remembered as the person who always wore the same thing.

---

2   Without, of course, coming across as a total pandering tool.

The Corporate Informational Interview

The informational interview is still a wonderful way to learn more about a particular career path or company, but it can take on a whole new meaning in the context of recruiting. Some companies, banks in particular, want you to visit "informally" with a number of different employees. While these meetings are generally positioned as non-evaluative, that's not true. Everything is evaluative, at least in a baseline kind of way. No one is trying to back-door the interview process or catch you off-guard, but every interaction you have with a potential employer matters. You might travel to the company's location and spend a day or more meeting with folks to discover your fit. Fortunately, you are not likely to get hit with a case or tough questions about your resumé.

> *Try to find out what the corporate philosophy is, what the company values, and what they want to see you emphasize in interviews.*
>
> *-- Jon, Haas '11 (Berkeley)*

Making you sit through a ridiculous number of these conversations has a few benefits for the company. For one, it allows you to demonstrate a sincere interest. If you don't want to spend 20+ hours chatting with potential colleagues, this probably isn't the right place for you. Also, for banks in particular, it is about discovering which division or subdivision is right for you. You will meet with people on a variety of trading desks or in different equity areas to see where there is mutual interest. It's like speed dating…only not so speedy. At any company, look for personal connections with one or two employees who might become early-stage mentors for you, if you join.

Use this time to get your questions answered. Ask about the work that is done, the dynamics of the group, and anything related to lifestyle.

Long hours are par for the banking course, but do a reality check— do you honestly want to be at the office from 6 am until 3 am on a semi-regular basis for the next few years? If so, express enthusiasm for midnight McDonald's runs. If not, maybe you need to consider a different employer or even a different line of work.

> *If you can come across as being hungry, you're good. Employers then know that you're not entitled and that you're willing to work hard.*
>
> *-- Dylan, Kenan-Flagler '11 (UNC)*

Ms. Manners Goes to Recruiting Events

Bizarrely, Emily Post failed to address company recruiting in any of her writings. Regardless, the rules of etiquette in corporate settings differ little from those in class, in the workplace, and in civilized society, so if you employ a bit of common sense, you will make yourself all that much more enjoyable and employable. Spot of tea?

Rule #1: Be polite to everyone. It's always a good idea to smile at the woman who is checking you in, to make eye contact with the person greeting you at the door, and to thank the bartender for your drink. Never treat assistants poorly (and not just because they're the ones who run the world). Assume that you are being judged on every one of your interactions; you don't know who might be listening in on your conversation or watching you from afar. Be aware what you say, even if you think you are in a secluded corner, gossiping about your study buddy and his recent hookup with your Econ professor. Definitely don't bad-mouth the company or any of its competitors; you wouldn't want your comments to be falsely attributed or taken out of context. Most importantly, employers want to find positive people. If you trash-talk the crab cakes at the first event, one can only imagine what you are going to have to say about Corporate's vacation policy a year in.

Rule #2: Don't be "that guy." Recruiting events are a time to show that you are interested in the company, smart, and fun to be around. They are not the time to show anyone up—be it a classmate, a professor, or, God forbid, a senior executive. This is also not the venue for you to walk someone through your resumé or provide a synopsis of your greatest achievements. Ask questions that are relevant and geared towards gathering more information about the company. Stay clear of things that you should know or could easily find out from the Internet.

Rule #3: You *are* there to make friends. This is similar to the previous point but more directed at how you interact with your peers. Say what you will about reality TV and, in particular, dating game shows—that they are responsible for the dumbing down of American culture, that they are a poor replacement for scripted programming, that they are the best (legal) guilty pleasure ever invented—but the one thing that these shows have taught us is the importance of not being a jerk. No one likes the know-it-all, the arrogant guy who thinks he has the competition locked up from the get-go, or whoever says, "I'm not here to make friends." On TV, these people are ostracized and ganged up upon by the rest of the crew—and rightfully so.

The lesson is that you should imagine that cameras are rolling at every event. Be respectful of the people around you and engage them in conversation, regardless of their position. You may learn something about the company or the industry from other classmates or from the support staff. If nothing else, you may fool people into thinking you have a decent amount of social dexterity.

Second years have a lot more influence than you think. You don't want to be a pompous jerk in front of them; they can be very good mentors.

-- Brian, Booth '11 (Chicago)

Rule #4: Be engaging, but don't be a stalker. Nearly all corporate presentations will provide some amount of mingling between students and company representatives. What usually happens is that a 45-minute PowerPoint is followed by another half-hour of questions and then informal chats. Inevitably, you will see your classmates make a beeline for the speaker. They will form very intense semi-circles around this person, slowly pushing him or her further and further back until the poor victim is swallowed up by the nearest window treatment. The representative will do his or her best to entertain the group and respond to all questions, but someone amongst the students will try to monopolize the entire conversation. The target will awkwardly try to engage others but the one student will not be halted. Eventually, the target will have drained his or her drink and will politely move towards the bar, hoping and praying not to be followed. No one likes a Stage 5 Clinger.

Most conversations with company representatives are, unfortunately, small talk. If, however, you sense that you might be getting somewhere with someone, go ahead and dig a little deeper. We're not talking about engaging in corporate espionage here, or asking for weird personal revelations. But if you discover that you and the company rep both sang in a cappella groups in college, then go ahead and glee out together. Just don't actually start singing.

Rule #5: Stick to a two-drink maximum. Sure, the alcohol is free and probably a lot better than what you will find at Happy Hour, but that doesn't mean you get to do shots on the company tab. (That comes once you have the expense account.) It is just fine to have a drink or two, but the last thing you want to be caught doing is slurring your words or placing your hand inappropriately on the senior partner's leg. Similarly, be mindful of what you are eating and the fact that you are probably going to be speaking fairly close to someone's face. Avoid garlic dip, stinky cheeses, and other foul-smelling foods. Why these even show up on the hors d'oeuvres table is mindboggling.

Note: These rules apply to the big events on campus, as well as any smaller events that may take place off-campus at any point in the recruiting/interviewing process. Expect that some of the bigger players will have dinners and other, more social, events for you to participate in. They might—oooh!!!—even invite students from other schools, so be sure to be friendly and outgoing. The same etiquette is called for when your competitors from other schools appear. Remember that these events are also part of the classic "airport test."[3]

Finessing the Follow-up

Had a good time? Met some interesting employees? Enjoyed the Gruyère? That's wonderful. We're happy for you. But if you want your association with your dream company to be more than a one-night stand, you need to follow up with your hosts.

The key to the post-recruiting email is to be timely, relevant, and memorable—and it all starts at the event itself. It goes without saying that, if you're talking to a representative of the company, you want to ask for his or her card. After you've finished the conversation, step off to the side and *jot a few notes* on the back. What did you and George talk about? Did he make any interesting points or observations? George is going to meet a bunch of people at that recruiting event; you want to make sure he has a way to recall you and your conversation when he gets your email.

> *You have to be exceptional always; in your follow-up, be exceptionally gracious and exceptionally professional.*
>
> *-- David Cooley, Associate Director,*
> *External Relations and Career Counselor, Anderson (UCLA)*

---

3   Given the reliability of airline travel these days, it's highly likely that, if your job involves travel, you will, at some point, be stuck with a co-worker at an airport for an ungodly amount of time. Your future employer wants to know that you're someone he or she could actually tolerate spending that time with.

The next question is when to send said email. The answer? The next day. Do not send a thank-you note via your smartphone as you walk home from the event; it comes across as insincere and reeks of "I had to do this, so I did it as quickly as I possibly could." That may very well be true, but it is not the message you want to convey.

Take time to hand-craft your message, referencing something specific about your interaction (this is where those handy business-card notes come into play). If you have a particular question, you can ask it here, in hopes of creating a conversation—but let the rules of informational interviews apply here, too, and don't ask anything that you could easily look up the answer to yourself.

> This isn't like tee-ball; not everyone gets a trophy. There are a limited number of jobs out there and you have to work to find one.
>
> -- Christine Gramhofer, Director, Academic Services, Booth (Chicago)

Whatever you do, be sure to read over the note before you hit "send." Read it aloud, slowly. Typos, grammatical errors, and other slips, Freudian or not, are all very easy ways to get your resumé tossed in the "reject" pile.

Now, cool your heels. Don't expect that you'll necessarily get a response to your note; it would be weird if every thank-you note begat some other thank-you note. Do, however, think about how you can maintain the relationship. If some time has passed and you haven't had any communication but read an article or hear a piece of news that would be relevant to the person you spoke with, feel free to drop him or her an email. If this begins the conversation anew, see about setting up a time to speak again, if you think there is a good reason or that you can find one.

CHAPTER 26:
INTERVIEWS…AND OFFERS!

All right. You have narrowed down your options and figured out what you want to do. You have made strategic use of company presentations and your personal network to meet a variety of connected folks in your chosen field. You have written cogent cover letters and polished your resumé to a mirror finish, so that it reflects you perfectly.

And now, interview season has begun. It's time to don the business suit for real.

Interviews are game time, the make-or-break of your immediate career plans, the purpose and culmination of mountains of work. How can you *not* be stressed? Before a launch, an astronaut was once asked whether he was nervous. In reply, he said something to this effect: "I'll be strapped to one of the largest bombs ever built, and it's going to blow up and fling me into space. If I'm not nervous, I'm not grasping reality."

Maybe "bomb" isn't the most uplifting metaphor in the context of interviews, but you get our point: it's totally natural to feel stress right now. The whole question is how you handle it.

Interviews come in two primary flavors.

1. ***Behavioral*** – In this traditional format, you are asked questions off of your resumé. You discuss past accomplishments and future

intentions, letting your intelligence, character and sunny personality shine through.

2. **Task-based** – If behavioral interviews are about the past and the future, task-based interviews are about the present, since you are asked to perform specific tasks in real time. For instance, consulting firms usually ask you to attack a *case*—not a booklet published by Harvard Business School, as you've become used to in class, but a miniature business problem nonetheless. As you try to solve the case, you ask questions, examine exhibits, and jot notes on paper—things you don't do in a typical behavioral interview.

   Other industries use tasks as well: for instance, a marketing division might want you to evaluate the marketing mix for a hypothetical brand launch, or a Wall Street recruiter might ask you to construct a pitch for a potential acquisition, using financial statements and other materials.

Oh, Behave

We have both taught scores of students how to do battle with the GMAT. In some ways, that test is just like a job interview—you face questions that adapt to you in real time, and you can't turn back the clock to change an answer. Sure, an interviewer won't ask you to solve for x, but you might feel something like "test anxiety" when you're asked about that gap in your work experience.

You may never have come to love the GMAT as we do, but you dealt with it, both ahead of time and in the heat of the moment. That's what you've done in countless other challenging situations. And that's what you'll do this time with these interviews.

As much as you can, mentally embrace the experience of an interview. Regardless of what you do, the adrenaline is going to rush into your bloodstream. What you have control over is whether the adrenaline paralyzes you in quivering fear, or whether it lends you the strength of giants. Do whatever you must in order to direct the energy positively. Some people psych themselves up; others chill themselves out. If you're in the former group, log some heart-racing physical activity. Pound the punching bag to "Eye of the Tiger," or go for a run with Rage Against the Machine on your iPod. You'll also respond to metaphors of sports and war, so arm yourself with them before you take the field.[1]

Conversely, if such metaphors leave you uninspired, try channeling your adrenaline in calmer ways. Go for that run, but put Vivaldi on your headphones. Call an old friend for a catch-up and some positive reinforcement. Drink a cream soda. You know best what you need—just go get it ahead of time.

In the interview itself, dig deep and find a way to be authentically warm. If you aren't feeling a love connection, the person across the table will notice. For one thing, real smiles—ones caused by true laughter or joy—cause involuntary muscles at the corners of your eyes to crease, whereas false smiles leave those muscles relaxed. So anyone can instantly tell whether you are smiling genuinely or not. And no, you can't control those eye muscles. That's what involuntary means. In general, it's tough to fake sincerity.

Then what do you do, when you can't seem to bond on a personal level with the interviewer? When all else fails, ask for help. Send a momentary mental plea to a higher power or an inner source of strength, something outside your conscious self. We're not advocating a specific religion here, or even religion at all—the Flying Spaghetti Monster will do just fine. Just ask the FSM for a bit of pastafarian guidance as you try to find common ground with your blank-faced interviewer. You might not receive any supernatural help, but you'll feel better. Or hungrier.

---

1   One of us got this interviewing advice from an intense Wall Street type: "You're a hand grenade. Pull your own pin, roll in the room and blow up all over the place." As ludicrous as this analogy is, you can't fault it for being dull. Perhaps it's even more effective because it's so ridiculous. Puh-*pow*.

One balance you need to strike is how to be yourself while you deliver semi-prepared responses and project a modicum of extra energy. One of us interviews 3-5 potential test-prep instructors a week, and he regularly sees candidates who fall too far to either end of this spectrum. Some are almost too comfortable and casual; the laidback vibe is nice, but you wonder where the enthusiasm is. Other candidates are over-the-top performers, court jesters with what seems to be a grafted-on persona.

Where you want to be is in the middle: "you plus." You're always authentically you, but you're just a little revved up, if for no other reason than you have fight-or-flight hormones coursing through your veins. Don't be too rehearsed. Remember to blink (people who never do are spooky) and to shift position in your chair. An overly rigid posture smacks of rigor mortis.

What if the interviewer throws you a serious curveball? First of all, think over your background. What could someone perceive as a foible or flaw? Know what you'll say if any of these issues are brought up. Few interviewers are unrepentant jackasses, but many will challenge you bluntly—after all, they're trying to evaluate your past experiences and also observe what you do when a ball is chucked at your head. Do you charge the mound in anger, or do you duck calmly, brush the dirt off your jersey and get ready for the next pitch?

If you're being probed, don't take it personally, even if it feels like it's coming from aliens or the TSA. Just state your case without apology and be ready to move on.[2] If the foible in question were enough on its own to get you dinged, you probably wouldn't be in the interview in the first place. So roll with the punch and shrug (mentally, not physically).

———————————

2   One of us earned some god-awful grades his junior year in college, grades he still feels guilty pangs about. When one consulting firm requested his undergrad transcript in advance of second-round interviews, he knew he could be in for a pummeling, and he girded up accordingly. Not one interviewer mentioned a thing until the end of the day. The last meeting was with the managing director, and the author had not even crossed the threshold of the office when the MD barked, "So what happened your junior year?" The author was able to blurt out a decent-enough answer to get a job offer from that same MD.

If you're transitioning from another career to finance or consulting, you may be asked, "What was your grade in Corp Fin?" even though your campus has a no-grade-disclosure policy. Be ready for this. In particular, off-campus recruiters will not care about closed vs. open grading—if they ask for your grades, they'll want an answer.

Finally, if a question completely throws you for a loop, stop and think. Pauses feel longer to you than to the person you've been talking with. Take a deep breath—we say that a lot because it's so darn useful. There's nothing like fresh oxygen in your lungs to restart your heart and unfreeze your mind. And take a sip of that glass of water you accepted earlier—it buys you a few seconds and forestalls a coughing fit. (That means that you should always accept water when it's offered.)

That Sounds Like a Case of the Mondays

The most common task-based interview is the infamous "consulting case." Your goal in this sort of interview is to show how you can structure an inquiry into an ill-defined problem, dig into promising areas, synthesize findings, and come up with creative alternatives. You play the role of a working consultant, while the interviewer acts the part of the client or another consultant.

Ahead of time, you must practice with second years. Don't just read books, and don't just kick cases around with other numbskull first years. It takes experience to administer a case well. To get into tip-top shape for consulting interviews, you have to have your butt kicked at least a few times by skilled second years. If your very first practice case goes well, it probably wasn't hard enough.

Be organized in your note-taking. If you're comparing a fast-food chain to its competitors along a bunch of dimensions, set up a quick table with a couple of columns. A little organization can help you unlock an insight.[3]

---

3   In a practice case one of us was wrestling with, the mystery boiled down to why a certain pair

During the case, ignore pernicious thoughts about how well the interview is going. Sure, you need to read signals about promising leads, but the other person may act completely deadpan, with not a shred of a smile or other positive feedback. Don't let that throw you. Smack yourself and stay in role as a consultant.

The big advantage of task-based interviews in general is that, in a sense, you're not the focus. Your skills are. It's less an explanation of past performances and more an actual tryout or audition. Thespians are given a scene to read, athletes are given sprints to run, and you'll be given a business problem to solve. As much as possible, you should even look for ways to enjoy the process. One of us remembers with weird fondness a cool case interview conducted at a whiteboard displaying a map of India: the problem was to determine where to situate cement plants and why.

Not every case will naturally reach out and grab you, but if you can find pleasure in solving the puzzle, all the better. Or in *trying* to solve it. You can feel as if you flubbed the case completely but still do well enough to move forward.[4]

All this case-interviewing advice holds for any kind of task-based interview. Prepare by actually doing similar activities with people who can hold you to account. On game day, get all dorky on the puzzle, do your best, and put the results in the hands of fate. In one final-round interview, one of us was sent into a room with a pile of written materials and a clunky computer and given 45 minutes to come up with a half-hour presentation she would then deliver. How did the presentation come out? About as clunky as the computer. But she got the offer anyway.

---

of numbers had a 2:1 ratio. The author stumbled into the answer only by virtue of organization: another row in his notes displayed a ratio of 1:2, which turned out to be the key.

4   In a first-round interview, one of us tackled a profit case by focusing exclusively on revenues, failing utterly to consider costs. That's about as basic a mistake as one could make (since Profits = Revenues – Costs, duh), but he still progressed to the next round.

Tips for Surviving Interview Season

Tip #1: Keep extra clothes in your locker. Sure, you're going to be chugging your coffee, trying to caffeinate before you face your executioner...er...interviewer. But what happens when your triple mocha latte spills all over your fresh pressed shirt? Uh-oh. Even if the stain is no match for your Tide-to-Go pen (keep one of those handy, too), at least you have a spare outfit in your locker. A quick switcheroo and no one will be the wiser.

Tip #2: Have a toothbrush and other grooming supplies on hand. In economics, certain preferences are known as ***hygiene requirements***: there's no reward for being extra clean, but you're severly penalized for being dirty. Guess what? Physical hygiene is a hygiene requirement, folks.

Interviews should be about fishing for answers, not fishing to get that piece of broccoli out of your molars. Before you meet with anyone, take some time to freshen up and make sure that you don't have a forest growing in your teeth or that your breath smells of the smokehouse. Now that there are throwaway toothbrushes, you have no excuse for just using a breath mint. (Although if you are ever offered one, take it. It just might be a message.)

Check yourself in the mirror just before you walk into an interview. Guys, this might mean carrying a compact.[5]

Tip #3: A little cologne/perfume goes a very long way. You want them to focus on you, not the way you smell. Keep antiperspirant or deodorant in a neutral or very mild scent handy—the aromatic equivalent of the color of your resumé paper. While you may live for *Eau de Greenbacks* or *Arbitrage: The Scent of the Deal*, it's possible that the smell

---

[5]   One of our classmates went into an interview, not knowing that a shaving nick on his neck had split open. Afterwards, he didn't know what was worse: that he looked as if Edward from the *Twilight* saga had savaged his jugular, or that the interviewer had watched him hemorrhage without saying a syllable. A mirror would have been useful. Another lesson: always carry a pack of Kleenex to stanch a bleeder or to fish out a "bat in the cave."

triggers migraines for your interviewer—or, worse yet, reminds him of his ex-girlfriend. (We heard one such horror story.)

Tip #4: Lie to your calendar. If you have an appointment at 4pm, put it in your calendar as being at 3:45. This way, you will be sure to give yourself extra time to get to wherever you're going, whether it's around the corner or around the globe. (If it's the latter, give yourself more than a 15-minute grace period.)

Tip #5: Always write a thank-you note. You may be completely drained from three hours of back-to-back interviews. Your mouth may feel like it's been stuffed with cotton and you're starting to wonder if that smile plastered on your face makes you look like The Joker from *Batman*. Good thing you don't have to be able to talk to write a thank-you note. Be sure to send one within 24 hours.

The Return of #2 Pencils

A newish trend in interviews is the use of either standardized tests or company-specific tests as a way to screen applicants. What? You thought you were done with those sorts of things when you torched your GMAT books? Sorry about that.

These tests allow companies to try to even the playing field between applicants from different schools, as well as isolate and measure particular skill sets. Depending upon the company and the test, you may or may not be able to prepare; ask for as much information as possible prior to the big day. This is also one of those areas where second years and professional clubs will be able to provide insight; don't be afraid to ask lots of questions.

Also know that, just like the GMAT, these sorts of tests provide just one data point. Rarely are they the determining factor in an employment decision. You want to show your abilities, but don't stress about getting a perfect score. It won't get you a higher signing bonus.

Grace Goes a Long Way

Whether you think you aced an interview or bombed it, you never really know until you get that next phone call or email. Try not to bite off all of your fingernails waiting—it's not good for your teeth.

Not advancing in an interview process or getting the job that you had your heart set on can be quite a blow, but there are good ways to handle bad news and not-so-good ways. Just remember, how you react can have a huge impact on whether the company permanently shuts the door on you or leaves it open for you the following year.

If you do get the "we're sorry that we're not going to be able to make you an offer" phone call, take a deep breath and tell your contact how sorry you are to hear such news. They might offer an explanation, such as that they're taking fewer interns than in the past or they don't see you as having a particular skill set that they need. If no explanation is forthcoming, you can ask politely whether it would be possible for you to receive a little feedback, so that you might be a better candidate down the line.

The person you're talking to may not be someone who interviewed you, or you may feel that you had a better connection with someone else at the company. If so, you may want to reach out to that person separately for comments. Whatever you do, take any critique you receive earnestly, not defensively. You are done interviewing at this point; it's over, so let it go. If you think something might have been overlooked, you can bring that up the next year.

Ask your contact whether you can stay in touch with him or her over the year. Send brief quarterly update emails about what you've been up to

> *Just as being admitted to a top MBA program is a seal of approval, so is being hired for a summer internship.*
>
> Sheryle Dirks,
> Associate Dean for Career
> Management, Fuqua
> (Duke)

and how you have grown in particular ways. Reconfirm your desire to speak with the company in the future about possible positions without coming across as obsessive.

Behind closed doors, feel free to cry, scream, yell, or devour that pint of ice cream. We know; we've been there. Don't eat too fast or you'll get one of those horrible brain-freeze headaches.

> *Be prepared that you might not get what you want, no matter how much you want it or how hard you worked for it. Luck is a very key factor.*
>
> *-- Ann, Booth '11 (Chicago)*

The Hard Part: Decision Time

Having survived months and months of interviewing, you now find yourself in the enviable position of having multiple offers. That's fantastic! You now know what it's like to be the most attractive person in the bar on a Friday night. As we like to say, this is a good problem to have.

But with so many options, how do you pick the right one? If you're lucky, you've already taken a course in decision analysis and know how to utilize various metrics to weigh your different priorities and offers. If you haven't, you can figure it out by going through the following exercise.

It may seem odd that such a crucial decision is done in such a mathematical way—yes, you will find Excel to be a useful tool here—but it's all about clarifying your own thoughts, which are probably a jumbled mess right about now. And while you may only be puzzling over a summer internship at the moment, knowing how to use this kind of analysis will be very helpful when you face even bigger decisions in the future, both in business and in the rest of life.

Even if you've been keeping a financial ledger since you were three years old and know exactly what you want to do, the stuff that follows is worth looking at. While some fabulous programs involve a whole twelve steps, this one has just five:

1) Identify and organize your criteria.

2) Define your scales and fill in any gaps in your knowledge.

3) Assess your preferences.

4) Decide what's important to you when making tradeoffs between the criteria.

5) Crunch the numbers and check your gut.

That last one really is important—but you only get there by going through the first four. Grab a pen and some paper or your trusty spreadsheet program and join us in this fun-filled exercise.

1) Identify and Organize Your Criteria

First, brainstorm a list of issues you find important for a summer internship. Group the issues loosely as you go, and add subpoints or categories as they occur to you. Don't worry about overlap between issues; it will get worked out. Some popular categories:

- Desired Industry

- Desired Function
    - Ability to see or try other functions
    - Position on a track for long-term career progression

- Company Environment
    - People I want to work with
    - Opportunities to access different people in the organization
    - Collaborative work environment

- Location
  - Where I want to be for the summer
  - Where I might want to be for a full-time position or access to such location

- Salary and Other Perks
  - Possibility of a full-time offer
  - Possibility of tuition reimbursement if I take said offer

- Work/Life Balance
  - Acceptable hours
  - Acceptable travel

General "fit and feel" aren't on this list for a reason. That's not to say they're unimportant; in fact, they are key. However, one point of this exercise is to push you to define "fit and feel" in more tangible terms:

- What does "fit" mean in terms of your personality and the company?

- What does "feel" mean in terms of a working environment?

Look back over your list. If the positions you are considering are essentially the same in some area, drop or refine the related criterion. For example, if all you are considering are offers from large management consulting firms, "desired function" and "desired industry" may be irrelevant. You may want to dig deeper into the differences of the firms and the nature of the work they do (i.e., length of engagements, size of average teams, etc.).

Now it's time to start drawing. Yes, you read that correctly. You are going to organize your list into an *issue tree*.[6] The purpose is to help you figure out how all the issues are related. Also, insert any very general preferences as they occur to you.

---

6   If you want to become a management consultant, get used to this sort of thing. Consultants *love* issue trees. This exercise may persuade you that you do not, in fact, wish to become a consultant. And that is *just fine*.

Here's an example:

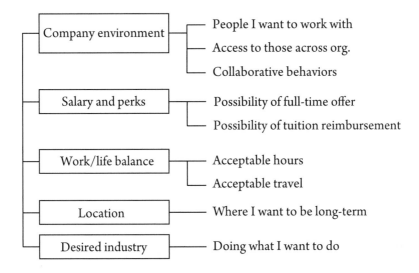

Your tree should cover everything of importance (*no gaps*), and the branches should be as distinct as possible (*no overlaps*).[7] That's hard to achieve perfectly, so just give it the old grad-school try.

2) Define Your Scales and Fill in Gaps

At this point, we need to define a *scale* or metric for each branch of the tree.

You're already set when the criterion is numeric to begin with, like the salary you're going to be paid. Just list the relevant values. For the sake of this exercise, we're assuming that you're choosing between two consulting companies and an investment bank:

	Brane	CBGB	GoldenStacks
Annualized base salary	$125,000	$120,000	$100,000

---

7   This characteristic is known to consultants as MECE (mutually exclusive and collectively exhaustive). See the Probability section in Chapter 16: Statistics.

Now move on to the "harder to measure" group. First, try to narrow down any broad categories. Then define levels qualitatively or use a *proxy measure*, a quantitative metric that corresponds approximately to the bigger issue:

	Brane	CBGB	GoldenStacks
Long-term lifestyle I want *(too broad)*			
Ability to limit travel *(more specific)*	Low	Medium	High
Percent of employee time spent at home office *(proxy)*	10%	20%	50%

Now, you may not know enough to do this for every issue and at every company, so it's time to go to your resources. Talk to second years who may have held these positions or call up your recruiter and ask (nicely) about the topics that are most important to you. As you gather info, you may need to redefine the scales and even the criteria themselves.

By the way, don't worry about ordering the criteria at this point. Just get them down on paper; you'll weigh them against each other later on.

When all is said and researched, you should have a table like the one below, though probably with more criteria:

	Brane	CBGB	GoldenStacks
Base salary	$125,000	$120,000	$100,000
Ability to limit travel	Low	Medium	High
Work environment	Collegial	Mixed	Competitive
Location	Acceptable	Barely Tolerable	Ideal

3) Assess Your Preferences

Now we need to start getting these measurements on the same footing. The first step is to assign *utility points*. Utility points just express how much you like something.

- What do you like the *most* in any row? Give that measurement 100 points.

- What do you like the *least* in any row? Give that measurement 0 points.

Now you have established a range for each row. For example:

Location	Acceptable	Barely Tolerable	Ideal
– Utility points	TBD	0 points	100 points

What is "best" will vary among the criteria and your personal preferences. If you notice, we choose to list judgments of the location, rather than the location itself. For some, Cleveland is ideal; for others, it might be less so. There is no right answer—except yours.

Now that you have your range defined, you have to assess the in-between measurements. You might start with a linear scale so that, if a measurement is halfway between "best" (100) and "worst" (0), you give it 50 points.

However, the differences might not be linear for you. You might feel being in your ideal city is twice as important as the difference between being somewhere that's just okay and somewhere that you're really not happy about. If so, give that "Acceptable" ranking just 33 points.

Location	Acceptable	Barely Tolerable	Ideal
– Utility points	33 points	0 points	100 points

This way, the difference between "Ideal" and "Acceptable" ($100 - 33 = 67$ points) is basically twice the difference between "Acceptable" and "Barely Tolerable" ($33 - 0 = 33$ points).

After you assign utility points, your chart might look something like this:

	Brane	CBGB	GoldenStacks
Base salary	$125,000	$120,000	$100,000
– Utility points	**100**	**67**	**0**
Ability to limit travel	Low	Medium	High
– Utility points	**0**	**50**	**100**
Work environment	Collegial	Mixed	Competitive
– Utility points	**100**	**50**	**0**
Location	Acceptable	Barely Tolerable	Ideal
– Utility points	**25**	**0**	**100**

To see whether you can easily eliminate any schools at this point, you can get out your graph paper and plot the relative performance of the offers:

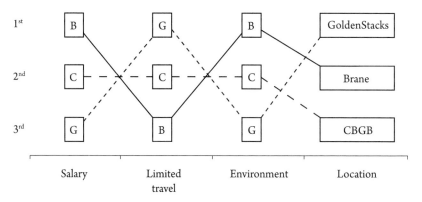

A "loser" at this point would be any company worse than another company in every way. The fancy term for this occurrence in decision analysis is **_domination_**. If job A scores above job B in every dimension, then B is dominated. None of the three companies above is dominated, so we keep them all.

4) Making Tradeoffs

Now, not all jobs were created equal—and not all criteria matter as much to you. You need to figure out how much different issues are worth to you. This involves some funky, hypothetical "horse-trading" as you assign weights to the criteria.

Imagine a set of hypothetical jobs. It doesn't matter what they are; all that matters is that you need to have one more job than you have criteria to weigh. So, if you have four criteria, you need five imaginary jobs. Got it? Good.

One job, the *Bad Benchmark,* ranks the worst on *all* of your criteria. The other jobs are equally bad on *all but one* criterion. That is, each job is tops in one area and tied with the rest of the crowd for last on every other issue. (It's all very black-or-white at this point.) The particular criterion that a given job is "best" in is then "swung" to the top of the pile to illustrate its superiority.

It's not as confusing as it sounds: one job is given the top mark for the category and the rest of the jobs all receive the same lowest mark for the category.

Make another table, forgetting about the utility points for now:

	Bad Benchmark	A	B	C	D
Base salary	$100,000	**$125,000**	$100,000	$100,000	$100,000
Ability to limit travel	Low	Low	**High**	Low	Low
Work environment	Compet.	Compet.	Compet.	**Collegial**	Compet.
Location	Barely Tolerable	Barely Tolerable	Barely Tolerable	Barely Tolerable	**Ideal**

If this chart was all that you had to go on, how would you rank the jobs? Obviously, the Bad Benchmark comes last—it's the worst in every way. But which of the others, given that each one highlights one particular criterion, comes in first? Second?

Take some time and think this through; this is, as they say, where the rubber meets the road. You need to determine what your "trump" criteria are.

Say that, after careful thought, you decide that you would select job B first, then C, then D, then A, *solely on the basis of these criteria*. Remember, these are completely fake jobs—don't try to extrapolate from them yet, and definitely don't try to cash any paychecks.

	Bad Benchmark	A	B	C	D
Base salary	$100,000	**$125,000**	$100,000	$100,000	$100,000
Ability to limit travel	Low	Low	**High**	Low	Low
Work environment	Compet.	Compet.	Compet.	**Collegial**	Compet.
Location	Barely Tolerable	Barely Tolerable	Barely Tolerable	Barely Tolerable	**Ideal**
YOUR ranking	5	4	1	2	**3**

Assign a weight of 0 to the Bad Benchmark and a weight of 100 to your top choice (Option B in this example).

Now come up with the intermediate levels. Going from the Bad Benchmark to the job B increased your happiness by 100 points. If instead, you were comparing the Bad Benchmark and job D, how many points happier would you be with D?

Again, it's all relative—and all based on your individual preferences—but when you're done, you'll end up with something like this:

	Bad Benchmark	A	B	C	D
Base salary	$100,000	**$125,000**	$100,000	$100,000	$100,000
Ability to limit ravel	Low	Low	**High**	Low	Low
Work environment	Compet.	Compet.	Compet.	**Collegial**	Compet.
Location	Barely Tolerable	Barely Tolerable	Barely Tolerable	Barely Tolerable	**Ideal**
YOUR ranking	5	4	1	2	3
YOUR points	0	25	100	60	50

These points are now your weights for the various criteria:

Criterion	Weight
Ability to limit travel	100
Work environment	60
Location	50
Base salary	25

Now it's time to leave your imaginary job offers and return to the ones you've got in your hot little hand.

5) Crunch the Numbers and Check Your Gut

Don't worry—you're almost done! C'mon, this should seem easy after all of those coffee chats, interviews, and presentations you had to go through. All that's left is for you to multiply each utility point score by the particular criterion's weight. Yes, this is the time to whip out the Excel and play along. High score wins.

	Brane	CBGB	GoldenStacks
Base salary	$125,000	$120,000	$100,000
Utility points	100	67	0
× 25	**2,500**	**1,675**	**0**
Ability to limit travel	Low	High	Medium
Utility points	0	100	50
× 100	**0**	**10,000**	**5,000**
Work environment	Collegial	Mixed	Competitive
Utility points	100	50	0
× 60	**6,000**	**3,000**	**0**
Location	Acceptable	Barely Tolerable	Ideal
Utility points	33	0	100
× 50	**1,650**	**0**	**5,000**
TOTAL	**10,150**	**15,675**	**10,000**

Congrats—You're going to work at CBGB! Rock on, Joey Ramone.

Now *check your gut.* Say it aloud: "I'm going to work for CBGB." How do you feel?

If you feel a sense of relief and joy, then fabulous!

The process has helped you clarify what you want—and why you want it. You want to work for CBGB because it's going to give you the best ability to limit your travel, which is what you have declared to be of primary importance. But that's not all; CBGB stacks up well on many of the other metrics you have deemed to be key.

However, if you're staring at that Excel screen and feeling a large pit starting to form in your stomach … if you find yourself wishing that the results came out differently…then re-examine your process. Question the utility points you assigned and the weights you gave the criteria. Were you being completely forthright with yourself along the way? You need to be honest here; lying to yourself is like cheating in a game of Solitaire. It's only going to hurt you, so you'd better do it right.

At the end of the day, it's your decision. Do what you want to do and accept the offer you really want to accept. We just think that you'll sleep better if you have done your homework and you know the real reasons that led you to choose one over another.[8]

Thanks, but No Thanks

Whether you had one interview or thirty with a company, you need to let the organization know as soon as possible if you won't be accepting an offer. Call up your HR contact and let him or her know. Express appreciation for the offer, admiration for the company, and general disappointment at not being able to accept. If asked, you should tell the company what offer you have accepted and, without getting too specific, why. Be careful not to burn any bridges.

To that end, you should also contact anyone else at the organization who championed or helped you along the way. Again, an expression of gratitude can do wonders, should you want to come back a year (or more) from now and look for fulltime employment opportunities.

What you don't want to do is hold off until the last possible minute, or take an offer and then back out before you ever start. That's rude and irresponsible—and it can get you blacklisted by your career services office. You wouldn't stand someone up on a Friday night; don't stand up a potential employer. As they say, karma's got sharp canines.

---

8   One of us, conflicted about where to go for undergrad, took a walk in a field to make up his mind. Just before reaching home, he came upon a large wooden contraption in the shape of a letter, the first initial of one of his choices. He took this as a signal from fate. Sometimes, you just gotta follow the signs.

CHAPTER 27:
ONE DOWN, ONE TO GO

It's hard to believe that you're now the old guard, the seniors, the venerable ones. You're halfway there. You're the club presidents, the TAs, the ones blowing off class to go to Jamaica.

We'd say you've earned it, but we don't really know if that's true. But we are happy that you're enjoying your time.

However, as quickly as the first half of business school went by, we promise the second half will move twice as quickly. And when it's all said and done, you're going to want to look back fondly—and look forward excitedly. This means that you need to both cross off the last of your "B-School To-Do's" and find a job. At the same time, you probably have a lot of responsibilities as you're now in charge of twelve clubs, eight conferences, and the weekly beer tap. Oh, and then there are those pesky classes, yet again.

> *First year, you get a little beat down, particularly when you don't know what you want to do. Second year, you have so much more confidence, both from your summer experience and your leadership roles; they give you a sense of responsibility.*
>
> *-- Tara, Kenan-Flagler '11 (UNC)*

If you are one of the lucky ones to both receive and accept an offer from your summer employer, congratulations! You have scored yourself hundreds of hours that you can now fill as you see fit, while the rest of your friends and classmates don their best pinstripes and eagerly look for future work. And if you're one of the suited folk, you've got yet another few weeks or months of cocktails and interviews. The good news is that you've probably gone through this all before and you know what you're doing; you're more determined now and more focused on finding the absolute right job. Godspeed.

> *Whoever told us that second year is a breeze—I want to slap them. If you don't have an offer, it's tough.*
>
> *-- Lisa, Stern '11 (NYU)*

The Last Hurrah

In many ways, the start of your second year is like the first. Even though you have a much better idea of what you're getting yourself into, there is the flurry of activities, the mad dash to the bar, and all of the newbies to meet.

> *First year is your "To-Do List"; second year is your "Bucket List." First year is tactical, but second year... I've already run that race. What do I really want to get out of this experience?*
>
> *-- Barr, Fuqua '11 (Duke)*

You're still paying big-time bucks to be in school, even if you're already focusing on signing bonuses and salaries to come. So make sure you commit to your second year just as much as you did to your first.

Don't ditch the calendar. In fact, hold it just as close to your body as you ever have. You may have more control over your class schedule—heck, you may have arranged it so that you only have to show up on campus a day or two a week—but that doesn't mean you have any fewer time commitments.

Plan for the whole year. As this is your final year, you want to make sure that you get everything in that you want to. Figure out what you want to accomplish, both before your time as a student ends and before you start back to work full time. This is your last chance (at least, for a while) to take advantage of flexible hours and a university environment.

Do one thing that scares the hell out of you. By now, you have hopefully realized that b-school is actually a very safe place to try things out.[1] Take a class you know will be arduous but fascinating, write a business plan for that company you've always dreamed of starting, go skydiving with your Army Ranger buddy if you can't stand heights[2], or perform in the school talent show if you have stage fright.

Be nice to the first years. It wasn't that long ago—only a year—that you were in their shoes. Remember how great the second years were to you? Good. Now you owe it to those who came before you to help those who come after you.[3] It's how the b-school system works.

> *I wish I'd been less scared about starting a business, that I would have gone for "it" more.*
>
> *-- Nadiyah, Booth '11 (Chicago)*

Go after the job of your dreams. If you haven't settled on your post-school plans, fine. Know what you want and go for it. You are soon to be a newly-minted MBA. Again, the degree grants you no particular license—which means that absolutely everything is on the table. Depending

---

1   That is, to try legal things out.

2   Don't worry—you won't be that high for that long.

3   "Help" is not the same thing as "rank the attractiveness of."

upon where you are in life, you may have a lot of freedom, or you may be constrained by responsibilities. Regardless, never forget that your MBA has been an investment in yourself, so factor your own happiness into whatever career you end up choosing. You'll thank yourself later.

Make a mark on your school. Whether your MBA class has 900 students or 90, you can always make an impact on the program if you choose to. Administrators look for you to offer suggestions and additions to the program. Now is a great time to take on a project that will be meaningful to you and leave a lasting impact on your program. Don't be pushy—but don't be shy. Your school won't hesitate to ask you for a donation next year, so why not get involved now in shaping the school's future?

The Long Road Ahead

So, business school hasn't really been the vacation you thought it would be—but it's been a pretty awesome experience nonetheless, right? Alas, the endgame has always been to return to the working world, where you'll exchange that backpack for a briefcase, your sweatpants for suits, and pizza lunches for power lunches. (Hey, it's not all bad.)

The key to success in the post-MBA world is to make as much of the skills—both hard and soft—that you learned while you were in school and to show as much passion and zeal for your career as you did for Happy Hour. You are launching a new life for yourself; it's time to get excited all over again. You remember how you felt when you first got that email

> *You have to do your first and second jobs really well; no one gets hired to be a CEO straight out of business school. You need to build those skills to do the job right and influence people.*
>
> *-- Naomi Tschoegl, Senior Associate Director, MBA Program Office, Wharton (U Penn)*

with your offer of admission? Your job offer letter is the same—only this time, someone's wanting to pay you.

Treat moving into your next job very much the same as you treated your move into business school (or by doing those things that you wished you had done). Go back and reread some of the stuff in Part I of this book; it's been a long time since you thought about those topics. Take time off to enjoy a real vacation, but give yourself long enough to get your life established before you begin punching the clock (with your fists). Make a list of goals for yourself, both personal and professional, and plot out a calendar. Don't forget to reconfirm how you want to introduce yourself to your new colleagues; they'll be asking your name a lot, just like during orientation week.

Remember that, as much as you've learned in your MBA studies, you're not the expert yet. Don't pretend to know what you don't, and be conscientious of those who have been at your new company for longer than you, whether they sit above or below you on some org chart. There's plenty you can learn from every person in the office.

> *What it takes to get a job is very different from what it takes to advance in that job. Think about how you manage others and yourself.*
>
> *-- Jennifer Brooks, Senior Associate Director, MBA Career Management Center, Kenan-Flagler (UNC)*

Where do you want your current job to take you? If you are in a rotational program or one that is a direct pipeline to another role, your track may be more or less prescribed for the near term. Still, think a few steps down the career path—how can you build towards your goal?

Begin cultivating advisors and mentors as soon as possible. Look for all kinds of connections, from shared alma maters to sports-team allegiances. Did you click with some of those folks you met way back in the informational interview process? What about someone at your new company? Even if your company provides you with a formal mentor and/or a direct supervisor, use some of those networking and people skills you perfected to create even more loyal supporters whom you can turn to down the line.

Lastly, be prepared to work hard. Few people go to business school with the intention of getting 9-5 jobs afterwards, so understand that the stresses of your career are what you signed up for. Of course, you're entitled to have bad days and make mistakes but, fundamentally, you should be happy. And if you're not, figure out why and make a change. You still have your degree, your "skill set," and, if you've done things right, a wide-ranging network of people to help you find the perfect position.

Never Lose Sight of the Trees

As you move on in life, you will hit many "greats"—you will do great things, meet great people, and encounter great challenges. You'll even screw up in great ways. Life will roll and coast like a rollercoaster—that's what it does best—and along the way, no matter how much success or failure you have, keep your eyes on what matters to you most.

At the beginning of this tome, we made a point of saying that the hardest thing about business school is balancing between changing and staying the same. In this regard, business school is a lot like life—this tension continues. But in school, you were constantly challenged to defend your thoughts, positions, and values. In life, you won't have the academic year, a regular recruiting season, and engaged classmates to prod you. You will have to force yourself to return to key questions again and again, making sure that your positions are firmly grounded.

As hokey as it sounds, write a letter to your future self. Right now. Then stick it in an envelope and put it in a drawer where you won't lose it. Two years ago, you were in a very different place. And two years from now, who knows where you'll be? So put a reminder on your calendar for two years from the day you graduate: *Read Letter to Self.* And when that reminder dings, go dig up the letter and read it.

Don't know where to start? Try this.

Date

Dear _____(your name):

It's been a long time. I wanted you to know where I stand on a few issues, now that I'm completing our MBA and about to launch our career. I'm taking this job doing... because...

I'm most excited about...

I'm most concerned about...

I know, looking forward, that I always want to be...

I value... and plan to incorporate it into our life by...

What do you think? Does all of this still make sense to you?

I wonder where you are reading this. I wonder if you're happy and fulfilled. And if you're not, I hope you'll take into account the things written here and get us back on track because, at the end of the day, we've got it pretty good.

Talk to you soon,
Me

APPENDIX

A. Twenty-Five Key Points

1) Befriend second years. They were just in your shoes, have all of the cheat sheets, and have figured out what's really important.

2) Plan to spend a large amount of your day (or all of it) at school. Even if you're only in class for 15 hours a week, you're a full time student, and campus is now your office.

3) If you want to do something about your job search before you go to school, do informational interviews—find out what people do, why they still do it, and what else they would consider doing.

4) Budget for the summers before, after, and during business school as though you won't have additional income.

5) Don't have the first hook up—everyone *will* know.

6) Don't get completely wasted too soon. Everyone will know about that, too.

7) Make sure to do a little bit of everything. Sometimes, you *should* blow off your friends to prepare a case, and sometimes you should blow off your case to go out with your friends.

8) Clubs: join a lot, but be committed to only a couple.

9) Ask a professor out…to lunch.

10) Listen more than you talk, particularly when working in teams. Out of conflict can come some great things, even if they're not what anyone originally wanted.

11) Recognize that you are making an investment in your future and your goals, which can mean spending money on travel and other learning opportunities. (Note: Bottles of Dom Perignon do not count as "learning opportunities," but dinners with classmates do.)

12) Figure out your personal organizational system ahead of time. Buy the necessary technology or notebooks to be productive and efficient. (TrapperKeeper, anyone?)

13) You're not an MBA just because you're getting one. Whatever you *do* do, don't forget who you are and why you're there.

14) Be prepared to be overwhelmed. It's okay to cry, just try not to do so in front of your professor or future manager.

15) Don't front about who you are. You'll be found out in a flash.

16) Before you graduate, take at least one course that scares the s#*t out of you.

17) Establish your team's expectations early and revisit them often. Adjustments are par for the course.

18) Don't be late. You said you'd be there, so be there.

19) Take stock of your public image. Professors, administrators and your classmates all know what Facebook is.

20) Recognize that every one of your classmates brings something to the table. Be willing to talk with all sorts of people, but also take the time to develop solid friendships.

21) Remember that your classmates are your colleagues, not your competition.

22) Travel.

23) Follow your passion, even if it isn't what you told the admissions committee it would be.

24) Don't take yourself too seriously, or no one else will take you seriously enough.

25) It's not life or death; it's business school.

B. Catechism of B-School Cliches

Ask these questions of someone in your class. Observe the extent to which we've all been trained like monkeys.

Outside of what should one try to think?
The box.

In order to avoid reinventing what?
The wheel.

How much does the gorilla weigh?
Eight hundred pounds.

Where is said gorilla?
In the room.

No, that's the elephant. The gorilla is in the marketplace. What does one do with the elephant in the room?
Ignore it.

What kind of fruit does one pick?
Low-hanging.

Because picking such fruit is a no-what?
Brainer.

Where on the envelope are the calculations?
On the back.

And from how many feet up is the big-picture view?
Thirty thousand. Occasionally just ten thousand.

If the situation is win-lose, to what number does the game sum?
Zero.

What kind of diligence does one always do?
Due.

In what direction does one circle to a previous comment?
Back.

What does one do with the loop?
Close it. Or at least stay in it.

And in what direction does one scale a successful process?
Up.

In this case, one hopes that the process will do what?
Scale.

Because it is … ?
Scalable.

In other words, it should demonstrate … ?
Scalability.

And finally the process achieves … ?
Scale.

Where does one make the pitch?
The elevator. Or the boardroom.

If one believes said pitch without questioning it, one is drinking what beverage?
The Kool-Aid.™

What kind of neck slows the operation down?
Bottle.

Is that not also a type of service?
Yes.

And if one is lucky, where does one have a seat?
At the table.

One's health, one's business model, and one's coffee should all be what?
Robust.

A paradigm shift occurs in a meeting where one is said to come to whom?
Come to Jesus.

At such a meeting, what two infernal things might be dispensed?
Fire and brimstone.

And which page should we all be on?
The same one.

C. Jargon Bingo

To play in a boring class. Check off each term as a classmate says it aloud. Once you complete a row or column, signal Bingo by making a comment that includes all five terms. Alternatively, incorporate the word "Bingo" or another agreed-upon term into your comment.

B	I	N	G	O
30,000-foot view	elevator pitch	drink the Kool-Aid	low-hanging fruit	paradigm shift
special sauce	think outside the box	thought leader	win-win	Web 2.0
mission-critical	zero-sum	80–20	net-net	elephant in the room
800-pound gorilla	scale	grow the pie	back of the envelope	bottleneck
best practices	due diligence	reinvent the wheel	skill set	core competency

D. Glossary of Common Terms

Accrual – A cruel, cruel accounting method wherein revenue and expenses are recognized when they are incurred, regardless of whether any cold, hard cash was involved. Accrual accounting is different from cash accounting, which follows the greenbacks.

Acme – The name given to any company in a simulation when the author was too lazy to come up with something more interesting. To its credit, Acme produces rocket sleds and superhero outfits for Wile E. Coyote.

Acquisition – When one company buys another. Or any time you acquire something… like your study partner's notes.

Amortize – To account for something over a long period of time. If you amortize the cost of your MBA over your entire lifetime, it's still crazy expensive.

Angel – An investor who comes in at the beginning stages of an enterprise and provides seed funding. Kind of like the classmate who saves your butt right before a midterm.

Arbitrage – Making a penny by buying a financial asset at $0.99 and instantly selling something equivalent for $1.00. Arbitrageurs try to do this over and over to make lots of pennies. Arbitrage is definitely not a French body spray.

Balance Sheet – A snapshot of a company's finances, including assets, liabilities, and shareholders' equity.

Bandwidth – What you're able to keep up with. Also what your Internet provider is operating on.

Barriers to Entry – The industry equivalent of a chastity belt. Barriers to entry such as high start-up costs keep potential competitors from joining the fray.

Benchmark – The standard by which something is judged. Or, to measure against those standards. Once upon a time, someone measured something by marks on a bench, and the rest is word history.

Beta – The Greek letter B (β), used to indicate (1) an early version of a product made available to customers, (2) the slope of a regression line in statistics, or (3) the risk of a financial asset, when it is added to a market portfolio. Also a very popular type of pet fish.

Bleeding Edge – Where the technological leading edge goes bad.

Blue Chip – A term for large, important companies, generally those that make up the Dow Jones Industrial Average. The most valuable poker chip (helps to keep a few up your sleeve).

Bond – A formal loan to a company or government, repaid with interest.

Book Value – A company's accounting assets minus its liabilities, often much different from its market value. Book value is not, technically, what you can sell your texts to first years for.

Bottom Line – The profit of a company, so called because it's listed on the bottom line of an income statement.

Brand Equity – The value of all of the warm-and-fuzzies that people feel towards a particular product or company.

Bricks and Mortar – Anything that isn't prefaced with an "e-"; a physical presence.

Buggy Whip – A general term used to describe obsolescent technology (e.g., buggy whips after the automobile was invented). The term *buggy whip* itself is becoming old-fashioned.

Business Cycle – The up-and-down swing of a national economy over the course of years.

Business Model – The way a company makes money, or the reasons why it should.

Business Plan – The document that (1) you write and that (2) no one reads and that (3) tries to explain how your startup will make money and the reasons why it should.

C-level – Refers to top-level executives, such as CEO, CMO, CTO. "C" is for "Chief."

Capital – Money gathered for investment.

Cartel – A group of sellers that work together to force prices higher than the market would otherwise dictate. OPEC is the cartel of oil-producing countries.

Cash Cow – What we would all love to have grazing in our pastures. A tried and true product that generates large profits without requiring much in the way of resources.

Commercial Paper – Short-term loans to companies. These loans are not secured by any specific asset as collateral.

Commodity – Undifferentiated stuff that is bought and sold, such as oil, soybeans, or copper.

Common Stock – Represents ownership in a company.

Comps – Also known as comparables. These are the numbers from the previous year that you use to assess current performance. *Comps* can also refer to the analysis of comparable companies in a pitch book.

Deck – A group of PowerPoint slides that guide a discussion or tell a story. Also known as a pack.

Deflation – A general fall in prices in an economy. Sounds good. Is bad.

Depreciation – The decline in value of a fixed asset.

Derivatives – Side bets in the casino of Wall Street, used either to lower risk (hedge) or take on more risk (speculate).

Discount Rate – An effective rate of interest, used to *discount* future cash flows to their present values.

Diversification – Holding different financial instruments as a way of spreading investment risk.

Economies of Scale – The corporate version of Costco; savings that can be achieved by doing something in bulk.

Elevator Pitch – The uber-quick spiel by which you sell yourself or your company while the elevator descends from Floor 19 to the lobby.

Equity – Ownership. In b-school, this term almost never means "fairness," perhaps not surprisingly.

Excel – The dominant spreadsheet program. Your best friend and worst enemy.

Expected Value – The long-run average value you'd get if you took a bet many, many times.

Federal Reserve – Also known as "The Fed." The central bank of the United States (really a system of banks), which controls the US money supply and acts like a super-bank to typical banks and to the US government. The Fed is run by a board of governors and a chairman, whose face shows up a lot in the *WSJ*. Not the same as "the Feds," i.e. federal agents.

Federal Funds Rate – The interest rate banks charge each other when they lend each other money overnight to meet reserve requirements. The Fed sets the target "fed funds" rate.

Fiscal Year – A 365-day time frame for a company. Fiscal years don't necessarily correspond to any calendar, whether Gregorian, Lunar, or Mayan.

Fixed Cost – Whether you make one widget or one million, your fixed costs stay the same. Hence the term "fixed." Nice how that works, no?

FOMO (*Fear of Missing Out*) – The irrational fear that nearly all business school students have at some point that they are not doing enough of whatever their classmates are doing a lot of.

Forward – An agreement to trade something for money at a future date.

Future – A type of standardized forward contract traded on an exchange.

Going Concern – The assumption that a company is going to continue operating indefinitely and is not in liquidation. Not always a good assumption.

Goodwill – A kind of intangible asset recorded on the books after an acquisition. Contrary to its use in everyday life, the term *goodwill* means nothing fuzzy or nice in accounting, partly because there is not much fuzzy or nice in accounting.

Hedge – To take an offsetting bet as a form of insurance, lowering your risk. In speech, to *hedge* is to be evasive, as in "beating around the bush."

Inflation – A rise in the general price level in an economy. A little bit of inflation is good; a lot of it is really bad. Many indulgences seem to work this way.

Initial Public Offering (IPO) – The sale of shares of a formerly privately-owned company to the general public. When the founders, angels, and venture capitalist investors get rich.

Investment – What you tell yourself these two years are, an investment in your future.

Just-in-time (JIT) – An approach to manufacturing that matches production with need in order to reduce inventory carrying costs. Justin Timberlake also matches production with need.

Karaoke – Rarely as good an idea as you think.

Keynes – Economist who gave his name to Keynesian economics, which argues for significant government intervention in the economy to try to smooth out business cycles.

Leverage – The use of debt to amplify a bet. It's just like borrowing money to gamble at a casino: you'd better do well. Sometimes *leverage* simply means "power," as in *The scandalous emails I accidentally received from my boss gave me leverage in our next salary negotiation.*

Liability – A debt that one is responsible for. A negative asset, like that guy in your study group.

Liquidation – Firesale! Get it before it's gone!

Liquidity – Ability to be converted into money. Cash is liquid. Try drinking some.

Marginal – Marginal cost means the cost of the very last unit produced. Marginal revenue means the revenue you get from the very last unit sold. In the real world, something "marginal" may be unimportant, but marginal quantities are super-important in economics.

Merger – When two companies become one. Unlike an acquisition, a merger is meant to happen between "equals." That's never true; there's always a winner and a loser.

Metric – A measure or number by which you grade performance.

Net Income – What you are left with after student loan payments.

Neoclassical – "Standard" economics, in which people always maximize utility in rational ways and prices instantly adjust in well-functioning markets throughout the economy.

Offline – When your printer is acting up, or when you should really continue the conversation at a later time with a smaller group.

Offshore Financial Center – See *Switzerland* or *Cayman Islands*. Where you put your money once you've got oodles of it.

Operating Income – Operating revenue, less operating expenses. Operating income excludes income generated by "non-operations," as well as interest and tax expenses.

Opportunity Cost – The benefits you missed on Road B, because you took Road A instead.

Option – The ability to buy or sell a financial asset at a fixed price.

Perfect Competition – The theoretical state of affairs in a perfect market, in which many, many buyers and sellers interact to rapidly set a market-clearing price, without any one player having control over that price.

Pitch Book – An analysis of a deal, made by an investment bank to convince a client to commit to said deal.

Poison Pills – Methods implemented by a company's board of directors, seeking to prevent hostile takeovers by shareholders who are unfriendly to current management or ownership.

Portfolio Play – Spreading your bets, as you do when you hold a portfolio of stocks (rather than just one stock).

Preferred Stock – A part-stock, part-bond claim on a company. Preferred stock is more risky than regular debt but less risky than common stock.

Prime Rate – A reference interest rate used by banks to calculate the interest rate on certain loans, such as student loans and adjustable-rate mortgages. In the US, the prime rate is derived from an even more basic interest rate, the federal funds target rate.

Profit – What's left once you subtract your expenses from whatever revenues you have earned. Being in the black. Makin' money. Rollin' in the dough.

Queue – A line you wait in. Although common in British English, the term *queue* is rarely used by Americans outside of technical contexts.

Resources – The expendable folks you throw at small projects. When you yourself are referred to as a *resource*, hide.

Salvage Value – What you can get for your roommate's computer or the assets of a company, if you sell them off after they've lived a useful life.

Scorecard (Balanced Scorecard) – A tool that shows you how an operation is doing relative to a whole set of benchmarks. The point is to judge performance from several perspectives, not just one.

Six Sigma – A process-improvement methodology adopted by many companies. The name refers to six standard deviations away from the mean. According to the normal curve, six-sigma events happen only once in a very blue moon.

Spot – Current, as opposed to future. The spot market for electricity is where electricity is bought and sold for immediate delivery. A spot price is a price in the spot market.

Supply Chain – A system by which materials move from suppliers through various intermediaries and finally to customers.

Sunk Cost – Like the ante in poker, a sunk cost is what you're already in for. A common mistake is to let sunk costs affect your decisions about future courses of action.

SWOT analysis – A strategic evaluation of a company's Strengths, Weaknesses, Opportunities and Threats. SWOT comes before the SWAT team but after signs of trouble.

Synergy – An overused word. In strategy class, *synergy* means pretty things like "working together, the whole is bigger than the sum of the parts," etc. In the real world, *synergy* is code for "who do we fire when we merge these groups?"

Teaching Assistant (TA) – An overqualified MBA or underqualified PhD student who leads review sections and grades the majority of papers.

Term Sheet – The outline of a business agreement. Often associated with private equity and venture capital deals.

Top Line – The revenue of a company (so called because it's on the top line of an income statement). *Marbles-R-Us is finally showing some top-line growth* means that revenues are increasing.

Value Chain – An end-to-end analysis of a business process, focusing on how much value is added at each stage of the process.

Value Proposition – Your big pitch to your customers. Why your offering is so much better than anyone else's.

Variable Cost – The non-fixed costs of production, such as materials and labor.

Vertical Integration – Owning all the links in the supply chain, starting from raw materials, all the way through distribution of finished products to end users.

Widget – What you call a random product when you don't care what it is, for the purposes of some academic exercise. Often made by Acme Co.

Yield Curve – A graphical relationship between the yield of some type of bond (its effective interest rate) and the time to maturity of the bond. This curve usually slopes upwards (longer-term bonds pay higher yields), because long-duration bonds are inherently riskier and because inflation is typically expected for the future.

E. Acronym Guide

Acronym	Meaning	Pronunciation
ABC	Always Be Closing	Pronounce each letter
B2B	Business-to-Business	Pronounce each letter/ number
B2C	Business-to-Consumer	Pronounce each letter/ number
BATNA	Best Alternative To Negotiated Agreement	"Bat-na"
CAGR	Compound Annualized Growth Rate	"Kag-err" (much like "kegger")
CAPM	Capital Asset Pricing Model	"Cap-M"
CAPX	Capital Expenditure	"Cap-X"
CLM	Career-Limiting Move	Pronounce each letter
COB	Close of Business	Pronounce each letter
COGS	Cost of Goods Sold	Rhymes with "hogs"
CRM	Consumer Resource Management	Pronounce each letter
CYA	Cover Your Ass	Pronounce each letter
DBA	Doing Business As	Pronounce each letter
DCF	Discounted Cash Flow	Pronounce each letter
DJIA	Dow Jones Industrial Average	Never spell this; call it "The Dow" or "The Dow Jones"
EBIT	Earnings Before Interest & Taxes	"E-bit"

Acronym	Meaning	Pronunciation
EBITDA	Earnings Before Interest, Taxes, Depreciation, & Amortization	"E-bit-da"
EPS	Earnings Per Share	Pronounce each letter
FIFO	First In, First Out	"Fife-oh"
FOMO	Fear Of Missing Out	"Foe-moh"
The FT	The Financial Times	Pronounce each letter
FX	Foreign Exchange	Pronounce each letter
FY	Fiscal Year	Pronounce as "Fiscal Year"
GAAP	Generally Accepted Accounting Principles	Say it like the t-shirt store or, as the London Tube reminds you, "Mind the ___."
IMF	International Monetary Fund	Pronounce each letter
IPO	Initial Public Offering	Pronounce each letter
IP	Intellectual Property or Internet Protocol	Pronounce each letter
IRR	Internal Rate of Return	Pronounce each letter
JIT	Just-in-time	Pronounce as "Just-in-time"
KISS	Keep It Simple, Stupid	Say it like the heavy metal band or what you do to your sweetie
KPI	Key Performance Indicators	Pronounce each letter
LBO	Leveraged Buyout	Pronounce each letter
LIBOR	London Interbank Offering Rate	"Lie-bore"
LIFO	Last In, First Out	"Life-oh"

Acronym	Meaning	Pronunciation
LLC	Limited Liability Company	Pronounce each letter
LY	Last Year	Pronounce as "last year"
M&A	Mergers and Acquisitions	Pronounce each letter
NDA	Non-Disclosure Agreement	Pronounce each letter
NPV	Net Present Value	Pronounce each letter
OTC	Over The Counter	Pronounce each letter
PE	Private Equity	Pronounce each letter
P/E ratio	Price-to-Earnings ratio	"P.E. ratio"
P&L	Profit and Loss (more common than Property & Liability, as in insurance)	"P and L"
R&D	Research and Development	"R and D"
ROI	Return on Investment	Pronounce each letter
S&P 500	Standard & Poor's	"S and P 500"
SKU	Stock Keeping Unit	"Skew," not "s-k-u"
VC	Venture Capital or Venture Capitalist or Variable Cost	Pronounce each letter Pronounce as "variable cost"
WACC	Weighted Average Cost of Capital	Exactly as in "That's whack!"
The WSJ	*The Wall Street Journal*	"The Wall Street Journal"
YOY	Year over year	Pronounce as "year over year"

ACKNOWLEDGEMENTS

We've had incredible help and support in writing this book.

Our student hosts and hostesses as at the schools we visited:

Matt and Dean (Fuqua/Duke), Elizabeth (Kenan-Flagler/UNC), Aderly, Lisa, and Brian (Booth/Chicago) , Carrol and Chris (Kellogg/Northwestern), Della and Mike (Haas/Berkeley), Maya (GSB/Stanford), Jim (Marshall /USC), Karen (Anderson/UCLA), Tripp and Jen (Ross/Michigan), Jessie, Tushar, Patty and Paul (Wharton/U Penn), Will and Jason (Sloan/MIT), Carolyn and Ari (HBS/Harvard), Mike and Sharon (CBS/Columbia), Craig (Stern/NYU).

And the administrators and faculty who were kind enough not to turn us away:

Blair Sheppard, Sheryle Dirks, Erin Gasch (Duke/Fuqua), Anna Millar, Catherine Nichols, Susan Brooks, Emily Wilkins, Tim Flood (Kenan-Flagler/UNC), Christine Gramhofer (Booth/Chicago), Susan Corley Judkins, David Cooley, Jennifer Chow Bevan (Anderson/UCLA), Peter Giulioni (Marshall/USC), Heather Byrne, Al Cotrone, Evonne Plantinga (Ross /Michigan), Naomi Tschoegl, Kembrel Jones (Wharton/U Penn), Debbie Berechman, Jenifer Marshall (Sloan/MIT), Marilena Botoulas, Nayla Bahri, Jilliann Rodriguez (CBS/Columbia).

Much love to our b-school alma maters. We hope it's obvious.

Outside of visits to specific schools, others who contributed ideas to the book include Josh Fischer, Greg Fowlkes, Katherine Boas, Laura Nelson, Helena Plater-Zyberk, and Joshua Fisher. Special thanks to Laura Wilcox, formerly of MIT Sloan, for her wonderful insights.

We also must thank the staff of Manhattan GMAT for all of their hard work on this project. Cathy Huang and Dan McNaney did absolutely incredible work to lay out the book from start to finish, create hundreds of complicated diagrams, wrestle with edits and editors, and get the job done. Eric Caballero read numerous drafts, offered great suggestions, and opened his Rolodex wide. Tom Rose, Robert Wilburn, Grace Wang, Sean Murphy, Whitney Garner, Abby Pelcyger, Carrol Chang, Patty Tritipeskul and Chris Brusznicki added valuable thoughts and shared leads. Belen Ferrer, Taniya Wilder, and Erica Busillo deciphered terribly scrawled handwriting and Whitney Garner mustered her statistics diagramming capabilities to push us over the goal line. Evyn Williams designed a fabulous cover (that drink looks good enough to drink), while Jessica Eliav and the rest of the Marketing team guided us to the title and provided important insights. Kelly Faircloth and Elizabeth Krisher gave us incredibly useful feedback, and Beretzi Garcia forced us to meet our deadline. Special thanks to Dan Gonzalez, Tarik Zahzah, Dave Mahler, Dan Bernstein, Gregg Lachow, and Danielle DiCiaccio for taking a fine-toothed comb to our final drafts. Sam Edla and the other IT guys built and steered our web presence. Andrew Yang supported the book from the get-go and provided the resources and space to get it done. And Zeke Vanderhoek made it all possible in the first place.

Carrie: When I first joined Manhattan GMAT as an instructor, I thought I had found a pretty great part-time job. Little did I know how much this company and my experiences as a teacher would change my life. Over the past three years, I have been inspired by my students' passion—maybe not for the GMAT, but for their futures—and I have been awed by my colleagues' dedication to the art of teaching. Never could I have imagined a company more supportive of its employees, as well as its clients, and

I am thankful for all of the opportunities Manhattan GMAT has given me, particularly with regard to creating this book. Working with Chris Ryan has been eye-opening; I've never met someone with so much talent, humor, and compassion, and so little ego.

I am endlessly grateful for all of the irrational actors in my life: friends and family who continually support me, no matter how crazy my endeavor or what I ask of them. Marcie Ulin, Tom Halford, and Meredith Lavendar for opening up their homes, Laura Nelson and Katherine Boas for being b-school sounding boards, Matt Lau for pointing out all sorts of errors, Bobbye Tigerman, Dana Lewis, Sugi Ganeshananthan, Carol Creighton, Jessica Sebeok, and Jackie Dechongkit for keeping me sane, and many, many others who have filled my life with humor, compassion, and zeal. A special shout out to Cluster H'07 and my CBS Follies family. To Barbara Belmont, for being my friend and my mentor (and my cousin, not that she had much choice in that one). To my parents, John and Stevie, who have always expressed faith in me, even when they probably shouldn't have, and to my brother, Scott, who has served as my primary teacher since the day I came home from the hospital. And lastly, to my nephew Oliver, who has reminded me how amazing it is to learn something new, each and every day.

Chris: It's been a humbling experience writing this book with Carrie. Her exceptional mind is only matched by her spirit, wit, and dedication. We'll miss her much round these parts. An additional metric ton of appreciation goes to all the instructors and staff at Manhattan GMAT, who recover so many of my fumbles and encourage me to play better.

Stepping back, I'd like to thank some of my teachers of yore: Mr. D'Angelo and Fr. Sliben for math and generosity, Mr. Pomeroy for physics and discipline, Sra. Finizio for Italian and joy, Mary Ellen Schauber for singing and more joy. Among others, Larry Murphy at BCDS and Jane Gutsell, Linda Sloan, and Tommy Webb at GDS taught me by deep example. Chris Johnson, Sacha Adam, and Scott Griffith somehow kept b-school funky. Many folks keep me on track, even when they don't know it; among them are Rob Weis, Josh Fischer, and Larry Finer (in it to win it). Vito, Jared, Will, Marsh, Pat, Brian, Neil, Norine, Isabel, Matt, Jon, Don, Ron, Eric C, Eric C, Eric V, Greg, Yissel, Jay, Robert, Jim, as well as wives & husbands—it's an honor.

Since I was raw clay, my parents Justin and Susan and my siblings Justin, Liz, and Tim have taught me to do X for practically all X; I am not who I am without them, and I love them dearly for it. Mark, Charlie, Julia, Caitlin, Duncan (and honoraries Ben & Sam), you're the future's gift to us—thanks for keeping us young. Finally, my wife Kathryn teaches me every day what it means to strive and to care. Her courage and love inspire me, and I am dumbly grateful for her presence in my life.

ABOUT THE AUTHORS

Carrie Shuchart holds a A.B. in Social Studies from Harvard University and an MBA from Columbia Business School. She has previously been an editorial analyst at *The Atlantic*, a freelance television producer, and an entrepreneur. While at Columbia, she focused her efforts on *Follies*, the school's semi-annual comedy show, for which she acted, directed, and made some pretty poor attempts at dancing.

She began teaching with Manhattan GMAT in 2008 as a way to fund her start-up habit and her shoe collection. Recently, Carrie joined the Los Angeles office of McKinsey & Co. as a consultant. She still can't explain what the job entails.

A native of the First State, Chris Ryan has an A.B. in Physics from Harvard University. Before getting an MBA from the Fuqua School of Business (Duke), he taught high school science through Teach for America and later in private schools. At Fuqua, Chris was head TA of the core Statistics and Finance courses, as well as Curriculum Representative and *FuquaVision* co-president.

After b-school, he worked for McKinsey & Co. in New York, then joined Manhattan GMAT, where he now serves as the Director of Product and Instructor Development. In his spare time, Chris writes moody music, tinkers with moody screenplays, and occasionally hangs out with his wife Kathryn at home in Brooklyn.